The Developer's Dilemma

T0323317

The United Nations University (UNU) World Institute for Development Economics Research (UNU-WIDER) was established by the United Nations University as its first research and training centre and started work in Helsinki, Finland, in 1985. The mandate of the institute is to undertake applied research and policy analysis on structural changes affecting developing and transitional economies; to provide a forum for the advocacy of policies leading to robust, equitable, and environmentally sustainable growth; and to promote capacity strengthening and training in the field of economic and social policy-making. Its work is carried out by staff researchers and visiting scholars in Helsinki and via networks of collaborating scholars and institutions around the world.

United Nations University World Institute for
Development Economics Research
(UNU-WIDER)
Katajanokanlaituri 6B, 00160 Helsinki,
Finland
www.wider.unu.edu

The Developer's Dilemma

Structural Transformation, Inequality Dynamics, and Inclusive Growth

Edited by

ARMIDA SALSIAH ALISJAHBANA

KUNAL SEN

ANDY SUMNER

ARIEF ANSHORY YUSUF

A study prepared by the United Nations University World Institute for Development Economics Research (UNU-WIDER)

OXFORD
UNIVERSITY PRESS

Great Clarendon Street, Oxford, OX2 6DP,
United Kingdom

Oxford University Press is a department of the University of Oxford.
It furthers the University's objective of excellence in research, scholarship,
and education by publishing worldwide. Oxford is a registered trade mark of
Oxford University Press in the UK and in certain other countries

World Institute for Development Economics Research of the United Nations University (UNU-WIDER),
Katajanokanlaituri 6 B, 00160 Helsinki, Finland

Enquiries concerning reproduction outside the scope of this licence
should be sent to the Rights Department, Oxford University Press, at the address above

Published in the United States of America by Oxford University Press
198 Madison Avenue, New York, NY 10016, United States of America

British Library Cataloguing in Publication Data
Data available

Library of Congress Control Number: 2022933842

ISBN 978–0–19–285529–9

DOI: 10.1093/oso/9780192855299.001.0001

Printed and bound by
CPI Group (UK) Ltd, Croydon, CR0 4YY

Links to third party websites are provided by Oxford in good faith and
for information only. Oxford disclaims any responsibility for the materials
contained in any third party website referenced in this work.

Foreword

Structural transformation—the movement of workers from lower-productivity to higher-productivity activities—has long been regarded as an essential feature of rapid and sustained growth but has been historically associated with rising income inequality. At the same time, inclusive growth is more likely with steady, or even falling, inequality, with the benefits of economic growth shared broadly, and especially with the poorest. In a nutshell, the 'developer's dilemma' is the potential trade-off between structural change and inclusive growth. How to manage this dilemma is a thorny question facing many developing countries pursuing economic development. In 2019, UNU-WIDER took up the challenge the dilemma presents by assembling a team of country experts to research the development challenges low-income and middle-income countries are facing with 'new' forms of structural transformation, including tertiarization and premature deindustrialization. By doing so, the book sets out a new research agenda that considers how inclusive growth and structural economic transformation are related in different country contexts. The genesis for the book was the rich discussions the four editors had in the workshops organized by the Economic and Social Research Council (ESRC) Research Network on Global Poverty and Inequality Dynamics in 2017 and 2018, in which many of the book's authors participated.

In the past, UNU-WIDER has done considerable research on structural transformation, as well as on inequality. In this volume, the editors bring these two strands of research together to examine the structural transformation–inequality relationship. To focus more squarely on the problem, a central remit of the research team was to produce knowledge and policy alternatives to address the challenges of different varieties of structural transformation and its implications for inequality and inclusive growth outcomes. And I believe the team has superbly fulfilled that remit, judging by the depth of studies and analyses within this book, each accompanied with well-thought-out policy conclusions and suggestions on moving forward for development.

I heartily thank the authors for sharing their research expertise with us on what is a hugely important and complex area. Also, I sincerely thank my fellow editors for exercising their sound analytical and editorial skills, so clearly evidenced in this important book in front of us.

UNU-WIDER gratefully acknowledges the support and financial contribution to its research programme by the governments of Finland, Sweden, and the United

Kingdom. Without this vital funding, our research and policy advisory work would be impossible.

Kunal Sen
Director, UNU-WIDER
Helsinki, March 2022

Acknowledgements

The editors would like to thank for comments and contributions participants at the UNU-WIDER project workshop, Bangkok, 10 September 2019 and the UNU-WIDER/UNESCAP conference, 11–13 September 2019, Bangkok.

We would also like to thank Lorraine Telfer-Taivainen, UNU-WIDER Editorial and Publishing Associate, for her constant support and remarkable commitment in preparing the manuscript. We have also benefited from the comments of three anonymous reviewers. Guidance, advice, and encouragement from our Oxford University Press editor, Adam Swallow, has been invaluable.

Armida Salsiah Alisjahbana, Kunal Sen, Andy Sumner, and *Arief Anshory Yusuf*

Contents

III. SUB-SAHARAN AFRICA

IV. LATIN AMERICA

V. LOOKING AHEAD

List of Figures

List of Tables

List of Abbreviations

AFC	Asian Financial Crisis
B-BBEE	broad-based Black economic empowerment
BBS	Bangladesh Bureau of Statistics
BGMEA	Bangladesh Garment Manufacturers and Exporters Association
BJP	Bharatiya Janata Party (India)
CCCP	Chinese Communist Party
CDF	cumulative distribution function
CFPS	China Family Panel Studies
CHN	China
CPD	Centre for Policy Dialogue
DevEA	developing East Asia
ECI	economic complexity index
EDIG	Economic Dialogue on Inclusive Growth
ERP	economic recovery programme
ESRC	Economic and Social Research Council
FDI	foreign direct investment
FERA	Foreign Exchange Rate Regulation Act
GDP	gross domestic product
GGDC	Groningen Growth and Development Centre
GLSS	Ghana Living Standards Survey
GNI	gross national income
GPID	Global Poverty and Inequality Dynamics
GPRS	Growth and Poverty Reduction Strategy
GSGDA	Ghana Shared Growth and Development Agenda
GVC	global value chain
HEI	higher education institution
HIC	high-income country
HIEA	high-income East Asia
HIES	Household Income and Expenditure Survey
ICT	information communications technology
IDC	Industrial Development Corporation
ILO	International Labour Organization
IMF	International Monetary Fund
INC	Indian National Congress
IND	India
IPAP	Industrial Policy Action Plan
ISI	import substitution industrialization
LA	Latin America

LDC	least-developed country
LEAP	Livelihood Empowerment against Poverty
LFP	labour force participation
LIC	low-income country
LMIC	lower-middle-income developing country
MDG	Millennium Development Goals
MFA	Multi-Fibre Arrangement
MIC	middle-income country
MRTP Act	Monopolies and Restrictive Trade Practices Act
NBS	National Bureau of Statistics
NDC	National Democratic Congress Party
NDP	National Development Plan
NEET	not in education, employment, or training
NESOB	National Economic and Social Development Board (Thailand)
NGO	non-governmental organization
NIC	newly industrialized country
NMW	national minimum wage
NPP	New Patriotic Party
NSO	National Statistical Office (Thailand)
NTB	non-tariff barrier
ODA	official development assistance
ODI	Overseas Development Institute
OEC	Observatory of Economic Complexity
OPEC	Organization of the Petroleum Exporting Countries
PDS	Public Distribution System
PNDC	Provisional National Defence Council
pp	percentage points
PPP	purchasing power parity
R&D	research and development
RMG	ready-made garments
SAP	structural adjustment programme
SSA	sub-Saharan Africa
SOE	state-owned enterprise
ST	structural transformation
TES	temporary employment services
TVE	township and village enterprise
UMIC	upper-middle-class income developing country
UNDP	United Nations Development Programme
UNFPA	United Nations Population Fund
UNSDGs	United Nations Sustainable Development Goals
UNU-WIDER	United Nations University-World Institute for Development Economics Research
WDI	World Development Indicators
WIID	World Income Inequality Database
WTO	World Trade Organization

Notes on Contributors

Armida Salsiah Alisjahbana is Under-Secretary General of the United Nations and Executive Secretary of the United Nations Economic and Social Commission for Asia and the Pacific (ESCAP). She is a member of the Indonesia Academy of Sciences and currently on leave from her position as Professor of Economics at Universitas Padjadjaran, Bandung, Indonesia. Her area of expertise and research interests are in development economics and sustainable development. She has published extensively on the subjects related to human resources development and environmental costs of sustainable development in Indonesia.

Richmond Atta-Ankomah is a research fellow at the Institute of Statistical, Social and Economic Research, University of Ghana. Richmond's research interests are in development and microeconomic issues pertaining to households and firms and, more recently, on poverty, inequality, and structural transformation in developing countries. He has been a Research Associate at the Ghana node of the African Centre of Excellence for Inequality Research since 2018.

Haroon Bhorat is Professor of Economics and Director of the Development Policy Research Unit at the University of Cape Town. He serves on the Presidential Economic Advisory Council and holds a prestigious SARChI Chair in Economic Growth, Poverty and Inequality Research. He is Non-resident Senior Fellow at the Brookings Institution, Research Fellow at IZA, and a member of the UCT College of Fellows. Prof. Bhorat sits on the editorial advisory board of the *World Bank Economic Review*, and he is Board Member of the National Research Foundation (NRF) and UNU World Institute for Development Economics Research (UNU-WIDER). He is a member of the WHO's High Level Commission on Health Employment and Economic Growth and was Head of Research for the UN's High-Level Panel on the Post-2015 Development Agenda. He has served as an economic advisor to past Ministers of Finance, and previous Presidents Thabo Mbeki and Kgalema Motlanthe. He has his PhD in Economics through Stellenbosch University, studied at the Massachusetts Institute of Technology, and was a Cornell University research fellow.

Sergio Firpo is Instituto Unibanco Professor of Economics and the Dean of Research at Insper. He received his PhD in economics from the University of California at Berkeley in 2003. His main research interests are microeconometrics, policy evaluation, labour economics, development economics, and empirical political economy. He is an Elected Fellow of the Econometric Society and Level 1 Researcher at CNPq. He is also Research Fellow at the Institute of Labor Economics (IZA), the Global Labor Organization (GLO), the Center for Evaluation and Development (C4ED), and the Center for Transdisciplinary Research in Education (CPTE-IU). He is an associate editor of the *Journal of Business Economics and Statistics*, the *Journal of Econometric Methods*, and the *Journal of Applied Econometrics*.

Sabyasachi Kar is RBI Chair Professor at the Institute of Economic Growth, Delhi, and Research Partner at the ESRC GPID research network based at the King's College, London. His research spans macroeconomics, economic growth, development economics, and political economy. He has published numerous books and research articles in these areas, with a particular focus on issues related to the Indian economy. He is co-editor of the *Journal of South Asian Development*.

Sunera Saba Khan is a research economist at the South Asian Network on Economic Modeling (SANEM). Her research interests are in the areas of international trade and development economics.

Kyunghoon Kim has recently completed his PhD in Development Studies-Political Economy at the Department of International Development, King's College London. Kyunghoon's research focuses on the role of state-owned entities in economic development. His recent publications include articles in *Structural Change and Economic Dynamics, Competition & Change*, the *Journal of Contemporary Asia*, and the *Pacific Review*. Kyunghoon received an M.Sc. from the London School of Economics and Political Science (LSE) and has worked as a research fellow at the Samsung Economic Research Institute (SERI), Korea.

Monica Lambon-Quayefio is a senior lecturer at the Department of Economics, University of Ghana. Her research is broadly in the area of applied microeconomics, with a focus on poverty and inequality analysis and impact evaluations. She has published in the fields of development economics and in particular, in the area of health and labour-related issues in developing country contexts.

Yanan Li is an assistant professor of economics at the Business School of Beijing Normal University. Her research is development economics, with a focus on education, health, and minimum wages. She has published in the *American Journal of Agricultural Economics* and the *Journal of Development Studies*.

Kezia Lilenstein is the Programme Manager and a Researcher at the Development Policy Research Unit (DPRU) at the University of Cape Town (UCT). During her time at UCT she tutored extensively for the School of Economics and worked as a researcher for the Southern Africa Development Research Unit (SALDRU). She also worked as an editor for an online community newspaper and managed an impact evaluation of a NUMERIC, an education-based non-profit organization. Her research interests include labour economics (especially youth unemployment) and development economics. She has an MA in applied economics from UCT.

Arriya Mungsunti is a researcher at the Centre for Economics and Development Studies, Padjadjaran University, Bandung, Indonesia. She is also a research associate at the Institute for Land, Water and Society, a research group at Charles Sturt University, Australia. Her research interests include irrigation water use management, environmental economics, and agricultural resource economics. She holds an MA in economics from the University of New England and has completed her PhD in applied economics from Charles Sturt University.

Rafaela Nogueira received her PhD in economics from Getulio Vargas Foundation (FGV). Currently, she is Public Policy Associate at Nubank.

Morné Oosthuizen is Chief Research Officer and Deputy Director of the Development Policy Research Unit at the University of Cape Town (UCT). He also holds the INSETA-UCT Research Chair—a formal research programme in partnership with the Insurance Sector Education Training Authority. His research interests include the generational economy (National Transfer Accounts), poverty, inequality, and labour markets. He has worked on issues of intergenerational transfers and the demographic dividend in several countries in Southern Africa and helped coordinate the multi-country research project, Counting Women's Work, which aims to value time spent in unpaid services and incorporate it into estimates of production and consumption over the life course. He holds a PhD in Economics from UCT.

Robert Darko Osei is an associate professor in the Institute of Statistical, Social and Economic Research (ISSER), University of Ghana, Legon and also the Dean for the School of Graduate Studies at the University of Ghana. Robert's main areas of research include evaluative poverty and rural research, structural transformation and its implications for poverty and inequality, and other economic development policy concerns.

Renan Pieri received his PhD in economics from São Paulo School of Economics—Getulio Vargas Foundation (FGV), with a post-doctoral position at Insper. Currently, he is lecturer at the Department of Business Administration of Getulio Vargas Foundation. His research focuses on applied microeconomics, microeconometrics, and labour economics. His special interest is on programme evaluation and subjects related to development.

Selim Raihan is a professor at the Department of Economics, University of Dhaka, Bangladesh, and the Executive Director of the South Asian Network on Economic Modelling (SANEM). He has worked and published widely in the areas of international trade, economic growth, poverty, labour market, macroeconomic policies, political economy, and climate change issues.

Saon Ray is a professor with the Indian Council for Research on International Economic Relations (ICRIER), New Delhi. An economist specializing in industry and international trade issues, her areas of interest include global value chains, technological upgrading of Indian industries, free trade agreements and trade creation effects, technology transfer, foreign direct investment, efficiency and productivity of firms, financial inclusion, energy, and climate change-related issues. She has published widely on these issues in books and journal articles.

Lukas Schlogl is a post-doctoral researcher at the Department of Political Science, University of Vienna. His research focuses on social and technological change, digitalization, (de)industrialization, and the changing nature of work. He publishes in the fields of development economics, political science, and comparative policy studies.

Kunal Sen is Director of United Nations University World Institute for Development Economics Research (UNU-WIDER), and Professor of Development Economics at the Global Development Institute, University of Manchester. Formerly, he was Joint Research Director of the Department for International Development-UK funded Effective States and Inclusive Development (ESID) Research Centre. His current research is on structural transformation, labour markets, and the political economy of development. Kunal's recent authored books are *The Political Economy of India's Growth Episodes* (Palgrave Macmillan, 2016), and *Out of the Shadows? The Informal Sector in Post-Reform India* (Oxford University Press India, 2016). He has published over 100 journal articles, including papers in the *Journal of Development Economics,* the *Journal of Development Studies* and *World Development.* He won the Sanjaya Lall Prize in 2006 and the Dudley Seers Prize in 2003 for his publications.

Andrés Solimano is the founder and chairman of the International Center for Globalization and Development, Santiago, Chile. His research and policy work focuses on macroeconomics, inequality, international economics, economic development, pension systems, art economics, and related themes. In 2020, he published *A History of Big Recessions in the Long Twentieth Century* (Cambridge University Press), and in 2021, *The Rise and Fall of the Privatized Pension System in Chile. An International Perspective* (Anthem Press) and *The Evolution of Contemporary Arts Markets: Aestethics, Money and Turbulence* (Routledge).

François Steenkamp is Senior Research Officer at the Development Policy Research Unit (DPRU) at the University of Cape Town (UCT). Previously, he worked as a lecturer at the School of Economics at UCT. His research interests include economic complexity, industrial relatedness, and structural transformation, industrial policy, patterns and determinants of international trade, trade policy, export diversification, and economic development. François obtained his PhD in economics from UCT in 2019.

Andy Sumner is Professor of International Development at King's College London. He has twenty years' international research experience using both qualitative and quantitative methods and has published extensively in the areas of poverty, inequality, and economic development. He is Director of the Economic and Social Research Council (ESRC) Global Challenges Strategic Research Network on Global Poverty and Inequality Dynamics. He is Non-Resident Senior Fellow at UNU-WIDER and is also Fellow of the Academy of Social Sciences.

Waleerat Suphannachart is an associate professor of economics at the Department of Agricultural and Resource Economics, Faculty of Economics, Kasetsart University. Her research is in development economics, with a focus on agricultural productivity and issues in development studies.

Amy Thornton is a post-doctoral fellow at the Southern African Labour and Development Research Unit and African Centre of Excellence in Inequality Research at the University of Cape Town (UCT). Previously, she worked as a researcher at the Development Policy Research Unit at the University of Cape Town, and at the African Microeconomic Research Unit at the University of the Witwatersrand. Her research interests are economic demography, labour economics, and data quality of household surveys with a regional focus on South Africa. Amy obtained her Ph.D. in Economics from UCT in 2021.

Peter Warr is John Crawford Professor of Agricultural Economics, Emeritus, at the Australian National University. He studied at the University of Sydney, the London School of Economics, and Stanford University, where he received his Ph.D. in Applied Economics. His current research is on the relationship between economic policy and poverty incidence in Southeast Asia. He is a Fellow of the Academy of Social Sciences in Australia and a Distinguished Fellow and Past President of the Australian Agricultural and Resource Economics Society.

Chunbing Xing is Professor at the School of Agricultural Economics and Rural Development, Renmin University of China. His research area is China's labour market, focusing on migration, education, wage structure, and income distribution. He has published over fifty journal articles in the fields of rural–urban migration, wage determination, and education policies.

Arief Anshory Yusuf is Professor of Economics at the Department of Economics, Padjadjaran University. He received his bachelor's degree in economics from Padjadjaran University, an MSc from University College London, and a PhD from the Australian National University. His research focuses on the economics of the environment and natural resource management, as well as on the various aspects of economic development, such as poverty and inequality. He is an Honorary Senior Lecturer at the Australian National University and also a visiting professor at King's College London. He is a member of the Indonesian Young Academy of Science (ALMI) and the current President of Indonesian Regional Science Association (IRSA), and is also on the editorial board of the *Bulletin of Indonesian Economic Studies*.

Gabriela Zapata-Román is a Postdoctoral Research Fellow at Universidad Diego Portales, Chile and Honorary Research Fellow at the Global Development Institute of the University of Manchester. Her research is focused on the areas of inclusive growth, inequality in the labour market, inequality of opportunities and educational achievement, intergenerational mobility, gender inequality and social cohesion.

1

The Developer's Dilemma

Armida Salsiah Alisjahbana, Kunal Sen, Andy Sumner,
and Arief Anshory Yusuf

1. Introduction

The developer's dilemma is this: developing countries are seeking economic development—that is, structural transformation (ST)—which is inclusive in the sense that it is broad-based and raises the income of all, especially the poor. Thus, inclusive economic growth requires steady, or even falling, income inequality if it is to maximize the growth of incomes at the lower end of the distribution. Yet, this is at odds with the Kuznets (1955) hypothesis that economic development tends to put upward pressure on income inequality, at least initially and in the absence of countervailing policies. Our book explores this developer's dilemma or 'Kuznetsian tension' between ST and income inequality.

The core questions of our book are: (i) What are the types or 'varieties' of ST that have been experienced in developing countries? (ii) What inequality dynamics are associated with each variety of ST? (iii) Lastly, what policies have been utilized to manage trade-offs between ST, income inequality, and inclusive growth? We answer these questions using a comparative case-study approach, contrasting nine developing countries, while employing a common analytical framework and a set of common data sets across the case studies. The intended intellectual contribution of the book is thus, first, to provide a comparative analysis of the relationship between ST, income inequality, and inclusive growth; second, to do so empirically at a regional and national level; third, to draw conclusions from the cases on the varieties of ST, their inequality dynamics, and the policies that have been employed to mediate the developer's dilemma.

This introductory chapter is structured as follows: Section 2 defines ST and inclusive growth. Section 3 discusses Kuznets seminal work and our approach. Section 4 outlines our methodology and limitations. Finally, section 5 presents the book's structure.

Armida Salsiah Alisjahbana et al., *The Developer's Dilemma*. In: *The Developer's Dilemma.*
Edited by Armida Salsiah Alisjahbana, Kunal Sen, Andy Sumner, and Arief Anshory Yusuf, Oxford University Press.
© UNU-WIDER (2022). DOI: 10.1093/oso/9780192855299.003.0001

2. Defining structural transformation and inclusive growth

Structural transformation refers to a shift of economic activity from a less to a more productive sector, which spurs economic development in the Classical School of economic theory (of Lewis 1954, 1972, 1979; Kaldor 1957, 1967, as well as pioneers of sectoral-based analysis in development economics such as Chenery 1960, 1975, 1979; Hirschman 1958; and Myrdal 1957a, 1957b, 1968). Compared to inclusive growth, ST in the sense we use the concept has received limited attention recently, with the exception of McMillan et al. (2016) and Pritchett et al. (2017), although the latter focuses more so on the political economy of economic development. In this book, ST refers solely to inter-sectoral transitions towards higher-productivity activities.

One reason for this disregard is that the neoclassical growth model (developed by Solow 1956) considers incentives for saving, physical and human capital accumulation, and innovation as drivers of growth rather than sectoral reallocation of economic activity, as the Classical School does. Consequently, while neoclassical economics acknowledges the significance of increasing productivity, it typically employs a one-sector model of economic growth, which does not examine between-sector movements or ST. This indifference to sectors stems from the conviction that an equilibrating process of marginal returns results in an optimal distribution of production factors, at least in the medium-to-long run. According to neoclassical economics, growth in poorer countries will be more rapid than in richer ones, and economies with access to the same technology will reach similar levels of income (see Sutirtha et al. 2016 for discussion).

In contrast, the Classical School perceives the development of specific sectors and activities—manufacturing, in particular—to be crucial for economic growth. This is based on the conviction that in fact a disequilibrium and a subsequent suboptimal allocation of production factors across sectors may exist in the long term, which hampers economic development.

This book also pays attention to 'inclusive growth'. Inclusive growth in developing countries has been much discussed in terms of who benefits from growth and by how much and why. The area of enquiry has evolved through a set of precursors in the early 1970s (see, for instance, Adelman and Morris 1973; Chenery et al. 1974) and was reframed several times during the following decades into 'growth with equity' (see, for instance, Fei et al. 1979; Jomo 2006; World Bank 1993), 'pro-poor growth' (see, e.g. Besley and Cord 2006; Grimm et al. 2007; Shorrocks and van der Hoeven 2004), and 'inclusive growth' (see Ali and Zhang 2007; Klasen 2010; McKinley 2010; Rauniyar and Kanbur 2010). The latter developed into the umbrella term for discussions on the beneficiaries of growth.[1] In this

---

[1] While being related, these terms describe slightly different concepts. For instance, 'growth with equity' generally refers to growth accompanied by steady or decreasing inequality (and is associated

book, inclusive growth refers to economic growth which entails steady or falling income inequality and/or falling income poverty.

3. Our approach: Kuznets revisited

Our book's approach draws on Kuznets (1955) influential paper on the link between economic development, ST, and income inequality. Kuznets predominantly examined labour and its transition from rural to urban 'sectors'. His work thus resembles the dualism of Arthur Lewis, since both scholars made use of a dual economy heuristic. Lewis investigated the shift of labour from the 'traditional' to the 'modern' sector, whereas Kuznets studied the significance of rural–urban movements of labour for economic development. Kuznets argued that the transition in employment would cause income inequality to initially increase and to later decrease. Thus, inequality would follow an inverted-U-shaped curve during economic development, referred to since as the Kuznets curve.

Kuznets thesis that inequality would rise first and then decline has been contested. However, it is crucial to acknowledge that his inferences were highly tentative, as he noted himself due to data limitations at the time. His theory that inequality increased was deduced from time-series data for the UK, the United States, and East as well as West Germany, and point estimates of inequality for Ceylon, India, and Puerto Rico. Less often recalled is that he inferred the hypothesized fall in inequality from an abstract arithmetic model rather than from data. Notwithstanding the paper's numerous caveats, Kuznets work is frequently reduced solely to the (in)famous curve. This is a shame given the richness of the paper beyond the inverted-U curve itself.

Kuznets argued that overall income inequality is driven by differences in income *between* the urban and rural sector as well as *within* each sector. He maintained that inequality could increase or decrease simply due to the inter-sectoral movement of labour:

[E]ven if the differential in per capita income between the two sectors remains constant and the intra-sector distributions are identical for the two sectors, the mere shift in the proportions of numbers produces slight but significant changes in the distribution for the country as a whole.

(1955: 14–15)

with World Bank 1993). In contrast, absolute 'pro-poor growth' is characterized by a decreasing poverty headcount (or by the incomes of the poor rising above a given poverty line or fractile line), relative pro-poor growth in turn by a decreasing poverty headcount plus declining inequality of outcome (see discussions in Bourguignon 2003: 3–26; Kakwani and Pernia 2000; Ravallion 2004). Finally, 'inclusive growth' describes a fall in monetary and non-monetary poverty. This might require the inclusion of the poor—or a greater societal faction as well as the poor—in growth processes by creating employment and enhancing capabilities (through improved access to public goods such as health care or education; see Sen 2014 for discussion) to decrease poverty and potentially also inequality of opportunity and/or outcomes.

Two sub-processes of ST—that is, labour leaving the rural sector—are responsible for rising inequality: (i) people moving from a sector with lower to one with higher mean income; and (ii) individuals transitioning from a sector characterized by low variance in income to one where the variance is higher. If both sub-processes follow the same trend, that is, if the sector that is left has both a low mean income and a low variance while the sector that is transitioned to is characterized by a higher mean income as well as a high variance, inequality will rise during ST. Kuznets argued that the urban sector, which tends to be more unequal and with higher wages, typically grows during economic development; thus, inequality would increase during economic growth. In contrast, if labour is moving from a sector characterized by low mean income but higher within-sector inequality to a sector where the mean income is higher but inequality lower, then it is less certain whether inequality will rise.

Anand and Kanbur (1993a), provide a diagrammatic exposition of the Kuznets process to make clear the contribution of between-sector (or group) inequality and within-sector (or group) inequality to overall inequality.[2] Let I be the overall measure of inequality in a given country and x the share of workers in the urban sector. Let the working population of the country be normalized to one. Define between-sector (or group) inequality as the inequality in the income distribution when the fraction x of the working population receives income u_1 and the remaining fraction, $1-x$, receives income u_2 (where between-group inequality is defined as the value of the inequality measure when everyone in the sector receives the mean income of the sector). Following Kuznets, we can assume that the mean income of the urban sector is higher than that of the rural sector, that is, $u_1 > u_2$.

It is clear from this that between-group inequality must be zero at both $x = 0$ and $x = 1$; that is, when all workers are either in the rural sector or in the urban sector, there can be no between-group inequality. However, in the range where x is higher than zero but less than one, inequality will first rise with increasing x, then fall (as captured in Figure 1.1). This is because when x is small, there are more workers in the low-income sector (in our example, rural) than in the high-income sector, so between-sector income differences are significant. However, once a larger proportion of labourers work in the high-income sector, between-group inequality starts falling until it reaches zero, when all workers are in the high-income sector.

If we consider the behaviour of within-group inequality and define within-group inequality as the difference between overall inequality and between-group inequality, its movement with increasing x will depend on the assumptions regarding within-group inequality in the urban sector versus the rural sector. If one

[2] This exposition depends on the assumption that the inequality measure we are considering is decomposable. Among the inequality measures available in literature, the variance of log income and the mean log deviation (which is Theil's second index) have such decomposition properties; see Robinson (1976) and Kanbur (2017).

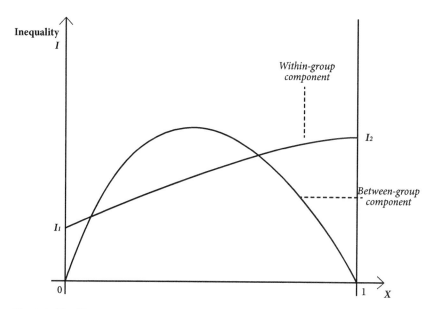

Fig. 1.1 The Kuznets process
Source: based on Anand and Kanbur (1993a).

assumes that there is higher within-group inequality in the urban sector than in the rural sector (as seems to be implied by Kuznets), then the within-group inequality component of overall inequality will strictly rise as x increases—that is, within-group inequality will increase with ST (as shown in Figure 1.1).

The combination of the behaviour of between-group inequality and within-group inequality may lead to the well-known inverted-U-shaped relationship between ST and inequality—in Figure 1.1, as x increases, there is an unambiguous increase in inequality. However, once a certain x is reached and the between-group component dominates the within-group component, inequality will start declining.

The curve's exact shape and the point when inequality starts to fall are contingent upon context-specific aspects. For instance, Kanbur and Zhuang (2013) illustrate that the rates of urbanization as well as the levels of between-sector and within-sector inequality differ considerably across countries. They show that these initial levels of between-sector and within-sector inequality in turn influence the extent of the effect that urbanization has on inequality.

Kuznets argued that inequality increases at first because growth will initially benefit those who are better off due to capital ownership and/or higher education levels. He argued that inequality would fall after a point due to increasing real wages in the urban sector, as a consequence of the growing number of workers leaving the rural sector. Thus, to counterbalance the dynamic of initially increasing inequality, Kuznets suggested that the answer was to increase the income share of those at the lower end of the distribution in the urban sector. Moreover, he assumed that in democracies, the political power of urban labour would grow, enabling them to collectively request wage increases, which would then result in legislation supporting a redistribution of income. Consequently, political forces are crucial to flattening inequality, which is why with progressing development, inequality would decrease. Some criticize Kuznets for not considering the significant effect of policy on inequality.

Kanbur (2017) flags this critique as unreasonable, since Kuznets (1955: 8–9, 16–17) discusses the option to use policy to counteract increasing inequality:

> One group of factors counteracting the cumulative effect of concentration of savings upon upper-income shares is legislative interference and 'political' decisions. These may be aimed at limiting the capital accumulation of property directly through inheritance taxes and other explicit capital levies. They may produce similar effects indirectly, … All these interventions, even when not directly aimed at limiting the effects of capital accumulation of past savings in the hands of the few, do reflect the view of society on the long-term utility of wide income inequalities.

Cross-country empirical evidence for the Kuznets curve has evolved over time as new data sets have become available and approaches to testing the thesis have changed. While a few studies in the 1970s supported the theory (Ahluwalia 1976a, 1976b; Ahluwalia et al. 1979), others from the 1980s and 1990s challenged it (Anand and Kanbur 1984, 1993a, 1993b). Deininger and Squire (1998) in turn questioned its universal validity, noting an inverted U in some, but not in other, countries. Thus, at present, the prevalent opinion suggests that there is no universal trajectory of inequality during economic development (also owing to the intervention of some governments, which is challenging to isolate in inequality data). Further, most studies have considered growth and inequality rather than ST and inequality. One recent exception is Baymul and Sen (2020), who conclude that a shift of labour to the manufacturing sector has equalized incomes no matter the country's level of ST. Labour moving into the services sector in turn has an unequalizing effect in structurally developing countries (i.e. countries where agriculture is the predominant sector by employment) but acts as equalizing in structurally developed countries (i.e. countries where manufacturing employment exceeds agricultural employment).

In this book, we go further and empirically identify a set of different varieties of ST developing these from Kim and Sumner (2019). These are based on the direction of movement of the shares of manufacturing employment and manufacturing value added. These stylized pathways of ST are: 'primary industrialization', 'upgrading industrialization', 'advanced industrialization', 'stalled industrialization', and 'secular deindustrialization' (see Figure 1.2).

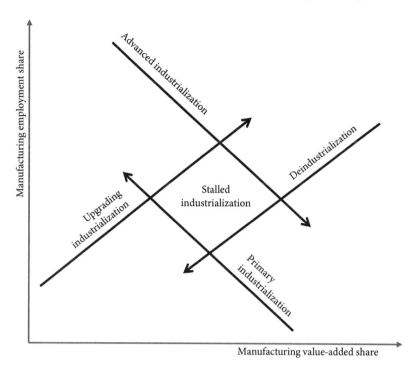

Fig. 1.2 Varieties of structural transformation
Source: developed from Kim and Sumner (2019).

Primary industrialization is characterized by a decreasing share of manufacturing value added but rising manufacturing employment (suggesting a decline in manufacturing productivity). During upgrading industrialization, both the value-added and employment shares of manufacturing are rising. Advanced industrialization proceeds contrary to primary industrialization, with the manufacturing value-added share growing while the employment share is falling (thus, productivity is increasing). Stalled industrialization is characterized by stagnating shares in both manufacturing value added and employment, while in the case of secular deindustrialization, both value-added and employment shares are declining.

Due to its focus on manufacturing, this typology is unsuitable to describe the development of very poor countries that are highly dependent on aid and remain predominantly agrarian or of developing economies with a significant mining sector. Furthermore, it is possible, and at times advantageous, that countries switch between the varieties of ST.

Subsequently, potential interactions of inequality trajectories and different forms of economic development can be investigated. Figure 1.3 illustrates our approach. The vertical axis of Figure 1.3 illustrates whether income inequality is rising or remains constant/is falling, while the horizontal axis depicts whether

		Growth-enhancing structural transformation	
		Weak	Strong
Income inequality	Increasing	Weak/'adverse'	Strong
	Stable or declining	Ambiguous	Weak/'benign'

Fig. 1.3 Typology of the Kuznetsian tension: income inequality trends versus growth-enhancing structural transformation

Note: Strong growth-enhancing ST is defined as more than 2 per cent gross domestic product (GDP) growth (using data from World Development Indicators, World Bank n.d.-b) and authors used other criteria, such as changes in value-added and employment shares in manufacturing, along with GDP growth.
Source: authors' compilation.

growth-enhancing ST is weak or strong. This yields four combinations of ST and inequality: (i) weak/'adverse' Kuznetian tension, characterized by rising inequality and weak growth-enhancing ST (see top-left cell in Figure 1.3); (ii) ambiguous Kuznetian tension with constant or falling inequality accompanied by weak growth-enhancing ST (see bottom-left cell); (iii) strong Kuznetian tension, where inequality is rising and strong growth-enhancing ST (see top-right cell); and (iv) finally, weak/'benign' Kuznetian tension, defined by constant or falling inequality with strong growth-enhancing ST (see bottom-right cell). Given that the interaction of inequality and ST varies according to time and context, countries can switch between these types over time.

4. The methodology and limitations of the book

This book is based on a set of comparative case studies which are bound together by the use of a common framework and common data sets. The book assembles a highly international set of scholars from around the world. When choosing the country cases, we sought to cover each of the developing regions in the world, to utilize the contributing scholars' country expertise, and additionally mix lower-middle-income and upper-middle-income developing countries (LMICs and UMICs, respectively) in order to consider countries which have experienced substantial ST. Of our nine cases, from East Asia, we consider Indonesia (a recent UMIC), China (UMIC), and Thailand (UMIC). In South Asia, we analyse India (an LMIC for some time) and Bangladesh (a recent LMIC). In sub-Saharan Africa, we focus on Ghana (a recent LMIC) and South Africa (a long-standing UMIC). Finally, in Latin America, we consider Brazil (a long-standing UMIC) and Chile (a country moving from UMIC recently to become a high-income country).

Clearly, as with any comparative case-study approach, there are limitations. Given practical constraints, we cannot cover all countries. Furthermore, matters change over time and the future may not be as the past. In order to broaden the coverage of this book, the survey chapter analyses the regions from which we chose cases. Without a doubt, there are other developing countries that would be interesting to look at in future work, such as Vietnam, Argentina, and Mauritius, to name just three. Furthermore, we do not cover the former Soviet Union and Eastern Europe, nor commodity-driven countries (some of our cases do have substantial commodities but their development has been via ST, at least historically). The former set of 'transition economies' has such a distinct shared history that it makes comparisons to other developing countries particularly challenging. And the latter, commodity-driven economies are not the focus of our study (for discussion, see Addison et al. 2018).

We also neither cover intra-sectoral ST nor the drivers of ST. Why not? Recent literature has highlighted the importance of within-sector productivity increases, which may occur in a period of economic change as less efficient firms exit the industry and more efficient firms increase in size (see World Bank 2013). This literature suggests that intra-sectoral movement of labour and capital may be the primary driver of productivity increases related to ST, especially in dual economies, where unproductive informal firms and more productive formal firms exist side by side in the same industry. While we acknowledge the importance of intra-sectoral reallocation of labour in driving overall productivity growth in developing countries, the foci of this book are ST in the Classical School sense, which is productivity-enhancing, inter-sectoral movement of labour and capital, and the relationship between ST and inequality dynamics.

The literature on the drivers of ST is vast and several notable contributions in mainstream economics have recently analysed the drivers of ST (Ngai and Pissarides 2007; Duarte and Restuccia 2010; and Herrendorf et al. 2014). Two classes of models have been developed: the first set of models assumes the drivers to be technological in nature and attributes ST to different rates of sectoral total-factor productivity growth. The second class of models prefers a utility-based explanation, where the movement of labour from the traditional sector (typically agriculture) to the modern sector (typically manufacturing) is caused by greater income elasticity of the latter via the so-called Engel effects (see Clark (1940) for an earlier exposition). While productivity growth and demand-side factors can be seen as proximate causes of ST, the fundamental determinants of ST are seen as related to economic globalization and technological change (see Rodrik 2016). In this book, we are less concerned with the drivers, whether proximate or fundamental, of ST, but rather we are interested in the consequences of ST and the implications for inequality and inclusive growth.

In our case studies, we make use of the same data sets across the book (with the exception of Bangladesh), namely the Groningen Growth and Development Centre (GGDC) 10-Sector Database (see, for discussion, Timmer et al. 2015). The

GGDC 10-Sector Database allows for analysis of changes in employment, productivity, and value added at a sectoral level in developing countries since the 1960s. This is supplemented with data from national sources if national data matches the GGDC 10-Sector Database. Data on inclusive growth is drawn from the World Bank's PovcalNet online analysis tool (World Bank 2019) and a standardized version of the United Nations University-World Institute for Development Economics Research (UNU-WIDER) World Income Inequality Database (WIID) (UNU-WIDER 2019). The GGDC data set broadly includes all employment regardless of formality or informality (Diao et al. 2017: 4–6), but the extent to which the value-added data do so depends on the quality of national sources (see Timmer et al. 2015).

The limitations of the PovcalNet data set are discussed in Edward and Sumner (2014, 2015) and relate to caveats that are common in poverty and inequality data, specifically, the use of purchasing power parity (PPP) conversion rates for cross-country income poverty estimation; the setting of poverty lines themselves; the comparability of income and consumption surveys; and the poor capture of income/consumption among the richest.

5. Book structure

Our book is structured thus: following this introduction, a survey chapter provides a regional overview. Subsequently, the case studies of nine countries are presented in a common format, organized by regions: first, East Asia, including Indonesia, China, and Thailand; second, South Asia, with India and Bangladesh; third, sub-Saharan Africa, thus Ghana and South Africa, finally, Latin America with Brazil and Chile. We then have a chapter relating to the future of the developer's dilemma. In the forward-looking chapter, scenarios for ST and the inequality dynamics implied are explored, as, it seems certain, developing countries will face new constellations of ST related to tertiarization, in particular amid new technologies such as artificial intelligence and the processes of automation. Finally, the concluding chapter draws together the themes of the book, focusing on the questions highlighted earlier in this introduction.

References

Addison, T., and A. Roe (2018). *Extractive Industries: The Management of Resources as a Driver of Sustainable Development*. Oxford: Oxford University Press.

Adelman, I., and C. Morris (1973). *Economic Growth and Social Equity in Developing Countries*. Stanford, CA: Stanford University Press.

Ahluwalia, M.S. (1976a). 'Inequality, Poverty and Development', *Journal of Development Economics*, 3: 307–342.

Ahluwalia, M.S. (1976b). 'Income Distribution and Development: Some Stylized Facts', *American Economic Review*, 66(2): 128–135.

Ahluwalia, M.S., N.G. Carter, and H.B. Chenery (1979). 'Growth and Poverty in Developing Countries', *Journal of Development Economics*, 6: 199–341.

Ali, I., and J. Zhang (2007). 'Inclusive Growth toward a Prosperous Asia: Policy Implications'. ADB Economics and Research Department Working Paper 97. Manila: Asian Development Bank.

Anand, S., and S.M.R. Kanbur (1984). 'The Kuznets Press and the Inequality–Development Relationship'. Discussion Paper 249. Colchester: University of Essex Department of Economics.

Anand, S., and S.M.R. Kanbur (1993a). 'The Kuznets Process and the Inequality–Development Relationship', *Journal of Development Economics*, 40: 25–72.

Anand, S. and S.M.R. Kanbur (1993b). 'Inequality and Development: A Critique', *Journal of Development Economics*, 41(1): 19–43.

Baymul, C., and K. Sen (2020). 'Was Kuznets Right? New Evidence on the Relationship between Structural Transformation and Inequality', *Journal of Development Studies*, 65(9): 1643–1662.

Besley, T., and L.J. Cord (eds) (2006). *Delivering on the Promise of Pro-Poor Growth: Insights and Lessons from Country Experiences*. Washington, DC: World Bank.

Bourguignon, F. (2003). 'The Growth Elasticity of Poverty Reduction: Explaining Heterogeneity across Countries and Time Periods'. In T. Eicher and S. Turnovsky (eds), *Inequality and Growth: Theory and Policy Implications*. Cambridge, MA: MIT Press, 3–26.

Chenery, H.B. (1960). 'Patterns of Industrial Growth', *The American Economic Review*, 50(4): 624–654.

Chenery, H.B. (1975). 'The Structuralist Approach to Development Policy', *The American Economic Review* 65(2): 310–316.

Chenery, H.B. (1979). *Structural Change and Development Policy*. New York: Oxford University Press.

Chenery, H.B., M. Ahluwalia, C. Bell, J. Duloy, and R. Jolly (1974). *Redistribution with Growth*. Oxford: Oxford University Press for the World Bank.

Clark, Colin. (1940). *Conditions of Economic Progress*. London: Macmillan.

Deininger, K., and L. Squire (1998). 'New Ways of Looking at Old Issues: Inequality and Growth', *Journal of Development Economics*, 57: 259–287.

Diao, X., M. McMillan, and D. Rodrik (2017). 'The Recent Growth Boom in Developing Economies: A Structural-Change Perspective'. NBER Working Paper 23132. Cambridge, MA: National Bureau of Economic Research.

Duarte, M., and D. Restuccia (2010). 'The Role of Structural Transformation in Aggregate Productivity', *The Quarterly Journal of Economics*, 125(1): 129–173.

Edward, P., and A. Sumner (2014). 'Estimating the Scale and Geography of Global Poverty Now and in the Future: How Much Difference Do Method and Assumptions Make?', *World Development* 58(C): 67–82.

Edward, P., and A. Sumner (2015). 'New Estimates of Global Poverty and Inequality: How Much Difference Do Price Data Really Make?' CGD Working Paper 403 (and data set). Washington, DC: Center for Global Development.

Fei, J.C.H., G. Ranis, and S.W.Y. Kuo (1979). *Growth with Equity: The Taiwan Case*. Washington, DC: World Bank.

Grimm, M., S. Klasen, and A. McKay (2007). *Determinants of Pro-Poor Growth: Analytical Issues and Findings from Country Cases*. Basingstoke: Palgrave Macmillan.

Herrendorf, B., R. Rogerson, and A. Valentinyi. (2014). 'Growth and Structural Transformation'. In P. Aghion and S. Durlauf (eds), *Handbook of Economic Growth*, Vol. 2. Amsterdam: Elsevier, 855–941.

Hirschman, A.O. (1958). *The Strategy of Economic Development*. New Haven, CT: Yale University Press.

Jomo, K.S. (2006). *The Great Divergence: Hegemony, Uneven Development, and Global Inequality*. Oxford: Oxford University Press.

Kakwani, N., and E. Pernia (2000). 'What Is Pro-Poor Growth?', *Asian Development Review*, 18(1): 1–16.

Kaldor, N. (1957). 'A Model of Economic Growth', *The Economic Journal* 67(268): 591–624.

Kaldor, N. (1967). *Strategic Factors in Economic Development*. Ithaca, NY: New York State School of Industrial and Labor Relations, Cornell University.

Kanbur, R. (2017). 'Structural Transformation and Income Distribution: Kuznets and Beyond'. IZA Discussion Paper 10636. Bonn: Institute of Labor Economics.

Kanbur, R., and J. Zhuang (2013). 'Urbanization and Inequality in Asia', *Asian Development Review* 30(1): 131–147.

Kim, K., and A. Sumner (2019). 'The Five Varieties of Industrialisation: A New Typology of Diverse Empirical Experience in the Developing World'. ESRC GPID Research Network Working Paper 18. London: ESRC Global Poverty and Inequality Dynamics Research Network (GPID).

Klasen, S. (2010). 'Measuring and Monitoring Inclusive Growth: Multiple Definitions, Open Questions, and Some Constructive Proposals'. ADB Working Paper Series. Manila: Asian Development Bank.

Kuznets, S. (1955). 'Economic Growth and Income Inequality', *American Economic Review*, 45(1): 1–28.

Lewis, W.A. (1954). 'Economic Development with Unlimited Supplies of Labour', *The Manchester School*, 22(2): 139–191.

Lewis, W.A. (1972). 'Reflections on Unlimited Labour'. In L.E. diMarco (ed.), *International Economics and Development. Essays in Honour of Raoul Prebisch*. New York: Academic Press.

Lewis, W.A. (1979). 'The Dual Economy Revisited', *The Manchester School* 47(3): 211–229.

McKinley, T. (2010). 'Inclusive Growth Criteria and Indicators: An Inclusive Growth Index for Diagnosis of Country Progress'. ADB Sustainable Development Working Paper 14. Manila: Asian Development Bank.

McMillan, M., D. Rodrik, and K. Sepuúlveda (2016). *Structural Change, Fundamentals, and Growth A Framework and Case Studies*. Cambridge: Cambridge University Press.

Myrdal, G. (1957a). *Rich Lands and Poor: The Road to World Prosperity*. New York: Harper & Row.

Myrdal, G. (1957b). *Economic Theory and Underdeveloped Regions*. London: Gerald Duckworth & Co. Ltd.

Myrdal, G. (1968). *Asian Drama: An Inquiry into the Poverty of Nations*. New York City: Pantheon.

Ngai, R., and C. Pissarides (2007). 'Structural Change in a Multisector Model of Growth', *American Economic Review*, 97(1): 429–443.

Pritchett, L., K. Sen, and E. Werker (2017). *Deals and Development. The Political Dynamics of Growth Episodes*. Oxford: Oxford University Press.

Rauniyar, G., and R. Kanbur (2010). 'Inclusive Development: Two Papers on Conceptualization, Application, and the ADB Perspective'. Cornell University Working Paper 2010-01. Ithaca, NY: Cornell University.

Ravallion, M. (2004). 'Measuring Pro-Poor Growth: A Primer'. World Bank Working Paper 3242. Washington, DC: World Bank.

Robinson, S. (1976). 'Income Distribution within Groups, among Groups, and Overall: A Technique of Analysis'. Research Program in Development Studies Discussion Paper 65. Princeton, NJ: Princeton University.

Rodrik, D. (2016). 'Premature Deindustrialization', *Journal of Economic Growth*, 21: 1–33.

Sen, K. (2014). 'Inclusive Growth', *Asian Development Review*, 31(1): 136–162.

Shorrocks, A., and R. van der Hoeven (eds) (2004). *Growth, Inequality and Poverty: Prospects for Pro-Poor Economic Development*. Oxford: Oxford University Press.

Solow, R.M. (1956). 'A Contribution to the Theory of Economic Growth', *Quarterly Journal of Economics* 70(1): 65–94.

Sutirtha, R., M. Kessler, and A. Subramanian (2016). 'Glimpsing the End of Economic History? Unconditional Convergence and the Missing Middle-Income Trap'. CGD Working Paper 438. Washington, DC: Center for Global Development.

Timmer, M.P., G.J. de Vries, and K. de Vries (2015). 'Patterns of Structural Change in Developing Countries'. In J. Weiss and M. Tribe (eds), *Routledge Handbook of Industry and Development*. London: Routledge, 65–83.

UNU-WIDER (2019). Standardized dataset based on World Income Inequality Database, WIID 4, version 22 February 2019. Helsinki: UNU-WIDER.

World Bank (n.d.-a). 'PovcalNet'. Online analysis tool for global poverty monitoring. Washington, DC: World Bank. http://iresearch.worldbank.org/PovcalNet/home.aspx

World Bank (2019). 'World Development Indicators' (data base). Washington, DC: World Bank.

World Bank (1993). *The East Asian Miracle: Economic Growth and Public Policy*. Washington, DC: World Bank.

World Bank (2013). *World Development Report: Jobs*. Washington, DC: World Bank.

2

The Developer's Dilemma

A Survey of Structural Transformation and Inequality Dynamics

*Armida Salsiah Alisjahbana, Kyunghoon Kim, Kunal Sen,
Andy Sumner, and Arief Anshory Yusuf*

1. Introduction

The 'developer's dilemma' is a tension emerging from the fact that developing countries are pursuing two goals which may generate a tension around income inequality. Developing countries, first, are seeking structural transformation and, second, are seeking broad-based economic growth to raise the incomes of the poor. Simon Kuznets (1955) originally hypothesized that structural transformation may have a tendency, in the absence of policy intervention, to put upward pressure on income inequality. However, broad-based economic growth requires steady, or even falling, income inequality to maximize the growth of incomes at the lower end of the distribution.

In this chapter, we analyse the empirical experience of the developing world in order to present a typology of 'varieties' of structural transformation and discuss the structural transformation–inequality relationship under different varieties of structural transformation. The chapter is structured as follows. Section 2 discusses the empirical experience of structural transformation in the developing world since 1960, section 3 discusses structural transformation and inequality dynamics, and section 4 concludes.

2. Empirical patterns of structural transformation

2.1 The role of structural transformation

McMillan and Rodrik (2011), in considering sectoral and aggregate labour productivity data between 1990 and 2005, demonstrate that the transfer of labour and

Armida Salsiah Alisjahbana, et al., *The Developer's Dilemma*. In: *The Developer's Dilemma*.
Edited by Armida Salsiah Alisjahbana, Kunal Sen, Andy Sumner, and Arief Anshory Yusuf,
Oxford University Press. © UNU-WIDER (2022). DOI: 10.1093/oso/9780192855299.003.0002

other inputs to higher-productivity activities fuels economic development. Their paper additionally notes that, conditional on the precise sectors to which labour is reallocated, structural transformation can either produce growth-enhancing or growth-reducing effects. This point is of substantial importance in terms of validating the hypotheses of the classical school, insofar as it highlights the sectoral movement of labour as a key catalyst in determining the trajectory of economic development. In this view, their paper attributes the growth-enhancing effects of structural transformation in Asia to the fact that labour transferred from lower to higher labour productivity sectors therein. They argue that the opposite was the case in sub-Saharan Africa and Latin America, where labour moved from higher- to lower-productivity sectors, which in turn constrained economic growth rates. Their paper also suggests that countries reliant on the commodities sectors have a tendency towards growth-reducing structural transformation. Even if these sectors achieve higher levels of productivity, they often struggle to absorb surplus workers from the agricultural sector.

Following on from their study, this section extends the time series and uses more fine-grained regional classifications to understand the different characteristics of structural transformation in the non-Western world. This section takes a close look at the varying empirical patterns of structural transformation in high-income East Asia, developing East Asia (excluding China), Latin America, sub-Saharan Africa, China, and India by considering sectoral value-added and employment shares, and sectoral labour productivity of around four decades up to 2010. China and India are analysed separately on the grounds that they have a large population and economy which are comparable to those of major regions. This chapter sometimes refers to these two countries as 'regions' for convenience.

Before we begin to analyse the structural transformation patterns, we present the country composition of each region according to economic structures. In this regard, Baymul and Sen (2020) provide an insightful classification of economies: (i) countries in which manufacturing employment is larger than agricultural employment are called 'structurally developed'; (ii) countries in which services employment is larger than agricultural employment are called 'structurally developing'; and (iii) countries in which agricultural employment is the largest are called 'structurally underdeveloped'. Using this classification and employment data from the Groningen Growth and Development Centre's (GGDC) 10-Sector Database (Timmer et al. 2015), we find clear regional variations (Table 2.1). In 2010, sub-Saharan Africa was mainly composed of 'structurally underdeveloped' countries and had no 'structurally developed' countries. Latin America and developing East Asia were mainly composed of 'structurally developing' countries and had no 'structurally underdeveloped' countries. High-income East Asia was composed of only 'structurally developed' countries. India was 'structurally underdeveloped', and China was 'structurally developing'.

Table 2.1 Employment composition in 2010 according to countries' variety of structural transformation

	Structurally underdeveloped	Structurally developing	Structurally developed
India	100	0	0
Sub-Saharan Africa	84	16	0
China	0	100	0
Developing East Asia	0	94	6
Latin America	0	62	38
High-income East Asia	0	0	100

Sources: authors' illustration based on Baymul and Sen (2020) and the GGDC 10-Sector Database Version 2015 (Timmer et al. 2015).

These different economic structures across the regions are the outcomes of different structural transformation patterns over the decades. The diverse patterns of structural transformation have also resulted in regional differences in labour productivity and economic growth rates. Using the methodology of McMillan and Rodrik (2011), Figure 2.1 shows the decomposition of average labour productivity growth into the components of structural transformation ('Between') and within-sector productivity growth ('Within') between *c.* 1970 and *c.* 2010. We also divide the time period into two—before and after 1990—to investigate any notable changes during the recent decades.

We find that there are significant differences in the regions' labour productivity growth rates between *c.* 1970 and *c.* 2010. The growth rate was the highest in China (6.6 per cent), followed by India (3.1 per cent), developing East Asia (2.5 per cent), and high-income East Asia (2.3 per cent). The growth rate was much lower in sub-Saharan Africa (0.5 per cent) and Latin America (0.4 per cent). We find that structural transformation played a relatively small role in sub-Saharan Africa, Latin America, and high-income East Asia, and its role weakened over time. As high-income East Asia is mainly composed of structurally developed countries, this pattern is somewhat expected. Despite this pattern, relatively strong economic growth was achieved in high-income East Asia, considering its stage of development, due to strong improvement in within-sector productivity. However, the case of sub-Saharan Africa is of particular concern as weak structural transformation prevented this economy from taking off. Between 1990 and 2010, the contribution of structural transformation to labour productivity growth was even negative in this region. In Latin America, many middle-income economies struggled to attain high-income country status due to weak structural transformation, especially after 1990. In comparison, we find that structural transformation played an important role in the economic development of developing East Asia, China, and India, albeit

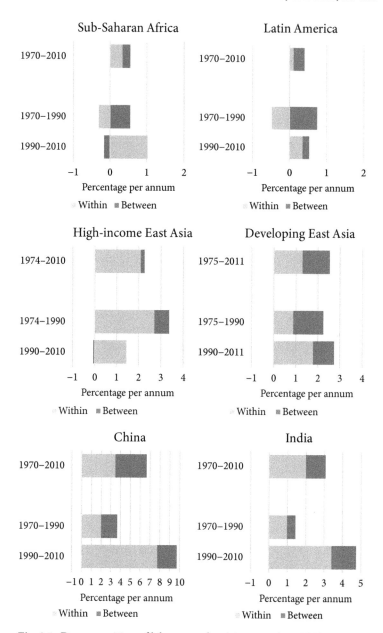

Fig. 2.1 Decomposition of labour productivity growth, *c.* 1970–*c.* 2010

Source: authors' calculations based on the GGDC 10-Sector Database Version 2015 (Timmer et al. 2015).

to varying degrees. For China and India, the contribution of structural transformation, in absolute terms, was larger in the latter period, enabling these two countries
to record impressive economic growth.

2.2 Varieties of structural transformation

With this regional variation in the role of structural transformation in mind, this
subsection conducts a detailed analysis of the diverse structural transformation
patterns. This subsection investigates some important differences and similarities in the trends of value-added and employment composition between regions
and classifies their diverse experience. In each case, five-year moving averages of
value-added (in 2005 constant prices) and employment shares are used in order to
smooth out annual fluctuations and find meaningful trends. The shares mentioned
in the text are also five-year moving averages, unless otherwise stated. In order to
show the changes in value-added shares and employment shares in proportion to
each other, the *x*-axis and *y*-axis have the same minimum and maximum scale values in each of the sectoral graphs in Figure 2.2, except in the graph on the mining
sector as it needs to display very small employment shares. The aggregates are built
thus (based on GGDC 10-Sector Database availability):

- sub-Saharan Africa: Botswana, Ethiopia, Ghana, Kenya, Malawi, Mauritius,
  Nigeria, Senegal, South Africa, Tanzania;
- Latin America: Argentina, Bolivia, Brazil, Chile, Colombia, Costa Rica,
  Mexico, Peru, Venezuela;
- developing East Asia (excluding China): Indonesia, Malaysia, Philippines,
  Thailand;
- high-income East Asia: Hong Kong, Japan, Singapore, South Korea, Taiwan.

Considering that agriculture is often the sector with the lowest labour productivity,
changes in this sector's shares can be an important proxy for assessing the magnitude of structural transformation (Figure 2.2(a)). We find that high-income East
Asia and Latin America experienced the 'later stage of de-agriculturalization' between 1980 and 2010. By 1980, Latin America and high-income East Asia already
had a small agricultural value-added share below 10 per cent. The value-added
share in Latin America stayed at 5–6 per cent during the following three decades
and the share in high-income East Asia declined slightly from 3.9 per cent in 1980
to 1.8 per cent in 2010. During this period, both regions saw a notable decline in the
agricultural employment share. The employment share in Latin America declined
from 33.4 per cent in 1980 to 16.3 per cent in 2010 and the share in high-income
East Asia from 17.5 per cent to 5.3 per cent.

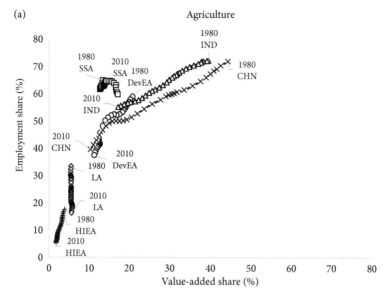

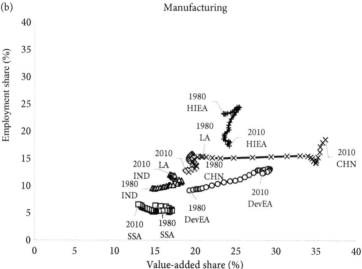

Fig. 2.2 Sectoral value-added (constant price) and employment shares, 1980–2010

Notes: (i) Business services: financial intermediation, renting, business activities; non-business services: (a) wholesale and retail trade, repair of motor vehicles and motorcycles, personal and household goods, hotels and restaurants; (b) transport, storage, communications; (c) public administration, defence, education, health, social work; and (d) other community activities, social and personal service activities, activities of private households. (ii) CHN: China; DevEA: developing East Asia; HIEA: high-income East Asia; IND: India, LA: Latin America; SSA: sub-Saharan Africa. (iii) Value-added and employment shares are five-year moving averages.
Source: authors' calculations based on the GGDC 10-Sector Database Version 2015 (Timmer et al. 2015).

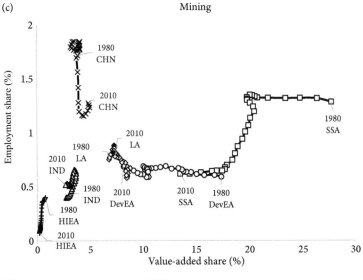

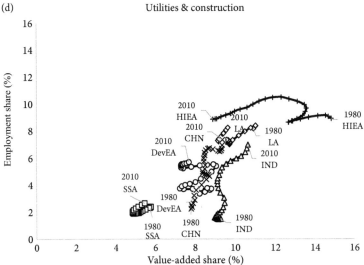

Fig. 2.2 *Continued*

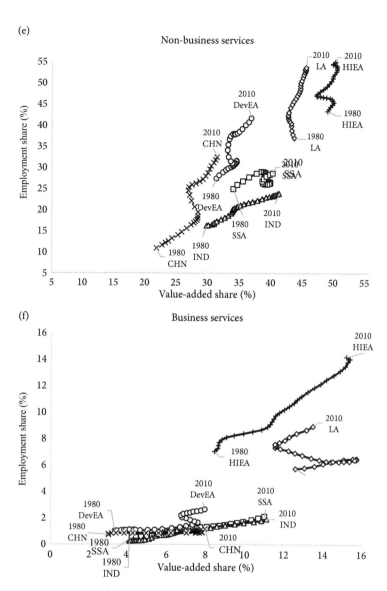

Fig. 2.2 *Continued*

In comparison, other parts of Asia displayed much larger declines in the shares of agricultural value added and employment as they experienced the 'earlier stage of de-agriculturalization'. China and India experienced particularly large declines in both agricultural shares. China's agricultural value-added share declined substantially from 44.2 per cent in 1980 to 10.3 per cent in 2010 and the employment share from 71.9 per cent to 39.6 per cent. In India, the value-added share shrunk from 39.4 per cent in 1980 to 17.2 per cent in 2010 and the employment share from 72.1 per cent to 55.1 per cent. Despite these large changes, India's agricultural shares were similar to those of sub-Saharan Africa in 2010, since its shares in 1980 were very large.

Unlike other regions, sub-Saharan Africa did not show a clear sign of de-agriculturalization between 1980 and 2010. Sub-Saharan Africa's agricultural value added grew faster than the overall economy, leading to a small increase in its share. The agricultural employment share was smaller in 2010 than in 1980, but the size of decline during this period was minuscule compared to other regions. In sub-Saharan Africa, the employment share declined by just 1.7 percentage points (pp) per decade (compare: China: 10.8 pp; developing East Asia: 7.2 pp; Latin America: 5.7 pp; South Asia: 5.7 pp; high-income East Asia: 4.1 pp). In sum, we find that all the regions, except sub-Saharan Africa, experienced notable de-agriculturalization between 1980 and 2010.

The rest of this subsection investigates which economic sectors drove economic and employment growth in the developing world. The aim is to explore which sectors 'filled in the gap' left by the shrinking agricultural sector. First, we analyse the patterns of the manufacturing sector (Figure 2.2(b)). In Asia, the manufacturing sector was an important driver of structural transformation if we look at the long-term trend between 1980 and 2010, yet its role changed over time if we focus on sub-periods. While all four Asian regions displayed a similar pattern during the 1980s, their pattern showed great diversity during the 2000s as they experienced different types of industrialization.

By focusing on the changes in manufacturing value-added and employment shares, we categorize countries' industrialization patterns between 1990 and 2010 into five types (see Figure 2.3). We name these varieties of industrialization as follows: 'primary industrialization', 'upgrading industrialization', 'advanced industrialization', 'stalled industrialization', and 'secular deindustrialization'. The categorization has been constructed based on the recent *direction of changes* in the manufacturing shares and not on the absolute *levels* of those shares. Therefore, a country with a lower manufacturing share may be categorized as going through industrialization, whereas a country with a higher manufacturing share may be categorized as experiencing deindustrialization.

We find four Asian regions in quadrant I in Figure 2.3, meaning that they all experienced concurrent expansion of manufacturing value-added and employment shares, or 'upgrading industrialization' during the 1980s. While China

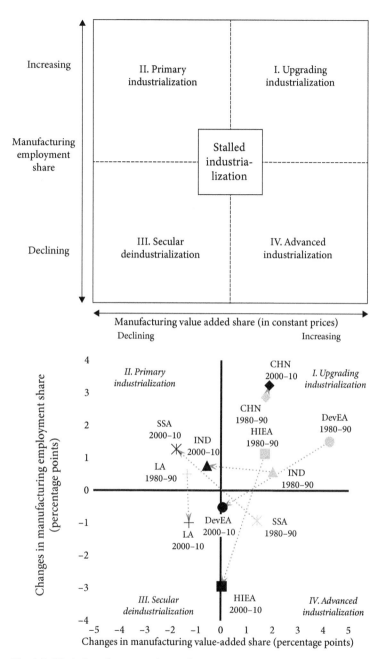

Fig. 2.3 Varieties of structural transformation

Note: (i) CHN: China; DevEA: developing East Asia; HIEA: high-income East Asia; IND: India; LA: Latin America; SSA: sub-Saharan Africa. (ii) Five-year moving averages of value-added and employment shares were used to calculate the changes. *Sources*: Kim and Sumner (2019); authors' calculations based on the GGDC 10-Sector Database Version 2015 (Timmer et al. 2015).

continued to experience 'upgrading industrialization' during the 2000s, the patterns in three other Asian regions changed. During the 2000s, high-income East Asia experienced 'advanced industrialization', with a large decline in the employment share but without a significant decline in the value-added share (quadrant IV in Figure 2.3). Therefore, this region maintained a large manufacturing value-added share, which averaged 23.9 per cent between 2000 and 2010. Developing East Asia experienced 'stalled industrialization' with no significant change in both shares (close to the origin in Figure 2.3), and India experienced labour-centred industrialization or 'primary industrialization', with an increase in the employment share but a decline in the value-added share (quadrant II in Figure 2.3).

In comparison, the manufacturing sector played less of a central role in the structural transformation of other regions. Focusing on the changes in value-added and employment shares, we find that sub-Saharan Africa went through a similar pattern to India during the 2000s and therefore experienced 'primary industrialization'. However, if we also consider the actual shares and not just the patterns, then it is more appropriate to conclude that industrialization has not yet taken off in sub-Saharan Africa (Figure 2.2(b)). Between 1980 and 2010, sub-Saharan Africa's manufacturing employment share never exceeded 7 per cent, despite the recent expansion, and the manufacturing value-added share in 2010 was just 13.5 per cent, which was the smallest share during the period under study. Finally, we find that Latin America experienced a concurrent decline in both value-added and employment shares or 'secular deindustrialization' during the 2000s (quadrant III in Figure 2.3).

The trends in the mining sector were also diverse across the regions. At an aggregate level, this sector is usually capital-intensive and therefore accounted for a small share of employment of around 1 per cent in most economies in 2010, while the value-added share was more varied. Figure 2.2(c) shows that the mining sectors' value-added and employment shares did not change significantly in Latin America, India, and high-income East Asia between 1980 and 2010, although the level of dependence on the sector varied across these regions. China also did not see a large change in its mining value-added share, but did experience a relatively large decline, compared to other regions, in the mining employment share, although the change was only less than half a percentage point. Value added in developing East Asia and sub-Saharan Africa was consistently more dependent on the mining sector, despite the recent shrinking of the sector's shares. In the case of developing East Asia, the mining employment share did not change much, while the mining value-added share halved from 17.4 per cent in 1980 to 8.2 per cent in 2010. In sub-Saharan Africa, the share of mining in both value added and employment shrank markedly, from 27.7 per cent in 1980 to 13.5 per cent in 2010, and from 1.3 per cent in 1980 to 0.6 per cent in 2010, respectively. In sum, the mining sector played a limited role in structural transformation in all the regions, as the value-added and employment shares were either small and remained relatively constant or were large and shrank.

Next, we analyse the utilities and construction sector (Figure 2.2(d)). This sector was an important job-creating industry for China and India between 1980 and 2010. During this period, this sector's employment share increased from 2.2 per cent to 7.3 per cent in China and from 1.5 per cent to 7.0 per cent in India. These notable increases in the employment shares were accompanied by some increases in the value-added share in both countries. Developing East Asia also experienced a notable increase in the employment share of the utilities and construction sector from 3.2 per cent to 5.7 per cent, but unlike China and India, the value-added share did not show a clear long-term trend. In contrast, the utilities and construction sector's shares did not show a significant change in Latin America and sub-Saharan Africa between 1980 and 2010. This sector's value-added and employment shares stayed particularly small in sub-Saharan Africa during this period. If we take a closer look, we find a short period of gentle recovery of both shares in these two regions during the second half of the 2000s, but it is yet inconclusive whether this was the beginning of a new long-term trend. In high-income East Asia, utilities and construction continued to be a large employer in the economy, with the employment share staying relatively stable and averaging 9.4 per cent between 1980 and 2010. However, the value-added share of this sector shrunk significantly from 14.8 per cent to 8.9 per cent.

Non-business services played an important role in structural transformation of all the regions. Figure 2.2(e) shows that non-business services experienced a concurrent and notable expansion of the value-added and employment shares in all the regions between 1980 and 2010. The expansion of the employment share was particularly large in high-income East Asia, Latin America, developing East Asia, and China. As a result, non-business services accounted for around one-half of total employment in high-income East Asia and Latin America and around one-third of total employment in developing East Asia and China. While there were limited changes in non-business services' value-added shares in high-income East Asia and Latin America, there were large increases in the value-added shares in developing East Asia and China, although these increases were smaller than the changes in the employment shares. In contrast, while the non-business services value-added and employment shares also both expanded notably in India and sub-Saharan Africa, the changes in the employment share were smaller than changes in the value-added share.

Finally, business services also played an important role in the structural transformation of all the regions (Figure 2.2(f)). For high-income East Asia, there was a simultaneous expansion of value-added and employment shares between 1980 and 2010. In Latin America, the employment share continuously expanded during this period, while the value-added shares were similar in 1980 and 2010, after some fluctuations. The patterns in four other regions are similar. The expansion of the business services' value-added share was significant in sub-Saharan Africa, India, China, and developing East Asia. In contrast, their business services' employment shares and their changes were much smaller. The expansion of the business services' value-added share was particularly large in sub-Saharan Africa and India, with the share exceeding 11 per cent in 2010, which was higher than China (8.1 per cent) and developing East Asia (8.0 per cent).

2.3 The dynamism of structural transformation

Next, this section analyses sectoral average labour productivities which provide important information on the dynamism of structural transformation. McMillan and Rodrik (2011: 60) state that labour productivity differences between the agricultural and non-agricultural sectors typically 'behave[s] non-monotonically during economic growth'. In their study, this economic logic is demonstrated using a U-shaped curve that has the ratio of agricultural to non-agricultural labour productivity on the y-axis against economy-wide labour productivity levels on the x-axis. At the very early stage of development, there is a small productivity gap between sectors, as there exists weak modern economy. Then, as economic development proceeds, relative labour productivity of the agricultural sector first declines, or the productivity gap between the agricultural and non-agricultural sectors widens, with investments in modern sectors. This is shown by the downward-sloping part of the U-curve. During this period, labour starts to shift from agriculture to modern sectors. Then, after the economy reaches a certain level of development, the productivity gap stops widening and starts to shrink or sectoral productivities begin to converge. This is represented by the turning point and the beginning of the upward-sloping section of the U-curve. This pattern appears as the labour movement between sectors becomes a major driver of economic development, while there exists a large productivity gap between sectors. At a later stage of development, structural transformation continues in advanced countries, often with workers moving from industries to services. Yet the contribution of structural transformation to labour productivity growth is now more limited due to smaller inter-sectoral productivity differences, shown as the high ratios of agricultural to non-agricultural labour productivity towards the end of the upward-sloping part of the U-curve. At this stage, within-sector labour productivity growth becomes a key factor which determines the overall labour productivity growth.

In this subsection, we analyse how relative labour productivity has changed across the regions. Figure 2.4 plots the ratio of agricultural labour productivity to non-agricultural labour productivity of the six regions under study. The curves for four Asian regions seem to represent the different sections of the U-curve which McMillan and Rodrik (2011) discuss. India displays a clear increase in the productivity gap, represented by its curve sloping downwards. The ratio almost halved from 28.8 per cent in 1975 to 15.9 per cent in 2010, during which labour productivity more than trebled. China also displays a clear downward trend, with the

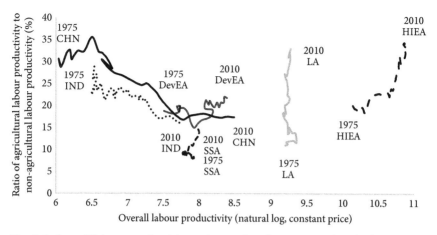

Fig. 2.4 Overall labour productivity and agricultural–non-agricultural relative labour productivity, 1975–2010

Note: CHN: China; DevEA: developing East Asia; HIEA: high-income East Asia; IND: India; LA: Latin America; SSA: sub-Saharan Africa.

Source: authors' calculations based on the GGDC 10-Sector Database Version 2015 (Timmer et al. 2015).

changes, in terms of the ratio and overall labour productivity, being even larger than those of India. The ratio peaked at 35.6 per cent in 1984 and declined to as low as 16.8 per cent in 2003. Between 2003 and 2010, the ratio did not show a significant change, with an average of 17.5 per cent suggesting that China was likely at the turning point of the U-curve. Between 1975 and 2010, China's labour productivity increased by a factor of more than 11. The trend for developing East Asia shows a small version of the U-shaped curve by itself, suggesting that this region went through the turning point and entered the upward-sloping part of the U-curve over the recent decades. Developing East Asia's ratio experienced a sharp decline from 19.9 per cent in 1987 to 14.9 per cent in 1992 and then the ratio started rising and recorded 21.7 per cent in 2010. While developing East Asia's labour productivity experienced healthy growth by increasing by a factor of 2.4 between 1975 and 2010, Figure 2.4 shows that it was caught up by China's labour productivity in 2009. High-income East Asia's ratio showed a clear upward trend between 1975 and 2010. The ratio recorded 18.5 per cent, the lowest level, in 1980 and from then on the ratio increased rapidly and recorded 32.9 per cent in 2010. This pattern indicates a convergence of agricultural and non-agricultural labour productivity. Between 1975 and 2010, high-income East Asia's overall labour productivity more than doubled.

In comparison, the patterns in Latin America and sub-Saharan Africa suggest that these two regions did not move along a similar path to Asia or the traditional development path based on dual-economy models between 1975 and 2010.

There was a rapid convergence in labour productivities of the agricultural and non-agricultural sectors from the early 1980s in Latin America and from the early 2000s in sub-Saharan Africa. While it may be too early to conclude that the increase in the ratio is a permanent feature in sub-Saharan Africa, the upward trend appears to be clearer for Latin America. In contrast to high-income East Asia, the productivity ratio of Latin America and sub-Saharan Africa increased at earlier stages of development and without much improvement in their economy-wide labour productivity. This pattern indicates that productivity convergence began without these two regions having fully enjoyed the benefits of structural transformation.

Next, we investigate the dynamism of structural transformation from the viewpoint of the relative sectoral productivity of modern sectors. In Figure 2.5, the *y*-axis shows the natural logarithm of the ratio of sectoral labour productivity to economy-wide labour productivity, and 0 indicates that sectoral labour productivity was the same as economy-wide labour productivity of the region in a given year.

Figure 2.5(a) shows that the manufacturing sector's labour productivity was continuously higher than economy-wide (or overall) labour productivity in all the regions. Therefore, a shift of labour from agriculture to manufacturing would have contributed to growth-enhancing structural transformation. As we discussed in subsection 2.2 Varieties of structural transformation, India, developing East Asia, and particularly China experienced an increase in the manufacturing employment share between 1980 and 2010, although the patterns during the 2000s were different to each other. In contrast, the manufacturing employment share did not change much in sub-Saharan Africa during the three decades. In Latin America and high-income East Asia, the employment share declined significantly but we find some notable differences between these two regions. The manufacturing employment share began to shrink at a much higher level in high-income East Asia compared to Latin America. Also, relative labour productivity of the manufacturing sector grew significantly in high-income East Asia, whereas it increased only slightly in Latin America. The small increase in manufacturing's relative labour productivity in Latin America was the result of a large fall in the overall labour productivity, rather than healthy manufacturing development. In fact, the absolute level of manufacturing labour productivity declined by 0.6 per cent in Latin America, while that in high-income East Asia increased by 170 per cent between 1980 and 2010. These patterns highlight the different performance under 'advanced industrialization', in the case of high-income East Asia, and 'secular deindustrialization', in the case of Latin America.

The mining sector's labour productivity was also consistently higher than economy-wide labour productivity in all the regions. Despite high labour productivity, the potential of this sector being the engine of growth-enhancing structural transformation is limited due to its small labour absorptive capacity. Furthermore,

(a)

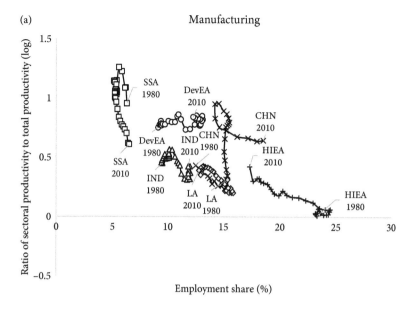

(b)

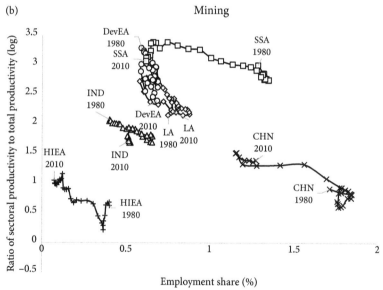

Fig. 2.5 Employment shares and relative labour productivity, 1980–2010

Notes: (i) Business services: financial intermediation, renting, business activities; non-business services: (a) wholesale and retail trade, repair of motor vehicles and motorcycles, personal and household goods, hotels and restaurants; (b) transport, storage, communications; (c) public administration, defence, education, health, social work; and (d) other community activities, social and personal service activities, activities of private households. (ii) CHN: China; DevEA: developing East Asia; HIEA: high-income East Asia; IND: India, LA: Latin America; SSA: sub-Saharan Africa. (iii) Employment shares are five-year moving averages.
Source: authors' calculations based on the GGDC 10-Sector Database Version 2015 (Timmer et al. 2015).

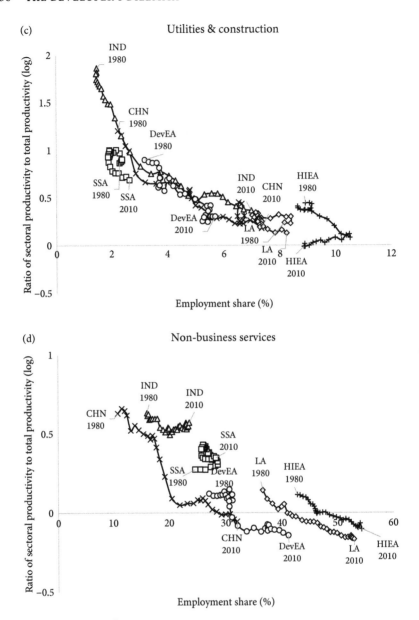

Fig. 2.5 *Continued*

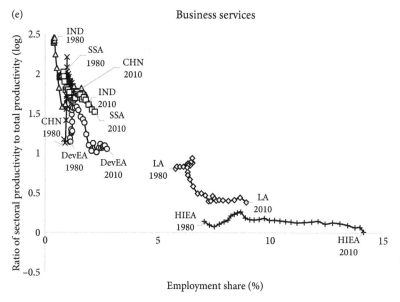

Fig. 2.5 *Continued*

Figure 2.5(b) shows that in regions where the mining employment shares were relatively large, such as China and sub-Saharan Africa, the shares actually declined between 1980 and 2010.

Labour productivity of utilities and construction was also high in all the regions. Except in high-income East Asia during the second half of the 2000s, sectoral labour productivity exceeded economy-wide labour productivity in all the regions. Figure 2.5(c) shows that this sector played a substantial role in employment generation and therefore growth-enhancing structural transformation in India and China, and to a lesser extent in developing East Asia. In contrast, this sector played a limited role in the structural transformation of high-income East Asia, Latin America, and sub-Saharan Africa, while it continued to be an important employer in high-income East Asia.

Next, we analyse labour productivity of services. Non-business services display labour productivity that is higher than economy-wide labour productivity at an earlier stage of development, such as in India and sub-Saharan Africa between 1980 and 2010 and also in developing East Asia up to 1994 and China up to 2005 (Figure 2.5(d)). Therefore, the shift of labour into this sector may play a positive role in poor countries if the workers are entering non-business services from sectors, such as agriculture, with lower labour productivity. However, as economic development progresses, labour productivity of non-business services seems to become lower than overall labour productivity. This pattern was apparent in Latin America and high-income East Asia for most of the period between 1980 and 2010 and in developing East Asia and China in the recent decade. Therefore, structural transformation that depends on non-business services will produce weak economic performance not only because there is a small productivity gap between non-business services and agriculture, but also because there is likelihood of labour shifting from high-productivity modern sectors into non-business services, in which case structural transformation will be growth-reducing. As Figures 2.3 and 2.5 show, the expansion of modern sectors in Latin America was concentrated in non-business services.

Finally, we take a look at the business services sector (Figure 2.5(e)). This sector's labour productivity was higher than economy-wide labour productivity in all the regions between 1980 and 2010. In China, India, sub-Saharan Africa, and developing East Asia, sectoral labour productivity of business services was particularly high. While these regions experienced an expansion of labour share in business services between 1980 and 2010, this sector has not yet played a pivotal role in structural transformation as the share remains small (not bigger than 3 per cent) in these regions. In comparison, Latin America, and especially high-income East Asia, experienced a notable expansion in the employment share of business services, suggesting that this sector played an important role in growth-enhancing structural transformation.

In sum, using the characteristics of structural transformation between 1980 and 2010 described in this section, we can categorize the six regions into three groups: (i) struggling transformer: sub-Saharan Africa; (ii) catching-up transformers: developing East Asia, China, and India and; (iii) mature transformers: Latin America and high-income East Asia. There are many similarities among the regions in each group but there are also some important differences.

Sub-Saharan Africa can be classified as a 'struggling transformer' as it experienced limited structural transformation and small productivity improvement in modern sectors. There were only slight changes in the value-added and employment shares of the agricultural sector and the adjustments within the modern sector were limited. Also, relative sectoral labour productivity of modern sectors recorded small changes during this period. While economic performance during this period was disappointing, high relative labour productivity of modern sectors indicates that the potential of growth-enhancing structural transformation is substantial in this region.

In the case of 'catching-up transformers' (China, India, and developing East Asia), both value-added and employment shares of the agricultural sector declined significantly. In these regions, the manufacturing, utilities and construction, and business services sectors consistently had labour productivity that was higher than economy-wide labour productivity and their employment shares expanded between 1980 and 2010. While there are some differences between these three regions and across time in terms of the magnitude of changes, we can conclude that a notable employment expansion of high-productivity sectors translated into a large contribution of structural transformation to labour productivity growth in these three economies. Considering these sectors' relatively high labour productivity during the most recent years, these sectors can continue to play an important role in growth-enhancing structural transformation. This is especially so for business services, in which the employment share has not yet expanded very much. However, there are also some notable differences between the three regions. During the 2000s, the manufacturing sector played a different role in structural transformation, as China experienced 'upgrading industrialization', India experienced 'primary industrialization', and developing East Asia experienced 'stalled industrialization'. Non-business services have also shown similarities and differences. This sector's employment share expanded in all three regions, but its relative labour productivity became lower than economy-wide labour productivity in developing East Asia and China during the recent period. As the sector's labour productivity remains relatively high in India, this sector may be able to play a positive role in growth-enhancing structural transformation for some time. If these diverse patterns in manufacturing and non-business services continue for a longer period in the future, it may be inappropriate to include these three regions in the same group.

The two regions with higher income, namely high-income East Asia and Latin America, experienced a rapid decline of the agricultural employment share, while recording a small agricultural value-added share. By 2010, the value-added and employment shares of the agricultural sector were much smaller compared to other regions. The different development outcomes between these two regions are striking, despite this similarity. The employment shares in lower-productivity non-business services and higher-productivity business services expanded in both 'mature transformers'. However, the non-business services sector was the main driver in the changes in employment composition in Latin America, whereas both business and non-business services played an important role in high-income East Asia. The contribution of business services to the changes in services sector employment share between 1980 and 2010 was 37.9 per cent in high-income East Asia, which was much higher than 16.1 per cent in Latin America. These patterns show that tertiarization was more growth-enhancing in high-income East Asia than in Latin America. Also, we find some similarities and differences in the two regions' manufacturing performance. The manufacturing employment share shrunk in both regions between 1980 and 2010 and the size of decline was actually much larger in high-income East Asia. However, the manufacturing sector's relative labour productivity increased significantly in high-income East Asia, whereas it did not change very much in Latin America. These patterns show the key difference between the 'advanced industrialization' of high-income East Asia and the 'secular deindustrialization' of Latin America. In sum, the pattern of structural transformation started to mature in Latin America before getting rich, and its recent stage of structural performance was less growth-friendly and sustainable compared to that of high-income East Asia. We next turn to the inequality dynamics of different types of structural transformation.

3. The Kuznetsian tension: the inequality dynamics of structural transformation

To recap, our analysis so far of the empirical regional experience of structural transformation shows very different trends in shares of sectoral value added and employment and relative labour productivity in high-income and developing East Asia (excluding China), China, Latin America, India, and sub-Saharan Africa.

What are the implications of the different regional experiences with structural transformation for the relationship between structural transformation and inequality dynamics? Figures 2.6 and 2.7 show the relationship between manufacturing/non-business services shares of employment and income inequality. Starting with sub-Saharan Africa, the weak experience with structural transformation, especially in manufacturing, and the relatively small movement of workers from agriculture to non-agriculture suggests that the Kuznetsian tension between structural transformation and inequality may not be evident as much as it is for the other regions.

Latin America witnessed deindustrialization, and, at the same time, there was a sustained increase in employment share of services. In this case, it is less evident how the tertiarization of Latin America may have impacted on inequality, and it would depend in part on which component of the services sector grew the fastest in the period 1980–2010. As Baymul and Sen (2020) argue, business services may have more of an inequality-enhancing effect than non-business services.

Developing East Asia (excluding China) has witnessed what may be termed as 'benign' structural transformation as the rapid increase in economy-wide productivity was accompanied by a notable increase in the share of manufacturing employment and a decline in the gross Gini. This pattern reflects a positive Kuznetsian dynamic of rapid structural transformation accompanied by job creation.

Finally, we note that in both China and India from about the mid-1980s there was a rise in the employment shares in manufacturing. We also see a rapid rise in non-business services' share of employment over the same period and a rise in the gross Gini.

We can summarize the various iterations of the structural transformation– inequality relationship or the Kuznetsian tension in a 2 × 2 matrix (see Figure 2.8), where the trend in income inequality is on the vertical side (i.e. increasing or stable/declining inequality) and the strength of growth-enhancing structural transformation (i.e. weak or strong) is on the horizontal. This produces four quadrants as follows:

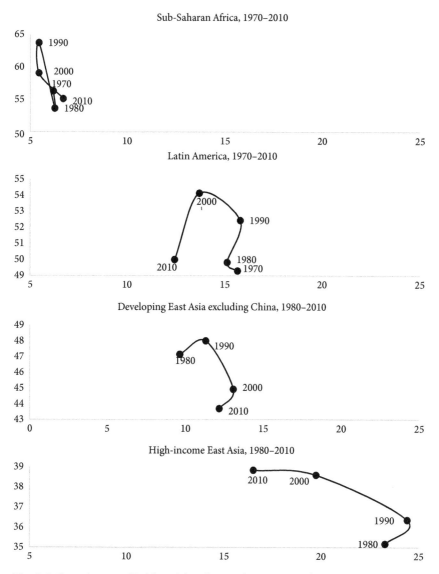

Fig. 2.6 Gross income Gini (*y*-axis) and manufacturing employment share (*x*-axis)

Notes: (i) The Gini coefficients are simple averages. If data were missing for specific years, the data for the closest year were used. (ii) Employment shares are five-year moving averages.

Source: authors' calculations based on the GGDC 10-Sector Database Version 2015 (Timmer et al. 2015) and UNU-WIDER World Income Inequality Database (WIID).

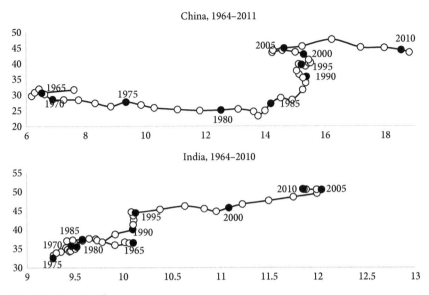

Fig. 2.6 *Continued*

- weak growth-enhancing structural transformation with increasing inequality (top-left quadrant in Figure 2.8);
- weak growth-enhancing-structural transformation with stable or declining inequality (bottom-left quadrant);
- strong growth-enhancing structural transformation with increasing inequality (top-right quadrant);
- strong growth-enhancing structural transformation with stable or declining inequality (bottom-right quadrant).

Each quadrant tells a different story about the structural transformation–inequality relationship or the Kuznetsian tension, and these can be mapped to the regional experiences noted above (with potential for movements over time between quadrants). For example, we can say that India and China have experienced a strong Kuznetsian tension as inequality has risen with strong growth-enhancing structural transformation. We can say developing East Asia (excluding China) has experienced a weak and benign Kuznetsian tension as it has experienced declining inequality with strong growth-enhancing structural transformation. In contrast, both Latin America and sub-Saharan Africa have experienced an ambiguous Kuznetsian tension in that inequality has been stable but growth-enhancing structural transformation has been weak. Finally, we can say that high-income East Asia fits into the weak and adverse Kuznetsian tension quadrant of rising inequality accompanied by weak growth-enhancing structural

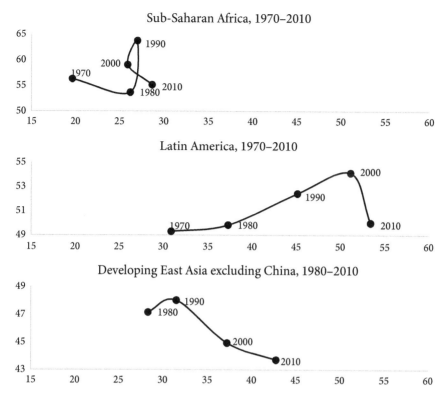

Fig. 2.7 Gross income Gini (*y*-axis) and non-business services employment share (*x*-axis)

Source: authors' calculations based on the GGDC 10-Sector Database Version 2015 (Timmer et al. 2015) and UNU-WIDER World Income Inequality Database (WIID).

transformation. This quadrant could even be thought of as an 'anti-Kuznetisian' tension at high income.

4. Conclusion

In this chapter, we analysed the empirical patterns of structural transformation in high-income East Asia, Latin America, developing East Asia (excluding China), China, India, and sub-Saharan Africa. We find that there is significant heterogeneity in the experiences of the six regions with respect to structural transformation. We propose a 'Varieties of structural transformation' typology to capture this heterogeneity.

Considering the trends of sectoral value-added and employment shares and relative productivity, we categorized six regions into three groups: 'struggling' (sub-Saharan Africa); 'catching-up' (developing East Asia, China, India); and

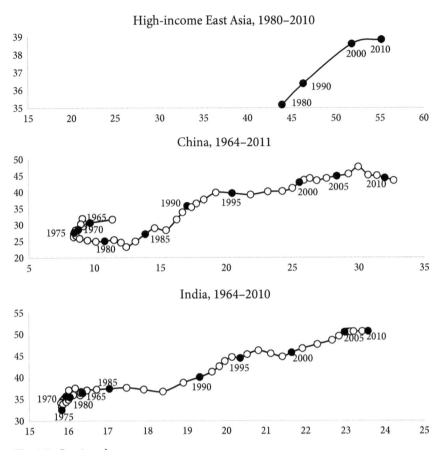

Fig. 2.7 *Continued*

'mature' (high-income East Asia, Latin America) transformers. While there were important similarities between regions within the same group, there were also some differences that explain the gap in the overall economic performance. More specifically, we find that all regions, with the exception of sub-Saharan Africa, witnessed a large decline in agricultural employment share (and, in the cases of India and China, agricultural value added as well) in the 1980–2010 period. With respect to manufacturing, China experienced an increase in employment and value-added shares, while in the case of India, manufacturing employment share increased; however, manufacturing value-added share declined from the late 1990s, after an initial increase. Developing East Asia's manufacturing value-added and employment shares expanded rapidly during the 1980s, but stalled over the recent decade. Latin America and sub-Saharan Africa experienced deindustrialization for a long period between 1980 and 2010. With respect to services, there was a significant increase in employment shares in high-income East Asia and Latin America, with the services value-added shares already high by the 1980s. Despite this similarity of the

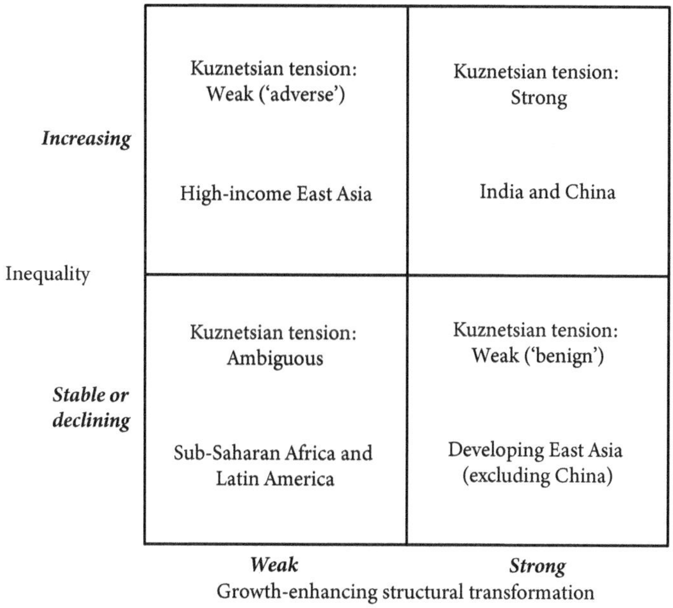

Increasing	Kuznetsian tension: Weak ('adverse') High-income East Asia	Kuznetsian tension: Strong India and China
Stable or declining	Kuznetsian tension: Ambiguous Sub-Saharan Africa and Latin America	Kuznetsian tension: Weak ('benign') Developing East Asia (excluding China)

Inequality

Weak   *Strong*
Growth-enhancing structural transformation

Fig. 2.8 The Kuznetsian tension: inequality trend vs growth-enhancing structural transformation
Source: authors' illustration.

two regions, a large productivity growth gap appeared because high-productivity business services played a more important role in the employment structural transformation of high-income East Asia. Developing East Asia and China experienced a notable increase in both the non-business services value-added and employment shares. In comparison, India and sub-Saharan Africa saw a more gradual increase in the non-business services employment share. The business services share expanded significantly in developing East Asia, China, and India in terms of value added but not in terms of employment.

Finally, we considered the inequality dynamics of structural transformation, noting different types of Kuznetsian tensions in each region. We developed a matrix of the possible iterations of the structural transformation–inequality relationship or the Kuznetsian tension based on the trend in income inequality and the strength of growth-enhancing structural transformation.

References

Baymul, C., and K. Sen (2020). 'Was Kuznets Right? New Evidence on the Relationship between Structural Transformation and Inequality', *Journal of Development Studies*, doi: https://doi.org/10.1080/00220388.2019.1702161.

Kim, K., and A. Sumner (2019). 'The Five Varieties of Industrialisation: A New Typology of Diverse Empirical Experience in the Developing World'. Economic and Social Research Council (ESRC) Global Poverty and Inequality Dynamics (GPID) Research Network Working Paper 18. London: ESRC Global Poverty and Inequality Dynamics Research Network (GPID).

Kuznets, S. (1955). 'Economic Growth and Income Inequality', *American Economic Review*, 45(1): 1–28.

McMillan, M.S., and D. Rodrik (2011). 'Globalization, Structural Change and Productivity Growth'. NBER Working Paper 17143. Cambridge, MA: National Bureau of Economic Research.

Timmer, M., G.J. de Vries, and K. de Vries (2015). 'Patterns of Structural Change in Developing Countries'. In J. Weiss and M. Tribe (eds), *Routledge Handbook of Industry and Development*. London: Routledge, 65–83.

UNU-WIDER (2019). Standardized dataset based on World Income Inequality Database, WIID 4, version 22 February 2019. Helsinki: UNU-WIDER.

PART I

EAST ASIA

3

Structural Transformation and Inclusive Growth

Kuznets 'Developer's Dilemma' in Indonesia

*Kyunghoon Kim, Arriya Mungsunti, Andy Sumner,
and Arief Anshory Yusuf*

1. Introduction

In this chapter, we focus on the 'developer's dilemma'—the distributional tension between structural transformation and inequality that Kuznets (1955) hypothesized—in Indonesia. We analyse how the quality of structural transformation and inclusive growth has evolved over time. We are particularly interested in how the manufacturing sector's role changed between the 1960s and the 2000s, and we relate the patterns of structural transformation to trends in poverty and inequality.

While Indonesia experienced weak Kuznetsian tension during the periods both before and after the 1997–1998 Asian Financial Crisis, there were notable differences in the economic outcomes in these periods. An important factor that can explain this economic growth differential is the performance of the manufacturing sector. This chapter demonstrates that the concurrent expansion of the manufacturing sector's value-added and employment shares, or 'upgrading industrialization', stimulated economic growth before the crisis, but that Indonesia experienced 'stalled industrialization' after the crisis (Figure 3.1). This pattern is similar to that of developing East Asia but is substantially different to that of high-income East Asia and China (see Figure 2.3, this volume).

The chapter focuses on the trends of structural transformation and inclusive growth from a historical perspective. A country's overall economic performance depends on the patterns and characteristics of structural transformation, which we define as the changes in an economy's value added, employment, and trade composition (McMillan et al. 2014; Sen 2019). We are particularly interested in the central role that the manufacturing sector plays in structural transformation and

Kyunghoon Kim, et al., *Structural Transformation and Inclusive Growth.* In: *The Developer's Dilemma.*
Edited by Armida Salsiah Alisjahbana, Kunal Sen, Andy Sumner, and Arief Anshory Yusuf, Oxford University Press.
© UNU-WIDER (2022). DOI: 10.1093/oso/9780192855299.003.0003

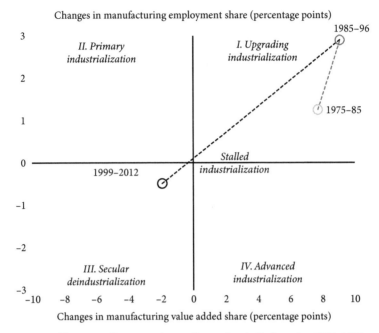

Fig. 3.1 Varieties of structural transformation in Indonesia, 1975–2012

Note: Five-year moving averages of value-added and employment shares were used to calculate the changes.

Sources: Kim and Sumner (2019); authors' calculations based on the Groningen Growth and Development Centre (GGDC) 10-Sector Database Version 2015 (Timmer et al. 2015).

inclusive growth. We focus on manufacturing because of the sector's special characteristics in terms of employment generation and productivity growth that enable the rapid and resilient economic catch-up of developing countries. We define inclusive growth as economic growth that benefits a broad section of the population, and particularly the poorer groups (Sen 2014). While these benefits can be identified using diverse measures, this chapter uses monetary poverty and inequality data to assess inclusive growth.

The chapter is structured as follows. Section 2 provides an overview of the developer's dilemma in Indonesia by analysing the patterns of structural transformation and inclusive growth. This section describes the key trends of the manufacturing sector and income inequality during the selected periods from the viewpoint of the Kuznetsian tension. Section 3 provides a historical narrative of Indonesia's economic performance before 1960—the period prior to Indonesia's modern structural transformation taking off. On the inclusivity front, the Indonesian economy experienced high levels of inequality along various dimensions during this period. Section 4 shifts the focus to the period between 1960 and 2010. It analyses the changing sectoral drivers of Indonesia's structural transformation and the poverty and inequality trends over time. This section finds that while Indonesia experienced 'upgrading industrialization' for most of the period before the Asian Financial Crisis, 'stalled industrialization' has been the major trend since the late 1990s, along with rising inequality. Section 5 finds that the combination of 'stalled industrialization' and rising inequality continued during the 2010s. It also analyses the policies adopted to fix the recent patterns of structural transformation and inclusive growth, and provides a comparison between the political economic environments in which the government pursued activist policies before and after the Asian Financial Crisis. Furthermore, this section highlights some of the key issues that could shape the future patterns of structural transformation and inclusive growth. Section 6 concludes.

2. The developer's dilemma in Indonesia: an overview

Before a detailed historical narrative is discussed in the later sections of this chapter, this section provides key evidence which shows Indonesia's twin development challenges of weakening structural transformation and inclusive growth. When we talk of the developer's dilemma, we can think about the changes in manufacturing value-added or employment shares and trends in income inequality, and their relationship. Figure 3.2 plots gross income Gini coefficients against the manufacturing value-added share in constant prices (Figure 3.2a) and the manufacturing employment share (Figure 3.2b). Figures 3.2a and 3.2b suggest that we can divide the period between the 1960s and the 2010s into three subperiods with distinctive patterns of manufacturing shares and inequality. The first period ('Cliff 1') is between the mid-1960s and the mid-1970s, when Indonesia's manufacturing sector was at an infant stage and recorded limited expansion, with the manufacturing value-added share hovering around 10 per cent. During this period, Indonesia's inequality rose rapidly. The second period ('Downhill') is between the mid-1970s and the mid-1990s. The manufacturing sector's value-added and employment shares expanded rapidly during these two decades. At the same time, Indonesia experienced a notable decline in inequality, with the Gini coefficient returning to a level similar to that of the mid-1960s. The final period ('Cliff 2') includes the 2000s and the early 2010s. The trend in this third period is somewhat similar to that in the first period ('Cliff 1'). The manufacturing value-added and employment shares stagnated during the first half of the 2000s and then declined slightly. During this period, inequality increased notably.

Analysing Indonesia's economic composition and inclusive growth, we do not find a period during which Indonesia experienced strong Kuznetsian tension, or a simultaneous increase in inequality and rapid growth-enhancing structural transformation (Figure 3.3). While Indonesia experienced weak Kuznetsian tension during the three periods, the outcomes were markedly different. During the

(a)

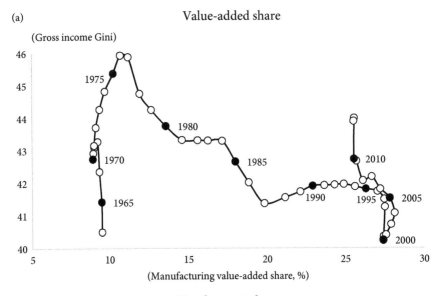

(b)

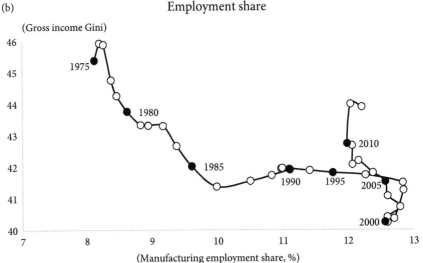

Fig. 3.2 Manufacturing development and inequality trends, Indonesia, 1964–2012 (a), 1975–2012 (b)

Notes: (i) The missing Gini coefficients were calculated using linear interpolation; see Kim et al. (2020) Figure 9 for the original data. (ii) Manufacturing value-added and employment shares are five-year moving averages; see Kim et al. (2020) Figures 4 and 6 for the original data.
Source: authors' illustration based on the GGDC 10-Sector Database Version 2015 (Timmer et al. 2015) and UNU-WIDER World Income Inequality Database (WIID).

second period ('Downhill'), Indonesia went through strong growth-enhancing structural transformation with notable growth of the manufacturing value-added and employment shares, or 'upgrading industrialization' (Kim and Sumner 2019).

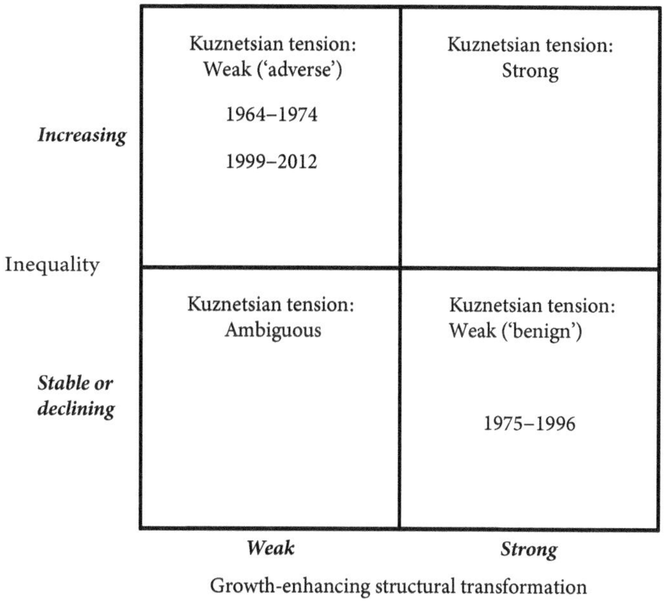

	Weak	Strong
Increasing	Kuznetsian tension: Weak ('adverse') 1964–1974 1999–2012	Kuznetsian tension: Strong
Stable or declining	Kuznetsian tension: Ambiguous	Kuznetsian tension: Weak ('benign') 1975–1996

Inequality

Growth-enhancing structural transformation

Fig. 3.3 Patterns of Kuznetsian tension in Indonesia, 1964–2012
Source: authors' illustration.

The economic situation was benign during this period, as the country experienced rapid GDP growth and improvement in living standards, as well as a decline in income inequality. In comparison, Indonesia experienced weak growth-enhancing structural transformation and a rise in inequality in the first and third periods ('Cliff 1' and 'Cliff 2') and therefore the situation was more adverse. During these two periods, Indonesia went through 'stalled industrialization', with limited change in the manufacturing value-added and employment shares.

As in the third period, the combination of stagnating manufacturing shares and rising inequality is the twin challenge that Indonesia is currently facing. In light of these two grand development challenges, governments face a dilemma in setting priorities and allocating valuable public resources accordingly. The rest of this chapter discusses the structural transformation and inclusive growth trends, the potential drivers, and the government's policies to solve development challenges.

3. Economic history up to *c.* 1960

3.1 Structural transformation: remaining static

Between 1900 and 1960, Indonesia's structural transformation was driven by the oil and gas sector. Based on the estimated value-added data in constant 2000 prices (Van der Eng 2010), the agricultural share declined gradually from 41.4

per cent in 1900 to 31.0 per cent in 1960. The industrial value-added share expanded from 17.1 per cent to 30.3 per cent. This expansion was driven by the oil and gas sector, with its share increasing from 0.8 per cent in 1900 to 17.6 per cent in 1960. During this period, Indonesia failed to achieve sustained industrialization or manufacturing-led structural transformation. Compared with the oil and gas sector, the change in manufacturing value-added share was less unidirectional. Overall, despite some spurts of industrialization, manufacturing remained small, with the share struggling to rise above 10 per cent between 1900 and 1960. Because of the limited manufacturing development, Indonesia's exports consisted mainly of natural resources and were concentrated in a few commodities during the first half of the twentieth century (Thomas and Panglaykim 1966). The services value-added share increased from 41.5 per cent in 1900 to 46.6 per cent in 1921. Then the share began to decline; it was recorded as 38.7 per cent in 1960. Overall, there was not a significant change in the services share between 1900 and 1960.

Comparing the 1930 and 1961 censuses, Jones (1966: 51–55) finds that there was limited labour shift from agricultural to non-agricultural sectors. The agriculture, forestry, and fishing sector's employment share did not change much, recorded at 73.9 per cent in 1930 and 73.3 per cent in 1961. The research suggests that the decline in the agricultural share may have been larger if one takes the methodological differences into account but, in any case, the decline would still be much smaller than that in other comparable developing countries. During this period, there were some notable changes within the non-agricultural sector. The manufacturing labour share declined from 11.5 per cent to 5.8 per cent and the mining share declined from 0.9 per cent to 0.3 per cent. The labour share of services (including utilities) expanded from 13.7 per cent to 18.8 per cent. The research suggests that this expansion is likely to have occurred among those employed in less productive services, such as rickshaw drivers and petty clerks.

Soekarno, the war leader during the struggle for independence and Indonesia's first president, struggled to stimulate structural transformation during his two decades in power between the mid-1940s and the mid-1960s. The President was preoccupied with dealing with internal political issues, namely the conflict between the communists and other political factions, even after he established an autocratic system in the late 1950s. The government pursued state-led development from the late 1950s onwards, after mass nationalization of Dutch companies, but the state enterprises were heavily used to serve the vested interests of the military and politico-bureaucrats. The government also lacked the additional capital necessary to spearhead structural transformation. During this period, private firms did not have the capacity to mobilize the resources needed to make meaningful investment in modern economic sectors and many struggled to survive, as infrastructure remained weak and the government mismanaged the economy (Lindblad 2008: 177–208; Robison 1986: 69–97). The inflation rate was recorded at 109 per cent in 1963 and 307 per cent in 1964, and reached 1,136 per cent in 1965.

Overall, structural transformation played a limited role in Indonesia's economic growth in the first sixty years of the twentieth century. The country continued to depend heavily on the natural commodity sector, and oil and gas in particular. Given the political and economic instability around 1960, it would have been difficult to imagine Indonesia joining the rank of Asia's rapidly growing economies in the near future.

3.2 Inclusive growth: slow progress

Numerous indicators show that there was slow progress in raising living standards during the first half of the twentieth century. Comparing socio-economic indicators for the 1930s and 1950s, Booth (2016: 52–55) demonstrates that life expectancy increased only slightly, from thirty-five years to thirty-seven-and-a-half years, and suggests that living standards may have deteriorated by highlighting a decline in Indonesia's real gross domestic product (GDP) per capita, Java's basic foods consumption per capita, and Jakarta's real monthly food expenditure per capita.

During this period, the level of inequality was high in Indonesia. Using income taxation data, Leigh and Van der Eng (2009) offer an estimation of the top income shares between 1920 and 1939. They find that the income share of the richest 1 per cent increased from 11.8 per cent in 1921 to 21.5 per cent in 1934. This research suggests that the sudden jumps in inequality in the early 1920s and the early 1930s were partly due to the large falls in the price of agricultural export products, which caused a significant decline in the relative incomes of farm households. While the price movements of agricultural products hit many rural households, they had limited impact on non-farm salary earners. Towards the end of the 1930s, the income share of the richest 1 per cent fell slightly, to 19.9 per cent in 1939. Van Leeuwen and Földvári (2016) confirm the high levels of inequality during the first half of the twentieth century. By estimating the expenditure Gini coefficients, this study finds that the overall inequality and rural–urban inequality rose rapidly between 1925 and 1939. Indonesia's overall inequality then declined between 1942 and 1959, with the effects of the war and the withdrawal of the Netherlands being the potential drivers of this change. Despite a decline in expenditure Gini during this period, it continued to be high, recorded at 51 in 1959.

High levels of inequality were also apparent between businesses, and this type of inequality had ethnic dimensions. During the first decade after independence in 1945, the private Indigenous capitalists struggled to compete against larger foreign firms and Chinese Indonesians. The government made efforts to foster the growth of Indigenous firms, yet its preferential support measures were often insufficient and inconsistent. While siding with Indigenous capitalists was important for maintaining political stability, the government continued to rely on foreign companies and Chinese Indonesians with capital and technology to sustain economic growth. This trend continued even during the period of strong economic nationalism and state-centred development between the late 1950s and the mid-1960s. While on the surface it was the conflict between the military and the communist party that was a primary cause in ending the Soekarno regime in 1967, the continuation of high levels of inequality and slow economic growth had gradually been weakening the regime's legitimacy over the previous two decades (Robison 1986: 36–98).

4. Economic development between *c.* 1960 and *c.* 2010

4.1 Structural transformation: from industrialization to tertiarization

The role of the manufacturing sector has transformed in Indonesia over the past five decades. This subsection first discusses Indonesia's industrialization before the Asian Financial Crisis. During this period of 'upgrading industrialization', the government policy focus shifted from import substitution during the 1970s and the early 1980s to export orientation during the late 1980s and the 1990s. The latter half of this subsection discusses how structural transformation became less growth-enhancing while Indonesia went through 'stalled industrialization' and tertiarization after the crisis (Figure 3.1; see Kim et al. 2020: Figures 4–6).[1]

Section 3. Economic history up to *c.* 1960 demonstrated that Indonesia had not begun modern structural transformation during the first six decades of the twentieth century. During the following decade or so, the Indonesian economy continued to depend heavily on natural resources. When Soeharto took over the control of the country in the mid-1960s, Indonesia's economy was in a dire situation. Therefore, rather than searching for direct methods of stimulating structural transformation, the immediate goal of the new regime under Soeharto was to stabilize the macroeconomic conditions. The government succeeded in calming the economic situation in the second half of the 1960s, after adopting liberalization measures and opening doors to foreign investors.

Using the 10-Sector Database of the GGDC, we find that agriculture dominated the economy and occupied approximately 35 per cent of value added at constant 2005 prices during the 1960s (Timmer et al. 2015: 65–83). The mining sector accounted for approximately 20 per cent of value added during the 1960s and was boosted during the oil boom of the 1970s. The merchandise exports–GDP ratio

---

[1] This subsection builds on Section 3 of Kim et al. (2018).

expanded rapidly from the early 1970s, and the share of fuel in total exports stayed above two-thirds for most years during the 1970s. The manufacturing sector was still in its infancy in the 1960s. At this time, the future trajectory of structural transformation continued to remain uncertain.

Then, the value-added shares of the agricultural sector and the mining sector began to decline from the late 1960s and the late 1970s respectively, and Indonesia's modern structural transformation and urbanization began. The growth of the manufacturing sector accelerated in the mid-1970s and contributed to the rapid economic development of the following two decades. The value-added share of the manufacturing sector increased from 11.6 per cent in 1975 to 27.9 per cent in 1995. The rise in the manufacturing sector's employment share was also notable—from 7.9 per cent in 1971 to 13.4 per cent in 1995. With the rise in the manufacturing value-added and employment shares, Indonesia experienced a period of 'upgrading industrialization'.

The manufacturing sector grew between the mid-1970s and the mid-1980s, along with the government's protectionist measures, import substitution policies, and significant state investments in manufacturing and infrastructure using revenues from oil exports. The government was a central investor in resource processing and capital-intensive industries. One notable feature in Indonesia's economic development during the oil boom is that the country did not suffer much from the Dutch disease because its policymakers seriously considered the importance of macroeconomic stability, structural transformation, and balanced growth (Lewis 2005: 106–112; Usui 1997).

However, the development strategy centred on active government intervention became unsustainable with the decline in international oil prices from the mid-1980s. Other international factors, such as the increase in the relative value of Indonesia's debt after the appreciation of the yen and a rise in global real interest rates, also put pressure on Indonesia's current account and fiscal position. In these circumstances, the Indonesian government took a decisive step to liberalize the economy. The rapid expansion of the manufacturing sector from the mid-1980s onwards was therefore related to a series of economic reform policies adopted by the government, including the restructuring of customs services and the lifting of foreign investment restrictions (Aswicahyono et al. 1996; Fane 1999; Feridhanusetyawan and Pangestu 2003).

During this period, there was a rise in export-orientated investment from higher-income Asian economies (see Chapter 2 for the discussion of these economies' structural transformation), whose companies sought potential industrial bases with low-cost labour as wages in their home countries increased. These companies were attracted to the economic liberalization policies adopted by the Indonesian government in the mid-1980s (Thee 1991). Further, the Plaza Accord in 1985 and Indonesia's currency devaluations in 1983 and 1986 had an important impact in making Indonesia more competitive in terms of labour costs. As a result,

Indonesia, having already built significant physical infrastructure in the 1970s, became an attractive place for foreign direct investment (FDI). Furthermore, the withdrawal of privileges from the North-East Asian economies in 1988 under the US General System of Preferences induced with even greater force the relocation of capital from North-East to South-East Asia.

Fujita and James (1997) show that a large increase in employment in the manufacturing sector from the 1980s onwards was due to the rapid growth of export-orientated industries. In particular, labour-intensive light manufacturing segments recorded impressive growth in output and created a large number of jobs. The manufacturing sector's share in merchandise exports also expanded rapidly from the early 1980s to the mid-1990s. Jacob (2005) shows that the surge in manufacturing exports was driven by resource-intensive manufacturing, including food and wood products, and labour-intensive manufacturing, such as garments and textiles.

However, the economic liberalization measures failed to put Indonesia on a sustainable path. At the end of the 1990s, it faced one of the most severe crises in its modern economic history, with a massive capital withdrawal from the country. The GDP growth rate plummeted to −13.1 per cent in 1998 and the economic recovery was slow, with GDP in constant prices reaching the pre-crisis peak only in 2003.

During and after the Asian Financial Crisis, the president's family businesses and private oligarchs were identified as the central culprits. Indonesia's oligarchs, many of whom were Chinese Indonesians with massive wealth and links with the dictator, had seen their businesses grow rapidly over the previous three decades. The Soeharto regime relied on the oligarchs to drive economic growth and provide political funding, especially during periods of fiscal difficulty. In return, the government offered them lucrative deals and subsidized credit and inputs. At the same time, Chinese Indonesian businesses depended heavily on the Soeharto regime, as they continued to be socially and politically vulnerable (Robison 1986: 271–277).

Economic liberalization from the mid-1980s provided Chinese Indonesian businesses with an environment for rapid growth. By this time, they had built a strong corporate and financial foundation that enabled them to compete against foreign firms. Also, strong financial power and political connections made Chinese Indonesian businesses an attractive partner for foreign investors during the liberalization period (Chua 2008; Robison and Hadiz 2004). Furthermore, Soeharto's children started to enter the business scene, while Indigenous capitalists became increasingly marginalized (Fukuoka 2015: 425–426).

During liberalization, the oligarchies expanded investment, often in rent-heavy industries, by sourcing external finance. As many conglomerates owned their own banks after the banking sector deregulation of the 1980s, channelling finance for their business expansion was not difficult. Also, the oligarchs' political connections meant that they could bypass financial sector rules, which were insufficient in any case, to allow their businesses and banks to take excessive risks. From the early 1990s, the foreign borrowing of Indonesian banks and private companies increased rapidly (Suhaedi and Wibowo 2011: 111–118). A large proportion of the increase in foreign debts was short-term loans (Radelet et al. 1998: 25–26). Large, foreign short-term debts made the Indonesian economy particularly vulnerable to financial panic. Financial liberalization also meant that moving capital out of the country had become easier for both domestic and foreign investors. The financial bubble and investment frenzy came to an end with the 1997 financial crisis, which involved rapid capital withdrawals and a substantial depreciation of the rupiah.

The economic turmoil, combined with political uncertainty after the end of Soeharto's thirty-two-year-long rule, destabilized Indonesia's business environment. The country's net FDI inflow was negative for four consecutive years. A lack of international capital had a significant impact on Indonesia's manufacturing sector, in which foreign companies had played an important role. After the crisis, the government embarked upon another wave of economic liberalization under the auspices of the International Monetary Fund (IMF).

During the 2000s, the manufacturing sector failed to return to the long-term growth experienced between the 1970s and the mid-1990s. After reaching a peak of 28.4 per cent in 2001, the value-added share of the manufacturing sector declined to 25.4 per cent in 2006 and flattened out. The manufacturing employment share declined from 13.1 per cent in 1997 to 11.3 per cent in 1998 and averaged 12.4 per cent up to 2012, with small annual fluctuations. In other words, Indonesia went through 'stalled industrialization'. Further, the share of manufacturing goods in merchandise exports declined rapidly following the Asian Financial Crisis. Due to weak manufacturing exports, combined with a rapid expansion of fuel imports, Indonesia's trade balance deteriorated during the 2000s.

However, the downturn of the manufacturing sector's value-added share cannot be solely attributed to the Asian Financial Crisis. There were already signs of slowdown in the manufacturing sector prior to the crisis. Szirmai (1994) and Timmer (1999) show that the productivity growth of Indonesia's manufacturing sector accelerated from the mid-1980s, but the pace did not match that of other industrializing economies in Asia. A number of studies recommended that the government deepen and broaden Indonesia's manufacturing base in the mid-1990s to make manufacturing-led structural transformation sustainable (Thee 2006). However, Indonesia's manufacturing sector continued to be concentrated in few labour-intensive and resource-based segments, in which global competition intensified with the entry of new contestants such as China during the 2000s.

Since the Asian Financial Crisis, the shares of two other industrial sectors—namely, the electricity, gas, and water supply sector (henceforth, utilities) and the construction sector—expanded, although their initial sizes were relatively small. The value-added share of the mining sector continued to decline, while the employment share averaged 1.0 per cent without much change during this period.

Next, we take a look at the growth pattern of the services sector since the 1960s. The value-added share of the services sector remained at approximately 30 per cent in the 1960s and 1970s. The services sector's value-added share only began to expand substantially during the 1980s after two decades of limited change: it increased from 30.9 per cent in 1980 to 36.1 per cent in 1990 and remained at approximately this level until the Asian Financial Crisis. The growth of services was led by the finance, insurance, real estate, and business services (henceforth, business services) sector in this period. The Indonesian government carried out major reforms in the banking industry in 1983 and 1988, and deregulation invigorated investments in finance-related sectors. The wholesale and retail trade, hotels, and restaurants (henceforth, trade services, included in 'non-business services') sector also showed significant growth.

Following the Asian Financial Crisis, Indonesia's services value-added share increased rapidly from 34.8 per cent in 2000 to 43.8 per cent in 2012, with a continuation of urbanization. The transport, storage, and communication (henceforth, transport services, included in 'non-business services') sector grew particularly rapidly. This sector's explosive growth can partly be attributed to regulatory reform in the telecommunications sector, which attracted large investments, and rising mobile phone and internet penetration in Indonesia. Trade services also recorded resilient growth. The community, social, and personal services (henceforth, personal services, included in 'non-business services') sector showed impressive growth during the 2000s after three decades of steady decline. Business services' share shrank by nearly one-quarter after the Asian Financial Crisis but began to recover in the early 2000s. The services-led structural transformation coincided with consumption-driven economic growth in Indonesia. During this period, the economically secure population and the middle class residing in urban areas expanded, and their ability to increase discretionary spending led to a rapid growth in demand for consumer services (Oberman et al. 2012).

The services sector's central role in the recent structural transformation is also evident in terms of employment. The long-term shift in the composition of sectoral employment was disrupted during the Asian Financial Crisis and its aftermath. The long-term trend of the declining employment share of the agricultural sector was halted between 1997 and 2005 as the crisis forced a considerable number of workers back into agriculture. During the crisis, a large number of workers in the industrial sector lost jobs and the lay-offs were particularly severe in manufacturing. When structural transformation began again in the mid-2000s, the services sector saw a rapid expansion in employment. The employment share of trade services and personal services increased rapidly, and the increase in business services was also significant, albeit from a low level. During this period, the manufacturing employment share plateaued.

The change of the main engine of structural transformation, and more specifically the expansion of the services sector in terms of both value added and employment, has had an important impact on Indonesia's economic growth. Labour productivity growth declined in Indonesia from 4.5 per cent per annum during 1985–1996 to 3.1 per cent per annum during 1999–2012 (see Kim et al. 2020: Figure 7). Furthermore, the share of the contribution of structural transformation to labour productivity growth shrank from 39.2 per cent to 29.8 per cent. These trends were caused by changes of the leading sectors in structural transformation.

Figures 3.4a and 3.4b show that the manufacturing sector recorded a simultaneous rise in both relative productivity *and* employment growth during 1971–1985 and 1985–1996. Construction and utilities and business services also showed a similar trend, yet their employment share was significantly smaller than that of the manufacturing sector. In comparison, all the economic sectors with higher-than-average labour productivity failed to experience a simultaneous rise in relative productivity *and* employment share in the most recent period (Figure 3.4c). The manufacturing sector saw both its relative productivity and its employment share decline between 1999 and 2012. The relative labour productivity of construction and utilities and business services also declined during this period. Non-business services saw a rapid expansion of its employment share, but this sector had labour productivity lower than that of the overall economy.

In sum, Indonesia's economic growth has lost dynamism compared with the past, as the manufacturing sector has stopped playing a central role in structural transformation. From the late 1990s, services drove Indonesia's structural transformation, with the services shares in value added and employment growing rapidly. However, the services subsectors that have led employment generation since the Asian Financial Crisis have so far displayed weak capacity to drive productivity growth. If the recent trends in structural transformation and productivity growth continue, it would be difficult for Indonesia to follow in the footsteps of the region's leading economies (see Chapter 2).

4.2 Inclusive growth: declining poverty amid waves of inequality

Inequality in Indonesia increased between the mid-1960s and the mid-1970s (see Kim et al. 2020: Figure 9). This period coincided with a period of slow growth-enhancing structural transformation ('Cliff 1' in Figure 3.2). Van der Eng (2009) suggests that the increase in inequality during this period may have been due to an increase in urban workers' skills premium, which was in turn caused by import substitution policies aimed at developing capital-intensive sectors. In contrast, from the mid-1970s, inequality declined for around a decade, and then the Gini coefficient was relatively stable between the end of 1980s and the end of 1990s, before suddenly declining in 1999. Low levels of inequality may be due to the positive effects of the government's agricultural development strategy starting

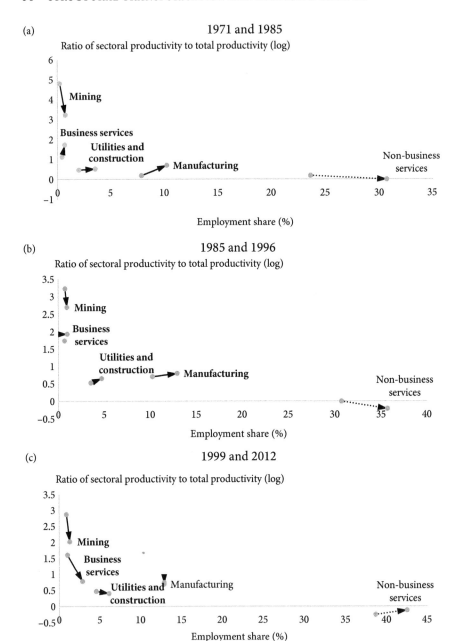

Fig. 3.4 Changes in employment share and relative productivity by sector, Indonesia, 1971–1985 (a), 1985–1996 (b), 1999–2012 (c)

Notes: (i) Business services are financial intermediation, renting, business activities; non-business services are (a) wholesale and retail trade, repair of motor vehicles and motorcycles, personal and household goods, hotels and restaurants; (b) transport storage and communications; (c) public administration, defence, education, health, and social work; and (d) other community activities, social and personal services activities, and activities of private households. (ii) Sectors with labour productivity higher than the economy-wide average labour productivity that experienced an increase in their employment share are in bold.
Source: authors' illustration based on the GGDC 10-Sector Database Version 2015 (Timmer et al. 2015).

to appear from the 1970s. Van der Eng (2009) notes that, thanks to large public expenditure and investment on rural development, agricultural productivity improved, along with a large increase in agricultural employment, although the share of agriculture in total employment continued to decline. Another factor that may have caused the decline in inequality is the expansion of labour-intensive manufacturing from the mid-1980s, which generated a substantial number of jobs ('Downhill' in Figure 3.2). In sum, Indonesia avoided Kuznetsian tension between the mid-1970s and the mid-1990s, during which time it experienced rapid growth-enhancing structural transformation.

The increase in inequality from the early 2000s to early 2010s ('Cliff 2' in Figure 3.2) cancelled out much of the decline in income inequality that Indonesia had experienced in the previous two decades. Yusuf et al. (2014: 251–252) suggest that there are three potential reasons for the rise in inequality in the post-crisis period: (i) the global commodities boom, which benefited mine owners and richer rural households disproportionately; (ii) the combination of stricter labor market regulations and a lack of formal employment generation; and (iii) the large proportion of regressive fuel subsidies in fiscal spending. Additionally, the World Bank (2014c) points out that the rising inequality during this period may be related to (i) richer households' access to assets; (ii) an increasing capital share and a declining labour share in national income; and (iii) a rise in wage inequality driven by a growing gap in returns to education. Finally, Akita (2017) demonstrates that while a decline in urban–rural education disparity contributed to reducing expenditure inequality, the expansion of higher education in urban areas may have been a key causal factor in raising expenditure inequality during the 2000s, as it increased both between educational groups and within the tertiary education group.

Next, we take a look at the trends in poverty. During the 1970s and 1980s, Indonesia experienced a notable poverty reduction. In a survey of studies on diverse poverty measures, Booth (1993: 69) notes that between the late 1960s and the late 1980s, 'whatever the poverty lines used and whatever the means adopted to adjust it for inflation, there seems to be little doubt that the proportion of the population living below the poverty line … declined in both urban and rural areas'. By taking a closer look at this period and extending the period to the 1990s, Booth (2016: 160–166) argues that economic growth became more pro-poor over time. Indonesia experienced economic growth that was more broad-based between 1976–1996 compared to 1966–1976. The potential drivers of broad-based growth were: (i) the government's rural development programmes; (ii) protection of poverty-related spending during the 1980s; and (iii) structural transformation that was led by labour-intensive sectors such as manufacturing, construction, trade, and transportation (Booth 2016: 165–166). It is also worth noting the government efforts to improve education services from the 1970s onwards, with a particular focus on primary education (Booth 2016: 79; Duflo 2001).

Indonesia experienced a sudden increase in the poverty rate during the crisis period of the late 1990s. After a sudden increase towards the end of the 1990s, Indonesia's poverty rates began to decline again (see Kim et al. 2020: Figure 10). The poverty rate at the US$1.90 poverty line declined rapidly from 66.6 per cent in 1998 to 9.4 per cent in 2014 and the poverty rate at the US$3.20 poverty line from 90.2 per cent to 37.9 per cent. This rapid decline in poverty was despite Indonesia's structural transformation losing dynamism and its overall economic growth slowing down during this period compared with the period before the Asian Financial Crisis. Suryahadi et al. (2012) compare the effects on poverty reduction of growth in value added in urban industry, urban services, rural agriculture, and rural services for 1984–1996 and 2002–2008. This research finds an increase in growth elasticities to poverty in the latter period. It demonstrates that urban services, followed by rural services, had the greatest effect on both rural and urban poverty reduction, and that the effect became stronger in the latter period.

While the services-centred structural transformation after the Asian Financial Crisis led to slower economic and productivity growth and coincided with a rise in inequality, there is no evidence to suggest that the power of economic growth to reduce poverty weakened. However, it is important to highlight that the poverty rates at higher thresholds have been stubbornly high. The poverty rate using the US$10.00 threshold has only declined slightly in the past two decades, and was recorded at 85.9 per cent in 2017. Moreover, if medium-paced growth and high inequality continue, then poverty reduction is expected to be much more challenging.

5. Development challenges and policies under democracy

5.1 Political economy and the developer's dilemma

Indonesia's political economy, and more precisely the politics of economic and social policymaking, has changed markedly since the late 1990s, when Indonesia became a democracy. When the democratic era began in Indonesia, the government initially focused on improving social protection provision and then gradually strengthened state activism with the aim of reviving growth-enhancing structural transformation. However, the process of strengthening state economic activism has been complex. Under the democratic political system, there has been strong competition among stakeholders, who prioritize different development goals. The government's annual fiscal allocation has also been influenced by the political schedule. Under the current system, whenever there are opportunities for the government to expand discretionary spending, the administration is pulled in different directions by stakeholders prioritizing diverse development programmes (see, e.g. Kim 2021). The growth-focused stakeholders point out the detrimental effects of lethargic structural transformation, while the equity-focused stakeholders emphasize Indonesia's low social spending compared with that of other middle-income countries. The precise balance of fiscal spending between these two broad goals will depend on voters' views on development priorities and also on the political power of different stakeholders in the policy process.

A more fundamental problem exists in Indonesia that limits the degree of state activism in dealing with development challenges. Indonesia's fiscal spending is low, as a percentage of GDP or in per capita terms, in major development areas such as infrastructure, health, and education.[2] The problem is not necessarily the small share of development spending in the total budget but the size of the fiscal budget itself. The government is legally required to allocate at least 20 per cent and 5 per cent of the total budget to education and health, respectively. From the mid-2010s, it has substantially reduced fuel subsidies and increased infrastructure investment. While further restructuring of the budget composition could make government policies more developmental, the key problem that constrains state activism is Indonesia's weak fiscal capacity. Although Indonesia's government debt-to-GDP ratio has stabilized around a relatively low level of 30 per cent, the government cannot substantially expand development spending without larger fiscal revenues due to the fiscal rule that caps its annual fiscal deficits at 3 per cent of GDP. Given these circumstances, the ability to pursue development policies depends on how much the government can expand fiscal revenues. Indonesia's government revenue and expenditure as a share of GDP are among the lowest in major developing countries, and are also low considering the country's income level (see Kim et al. 2020: Figure 15). Without substantially expanding fiscal revenue, the Indonesian government will have limited resources with which to stimulate growth-enhancing structural transformation and inclusive growth.

Finally, it is important to highlight the continued influence of the oligarchs, many of whom strove during the Soeharto era, survived the Asian crisis, and have flourished over the past two decades. Robison and Hadiz (2017) argue that the oligarchs, who hold massive material wealth, continue to influence Indonesia's economic policies and how government resources are allocated. They suggest that the recent economic protectionism has been the government's response to oligarchs' demands. From this viewpoint, the government's goal is understood as prioritizing the growth of oligarchs' wealth rather than providing public goods and stimulating national development. At the same time, the influence of the demands of median voters on the government's development strategy cannot be overlooked in a democratic Indonesia which holds regular elections. Considering these issues, the future trajectory of Indonesia's structural transformation and inclusive growth

---

[2] See World Bank (2013) on infrastructure spending, World Bank (2014a) on health spending, and World Bank (2018) on education spending.

will depend on whether, and how, the government aligns the interests of oligarchs, political elites, and the voters.

The rest of this section reviews some of the major policies that the government has adopted to fix the patterns of structural transformation and inclusive growth over the past decade within this changed policymaking environment.

5.2 Structural transformation policies

In this section, we first extend the analysis of structural transformation to the most recent period using the data on value added in constant 2010 prices and employment from Indonesia's central statistics office. We find the following trends during 2010–2017. First, structural transformation has continued, with the agricultural sector's value-added share declining from 14.3 per cent in 2010 to 13.2 per cent in 2017 and its employment share declining from 38.3 per cent to 29.7 per cent. Second, the stagnation of the manufacturing value-added and employment shares, or 'stalled industrialization', has continued. The value-added and employment shares averaged 22.3 per cent and 13.4 per cent, respectively, between 2010 and 2017, with no clear upward or downward trend. The relative productivity of the manufacturing sector continued to decline in this period. Third, services-led structural transformation has continued, with the value-added share increasing from 41.8 per cent in 2010 to 45.0 per cent in 2017 and the employment share from 42.3 per cent to 48.1 per cent. This expansion, again, was led by services subsectors with relatively low productivity, namely trade services and personal services.

From the late 2000s onwards, the Indonesian government began to strengthen state economic activism with the aim of stimulating structural transformation. The aim has been to move away from 'stalled industrialization' towards 'upgrading industrialization'. The key aspects of Indonesia's economic development strategy during the 2010s are as follows. First, the government has adopted various non-tariff measures and investment regulations to support or protect Indonesia's lagging sectors such as resource-processing and labour-intensive manufacturing industries (Hardum and Halim 2016; PwC Indonesia 2018a). Second, while strengthening regulations in certain sectors, the government has also implemented liberalization measures in others in order to attract private investment. Between September 2015 and November 2018, the government adopted sixteen sets of stimulus packages, which mostly contained plans to open up the Indonesian economy and streamline bureaucratic procedures in order to accelerate the investment process (Indonesia Investments 2018; PwC Indonesia 2018b). Third, the government started to directly lead infrastructure development during the second half of the 2010s. The Indonesian government increased infrastructure investment significantly after cutting the fuel subsidies that had burdened the fiscal budget of previous administrations. It also actively mobilized state-owned enterprises to invest in and construct infrastructure and expanded development financial institutions—so-called development banks—to finance projects (Kim 2020; World Bank 2017a).

In sum, the pattern of structural transformation during the 2010s has not changed much from that of the previous decade. Therefore, medium-paced economic growth has continued. The Indonesian economy is yet to see the effects of the government's strategy to improve the overall pattern of structural transformation or to achieve 'upgrading industrialization'.

5.3 Inclusive growth policies

Around the mid-2010s, there was a meaningful change in Indonesia's inequality trend. The rising trend in inequality ended in the early 2010s and the Gini coefficient stabilized during the first half of the 2010s. The data between 2013 and 2017 suggest that the trend may even have reversed: the gross income Gini coefficients declined by 0.54 points (see Kim et al. 2020: Figure 9). Poverty reduction has continued, and considering the recent pace of this, it would be reasonable to expect Indonesia to be close to eradicating extreme poverty at the US$1.90 poverty line by 2030. Yet reducing poverty rates at higher thresholds would be most challenging, especially if inequality stays high.

The government has also been strengthening its role in stimulating inclusive growth. First, an array of social assistance programmes has been implemented since the 2000s. As the public debt position began to stabilize in the mid-2000s, the government started to expand fiscal spending on social assistance programmes (see Kim et al. 2020: Figure 16). On annual average, the size of central government expenditure (in real terms) on social assistance programmes increased from 29.7 trillion rupiah in 2005–2009, to 37.2 trillion rupiah in 2010–2014, to 55.5 trillion rupiah in 2015–2016. Steps were taken to shrink large, untargeted subsidies during the 2010s, and the saved fiscal resources were redirected to several targeted programmes, such as health insurance for the poor and cash transfer for poor and at-risk students (World Bank 2017b). Second, the Indonesian government has been trying to support the poor by expanding health coverage. The government institutionalized the single-payer insurance administrator and the unified national health insurance programme in 2014 and set a goal to expand coverage to the entire population by 2019 (Pisani et al. 2017; World Bank 2014b, 2015). Third, many infrastructure projects that were implemented during the second half of the 2010s were aimed at solving regional inequality. While criticism continues that infrastructure development is Java-centric, the government has also focused on infrastructure projects outside Java, such as the Trans-Sumatra toll road. Also, it has implemented various programmes such as 'One Fuel Price' and 'Bright Indonesia' to reduce the price gap between regions (Kim 2021).

Indonesia's future inclusive growth will depend on how rapidly government spending on social programmes can expand, and on these programmes' ability to target the poor. Significant improvements seem necessary, as the ability of Indonesia's fiscal policy to reduce inequality in the early 2010s lagged behind that of many developing countries (World Bank 2016). Also, whether the Indonesian economy will experience broad-based, growth-enhancing structural transformation will determine inequality and poverty trends. Dynamic structural transformation that creates a large number of formal jobs in high-productivity sectors could contribute to bringing down the poverty rates at higher thresholds that have shown a relatively smaller decline in recent decades (see Kim et al. 2020: Figure 12–14).

5.4 Looking ahead

We end this section by highlighting some of the key issues that are expected to influence the future trajectory of Indonesia's structural transformation and inclusive growth. First, as China tries to shift towards 'advanced industrialization' that relies more on capital-intensive, as opposed to labour-intensive, manufacturing sectors, South-East Asian economies, including Indonesia, must compete to attract the bulk of the manufacturing investment that is seeking low-cost production bases. Several countries in the region that have experienced 'stalled industrialization' in recent decades view this as an opportunity to stimulate growth-enhancing structural transformation (see Chapter 2, this volume). The most practical option to achieve this over a short period may be to join the global value chain (GVC). However, the Indonesian government should remember that the effects on sustainable industrialization and inclusive growth of relying on the GVC are uncertain. Therefore, it should actively negotiate terms with multinational companies in the short term, while seeking ways to build strong domestic industries in the longer term. Second, the Indonesian government views rural–urban inequality as a structural problem that small-scale policies will struggle to solve. Therefore, it has floated the idea of relocating the capital city from Java to Kalimantan. While the motivation seems to be clear, there are many uncertainties regarding the actual effects on inequality, as Jakarta would remain the economic centre of the country for decades to come. Research on these issues will improve our understanding of the future patterns of structural transformation and inclusive growth in Indonesia.

6. Conclusions

Its remarkable performance in structural transformation and inclusive growth between the 1970s and the first half of the 1990s made Indonesia one of the eight high-performing Asian economies that the World Bank (1993) touted as a miracle. For two decades from the mid-1970s onwards, Indonesia's growth-enhancing structural transformation was dynamic, with the manufacturing sector driving productivity and employment growth. The poverty rate declined significantly, with declining or low and stable inequality. The Kuznetsian tension (Kuznets 1955) was weak and the economic situation was benign. In comparison, the post-Asian Financial Crisis period saw structural transformation losing dynamism, with relatively low-productivity services subsectors soaking up many workers. The inequality level increased until the mid-2010s, returning to a level similar to that recorded in the mid-1970s. Poverty has declined notably, but it could have fallen faster if inequality had not risen as rapidly as it did during the 2000s. The Kuznetsian tension was also weak during this period but the economic situation was much adverse compared to the previous period.

In response to the recent trends in structural transformation and inclusive growth, the Indonesian government began to take a stronger role in tackling development challenges during the 2010s. The ultimate goal is to turn the structural transformation and inequality trends of the past two decades, which can be described as a 'cliff', into a 'downhill' similar to the one that Indonesia experienced between the mid-1970s and the mid-1990s (Figure 3.2). To achieve this, the government needs a strategy to create more formal jobs through the expansion of high-productivity activities. While this strategy is important in terms of structural transformation and inclusive growth, it could also have a positive effect on raising the government revenue that is much needed in order to pursue development policies.

References

Akita, R. (2017). 'Educational Expansion and the Role of Education in Expenditure Inequality in Indonesia since the 1997 Financial Crisis', *Social Indicators Research*, 130(3): 1165–1186.

Aswicahyono, H., K. Bird, and H. Hill (1996). 'What Happens to Industrial Structure When Countries Liberalise? Indonesia since the Mid-1980s', *Journal of Development Studies*, 32(3): 340–363.

Booth, A. (1993). 'Counting the Poor in Indonesia', *Bulletin of Indonesian Economic Studies*, 29(1): 58–83.

Booth, A. (2016). *Economic Change in Modern Indonesia: Colonial and Post-Colonial Comparisons*. Cambridge: Cambridge University Press.

Chua, C. (2008). *Chinese Big Business in Indonesia: The State of Capital*. London and New York: Routledge.

Duflo, E. (2001).'Schooling and Labor Market Consequences of School Construction in Indonesia: Evidence from an Unusual Policy Experiment', *American Economic Review*, 91(4): 795–813.

Fane, G. (1999). 'Indonesian Economic Policies and Performance, 1960–98', *The World Economy*, 22(5): 651–668.

Feridhanusetyawan, T., and M. Pangestu (2003). 'Indonesian Trade Liberalisation: Estimating the Gains', *Bulletin of Indonesian Economic Studies*, 39(1): 51–74.

Fujita, N., and W. James (1997). 'Employment Creation and Manufactured Exports in Indonesia, 1980–90', *Bulletin of Indonesian Economic Studies*, 33(1): 103–115.

Fukuoka, Y. (2015). 'Who Brought Down the Dictator? A Critical Reassessment of So-Called "People Power" Revolution in the Philippines and Indonesia', *Pacific Review*, 28(3): 411–433.

Hardum, S., and D. Halim (2016). 'New Local Content Rule for Smartphones Paves Way for Creative Economy: Minister', *Jakarta Globe*, 3 September.

Indonesia Investments (2018). '16th Economic Policy Package Indonesia: Investment, Tax Holiday and Export Earnings'. *Indonesia Investments*, 19 November.

Jacob, J. (2005). 'Late Industrialization and Structural Change: Indonesia, 1975–2000', *Oxford Development Studies*, 33(3/4): 427–451.

Jones, G. (1966). 'The Growth and Changing Structure of the Indonesian Labour Force, 1930–81', *Bulletin of Indonesian Economic Studies*, 2(4): 50–74.

Kim, K. (2020). 'The State as a Patient Capitalist: Growth and Transformation of Indonesia's Development Financiers', *Pacific Review*, 33(3–4): 635–668.

Kim, K. (2021). 'Indonesia's Restrained State Capitalism: Development and Policy Challenges', *Journal of Contemporary Asia*, 51(3): 419–446.

Kim, K., and A. Sumner (2019). 'The Five Varieties of Industrialisation: A New Typology of Diverse Empirical Experience in the Developing World'. ESRC GPID Research Network Working Paper 18. London: Global Poverty and Inequality Dynamics Research Network (GPID).

Kim, K., A. Sumner, and A.A. Yusuf (2018). 'Is Structural Transformation-Led Economic Growth Immiserising or Inclusive? The Case of Indonesia'. ACDE Working Paper in trade and development 2018-11. Canberra: Australian National University.

Kim, K., A. Mungsunti, A. Sumner, and A.A. Yusuf (2020). 'Structural Transformation and Inclusive Growth: Kuznets' 'Developer's Dilemma' in Indonesia'. WIDER Working Paper 2020/31. Helsinki: UNU-WIDER.

Kuznets, S. (1955). 'Economic Growth and Income Inequality', *American Economic Review*, 45(1): 1–28.

Leigh, A., and P. Van der Eng (2009). 'Inequality in Indonesia: What Can We Learn from Top Incomes?', *Journal of Public Economics*, 93(1–2): 209–212.

Lewis, P. (2005). *Growing Apart: Oil, Politics, and Economic Change in Indonesia and Nigeria*. Ann Arbor, MI: University of Michigan Press.

Lindblad, J. (2008). *Bridges to New Business: The Economic Decolonization of Indonesia*. Leiden: KITLV Press.

McMillan, M., D. Rodrik, and Í. Verduzco-Gallo (2014). 'Globalization, Structural Change, and Productivity Growth, with an Update on Africa', *World Development*, 63(C): 11–32.

Oberman, R., R. Dobbs, A. Budiman, F. Thompson, and M. Rossé (2012). *The Archipelago Economy: Unleashing Indonesia's Potential*. Jakarta: McKinsey Global Institute.

Pisani, E., M. Kok, and K. Nugroho (2017). 'Indonesia's Road to Universal Health Coverage: A Political Journey', *Health Policy and Planning*, 32(2): 267–276.

PwC Indonesia (2018a). *Mining in Indonesia: Investment and Taxation Guide*, 10th edn. Jakarta: PwC Indonesia.

PwC Indonesia (2018b). *New Negative List of Investment: Opening New Opportunities for Foreign Investment*. Tax Indonesia 2018/15. Jakarta: PwC Indonesia.

Radelet, S., J. Sachs, R. Cooper, and B. Bosworth (1998). 'The East Asian Financial Crisis: Diagnosis, Remedies, Prospects', Brookings Papers on Economic Activity 1. Washington, DC: Brookings Institution Press.

Robison, R. (1986). *Indonesia: The Rise of Capital*. Sydney: Allen and Unwin.

Robison, R., and V. Hadiz (2004). *Reorganising Power in Indonesia: The Politics of Oligarchy in an Age of Markets*. New York: Routledge Curzon.

Robison, R., and V. Hadiz (2017). 'Indonesia: A Tale of Misplaced Expectation', *Pacific Review*, 30(6): 895–909.

Sen, K. (2014). 'Inclusive Growth: When May We Expect It? When May We Not?', *Asian Development Review* 31(1): 136–162.

Sen, K. (2019). 'Structural Transformation around the World: Patterns and Drivers', *Asian Development Review*, 36(2): 1–31.

Suhaedi, P.P., and P.A. Wibowo (2011). 'The Financial System: Balancing Financial Stability and Economic Growth'. In A. Ananta, M. Soekarni, and S. Arifin (eds), *The Indonesian Economy: Entering a New Era*. Singapore: Institute of Southeast Asian Studies.

Suryahadi, A., G. Hadiwidjaja, and S. Sumarto (2012). 'Economic Growth and Poverty Reduction in Indonesia before and after the Asian Financial Crisis', *Bulletin of Indonesian Economic Studies*, 48(2): 209–227.

Szirmai, A. (1994). 'Real Output and Labour Productivity in Indonesian Manufacturing, 1975–90', *Bulletin of Indonesian Economic Studies*, 30(2): 49–90.

Thee, K. (1991). 'The Surge of Asian NIC Investment into Indonesia', *Bulletin of Indonesian Economic Studies*, 27(3): 55–88.

Thee, K. (2006). 'Technology and Indonesia's Industrial Competitiveness'. ADB Institute Research Paper Series 72. Tokyo: Asian Development Bank (ADB) Institute.

Thomas, T., and J. Panglaykim (1966). 'Indonesian Exports: Performance and Prospects 1950–1970, Part I', *Bulletin of Indonesian Economic Studies*, 2(5): 71–102.

Timmer, M. (1999). 'Indonesia's Ascent on the Technology Ladder: Capital Stock and Total Factor Productivity in Indonesian Manufacturing, 1975–95', *Bulletin of Indonesian Economic Studies*, 35(1): 75–97.

Timmer, M.P., G.J. de Vries, and K. de Vries (2015). 'Patterns of Structural Change in Developing Countries'. In J. Weiss and M. Tribe (eds), *Routledge Handbook of Industry and Development*. Abingdon: Routledge, 65–83.

UNU-WIDER (2019) Standardized dataset based on World Income Inequality Database, WIID 4, version 22 February 2019. Helsinki: UNU-WIDER.

Usui, N. (1997). 'Dutch Disease and Policy Adjustments to the Oil Boom: A Comparative Study of Indonesia and Mexico', *Resources Policy*, 23(4): 151–162.

Van der Eng, P. (2009). 'Growth and Inequality: The Case of Indonesia, 1960–1997'. MPRA Paper 12725. Munich: Munich Personal RePEc Archive.

Van der Eng, P. (2010). 'The Sources of Long-Term Economic Growth in Indonesia, 1880–2008', *Explorations in Economic History*, 47(2010): 294–309.

Van Leeuwen, B., and P. Földvári (2016). 'The Development of Inequality and Poverty in Indonesia, 1932–2008', *Bulletin of Indonesian Economic Studies*, 52(3): 379–402.

World Bank (1993). *The East Asian Miracle: Economic Growth and Public Policy*. Washington, DC: World Bank.

World Bank (2013). *Indonesia Economic Quarterly: Pressures Mounting (March 2013)*. Washington, DC: World Bank.

World Bank (2014a). *East Asia Pacific at Work: Employment, Enterprise, and Well-Being*. Washington, DC: World Bank.

World Bank (2014b). *Indonesia Economic Quarterly: Hard Choices (July 2014)*. Washington, DC: World Bank.

World Bank (2014c). *Indonesia Economic Quarterly: Delivering Change (December 2014)*. Washington, DC: World Bank.

World Bank (2015). *Indonesia Economic Quarterly: In Times of Global Volatility (October 2015)*. Washington, DC: World Bank.

World Bank (2016). *Indonesia Economic Quarterly: Resilience through Reforms (June 2015)*. Washington, DC: World Bank.

World Bank (2017a). *Indonesia Economic Quarterly: Closing the Gap (October 2017)*. Washington, DC: World Bank.

World Bank (2017b). *Indonesia Social Assistance Public Expenditure Review Update: Towards a Comprehensive, Integrated, and Effective Social Assistance System in Indonesia*. Washington, DC: World Bank.

World Bank (2018). *Indonesia Economic Quarterly: Towards Inclusive Growth (March 2018)*. Washington, DC: World Bank.

Yusuf, A., A. Sumner, and I. Rum (2014). 'Twenty Years of Expenditure Inequality in Indonesia, 1993–2013', *Bulletin of Indonesian Economic Studies*, 50(2): 243–254.

4

Getting Rich and Unequal?

Structural Transformation, Inequality, and Inclusive Growth in China

Yanan Li and Chunbing Xing

1. Introduction

Economic growth is often accompanied by significant structural transformation, the pattern of which, to a large extent, determines its inclusiveness.[1] For example, some developing countries that have experienced tertiarization without fully developed industrialization (i.e. premature tertiarization) tend to have high levels of inequality and poor performance in poverty reduction (Rodrik 2016; Felipe et al. 2018). In contrast, the decrease in inequality and the rising living standards of a growing middle class in some industrialized countries are often attributed to a growing manufacturing sector. China is an important case of a country which has experienced record high economic growth and significant structural transformation over the past four decades. Its aggregate economy increased fivefold between 1978 and 2016, and its gross domestic product (GDP) per capita increased by twenty-one times. Behind this lie significant structural changes, rising income inequality, and great success in poverty reduction. Examining the interlinkages between these aspects is our major task in this chapter, which provides valuable lessons for other developing countries and will be important for China's policymaking when its growth slows down.

First, we document China's structural transformation across several dimensions. We show a significant decline in the low-productivity primary, or agricultural, sector and sizeable increases in the secondary and tertiary sectors. Meanwhile, the Chinese economy has become more export oriented, urban concentrated, and skill biased. These changes are supported by increased productivity in rural China, restructuring of ownership in urban areas, urbanization (rural–urban migration), and China's entry into the World Trade Organization (WTO).

---

[1] We acknowledge the constructive suggestions from Andrew Sumner and the help on the figures from Kyunghoon Kim. All errors are our own.

Yanan Li and Chunbing Xing, *Getting Rich and Unequal?*. In: *The Developer's Dilemma.*
Edited by Armida Salsiah Alisjahbana, Kunal Sen, Andy Sumner, and Arief Anshory Yusuf, Oxford University Press.
© UNU-WIDER (2022). DOI: 10.1093/oso/9780192855299.003.0004

We then show the trends in employment, inequality, and inclusiveness. China's economic growth is largely inclusive, with impressive success in poverty reduction due to increased productivity in rural and urban areas, relaxation of the restrictions on labour mobility, and increased opportunities for education. These changes have increased job opportunities for rural residents with low levels of education and have ensured that more people can benefit from a modernized economy. We also show that income inequality first increased significantly during the structural transformation and then seems to have plateaued since the late 2000s. However, we do not have convincing evidence that China's inequality will move to the downward segment of the Kuznetsian curve soon. We discuss related public policies during this period and analyse the political economy of structural transformation, inequality, and poverty reduction.

2. Trends in China's structural transformation after 1978

In this section, we discuss China's structural transformation during the reform period. During this period, China witnessed record economic growth. Between 1978 and 2016, the Chinese economy grew by a multiple of thirty-two times. China not only continued to transform from an agricultural to an industrialized economy; it also transitioned from a planned economy to a socialist market economy. Major reforms were first carried out in rural areas, which were followed by major reform measures in urban areas. We divide the reform period into three sub-periods (1978–91, 1992–2001, and 2002–present) to facilitate our discussions.

2.1 Trends of sectoral value-added and employment shares

Using the Groningen Growth and Development Centre's (GGDC's) 10-Sector Database (Timmer et al. 2015), the two graphs in Figure 4.1 show that labour and resources rapidly shifted away from the agriculture to the non-agricultural sector from 1978. In the period 1978–1991, agriculture's share of total employment fell from 70.5 per cent to 59.7 per cent. Most of the reallocated workers did not move to urban centres. Instead, they went to work in rural industrial enterprises, called township and village enterprises (TVEs), which were set up by township and village-level governments (Zhu 2012). While the manufacturing share of employment increased dramatically during this period, labour productivity was relatively steady (relative to US manufacturing productivity). In addition to manufacturing, non-business services (e.g. wholesale and retail, transport, public administration, education, and so on) also expanded and promoted the process of transformation from agriculture to non-agriculture. The non-business services employment share increased significantly from 11.3 per cent in 1978 to 18.7 per cent in 1991, as shown in Figure 4.1b.

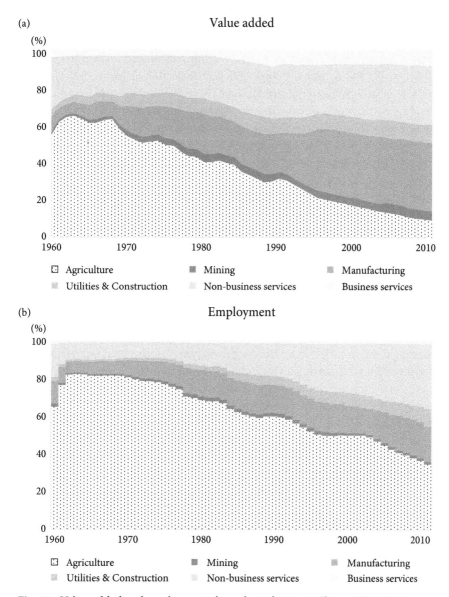

(a) Value added

(b) Employment

Fig. 4.1 Value-added and employment shares by industry in China, 1960–2011

Note: Business services: financial intermediation, renting, business activities; non-business services: (a) wholesale and retail trade, repair of motor vehicles and motorcycles, personal and household goods, hotels and restaurants; (b) transport, storage, communications; (c) public administration, defence, education, health, social work; and (d) other community activities, social and personal service activities, activities of private households.

Source: authors' illustration based on the GGDC 10-Sector Database Version 2015 (Timmer et al. 2015).

The 1990s followed a different structural transformation path to that of the 1980s. This period saw a slightly declining manufacturing employment share but a rapid increase in the share of manufacturing value added. Although industrialization was still at an early stage, this transformation characteristic coincides with so-called 'advanced industrialization' (Kim and Sumner 2019). As shown in Figure 4.1a, the value-added share of manufacturing went up from 24.3 per cent to 34.5 per cent during the period 1991–2000, and the manufacturing employment share decreased from 15.0 per cent to 14.5 per cent. The different trends of employment and value-added shares were probably driven by the restructuring of state-owned enterprises (SOEs), which increased labour productivity but led to mass lay-offs.

Agricultural labour continued to shift into the non-agricultural sectors in the early 1990s and decelerated thereafter. Until 2003, the agricultural employment share remained at around 50 per cent. In terms of value-added shares, however, the manufacturing sector surpassed agriculture from 1994. With declining agriculture employment and slow growth in manufacturing employment, the share of employment in non-business services increased from 17.9 per cent to 26.4 per cent in the 1990s.

China's structural transformation entered a new era in 2002, following China's entering the WTO. Driven by rapidly growing exports, the Chinese economy experienced a manufacturing boom and shifted a substantial amount of agricultural labour to the manufacturing sector. In contrast to the earlier period, the manufacturing shares of both employment and value added increased steadily. Specifically, the employment share grew by 4.7 percentage points (from 13.5 per cent in 2002 to 19.2 per cent in 2010) and the value-added share rose by 1.4 percentage points (from 35.1 per cent in 2002 to 36.5 per cent in 2010). Thus, the economy experienced an 'upgrading industrialization' during this period (Kim and Sumner 2019). Still, the manufacturing employment share outgrew the value-added share, highlighting the labour-intensive nature of China's manufacturing sector in the 2000s. Non-business sectors further developed during this period. The services sector's share of employment increased from 27.5 per cent to 33.2 per cent from 2002 to 2010, and the value-added share went up by 1.7 percentage points (29.7 to 31.4 per cent). Figure 4.2 summarizes the pattern of structural transformation between 1978 and 2011 in China.

2.2 Structural transformation and labour productivity

Having observed the structural transformation trend from 1978, a closely related question is whether the transformation is growth enhancing or growth reducing. As argued by McMillan et al. (2014), Asian countries have experienced productivity-enhancing structural change, which is in contrast to the

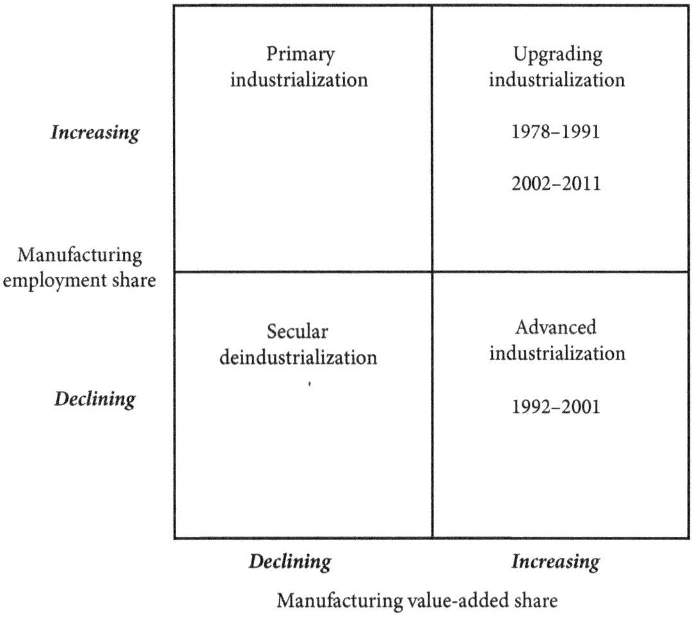

	Declining	Increasing
Increasing	Primary industrialization	Upgrading industrialization 1978–1991 2002–2011
Declining	Secular deindustrialization	Advanced industrialization 1992–2001

Manufacturing employment share

Declining   Increasing

Manufacturing value-added share

Fig. 4.2 Varieties of structural transformation in China, 1978–2011
Source: authors' illustration.

productivity-reducing structural change in Latin America and Africa. They further attribute the growth-enhancing effects of structural transformation in Asia to the fact that the labour has transferred from low to high labour-productivity sectors.

To empirically examine whether this holds true for China, we split labour productivity growth in each period into within-sector and between-sector growth.[2] The annual labour productivity growth from 1978 to 2011 was, on average, 7.6 per cent, of which 2.3 percentage points were driven by between-sector reallocation. This suggests that the result of labour transferring from the lower-productivity agricultural sector to higher-productivity modern sectors was *productivity-enhancing* structural transformation in China. If we look at each economic period, the growth-enhancing structural transformation contributed significantly to the total productivity growth in both the 1980s and the 2000s, whereas structural transformation in the 1990s made a minor contribution to total labour productivity growth. The 1990s period was different because, as we discussed in section 2.1 it went through the privatization of SOEs and did not see a large increase in manufacturing employment. This finding is also consistent with the growth model

---

[2] See Figure 4 in Li and Xing (2020).

proposed by Song et al. (2011), who found that about 70 per cent of the total factor productivity growth in manufacturing between 1998 and 2005 was driven by factor reallocation from less efficient (SOE) firms to the more efficient (private) ones.

We plot changes in labour productivity against employment shares for each period in Figure 4.3. Figure 4.3a shows that only the business sector recorded a simultaneous rise in relative productivity and employment growth during the first period. Construction and non-business services also showed an increase in their employment shares, but their relative productivity decreased. The manufacturing sector showed a large increase in the employment share, but no increases in productivity compared to other sectors. In the second and third periods, no economic sector experienced a simultaneous rise in relative productivity and employment share (Figure 4.3b and Figure 4.3c). In the second period, the most striking changes occurred in the manufacturing sectors (Figure 4.3b). As we discussed earlier, employment shares slightly declined despite a rise in relative labour productivity. The same pattern also occurred in the mining sector, which saw a rise in labour productivity but a declining employment share. In the most recent period, manufacturing and non-business services produced a large number of jobs, and employment shares further increased, but they did not see an increase in productivity. Notably, in all three periods, the non-business sector remained the largest job provider in China, and it grew rapidly over time. This pattern is in sharp contrast to many countries in Latin America and South Asia, where the expanded services sector had large added values but limited capacity for creating jobs.

In summary, over the past four decades, China's economy has experienced rapid structural transformation away from agriculture towards manufacturing and services. The contribution of manufacturing and services to the total value-added growth rate has been above 74 per cent since 1990.[3] The economic development has exhibited clear trends in upgrading industrialization and tertiarization. Since 2015, the size of agricultural employment has become smaller than the other two sectors, making China a 'structurally developed' country, according to the definition by Baymul and Sen (2020). During this process, China also witnessed significant restructuring of the ownership structure of the enterprises, rapid urbanization, and deepening integration into the world economy.

2.3 Urbanization

As shown, China has experienced a rapid structural transformation away from agriculture towards manufacturing and services in the past four decades. The economic development has also exhibited upgrading industrialization and tertiarization. An integral feature of structural change in China is the rapid urbanization

---

[3] See Figure 6 in Li and Xing (2020).

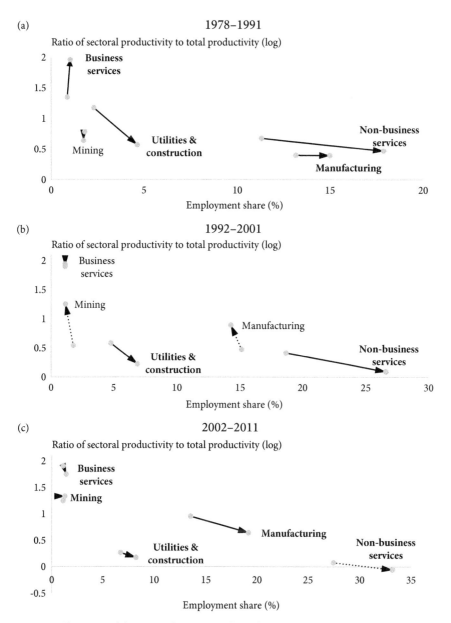

Fig. 4.3 Changes in labour productivity and employment share, China, 1978–2011

Note: Sectors with higher than economy-wide average labour productivity that experienced an increase in employment share are in bold.

Source: authors' illustration based on the GGDC 10-Sector Database Version 2015 (Timmer et al. 2015).

that has taken place over the past four decades. The urban percentage of the total population in China went up from 20.9 per cent in 1982 to 36.2 per cent in 2000, 49.7 per cent in 2010, and 58.72 per cent in 2017. This means more than 600 million people either migrated from rural to urban areas or were reclassified as urban residents due to city expansion over the period 1982–2017.[4] The large flow of rural residents into urban areas provided a sufficient labour force (at a competitive cost) for the economy during the economic transition period.

China's urbanization process has its unique feature due to the household registration system (*Hukou*). Despite the seemingly high urbanization rate, there are a large number of rural–urban migrant workers who temporarily live in urban areas and do not have urban household registration (*Hukou*). According to the National Bureau of Statistics, the number of rural–urban migrant workers increased from under 50 million in the late 1990s to 172 million in 2017. It is a pressing issue for China to make sure that the large migrant population integrates well into urban society. Failure to do so will slow down the structural transformation, as suggested by many studies (Ngai et al. 2016; Tombe and Zhu 2019).

3. Inclusive growth? Declining poverty and rising inequality

3.1 China's great achievement in poverty reduction

China's structural transformation (and growth) has been largely inclusive in terms of the impressive success in poverty reduction. China experienced a relatively long period of a boom in low-cost manufacturing, which provided substantial labour-intensive employment opportunities. Thus, rural residents, rural–urban migrant workers, and other disadvantaged groups, such as the youth, elders, and females, were all able to benefit from the structural transformation.

The headcount poverty ratio by the international standard (US$1.90 a day, 2011 purchasing power parity (PPP)) decreased from 88 per cent in 1981 to 41 per cent in 1999, and further to 0.7 per cent in 2015. Accordingly, by this standard, the size of the poor population decreased from 750 million in 1990 to 10 million in 2015. However, if we use the World Bank's new poverty standard of US$3.2, then the poverty rate in 2015 would be 7 per cent (see Figure 7 in Li and Xing, 2020).

If we further raise the poverty line to US$10 a day, an interesting pattern appears. Almost all the population (98–100 per cent) in China were living on US$10 or less a day before 1999. The share dropped markedly in the new century and fell from 98 per cent in 1999 to 80 per cent in 2010, and then to 60 per cent in 2015.

---

[4] Natural growth in the population played a minor role because urban residents had a low fertility rate under the one-child policy.

Although living standards have improved tremendously over the past two decades, the majority of the population in China is still relatively poor.

3.2 Income inequality

While China has performed exceedingly well in poverty reduction, its economic growth has been far from inclusive in relative terms: the disadvantaged groups have lagged, while others have enjoyed faster growth in income and wealth. China's income inequality during the 1950s–1970s was low by historical and international standards. Since the beginning of the market reform process, however, income inequality has increased markedly. In this section, we present evidence on the trend of income inequality from different perspectives and discuss its relationship with structural transformation.

Evaluating inclusiveness in relative scales is more challenging as it requires complete information on the income distribution, which is demanding due to missing high-income observations or misreporting. First, we obtain the Gini coefficients of income inequality from the official source, the National Bureau of Statistics (NBS) of China. The NBS only released national Gini coefficients after 2003. Fortunately, Ravallion and Chen (2007) estimate Gini coefficients for China based on household surveys in both rural and urban areas conducted by the NBS between 1980 and 2001. We combine these two sources and treat them as an official source.

China's Gini coefficient was mostly below 30 in the early 1980s, close to the most egalitarian Nordic countries (Piketty et al. 2019). Then the most significant increase took place between the mid-1980s and the mid-2000s, concurrent with the rapid structural transformation. According to Ravallion and Chen (2007), China's Gini index increased from 31 in 1981 to 45 in 2001. The statistics released by the NBS suggest that the Gini coefficient kept increasing in the following years and reached 49.1 by 2008. In the following decade, the inequality first declined to 46.2 in 2015 and then increased to 46.8 in the most recent years.

Combining the previous discussions on structural transformation, we discuss the Kuznetsian tension between growth-enhancing structural transformation and rising inequality for each economic period (see Figure 4.4 for the pattern). In the early 1980s, income inequality was relatively stable, despite a fast shift of labour from the agricultural to the non-agricultural sectors. After 1984, however, the Kuznetsian tension started to appear. The gross Gini coefficient rose from 25 in 1984 to 36 in 1990, probably driven by the privatization of state sectors and the burgeoning of private enterprises.

The second period, the 1990s, witnessed a further increase in income inequality. The structural transformation in this period was not growth enhancing. Thus,

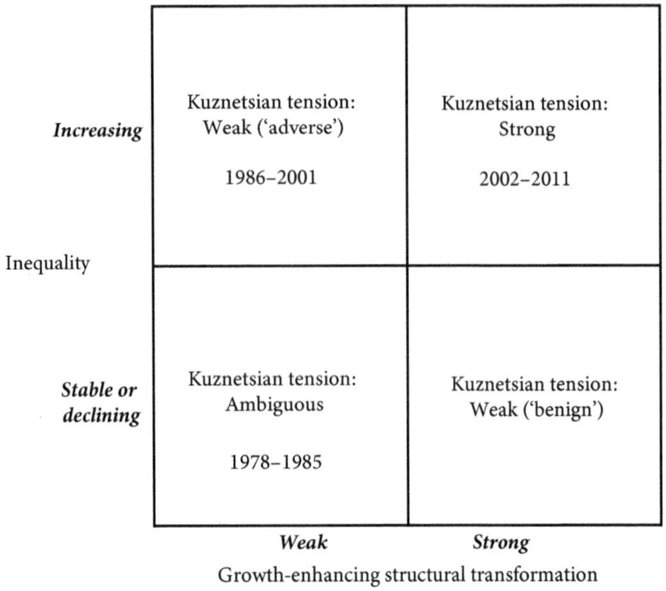

	Weak	Strong
Increasing	Kuznetsian tension: Weak ('adverse') 1986–2001	Kuznetsian tension: Strong 2002–2011
Stable or declining	Kuznetsian tension: Ambiguous 1978–1985	Kuznetsian tension: Weak ('benign')

Inequality

Weak   **Strong**
Growth-enhancing structural transformation

Fig. 4.4 Patterns of Kuznetsian tension in China, 1978–2011
Source: authors' illustration.

the Kuznetsian tension was weak, but in an adverse sense. The many business opportunities brought by the restructuring of the SOEs caused inequality to rise. Concurrent with the increasing inequality was a shrinking share of manufacturing employment with an increasing share of manufacturing value added (see Figures 4.5 and 4.6) and a higher share of non-business service employment with a stagnant value-added share (see Figures 4.7 and 4.8). Income inequality between the coastal and inland areas, and between rural and urban areas, increased.

The Kuznetsian tension became stronger in the early 2000s, following China's accession to the WTO. Inequality increased between 2003 and 2007, with an increasing share of manufacturing employment and value added (see Figures 4.5 and 4.6). The Gini income coefficient reached a record high of 48 in 2007. As we discuss in the following, the benefits from exports were heterogeneous across regions, hence generating vast spatial inequality during the manufacturing boom.

Since the late 2000s, inequality has shown a declining trend and the Kuznetsian tension seems to have weakened benignly. This trend has been documented in a couple of studies. Luo et al. (2018), using the China Household Income Project (CHIP) data, found that the Gini coefficient declined from 49.0 in 2007 to 43.3

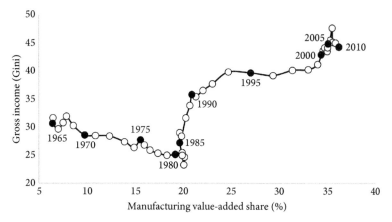

Fig. 4.5 Gross income Gini and manufacturing value-added share, China, 1964–2011

Notes: (i) The missing Gini coefficients were calculated using linear interpolation.
(ii) Manufacturing value-added and employment shares are five-year moving averages.
For example, the data for 1975 is an average of data for 1971–1975. See Fig. 4.1 for the
original data. These notes apply to Figs 4.5, 4.6, 4.7, and 4.8.
Source: authors' calculations based on the GGDC 10-Sector Database Version 2015
(Timmer et al. 2015) and UNU-WIDER World Income Inequality Database (WIID).

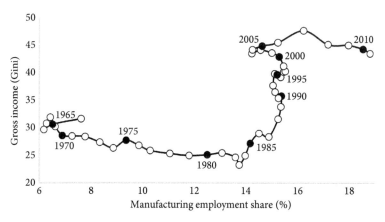

Fig. 4.6 Gross income Gini and manufacturing employment share, China, 1964–2011

Source: authors' calculations based on the GGDC 10-Sector Database Version 2015
(Timmer et al. 2015) and UNU-WIDER World Income Inequality Database (WIID).

in 2013, after a continual increase between 1988 and 2007. Kanbur et al. (2017),
using the China Family Panel Studies (CFPS) data, found that the Gini coefficient

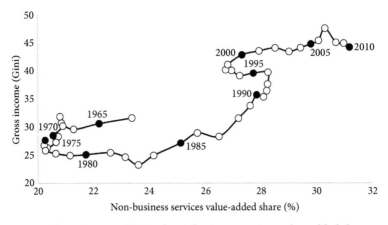

Fig. 4.7 Gross income Gini and non-business services value-added share, China, 1964–2011

Source: authors' calculations based on the GGDC 10-Sector Database Version 2015 (Timmer et al. 2015) and UNU-WIDER World Income Inequality Database (WIID).

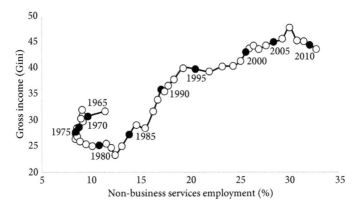

Fig. 4.8 Gross income Gini and non-business services employment share, China, 1964–2011

Source: authors' calculations based on the GGDC 10-Sector Database Version 2015 (Timmer et al. 2015) and UNU-WIDER World Income Inequality Database (WIID).

decreased from 53.3 in 2010 to 49.5 in 2014, and concluded that China's income inequality has turned around and started to decline.[5] The decline reflects the success

---

[5] Despite these uplifting findings, some opposite opinions exist. For instance, Xie and Zhou (2014) show that the Gini coefficients were increasing to very high levels between 2005 and 2012 and forecast an alarmingly increasing trend of inequality down the road. However, their inequality observations come from multiple data sources, some of which are incomparable, hence the increasing trend might be spurious. For example, the CFPS data tend to have higher inequality than CHIP data, and the former are more recent than the latter. It is hard to judge how much of the increase was real and how much was a result of sampling differences.

of numerous welfare policies targeting the low-income population during this period. As explained by Kanbur et al. (2017), the possible drivers of this turnaround are urbanization, transfer and regulation regimes, and tightening rural labour markets.

However, none of the previous studies have covered the most recent years, that is, after 2015. In fact, according to the official data from the NBS, Gini coefficients slightly rebounded after 2016. Therefore, it seems too early to conclude that China is already on the downward segment of the Kuznets curve.

The increase in income inequality is also manifested in other dimensions such as regional and rural–urban income gap, income shares owned by top income households, and the earnings gap between less educated and educated workers. Although regional income gap has declined recently, the educational gap and the share distribution of income has remained high; see Li and Xing (2020) for detailed discussions.

4. Policies that shaped structural transformation and inclusive growth between 1978 and 2016

Three underlying forces—technological change, institutional reforms, and globalization—have shaped the trends of structural transformation and the inclusiveness of growth in China. For the first two periods of economic development (i.e. the 1980s and 1990s), the focus was on economic efficiency. Concurrent with the rapid structural transformation were rising income inequality and reduced poverty incidence. Since the early 2000s, the Chinese government has paid more attention to social equity and has aimed to achieve inclusive growth. We discuss the policies that shape structural transformation, inequality, and inclusive growth for each period.

4.1 Rural reforms

The *first* economic period, 1978–1991, can be summed up by Deng Xiaoping's famous quote: 'Let some people get rich first' (Naughton 1993). The Chinese government implemented a series of reforms to get structural transformation started.

The first policy was the abolition of the commune system and the establishment of the Household Responsibility System. The attempt to change first occurred on a small scale in Anhui province in 1978, with their participants (all farmers) taking the immense risk of being punished for deviating from the orthodox. The new arrangement allowed rural households to have land use rights and to claim residuals after paying tax. Despite the political challenges in the early phase, this practice later won the recognition of the authority and was named the Household

Responsibility System, which gained considerable success. By providing incentives for rural residents to invest in their allocated land and utilize new kinds of technology and fertilizer, it increased agricultural productivity growth and alleviated China's subsistence food constraints, which in turn created surplus labour for later development in the non-agriculture sector. McMillan et al. (1989) showed that over 75 per cent of the measured productivity increase in China's agriculture after 1978 was due to the Household Responsibility System and the remainder to price increases. This reform signified a significant transition in China's economic model and opened a new era for the country's agricultural economy and rural development.

The second concurrent policy was allowing the entry of non-SOEs, such as collective and small-scale individual businesses. TVEs then flourished and expanded remarkably from the late 1980s, absorbing a large amount of surplus rural labour. In the early years of the reform period, the relocation of labour from agriculture to non-agriculture was mainly within rural areas. According to Zhu (2012), during 1978–1984, more than 49 million workers (19 per cent of the total work force) reallocated out of the agricultural sector, and most of them went to work in the rural industrial enterprises set up by township and village-level governments.

In terms of inclusive growth policies, the Chinese government implemented an education policy that had long-standing effects—the Compulsory School Law in 1986. It stipulated that all children over seven years had to enter primary school and complete the nine years of free schooling. This far-reaching policy improved the average education of the rural population and of females. Human capital accumulation laid the foundation for the manufacturing boom in the 2000s. The *Hukou* system also witnessed relaxation in the mid-1980s so that rural residents could find employment in urban areas without changing *Hukou* status, but, until the end of this period, strict control of migration remained.

4.2 Privatization: growth in private enterprises

The *second* stage of structural transformation, between the early 1990s and 2001, featured the restructuring of ownership of SOEs (or privatization) in urban areas. Before the economic reforms in 1978, SOEs accounted for 80 per cent of the total urban employment and more than 75 per cent of industrial output (Zhu 2012), and such dominance had led to the low efficiency of the urban economy and had limited the occurrence of large-scale rural–urban migration. The situation persisted into the early 1990s, despite efforts to reform the urban sector.[6] The fourteenth Congress of the Chinese Communist Party (CCCP) in 1992 set up the goal

---

[6] The main reformed areas include empowering the decision making of SOEs, increasing employment flexibility of enterprises, and encouraging the development of non-SOEs in urban areas (Cai et al. 2009).

of China's economic reform as establishing the socialist market economy, which meant that the role of non-public ownerships was officially recognized. Starting from 1992, the government took a series of measures to implement the ownership reform and to expand the market economy. The labour force started to be reallocated from the SOEs or collectively owned enterprises to the private sector from then, but still at a low pace. The fifteenth CCCP held in 1997 accelerated the process by further legalizing the development of private enterprises and by initiating a massive restructuring of the SOEs. Between 1995 and 2001, the state sector's share of total employment declined from 17 per cent to 12 per cent (Zhu 2012). With a reduction in legal barriers, private enterprises grew remarkably. Meanwhile, the SOE reforms also necessitated a large body of laid-off or unemployed workers (Appleton et al. 2002).

The ownership reform had a far-reaching impact on urban inequality, first because the income levels differed across enterprises of different ownerships and wage inequality was higher in the private than in the public sector. As increasing numbers of the labour force found employment in the private sector, wage inequality increased significantly. Whalley and Xing (2016) quantified this impact using the CHIP data. They found that ownership restructuring caused 40 per cent and 65 per cent of the increases in wage inequality measured as variance of log wages for the periods of 1995–2002 and 2002–2007, respectively. However, the results are sensitive to the inequality measure, and the corresponding contributions would be 16 per cent and 18 per cent if they used Gini coefficients.

Second, the SOE reforms caused unemployment and employment pressure for urban workers, which explains the low wage growth during this period and the narrowing of the rural–urban income gap. However, the reform made room for private enterprises and for rural–urban migration, which started to increase, especially in the late 1990s. In this period, there was also huge growth in agricultural labour productivity, pushing surplus labour away from agriculture. Government interventions in the agricultural sector were significantly reduced, and market liberalization provided farmers with strong incentives to adopt new technologies. As a result, the annual growth rate of total factor productivity in agriculture reached 5.10 per cent between 1988 and 1998 (Zhu 2012). Agriculture's share of total employment reduced from 60 per cent in 1990 to 50 per cent in 2000 (see Figure 4.1b). According to Cao and Birchenall (2013), agricultural total factor productivity growth accounted for the majority of the output and employment redistribution towards non-agriculture (between 1989 and 2009).

A major policy, which had the dual role of promoting structural transformation and inclusive growth, was the expansion of higher education in 1999. This policy was first implemented to postpone the entrance of youths into the labour market to extenuate the employment pressure caused by the SOE reform and the impact of the Asian Financial Crisis. Chinese households embraced this policy enthusiastically, and the expansion persisted into the 2010s, changing the Chinese labour market tremendously. We will discuss the further expansion later in more detail.

4.3 Globalization: growth in the export sector

The *third* stage of structural transformation, 2002–2011, featured trade liberalization. This period started with China's entrance into the WTO. From then, trade shares in total GDP increased steadily until 2008. Taken together with rising manufacturing employment in the mid-2000s, this clearly shows that export growth was a key driver for shifting the labour force away from agriculture and moving to modern sectors (Erten and Leight 2019).

The Chinese government has made continuous efforts to open the door to foreign businesses and to embrace globalization since 1978. Wan et al. (2007) gave a brief description of China's journey to globalization in terms of trade and tourism, foreign direct investment (FDI), and movement of people, etc. After joining the WTO, China further reduced the tariff rates for more than 5,000 products in 2002. The reduced tariff barrier was accompanied by substantial trade deregulation, a narrowing of the scope of quota limits, and increasing inflow of FDI.

The composition of exports has also been changing over time. The share of manufacturing goods in export products was 75.7 per cent in 1991, which increased to 88.6 per cent in 2001 and to 93.6 per cent in 2010. There is no doubt that China became the world's factory in the early 2000s. However, more recent findings suggest that China's export products are becoming more sophisticated, increasingly moving away from agriculture and textiles to machinery, electronics, and assembly (Amiti and Freund 2010).

Another feature of China's trade is the unevenness of regional exposure to globalization. Most of the trade activities were concentrated in the coastal regions. The share of exports in GDP was much higher in coastal provinces such as Beijing, Fujian, Guangdong, Jiangsu, Shanghai, Tianjin, and Zhejiang. In central and western provinces, export shares were much lower, seldom more than 10 per cent. Import shares showed similar patterns. In addition, growth in trade activities was also higher in coastal provinces than in non-coastal provinces. Take Jiangsu as an example. Its export/GDP ratio was 30 per cent in 2002, and the ratio more than doubled in 2007, reaching 61 per cent. The differential in exposure to globalization led to different patterns of structural changes and urbanization.

During the rapid economic growth period, local government officials, driven by promotion incentives, were actively engaged in competition over GDP growth (Yu et al. 2016). They competed for foreign or domestic capital investment by offering incentives such as low tax rates and unregulated labour markets. This resulted in a large loss of efficiency. Due to a lack of labour protection policies, the majority of rural migrant workers in urban manufacturing firms were living in poor environments and receiving low pay. And more broadly, the large rural and disadvantaged population groups had been left behind and forgotten. Social inequality was increasingly becoming a salient issue.

In the late 2000s, the Chinese government was concerned more about the widening wealth and income gaps and adopted more egalitarian and populist policies. These welfare policies covered education, labour protection, medical insurance, and pensions, among other areas. First, education expansion, particularly that in higher education, continued. Second, in the labour market, the government enacted and strengthened the enforcement of the Labour Contract Law in 2007 and frequently increased minimum wages. Third, China had achieved universal health care coverage and significantly increased old-age pension coverage by the late 2000s. Finally, the government strengthened the poverty eradication polices and implemented the 'poverty-alleviation with precision (*JingZhunFuPin*) programme', which aimed to eradicate absolute poverty by 2020.

4.4 *Hukou* reform and rural–urban migration

The *Hukou* system has been a fundamental institutional arrangement in China, and its reform, far from being once and for all, continued in the whole reform period. In the early phase of the 1978–1991 period, the *Hukou* was restrictive so that surplus rural labour could not move to cities where the employment pressure was already high. The government started to relax the *Hukou* restriction from the mid-1980s, when the demand for surplus rural labour increased in urban areas due to the increased autonomy of SOEs and the emergence of the private economy. However, as the economy was suffering the lowest growth since 1978, the relaxation trend reversed in the late 1980s (see Cai et al. 2009). Then, the 1992–2001 period (or, roughly speaking, the 1990s) witnessed a series of reforms of the *Hukou* system when the government realized that it would be unachievable to block migration in a socialist market economy. The government started to emphasize the management of rural–urban migration (who were allowed to move without changing their *Hukou* status), and the number of migrants increased.

The most significant increase in the number of migrants happened after China's entry into the WTO in 2002, the third period in our analysis. As stated earlier, the regional gap increased significantly in the following years, encouraging a large number of rural residents to migrate. These migrants have often been seen as one of the significant comparative advantages of the Chinese economy. The cheap labour of migrants proved crucial for the development of the receiving regions, which explains why they were allowed access to cities. On the other hand, as urban income was essential for raising the rural living standard, the government of sending regions encouraged migration. As a consequence, rural–urban migration reduced rural poverty significantly. However, changing *Hukou* status remained difficult, and migrants without local *Hukou* status were not entitled to many local benefits and were vulnerable to expulsion.

Over the past ten years, the migration pattern and typical demographics of migrant workers have changed significantly. The age of the average migrant worker has increased significantly, from 34 in 2008 to 38.6 in 2015. Over the same period, the share of migrant workers aged between sixteen and twenty decreased from 11 per cent to 4 per cent, and the share of those aged above forty increased from 30 per cent to 44 per cent. Today, migrant workers are still generally less educated than the urban labour force, but their education levels have increased rapidly. By 2015, one-quarter of rural-to-urban migrants had at least a high school degree, and 8.3 per cent of them had a college degree.

4.5 Higher education expansion and the increase in educated workers

China has increased its supply of educated labour in response to the rising demand for skilled labour. From 1990 to 2015, China's GDP grew at an annual rate of 10 per cent, and private and public expenditures on education grew even more rapidly. In the mid-1990s, government expenditures on education amounted to less than 2.5 per cent of GDP. By 2011, they had reached 4 per cent of GDP. As a result of the rising expenditure on education by both the Chinese government and individual households, the average education level of the Chinese labour force has increased rapidly.

In the recent two decades, the number of graduates with tertiary degrees increased tremendously. In 1990, 0.6 million students graduated from higher education institutions (HEIs). In 2017, the number of HEI graduates reached over 7 million. The rapid higher education expansion transformed China's higher education from elite education to mass education. When globalization and technological change increased the demand for skilled workers in the following years, students of different socio-economic backgrounds were able to benefit from economic growth. More importantly, the college expansion policy also advanced rural–urban mobility because rural residents with a college degree could change their *Hukou* status to urban *Hukou*. Therefore, this policy promoted inclusive growth.

5. Conclusion

China has achieved tremendous economic development since its reform and opening-up policy in 1978. The economy has transformed from an agricultural to an industrialized economy and is now further shifting towards a service economy. We have documented the transition process for each period, high-lighting the macro drivers of the economic transition and government policies. To summarize, the transition started in 1978, following the introduction of the Household Responsibility System, which greatly increased agricultural produc-tivity, and the *Hukou* reform, which relaxed rural–urban migration restrictions. The second transition period, from the early 1990s until 2001, featured the pri-vatization of SOEs. The third period, from China's entry into the WTO in 2001 until 2010, was a critical period for the country to achieve upgrading struc-tural transformation from an agricultural to an industrialized economy. Driven by growth in exports, globalization, and cheap labour costs, China enjoyed a manufacturing boom during this stage, along with higher urbanization rates and the expansion of higher education. Since the 2010s, the economy has en-tered a new era of declining manufacturing and exports and a growing services sector.

China has also achieved great success in reducing poverty rates over the whole reform period. However, income inequality has increased dramatically. Between the early 1980s and early 2000s, the income and wealth gaps had widened. Since the late 2000s, inequality seems to have plateaued, first showing a slight decline and then rebounding slightly. Therefore, it still seems early to conclude that China's development is an exemplar of the Kuznets hypothesis.

In the future, the Chinese economy seems to be gradually transitioning into a service economy. The services sector will outgrow the manufacturing sector in terms of their shares of value and employment, which is signalled by the rapidly growing gig economy in recent years. Automation and the use of robots are rising in all industries. Economic growth will be more reliant on domestic consumption than on exports.

With ongoing economic transitions, the tension between economic transition and inclusive growth is likely to persist. Absolute poverty is very likely to be erad-icated in the new era due to the 'poverty reduction with precision' campaign, but relative poverty will remain. Hopefully China keeps reforming the existing social security policies and public finance system, and pays more attention to disadvan-taged groups, which according to past evidence could help to further reduce social inequality and achieve inclusive growth.

References

Amiti, M., and C. Freund (2010). 'The Anatomy of China's Export Growth'. In R.C. Feenstra and S.-J. Wei (eds), *China's Growing Role in World Trade*. National Bureau of Economic Research. Chicago and London: University of Chicago Press, 35–56

Appleton, S., J. Knight, L. Song, and Q. Xia (2002). 'Labor retrenchment in China: Determinants and consequences'. *China Economic Review*, 13(2–3): 252–275.

Baymul, Ç., and K. Sen (2020). 'Was Kuznets Right? New Evidence on the Relationship between Structural Transformation and Inequality', *Journal of Development Studies*, 1–20. doi: https://doi.org/10.1080/00220388.2019.1702161.

Cai, F., D. Yang, and M. Wang (2009). 'Migration and Labor Mobility in China'. Human Development Research Paper 2009/09. New York: UNDP.

Cao, K.H., and J.A. Birchenall (2013). 'Agricultural Productivity, Structural Change, and Economic Growth in Post-Reform China', *Journal of Development Economics*, 104: 165–180. doi: https://doi.org/10.1016/j.jdeveco.2013.06.001.

Erten, B., and J. Leight (2021). 'Exporting out of agriculture: The impact of WTO accession on structural transformation in China', *Review of Economics and Statistics*, 103(2), 364–380. doi: https://doi.org/10.1162/rest_a_00852.

Felipe, J., A. Mehta, and C. Rhee (2018). 'Manufacturing Matters … But It's the Jobs that Count', *Cambridge Journal of Economics*, February. doi: https://doi.org/10.1093/cje/bex086.

Kanbur, R., Y. Wang, and X. Zhang (2017). 'The Great Chinese Inequality Turnaround'. SSRN Scholarly Paper ID 2962268. Rochester, NY: Social Science Research Network, https://papers.ssrn.com/abstract=2962268 (accessed 17 February 2020).

Kim, K., and A. Sumner (2019). 'The Five Varieties of Industrialisation: A New Typology of Diverse Empirical Experience in the Developing World', https://www.gpidnetwork.org/wp-content/uploads/2019/06/WP_18.pdf (accessed 17 February 2020).

Li, Y., and C. Xing (2020). 'Structural Transformation, Inequality, and Inclusive Growth in China'. WIDER Working Paper 33/2020. Helsinki: UNU-WIDER. doi: https://doi.org/10.35188/UNU-WIDER/2020/790-3.

Luo, C., S. Li, and T. Sicular (2018). 'The Long-Term Evolution of Income Inequality and Poverty in China'. WIDER Working Paper 2018/153. Helsinki: UNU-WIDER. doi: https://doi.org/10.35188/UNU-WIDER/2018/595-4.

McMillan, J., J. Whalley, and L. Zhu (1989). 'The Impact of China's Economic Reforms on Agricultural Productivity Growth'. *Journal of Political Economy*, 97(4): 781–807.

McMillan, M., D. Rodrik, and Í. Verduzco-Gallo (2014). 'Globalization, Structural Change, and Productivity Growth, with an Update on Africa'. *World Development*, 63(November): 11–32. doi: https://doi.org/10.1016/j.worlddev.2013.10.012.

Naughton, B. (1993). 'Deng Xiaoping: The Economist'. *The China Quarterly*, 135: 491–514.

Ngai, L.R., C.A. Pissarides, and J. Wang (2016). 'China's Mobility Barriers and Employment Allocations', *Journal of the European Economic Association*, 17(5): 1617–1653. doi: https://doi.org/10.1093/jeea/jvy035.

Piketty, T., L. Yang, and G. Zucman (2019). 'Capital Accumulation, Private Property, and Rising Inequality in China, 1978–2015', *American Economic Review*, 109(7): 2469–2496. doi: https://doi.org/10.1257/aer.20170973.

Ravallion, M., and S. Chen (2007). 'China's (Uneven) Progress against Poverty', *Journal of Development* Economics, 82(1): 1–42. doi: https://doi.org/10.1016/j.jdeveco.2005.07.003.

Rodrik, D. (2016). 'Premature Deindustrialization', *Journal of Economic Growth*, 21(1): 1–33. doi: https://doi.org/10.1007/s10887-015-9122-3.

Song, Z., K. Storesletten, and F. Zilibotti (2011). 'Growing Like China', *American Economic Review*, 101(1): 196–233. doi: https://doi.org/10.1257/aer.101.1.196.

Timmer, M., G. de Vries, and K. de Vries (2015). 'Patterns of Structural Change in Developing Countries'. In J. Weiss and M. Tribe (eds), *Routledge Handbook of Industry and Development*. London: Routledge, 65–83.

Tombe, T., and X. Zhu (2019). 'Trade, Migration, and Productivity: A Quantitative Analysis of China'. *American Economic Review*, 109(5): 1843–1872. doi: https://doi.org/10.1257/aer.20150811.

UNU-WIDER (2019). Standardized dataset based on World Income Inequality Database, WIID 4, version 22 February 2019. Helsinki: UNU-WIDER.

Wan, G., M. Lu, and Z. Chen (2007). 'Globalization and Regional Income Inequality: Empirical Evidence from Within China', *Review of Income and Wealth*, 53(1): 35–59.

Whalley, J., and C. Xing (2016). 'Ownership Restructuring and Wage Inequality in Urban China'. *International Labour Review*, 155(1): 57–72. doi: https://doi.org/10.1111/ilr.12005.

Xie, Y., and X. Zhou (2014). 'Income Inequality in Today's China', *Proceedings of the National Academy of Sciences*, 111(19): 6928–6933. doi: https://doi.org/10.1073/pnas.1403158111.

Yu, J., L.-A. Zhou, and G. Zhu (2016). 'Strategic Interaction in Political Competition: Evidence from Spatial Effects across Chinese Cities', *Regional Science and Urban Economics*, 57(March): 23–37. doi: https://doi.org/10.1016/j.regsciurbeco.2015.12.003.

Zhu, X. (2012). 'Understanding China's Growth: Past, Present, and Future', *Journal of Economic Perspectives*, 26(4): 103–124. doi: https://doi.org/10.1257/jep.26.4.103.

5

Benign Growth

Structural Transformation and Inclusive Growth in Thailand

Peter Warr and Waleerat Suphannachart[1]

1. Introduction

Structural change is a ubiquitous feature of growing economies (Timmer 2014). Thailand certainly qualifies as a growing economy. In 2017, real gross domestic product (GDP) per person was thirteen times its level in 1951, having grown for two-thirds of a century at an average annual rate of 4 per cent. Between economic sectors and between regions, growth has been far from uniform over time. The structure of the Thai economy has transformed radically, with agriculture contracting as a share of both GDP and employment, while the combined shares of industry and services have correspondingly expanded. The rate of this structural change has been strongly correlated with the overall rate of growth—the faster the growth, the more rapid the structural change. Not surprisingly, structural change in sectoral terms has also been correlated with the rate of urbanization.

Economic growth has also coincided with a massive reduction in the incidence of poverty. The rate of poverty reduction has been strongly correlated with changes in the overall rate of growth (Warr 2020) and structural change has undoubtedly affected this relationship. Earlier empirical research has indicated that the degree to which aggregate poverty incidence is reduced by a one per cent contribution from a given sector to aggregate GDP growth is highest for agriculture, followed by services, with industry far behind (Ravallion and Datt 1996; Warr 2014a). The decline in the GDP share of agriculture has meant that agriculture's contribution to overall GDP growth has similarly contracted. Do these structural changes mean that the poverty-reducing power of economic growth has also fallen?

[1] Helpful suggestions from Andy Sumner, data and graphical assistance from Kyunghoon Kim and Arief Anshory Yusuf, and computational assistance from Huong Lien Do are gratefully acknowledged.

Peter Warr and Waleerat Suphannachart, *Benign Growth*. In: *The Developer's Dilemma*.
Edited by Armida Salsiah Alisjahbana, Kunal Sen, Andy Sumner, and Arief Anshory Yusuf, Oxford University Press.

The story on economic inequality is more nuanced. Thailand's recorded level of economic inequality is high, by international standards, both across regions and across households. Average incomes per person among people living in or close to the capital city, Bangkok, have remained well above those of residents elsewhere in the country, especially the north and north-east regions. At the national level, measured economic inequality between households has declined over the long term. Over the medium term, it increased from the early 1960s until about 1986, then levelled off until about 1992, and subsequently declined steadily until 2017, reaching a level lower than any previously recorded. In his celebrated 1955 article, Simon Kuznets (1955) advanced the hypothesis of an inverted-U-shaped medium-term relationship between economic inequality and levels of national income. The Thai data are consistent with this account.

Our interest in this study is in the medium-to-long-term relationships between growth and structural transformation on the one hand, and the outcomes of poverty incidence and inequality on the other. We are less interested in the short-term, year-to-year, fluctuations in these variables, which are sensitive to other short-term shocks, unrelated to the underlying relationships of interest. Accordingly, the Thai historical data are divided into four distinct periods, according to the country's aggregate economic performance. We shall study whether a correlation exists between average annual rates of growth and structural change within each of these four periods and the corresponding poverty and inequality outcomes.

Sections 2 and 3 of the chapter summarize the record of Thailand's aggregate economic growth and structural change, respectively. Section 4 reviews the evidence on poverty incidence and economic inequality in Thailand and their possible relationship to growth and structural change. Section 5 explores the political economy implications of economic growth and structural change, as experienced in Thailand. The discussion stresses the regional dimensions of both economic growth and structural change as a driver of political events in Thailand. Section 6 concludes.

2. Aggregate economic growth

Figure 5.1 depicts Thai economic growth since 1951, when national accounts were first produced. The diagram shows both the level and growth rate of real GDP per person over this interval, identifying four distinct periods, labelled I–IV. Table 5.1 summarizes these four periods in terms of the average growth rates of real GDP (not per capita) and its sectoral components.[2] For comparison with other chapters in this volume, Figure 5.2 characterizes the varieties of structural transformation in Thailand.

---

[2] For comparison with later discussion, Period I is truncated in Tables 5.1, 5.2, 5.3, and 5.4 to 1981–1987.

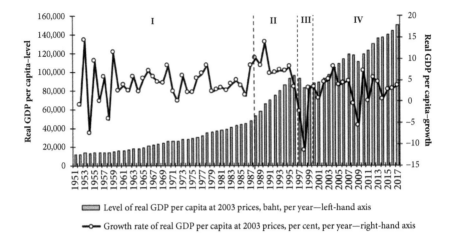

Fig. 5.1 Thailand: real GDP per capita and its growth rate, 1951–2017

Source: authors' calculations, using data from National Economic and Social Development Board (NESDB), Bangkok, http://www.nesdb.go.th/ (accessed 17 June 2019; new address https://www.nesdc.go.th).

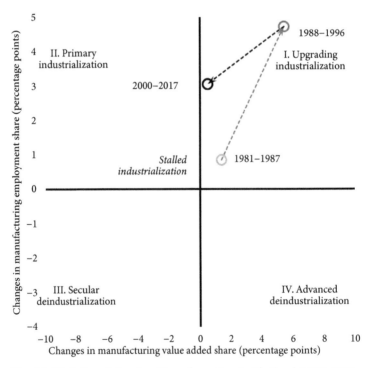

Fig. 5.2 Varieties of structural transformation in Thailand, 1964–2011

Source: data from the Groningen Growth and Development Centre (GGDC) 10-Sector Database Version 2015 (Timmer et al. 2015).

Table 5.1 Growth and structural change (% per annum)

Period	Real GDP growth and its sectoral components				Structural change by output shares		Structural change by employment shares	
	Total GDP	Agriculture	Industry	Services	Overall rate	Industrialization component	Overall rate	Industrialization component
I. Pre-boom 1981–1987	6.7	4.5	8.5	6.8	−0.57	−1.03	−0.25	−0.11
II. Boom 1988–1996	9.3	2.7	12.7	8.6	−0.68	−1.44	−2.07	−0.55
III. Crisis 1997–1999	−1.9	1.7	−2.9	−2.4	0.34	0.23	−0.33	1.44[a]
IV. Post-crisis 2000–2017	4.1	2.0	3.8	4.4	−0.22	−0.18	−1.00	−0.32
Whole period 1981–2017	5.7	3.0	4.4	5.8	−0.33	−1.09	−1.02	−0.35

Note: Roman numerals refer to the periods identified in Figure 5.1, except for Period I, which is truncated in this table and in Tables 5.2, 5.3, and 5.4. [a] During the crisis period (1996–2000, Period III), agriculture's employment share declined by 1.32 percentage points and industry's share declined by 1.88 percentage points. The workers released from these two sectors were partially absorbed by services, partially unemployed.
Source: Authors' calculations.

2.1 Period I: post-war recovery and sustained, moderate growth, 1951–1987

During the recovery from the Second World War and until the late 1950s, annual growth of economic output per person fluctuated widely, averaging 2.5 per cent per annum over this period. The policy priority of this time was not fostering growth but containing price inflation, which had reached almost 100 per cent per annum at the end of the Second World War (Ingram 1971; Nidhiprabha 2018). From 1959 to 1986 the average annual growth rate of real GDP per person was 4.3 per cent, compared with an average of just over 2 per cent for all low-income and middle-income countries over the same period, according to World Bank data. This was an extended period of moderate growth combined with macroeconomic stability.

2.2 Period II: economic boom, 1988–1996

Over this critical decade, the Thai economy was the fastest growing in the world, with real GDP per person growing at an average annual rate of 7.3 per cent. The boom was fuelled by very high rates of private investment, at around 40 per cent of GDP. During this boom earlier, negative assessments of Thailand's prospects were replaced by euphoric predictions that it would soon become a 'Fifth Tiger', following in the footsteps of Korea, Taiwan, Hong Kong, and Singapore. In 1993, the country was identified by the World Bank as one of East Asia's 'miracle' economies (World Bank 1993). By 1996, Thailand had experienced almost four decades without a single year of negative real GDP growth (Warr and Nidhiprbha 1996).

2.3 Period III: Asian Financial Crisis, 1997–1999

The Asian Financial Crisis (AFC) was a turning point for Thailand, in both economic and political terms. Over the two years 1997 and 1998, real GDP per person fell by a cumulative 14 per cent. In the simplest terms, the crisis was the collapse of the investment-driven economic boom of the preceding decade. Over-confident macroeconomic policy—including mis-management of the fixed exchange rate policy in combination with an open capital account—was central to this collapse (Warr 1999; Vines and Warr 2003).

2.4 Period IV: recovery from the Asian Financial Crisis, the global financial crisis, and moderate growth, 2000–2017

Following the AFC, the rate of economic recovery was moderate, and has remained so ever since. Thailand has never fully recovered from the loss of business confidence caused by the AFC, reflected in declining rates of private investment, combined with a loss of public confidence in the capacity of the traditional Thai elite to manage economic change and the expectation of political instability. From 2000 onwards, growth of real GDP per person was positive in all years except 2009 (the global financial crisis), but below its long-term trend. It was not until 2003 that the level of real GDP per capita regained its pre-crisis level of 1996. Both private domestic investment and, to a lesser extent, foreign direct investment (FDI) remained sluggish. Nevertheless, despite the slower-than-expected recovery, moderate growth did occur. By 2007, real economic output per person was 20 per cent above its 1996 pre-crisis level and almost ten times its level of 1951 (Warr 2013).

Between 2010 and 2017, the average annual growth rate of real GDP per person recovered to 3.4 per cent. The first half of this interval was a period of political turbulence, culminating in a military coup in May 2014.[3] The average rate of GDP growth per person was 3.6 per cent, slightly below the long-term average since 1951, 4 per cent. Over the four years of military government up to the end of 2017, the average rate of GDP growth per person was just under 3.1 per cent.

3. Structural transformation

We define *structural transformation* (ST) to mean a relocation of sectoral activity that raises overall output. The definition means that ST is not synonymous with industrialization, although the latter can be expected to be an especially important component of ST. Reallocation of sectoral activity can be described in terms of output or employment. Consider a three-sector classification of the total economy: agriculture, industry, and services. Structural change almost always corresponds to a reduction in agriculture's share of both output and employment (Timmer 2009). This reduction necessarily coincides with an increase in the combined output share of industry and services as well as an increase in their combined employment share, but the mix of industry and services in this structural change varies greatly and the mix may be very different for output and employment.[4] The distinction between these two dimensions of structural change (output and employment) will prove to be an important aspect of Thailand's experience.

---

[3] The military government remained in place until new elections were held in March 2019, when it was replaced by a coalition civilian government led primarily by members of the former military regime.
[4] Figure 1.1 (this volume) classifies countries and periods by the pattern of industrialization. In Thailand, disregarding the special case of the Asian Financial Crisis (period III), both output and employment shares in manufacturing increased in each of the other three periods (Table 5.1), but the increases in manufacturing's employment share was significant only in periods II and IV and the increase in its value-added share was significant only in period II. In Figure 5.2 period II is characterized as 'upgrading industrialization' and periods I and IV as 'stalled industrialization'.

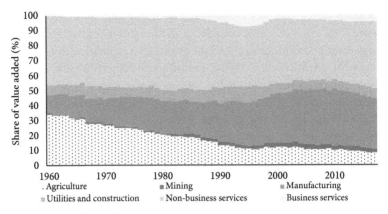

Fig. 5.3 GDP shares by sector, 1960–2017

Source: authors' calculations using data from the GGDC 10-Sector Database Version 2015 (Timmer et al. 2015).

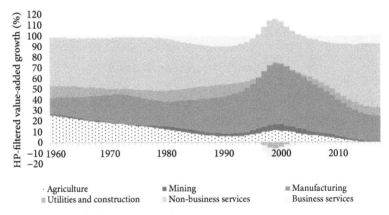

Fig. 5.4 Growth decomposition by sector, 1960–2017

Source: authors' calculations using data from the GGDC 10-Sector Database Version 2015 (Timmer et al. 2015).

3.1 Output shares

Figure 5.3 describes sectoral output (value-added) shares from 1960 to 2017. Agriculture's share of GDP (agricultural value-added/GDP) declined from 34 to 8 per cent. At the same time, the share of manufacturing industry rose from 13 to 34 per cent and the share of non-manufacturing industry rose marginally, from 7 to 9 per cent, while the share of services remained almost unchanged at 46 per cent. The decline in agriculture's share of output was taken up almost entirely by an increase in the share of manufacturing. Nevertheless, services accounted for more than one-half of all growth (Figure 5.4).

In this study, we are particularly interested in the possible relationship between structural change and other variables of interest. To facilitate this, the characteristics of structural change need to be quantified. The above discussion identifies two principal components of structural change: (i) the rate of decline of agriculture's share of GDP; and (ii) the proportion of that decline that is taken up by industry, on the one hand, and services, on the other.

The overall rate of structural change over a given period will be defined as the average annual change of agriculture's output share:

(a) *Overall rate of structural change (output shares in agriculture):*

$$= [S_t^{YA} - S_{t-\tau}^{YA}]/\tau, \tag{1}$$

where S_t^{YA} denotes the output (Y) share of agriculture (A) in year t and τ is the number of years comprising that period. A decline in the output share of agriculture will, of course, necessarily be matched by an increase in the combined output shares of industry and services.

The industrialization component of that mix, over the same period, is given by:

(b) *Industrialization component of structural change (output shares):*

$$= [S_t^{YI} - S_{t-\tau}^{YI}]/[S_t^{YA} - S_{t-\tau}^{YA}]. \tag{2}$$

The industrialization component index will be a proportion—possibly, but not necessarily, lying between 0 and 1.

Table 5.1 summarizes the data on these two output-based measures of structural change. Over the full period, 1981–2017, agriculture's share of GDP declined at an average rate of 0.33 percentage points per year. This decline was most rapid during the pre-boom and boom periods, especially the latter. During the years of the AFC, agriculture's output share increased, making this a period of reverse structural change. During the post-crisis period, the contraction of agriculture's output share resumed, as before the crisis, but at roughly half of its pre-crisis rate.

The industrialization component of structural change based on output shares (measure (b) above) indicates that over the entire period from 1981–2017 industrial growth accounted for all of the contraction of agriculture (index 1.09). But this proportion varied over time. The industrialization component was particularly strong during the pre-crisis period, especially during the boom decade, when the index reached 1.44. The increase in industry's output share coincided with a decline in the output shares of both agriculture and services, but the industrialization component declined following the AFC. In this post-crisis period, some export-oriented manufacturing industries performed very well, as discussed in this section below, but the decline in agriculture's output share following the crisis was taken up primarily by an expansion of services, rather than industry.

3.2 Employment shares

A typical feature of middle-income developing economies is that agriculture's employment share far exceeds its share of GDP and that the discrepancy between these shares persists during much of the process of economic development. The difference disappears only when the country has reached high income levels like those of Japan, Western Europe, and the United States today (Timmer 2014). Thailand's experience shows that in middle-income economies this disparity can actually increase as growth proceeds.

Whereas the employment share of agriculture was 81 per cent in 1960 (Figure 5.5), its share of output (agricultural value-added/GDP) was 34 per cent (Figure 5.3). Agriculture's employment share was 2.3 times as large as its output share. These facts alone imply that incomes within agriculture were far below the average of those of people employed elsewhere. In 1986, these shares were 66 and 18 per cent, respectively, a ratio of 3.7. In 2000, the shares were 48 and 12, a ratio of 4, and in 2017 the shares were 32 and 8 per cent, respectively, still a ratio of 4. Over almost six decades, the ratio of these two shares has increased.

This feature of Thailand's ST has consequences for the distributional effects of economic growth. As economic growth and structural change proceed, the incidence of absolute poverty declines everywhere, including within agriculture, but agricultural incomes continue to lag behind average incomes. The remaining pocket of people with incomes below the poverty line is increasingly concentrated in rural areas. Moreover, in Thailand, these poor rural households are highly concentrated within the north and north-east regions. As we will argue in Section 5, these raw statistical facts have had significant political consequences within Thailand.

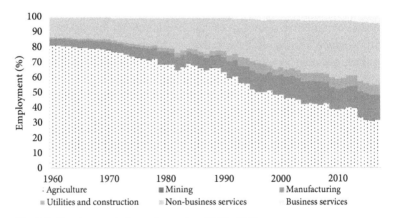

Fig. 5.5 Employment shares by sector, 1960–2017

Source: authors' calculations using data from the GGDC 10-Sector Database Version 2015 (Timmer et al. 2015).

Figures 5.3 and 5.5 reveal another crucial difference between structural change measured in terms of output and employment. Whereas the declining GDP share of agriculture was mirrored by an increasing GDP share of manufacturing, with the share of services barely changing, the opposite was true of employment. The decline of agricultural employment was mirrored by an expansion of services, not manufacturing. Between 1960 and 2017 agriculture's employment share contracted by almost 50 per cent of the total workforce (from 81.3 to 31.5 per cent). The employment share of manufacturing expanded by 12.4 per cent (4.3 to 16.7). But the employment share of services expanded by 32.2 per cent (13.5 to 45.7). For most of the five decades covered, employment grew more rapidly in manufacturing than in services, but it started from a much lower base.

Rates of structural change, measured in terms of employment shares, can be defined in an identical manner to output shares, as above. Using superscript E to signify employment:

(c) *Overall rate of structural change (employment shares in agriculture)*

$$=[S_t^{EA} - S_{t-\tau}^{EA}]/\tau. \tag{3}$$

(d) *Industrialization component of structural change (employment shares)*

$$= [S_t^{EI} - S_{t-\tau}^{EI}]/[S_t^{EA} - S_{t-\tau}^{EA}]. \tag{4}$$

Table 5.1 also summarizes the data on these two measures. Over the full period, agriculture's employment share contracted at an average of around one percentage point per year. The pre-boom rate was only one-quarter of this long-term rate, but during the boom the rate accelerated to double the long-term rate. After the crisis, the long-term average rate resumed. Over the full period, industrial employment absorbed 35 per cent of the workers released from agriculture. This proportion was 55 per cent during the boom, but only 11 per cent pre-boom. Clearly, industrial development dominated the boom period. During the AFC, industrial employment collapsed. Subsequently, the contraction of agriculture's employment share resumed at roughly the long-term rate.

Over the half-century ending in 2017, abstracting from growth of the total population, for every 100 workers leaving agriculture, 25 went to employment in manufacturing, 65 to services and the remaining 10 to non-manufacturing industry. These proportions varied markedly over time. It would be crudely inaccurate to describe this process as relocation of workers from agriculture to manufacturing (or industry). Relocation from agriculture to services was far more important. Structural transformation looks very different when viewed in terms of employment, rather than output. The reason is that manufacturing is so much more capital-intensive than any other major sector. Its expansion absorbs a high

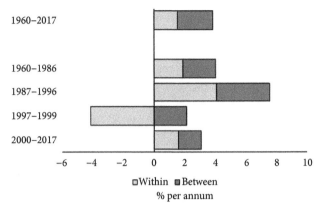

Fig. 5.6 Sources of labour productivity growth: within and between sectors

Source: authors' calculations, with assistance from Kyunghoon Kim, using data from a standardized version of UNU-WIDER World Income Inequality Database (WIID).

proportion of new investment in physical capital, generating a high proportion of new output, but it absorbs a much smaller proportion of relocated employment.

The ranking of the four main periods by rates of structural change measured in employment shares differs from their ranking in terms of output shares. From Table 5.1, the ranking by the overall rate of structural change measured in employment shares is: II, IV, III, I and ranking by the industrialization component is: II, IV, I, III. The crisis period (III) might be ignored for the purpose of these rankings, but even then the ranking of the other three periods is different when output shares and employment shares are used as the basis for calculating structural change.

Finally, Warr and Suphannachart (2020) describe a decomposition of the growth of aggregate labour productivity into within-sector productivity growth and between-sector productivity growth, the latter arising from the relocation of labour from low-productivity agriculture to higher-productivity industry and services. The findings are summarized in Figure 5.6. Structural change, measured in employment terms, contributed to labour productivity growth in all periods (leaving the crisis period aside) and accounted for over half of the growth of aggregate labour productivity over the full period 1960–2017.

4. Poverty, inequality, and inclusive growth

Two, quite different definitions of inclusive growth can be found in the literature, turning on whether they focus on poverty reduction or inequality reduction. As with the earlier term 'pro-poor growth', some authors interpret inclusive growth to mean growth that benefits the poor in absolute terms (poverty-reducing), while others define it as growth that benefits the poor proportionately more than the rich (inequality-reducing).[5] We will show that Thailand's growth has been unambiguously inclusive according to the first definition. According to the second definition, growth has been inclusive in the long term, as covered by our data, but not in every sub-period.

The definitions are arbitrary. In this study, inclusive growth is defined to mean growth of real GDP per capita that reduces poverty, whether or not it also reduces inequality. Nevertheless, changes in inequality are of interest in themselves and warrant attention, whether inequality is incorporated in the definition of inclusive growth or not. Regarding inclusive growth measured in terms of poverty reduction, the important question is not simply the binary one of whether growth is or is not inclusive. Most instances of positive growth of real GDP per capita do coincide with some decline in poverty incidence. Exceptions are rare. The more important empirical question is the *degree* to which growth reduces poverty. Accordingly, we will define the *growth inclusiveness index* to be the reduction of poverty incidence (change in the headcount measure, expressed as a percentage of the total population) per unit change in the level of GDP per capita. By construction, the change in poverty incidence over a given period is the product of the rate of growth of GDP per capita over that period and the inclusiveness index of that growth.

4.1 Poverty incidence

Figure 5.7 summarizes PovcalNet (World Bank n.d.) data on poverty incidence in Thailand for the period 1981–2017, using four poverty lines—US$1.90, US$3.20, US$5.53, and US$10.00, all at 2011 purchasing power parity (PPP). US$1.90 and US$3.20 are the World Bank's recommended poverty lines for low-income and middle-income countries, respectively. US$5.53 is a poverty line computed by the authors from the PovcalNet online tool to replicate the Thai government's official poverty line. This was done, using PovcalNet, by finding the poverty line that produced a level of poverty incidence for Thailand in 2015 that matched the Thai government's reported headcount level of poverty incidence for that year, 7.6 per cent. US$10.00 is another poverty line specified in World Bank's PovcalNet .

The estimated level of poverty incidence is necessarily higher using a higher poverty line, but the four series are otherwise similar. At all four poverty lines, measured poverty incidence declined continuously from 1981 to 2015, except during the economic contraction of the AFC, when all four series increased.

---

[5] The analytical relationship between these two definitions is discussed in detail in Warr (2005).

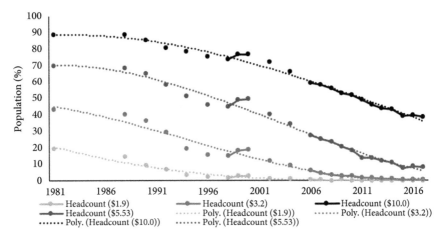

Fig. 5.7 Poverty incidence, 1981–2017

Note: 'Headcount ($X)' means the headcount measure of poverty incidence, as a percentage of the total population, at a poverty line of $X per person per day at 2011 PPP. 'Poly. (Headcount ($X))' (shown by the four dotted lines) means a polynomial function fitted to the time series data of Headcount ($X).

Source: authors' calculations, with assistance from Kyunghoon Kim, using PovcalNet (World Bank n.d.).

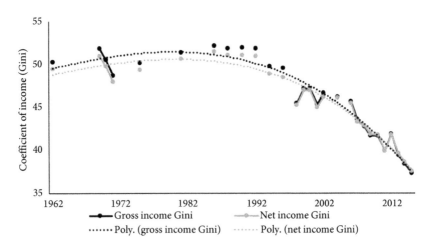

Fig. 5.8 Gini coefficient of incomes, gross and net, 1962–2017

Note: The dotted lines connecting the data points are a polynomial function of order 3 (labelled 'Poly.') fitted to the data.

Source: authors' calculations, with assistance from Kyunghoon Kim, using data from a standardized version of UNU-WIDER World Income Inequality Database (WIID).

4.2 Income inequality

Figure 5.8 shows the Gini coefficient of income inequality at the national level, covering the years 1962–2017.[6] Gross Gini and net Gini mean that the calculation is based on incomes before and after taxes and transfers, respectively. The two measures tell a very similar story, except that the level of the net Gini is slightly lower. In summarizing the data, we shall focus on the gross Gini coefficient and overlook short-term fluctuations.

1. Over the long-term (five-and-a-half decades covered by these data) the measured Gini fell from 0.503 in 1962 to 0.380 in 2017).
2. Over the medium term, two sub-periods can be identified:[7]
   (i) 1962–1986: Gini rose from 0.503 to 0.521;
   (ii) 1986–2017: Gini fell from 0.521 to 0.380.

For comparison with other chapters in this volume, Figure 5.9 summarizes the combinations of income inequality and ST in different periods in Thailand. One possible description of this pattern is that high levels of output growth, labour productivity growth, and ST lead to rising income inequality and lower levels of these drivers lead to reduced inequality. Sub-periods (i) and (ii) above seemingly fit the hypothesis. But within sub-period (ii), the boom years 1986–1992 showed the highest rates of growth and structural change but a small decline in the Gini coefficient. The large decline in the Gini from these high levels began after 1992, when growth began to slow. A seemingly more accurate description of these data would emphasize changes rather than levels: rising (slowing) growth rates coincide with increasing (declining) levels of inequality.

Another, not necessarily inconsistent, hypothesis would rest on changes in the functional distribution of incomes: when labour's share rises inequality falls, and *vice versa*. Figure 5.10 shows the share of GDP at factor cost received by labour, including all wages and imputed family labour used on family farms and small businesses, and the residual return to capital, covering the years 1971–2014. Over the full period, labour's share fell from 0.454 in 1971 to 0.393 in 2014, while the Gini coefficient also fell. This long-term observation is not consistent with the hypothesis that structural change raises inequality. Nevertheless, over the medium term, this hypothesis performs relatively well. Sub-periods (i) and (ii) fit the account well. The turning point for both variables was roughly similar: 1986–1992 for the Gini and roughly 1990 for labour's share.

---

[6] The data presented are drawn from UNU-WIDER (2019) based on the Socio-Economic Survey, conducted by the Thai government's National Statistical Office (NSO). The NSO survey data were first collected in 1957 but were not processed in digital format until the 1988 survey.

[7] Both the gross and net Gini values reported reached their maxima in 1986. The numbers refer to the gross Gini.

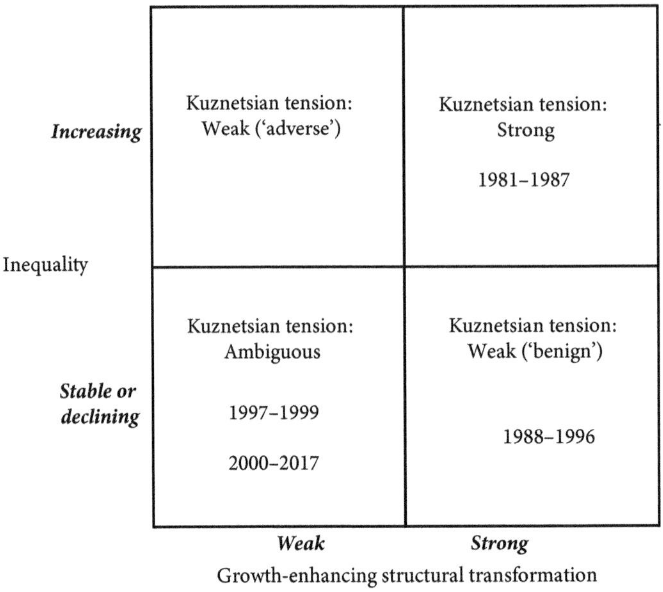

	Weak	**Strong**
Increasing	Kuznetsian tension: Weak ('adverse')	Kuznetsian tension: Strong 1981–1987
Stable or declining	Kuznetsian tension: Ambiguous 1997–1999 2000–2017	Kuznetsian tension: Weak ('benign') 1988–1996

Inequality

Weak   *Strong*

Growth-enhancing structural transformation

Fig. 5.9 Patterns of Kuznetsian tension in Thailand, 1981–2017

Source: data from the GGDC 10-Sector Database Version 2015 (Timmer et al. 2015) and UNU-WIDER (2019).

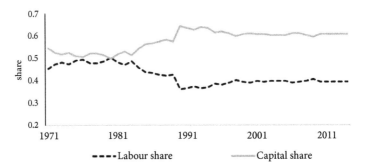

Fig. 5.10 Labour and capital shares of GDP at factor cost, 1971–2014

Source: authors' calculations using data from Penn World Tables Version 9.0. Feenstra, Inklaar and Timmer (2015).

Neither of the above explanations is fully consistent with the data and the two are not mutually exclusive. Other factors, not considered in the above discussion, undoubtedly influenced changes in economic inequality as well. Overall, the notion that growth and structural change drive changes in inequality in the medium term is not well supported by the empirical evidence and it is strongly rejected in the long term.

Two further points are important. First, in the Thai context, the important story is not so much about *changes* in inequality over time, but rather the high *level* of inequality over the entire period. Warr and Supphannachart (2020) show that the high level of inequality meant that over the three decades of economic growth (overlooking the AFC), the *absolute* gains per person received by the richest quintile were 4.6 times as large as the poorest quintile. The richest decile gained fourteen times as much per person as the poorest quintile and the richest centile gained thirty-eight times as much per person. Because the level of economic inequality remained high, the benefits of economic growth were received disproportionately by the rich.

The second point is that the component of economic inequality that is most politically sensitive within Thailand is not inequality between rich and poor *households*, but between rich and poor *regions* of the country. Section 5 develops this theme.

4.3 Inclusive growth: the growth inclusiveness index

Was Thailand's economic growth inclusive? The answer depends on the definition. If we use the definition that inclusive growth means growth that reduces inequality, the answer lies in Figure 5.8. Since inequality declined over the full period, the answer is yes, for the entire period, taken as a whole. Inequality increased prior to 1986 and declined thereafter, so according to this definition the growth was inclusive after that year but not before.

If we adopt the definition that inclusive growth is growth that reduces poverty, the answer is yes for the full period and for every sub-period excluding the crisis years, when growth was negative and poverty incidence increased. The average rate of poverty reduction over the full thirty-four years of the data was 2.40 percentage points per year. But what was the poverty-reducing power of the growth? Consider the degree to which poverty incidence declines per unit of GDP growth per person. We shall call this the growth inclusiveness index and compute it for each of the four periods shown and, crucially, for each of the four poverty lines shown in Figure 5.7.

The growth inclusiveness index is defined as:

$$I^L_{t,t-\tau} = (P^L_t - P^L_{t-\tau})/(Y_t - Y_{t-\tau}), \tag{5}$$

where P^L_t denotes the headcount measure of poverty incidence using poverty line L in year t. Year $t - \tau$ is the first year of each period shown, year t is the last year of that period, and τ is the number of calendar years in each period. Similarly, Y_t and $Y_{t-\tau}$ denote real GDP per capita in the corresponding years.

Table 5.2 summarizes the growth inclusiveness index over the four periods and shows that in all periods of positive growth (I, II, and IV) the index was negative because poverty incidence declined.[8] But the striking point is that the ranking of these three periods according to the index depends heavily on the poverty line that is chosen. At the lowest poverty line (US$1.90), growth during the pre-boom period I (1981–1987) was the most inclusive and growth during the post-crisis period IV (2000–2017) the least so. At the highest two poverty lines (US$5.53 and US$10.00), the opposite applies. At a poverty line of US$3.20, the boom period (1988–1996) shows the most inclusive growth.

The reason for the apparent anomaly is that (i) the four poverty lines detect changes in different segments of the distribution of incomes; and (ii) the measured responsiveness of poverty incidence to growth is necessarily different in these segments. Consider a graph of the cumulative distribution function (CDF) showing the logarithm of real incomes per person on the horizontal axis and on the vertical axis the cumulative proportion of households with incomes below the levels shown on the horizontal axis. The poverty line is a vertical line corresponding to the logarithm of a specified level of real income. Measured poverty incidence is the value on the vertical axis where the poverty line intersects the CDF. The CDF is typically S-shaped—relatively flat at the bottom and the top, and much steeper in between. This simple geometric fact explains the above findings.

The change in measured poverty incidence when growth shifts the CDF to the right depends on the slope of the CDF in the local neighbourhood of the poverty line.[9] The S-shape means that this slope is very different in different parts of the distribution. This in turn means that different poverty lines, intersecting different parts of the CDF, may imply very different changes in poverty incidence for any given horizontal shift in the CDF. At times when average incomes are low, low poverty lines intersect the CDF in its (middle) steeper region. They consequently show a greater responsiveness of poverty incidence to growth (a higher growth inclusiveness index). At such times, high poverty lines do the opposite because they intersect the CDF in its (upper) flatter region. As average incomes rise, the poverty line that shows the highest growth inclusiveness index is the one that intersects the CDF closest to its inflection point, where the slope of the CDF is highest.

At low poverty lines, measuring extreme poverty, the decline of agriculture's share of GDP as economic growth proceeds means that the contribution that economic growth makes to poverty reduction also declines. But at high poverty lines, this conclusion is reversed. This pattern is shown clearly in Table 5.2. There is a clear message. If we are to define the inclusiveness of growth to mean the reduction in poverty incidence per unit of economic growth, it is meaningful to discuss

---

[8] The index was also negative when growth was negative (period III) because poverty incidence increased.

[9] The slope of the CDF in the neighbourhood of the poverty line corresponds, inversely, to the degree of income inequality within this neighbourhood. The higher the slope, the lower the local inequality. It is this slope—the *local* degree of inequality—that determines the poverty-reducing effect of growth, and not the *overall* level of inequality.

Table 5.2 Annual change in inequality and poverty and the Growth Inclusiveness Index

Period	Change in Gini index per year	Change in poverty incidence per year				Growth Inclusiveness Index			
		Poverty line				Poverty line			
		$1.90	$3.20	$5.53	$10.00	$1.90	$3.20	$5.53	$10.00
I. Pre-boom 1981–1987	0.07	−0.75	−0.45	−0.16	−0.04	−0.35	−0.21	−0.07	−0.01
II. Boom 1988–1996	−0.29	−1.51	−3.09	−2.88	−1.66	−0.28	−0.58	−0.54	−0.31
III. Crisis 1997–1999	−0.59	0.08	0.85	0.87	0.27	−0.04	−0.44	−0.45	−0.14
IV. Post-crisis 2000–2017	−0.54	−0.13	−1.07	−2.43	−2.22	−0.04	−0.29	−0.67	−0.61
Whole period 1981–2017	−0.37	−0.54	−1.19	−1.72	−1.39	−0.17	−0.38	−0.55	−0.45

Note: The growth inclusiveness index is the change in the headcount poverty incidence (% of population) per unit change in GDP per capita per year (thousands of baht per year). The poverty line is measured in US$ per person per day at 2011 PPP. During the crisis period (1997–1999), the change in real GDP per capita was negative and the change in poverty incidence was positive.
Source: Authors' calculations.

the inclusiveness of growth over time only in relation to a particular poverty line. The data for Thailand demonstrate that changing the poverty line can easily reverse the qualitative conclusions that might otherwise be drawn about the inclusiveness of growth in different periods.

4.4 Structural transformation and inclusive growth

Is there a tension between ST and inclusive growth? Our interest is in the medium-term and long-term relationships among these variables, rather than annual fluctuations. Regarding the long term, radical structural change in Thailand has coexisted with both massive reductions in poverty incidence and a moderately large long-term reduction in income inequality, according to the available data. The Thai experience therefore contradicts a long-term tension between structural change and inclusive growth, whether the definition of inclusive growth includes inequality or not.

Regarding the medium term, the conclusions depend heavily on the definition of inclusive growth. The approach of this chapter has been to divide the historical period 1981–2017 into four distinct sub-periods, as in Figure 5.1, and to compare the rankings of these four sub-periods in terms of the variables of interest. The empirical findings are summarized in Tables 5.3 and 5.4. A crucial point from Table 5.3 is that the rankings of the four periods in terms of GDP growth per capita and two output-based measures of structural change (the overall rates of structural change and the industrialization component) are identical. Because these variables are so highly correlated in the data, it is not possible to isolate the impact of structural change from any of those other variables: they move together. We are at best looking at the joint effect of changes in all of those variables, taken together, not just structural change. We shall call this joint variable growth/structural change.

Turning to the distributional outcomes of interest, Table 5.4 shows first the ranking of the four periods, measured in rates of poverty reduction per year. At a poverty line of US$1.90 per day, the ranking of the four periods is again identical to their ranking according to growth, ST, and so forth in Table 5.3. At this poverty line, no tension is evident between the annual rate of poverty reduction and rates of growth/structural change. The faster the growth/structural change, the better. The same conclusion applies to the growth inclusiveness index.

At a poverty line of US$1.90, faster growth/structural change means faster poverty reduction per unit of growth as well. Comparing the pre-boom (1981–1987) and post-crisis (2000–2017) periods, I and IV, at the poverty line of US$1.90, the annual rate of poverty reduction in the former was almost six times the latter.[10]

---

[10] Remarkably, the growth inclusiveness index during the pre-boom period was double its value post-crisis.

Table 5.3 Summary of period rankings: growth, labour productivity, and structural transformation

Period	GDP growth per capita	Labour Productivity growth	Rate of structural change (output measure)		Rate of structural change (employment measure)		Growth contributions	
			Overall rate	Industrial'n component	Overall rate	Industrial'n component	Sectoral productivity	Structural change
I. Pre-boom 1981–1987	2	2	2	2	4	3	2	2
II. Boom 1988–96	1	1	1	1	1	1	1	1
III. Crisis 1997–1999	4	4	4	4	3	4	4	4
IV. Post-crisis 2000–2017	3	3	3	3	2	2	3	3

Note: Rankings of GDP growth per capita, labour productivity growth, rates of structural change, and growth contributions are summarized from Warr and Suphannachart (2020), Figure 1 and Tables 3, 2, and 4.
Source: Authors' calculations.

Table 5.4 Summary of period rankings: annual changes in poverty and inequality and the Growth Inclusiveness Index

Period	Annual reduction in poverty incidence Poverty line (US$ per person per day at 2011 PPP)				Growth inclusiveness index Poverty line (US$ per person per day at 2011 PPP)				Annual increase in inequality (Gini index)
	US$1.90	US$3.20	US$5.53	US$10.00	US$1.90	US$3.20	US$5.50	US$10.00	
I. Pre-boom 1981–1987	2	3	3	3	1	4	3	3	1
II. Boom 1988–1996	1	1	1	2	2	1	2	2	2
III. Crisis 1997–1999	4	4	4	4	n.a.	n.a.	n.a.	n.a.	4
IV. Post-crisis 2000–2017	3	2	2	1	3	3	1	1	3

Notes: Annual changes in poverty incidence and inequality are summarized from Warr and Suphannachart (2020: Table 8). The growth inclusiveness index is summarized from Warr and Suphannachart (2020: Table 9).
n.a. means not applicable. The crisis period is not included in the ranking of the growth inclusiveness index because it could be misleading. In periods I, II, and IV, a negative number means a reduction in poverty incidence per unit of positive growth (a desirable outcome). But in the crisis period, a negative number means an increase in poverty incidence per unit of negative growth (hardly desirable).
In the final column, periods are ranked by the average change in the Gini coefficient per year, based on the data in Fig. 5.8. Period I is ranked 1 because the Gini increased in that period, while it declined in all other periods. The largest absolute reduction occurred in period IV but the largest reduction per year occurred during the crisis, period III.
Source: Authors' calculations.

But inequality increased during period I and declined in period IV. These outcomes coincided with average growth rates of real GDP per capita of 3.41 per cent and 3.13 per cent during these two periods, respectively. The explanation for the difference in poverty outcomes is not that this small difference in growth rates was sufficient to overcome the difference in inequality outcomes. The main explanation is that at a poverty line of US$1.90 we are examining different segments of the cumulative distribution of incomes in the two periods: the middle, upward-sloping segment in period I and the lower, flat segment in period IV. All this has very little to do with changes in overall levels of inequality.

At higher poverty lines, the above empirical observations change to a surprising extent. The crisis period was the worst, in terms of poverty incidence, at all poverty lines. The boom period was the best at all poverty lines except US$10.00, when it was second best. Leaving aside the crisis period, when poverty incidence increased, at a poverty line of US$10.00 per day the rankings of the other three periods are exactly reversed from their ranking at US$1.90. As noted above, a meaningful definition of inclusive growth must specify not just whether changes in inequality are to be counted. If the definition is to rest on changes in poverty incidence, it must also spedify the poverty line at which poverty incidence is to be measured.

Finally, the ranking of the four periods by annual changes in overall inequality is summarized in the last column of Table 5.4. It is different from the ranking by either annual rates of poverty reduction or the growth inclusiveness index, for any poverty line. The crisis period recorded the most rapid reduction in inequality of any of the four periods. Its effects on the incomes of Thai people were negative among all income groups, but the proportional change was largest among those better-off households with capital to invest, causing measured inequality to decline significantly. Even when the crisis period is disregarded, a ranking according to changes in overall inequality is inconsistent with a ranking by annual rates of poverty reduction or the growth inclusiveness index at any poverty line. The reason is clear from the earlier discussion: the impact that growth has on poverty incidence depends on local inequality in the neighbourhood of the poverty line—as given by the local slope of the CDF—and not overall inequality. Changes in overall inequality over time are a poor predictor of changes in poverty incidence or the inclusiveness of growth.

5. The political economy of structural change and inclusive growth

Since the Asian Financial Crisis, Thailand has experienced political turmoil. A succession of mass demonstrations against elected governments, two military coups (September 2006 and May 2014), followed by military-led governments, has coincided with a rate of GDP growth below the long-term average, itself mainly attributable to a reduced rate of private investment (Warr 2020). At the risk of some oversimplification, the view advanced here is that the primary distributional conflict in Thailand is *regional*.[11]

On one side is the central region, including the capital, Bangkok, plus the southern region, loosely called 'yellow shirt'. On the other side are the north and north-east regions, loosely called 'red shirt'. There are yellow-shirt supporters in the north and north-east, but not many. There are also vast numbers of red-shirt supporters residing in Bangkok and surrounding regions, but most are relatively recent migrants from the north and north-east, with political affiliation to their home region.

The essential distributional conflict is not between rich and poor households. Because the 'red-shirt'-supporting north and north-east regions are on average considerably poorer than the 'yellow-shirt'-supporting central and southern regions, external observers have often mistaken the conflict as one between better-off and worse-off people. This interpretation misses the main point. Economic inequality is high within regions as well as between them. The primary distributional conflict is not between rich and poor within the central and southern regions or within the north and north-east regions. It is regional and crosses income distributional boundaries within regions.

Regional tensions are not new to Thailand. They extend back at least to the nineteenth century and earlier (Baker and Phongpaichit 2014).[12] Additionally, the debacle of the Asian Financial Crisis undermined confidence in the competence of the traditional ruling Bangkok elite to manage economic change. Expanded democracy, post-crisis, gave a political voice to these grievances. Underlying regional resentments emerged and Thai politics changed permanently. A new political group appeared, led by the successful and extremely wealthy entrepreneur Thaksin Shinawatra, a native of the northern city of Chiang Mai. He saw a political opportunity arising from the crisis and exploited it brilliantly. He claimed that the north and north-east remained poor, relative to the rest of the country, because of unfairness in the regionally biased way the government operated. In particular, it favoured the Bangkok-based elite, leading to better public infrastructure, better public educational facilities, and better public health care (Warr 2014b). There is abundant empirical evidence to support these claims of regional bias in public expenditure policy (Webster 2005).

---

[11] Through 2020 and into 2021, after this discussion was drafted, serious political conflict developed regarding the democratic legitimacy of the ruling military-based government and the role of the Thai monarchy. Distributional issues were not central to these events.

[12] Baker and Phongpaichit (2014) note that since the end of absolute monarchy in 1932 Thailand has experienced twelve military coups, with twenty-one charters or constitutions, an average of one every four years.

According to Thaksin Shinawatra, the north and north-east lost out because they lacked a political champion. He and his new political movement offered themselves in that role. The message worked spectacularly. With a combined population of 52 per cent of the national total, the voting power of the north and north-east, combined with Thaksin's huge popularity there, enabled his 'red shirt' political parties to win every election contested between 2001 and 2011.

Thaksin Shinawatra's message has been described as populist in that he successfully portrayed the problems of the country as a consequence of the dominance of the traditional political elite. Thaksin was divisive. The 'yellow-shirt' establishment both feared and hated him. There was an important redistributive component to his policies. His governments introduced highly successful moves towards universal health care (the 30 baht health card), reduction of farmer debt (through debt reduction-subsidized loans), and a system of fiscal transfers to rural villages (the village fund programme).

There was a rural–urban dimension to this conflict. The central region, especially Bangkok, is heavily urbanized. The north and north-east regions are more heavily rural. The most popular policy measures of the 'red-shirt' government of Thaksin Shinawatra (2001–2006) were ones that favoured, or were meant to favour, rural people. Thaksin, and later his younger sister Yingluck, also presided over a disastrous attempt to assist their rural base by supporting the producer price of rice through a government rice-purchasing scheme. This scheme was not about assisting poor people. The price supports favoured those farmers who were the largest sellers of rice, the largest farmers—not poor farmers, whose net sales of rice were small, or even zero. While rural–urban differences within the central region and within the north and north-east regions certainly exist, they have not been the principal focus of distribution-based political conflict, which has been predominantly about differences between regions.

Warr and Supphannachart (2020) present data summarizing income differences between regions over the three decades since 1986. Bangkok metropolitan region remained the wealthiest, followed by the central and south regions, with the north and north-east well behind and not catching up. In 1986, average income in Bangkok was 2.5 times the average in the north region and 2.8 times the average in the north-east. These differences barely changed in the succeeding three decades. Regional tensions can be expected to continue as long as these regional disparities are ignored.

6. Conclusions

Over the six-and-a-half decades between 1951 and 2017, Thailand's real GDP per person grew at an average annual rate of 4 per cent. In the process, the structure of the Thai economy changed radically, but this structural change looks very different when measured in output or employment terms. The output share of agriculture contracted and the share of manufacturing expanded, almost continuously. The employment share of agriculture also contracted, even more rapidly than its output share, but starting from a much higher level. The employment share of services grew correspondingly.[13] Structural change contributed to economic growth, as relatively unskilled people moved from low-productivity rural employment to more productive urban and peri-urban employment in industry and services. The social and economic flexibility to undergo this dramatic structural change clearly facilitated the massive reduction in extreme poverty that occurred.

Economic policy contributed to urbanization through infrastructure and policy decisions. Physical transport infrastructure facilities linking the various parts of Thailand are excellent by developing country standards, even within rural areas, and have been so since the 1960s. In addition, public policy did not obstruct the relocation of workers to the new industrial regions, even though urban areas were already highly congested.

Did Thailand's ST affect inclusive growth and inequality? The Thai data on growth of output, growth of labour productivity, and structural change are so highly correlated that it is analytically impossible to separate their individual impacts. Growth and structural change must be conceived as a joint package. The Thai experience suggests that in the long run, Thailand's growth and structural change have promoted inclusive growth and have also coincided with reduced inequality.

In the medium term, the Kuznets hypothesis of an inverted- U-shaped pattern of inequality is supported by the Thai data. Somewhat surprisingly, the medium-term impact that growth and structural change have on inclusive growth depends heavily on the poverty line used in the calculation of poverty incidence. The reasons are described in this chapter. This finding is apparently new. Regarding what has recently been called 'Kuznetsian tension' (Alisjahbana et al. 2020) (the coexistence of high rates of structural change and increased levels of inequality), the Thai data do not support such a relationship over the medium term. Over the long term, they suggest the opposite.

The common but false claim that declining inequality maximizes the rate of poverty reduction rests on two errors. First, it ignores the possible trade-off between rates of growth and changes in inequality. If more rapid growth leads to rising inequality, then it is possible that the highest rates of poverty reduction are achieved when growth is most rapid, even if inequality increases. The Thai data demonstrate exactly this outcome. Second, by focusing wrongly on the overall level of inequality, it ignores the fact that changes in poverty incidence in response to

---

[13] In Chapter 2, the editors of this volume distinguish countries in which agricultural employment is larger than either services or industry ('structurally underdeveloped') from those in which services employment exceeds agriculture ('structurally developing'). Table 1.1 shows that most countries of developing East Asia belong to the second category. By these definitions, Thailand was 'structurally underdeveloped' until about 2008 and became 'structurally developing' only after 2012.

growth depend solely on inequality in the neighbourhood of the poverty line (the slope of the cumulative density function in this region) and not on the overall level of inequality. For example, changes in the extreme ends of the distribution can have large effects on measured overall inequality, one way or the other, but if they do not change the distribution in the neighbourhood of the poverty line they have no impact on measured poverty incidence or on the responsiveness of poverty incidence to growth.

The available data show that the incomes of people living in or near the capital, Bangkok, and in the southern region (with the exception of the three southern-most, predominantly Muslim provinces) have remained much higher than those of people in the heavily rural north and north-east regions, despite massive inflow of poorly educated, low-skilled people from other parts of the country. The dif-ferentials between these income levels have barely changed over recent decades. The fruits of economic growth, especially industrial growth, have accrued over-whelmingly to residents of the central and southern regions, especially the capital, Bangkok, and its surrounds, including massive numbers of new residents, re-cently migrating from other regions. The important point is the persistence of a high *level* of regional inequality, not changes in it. If there is a 'developer's dilemma' in Thailand, it is seemingly not that growth and ST accentuate the gap between rich and poor households. It is that economic development has not di-minished the longstanding and politically toxic disparities between rich and poor regions.

References

Alisjahbana, A., K. Kim, K. Sen, A. Sumner, and A. Yusuf (2020). 'The Developer's Dilemma: A Survey of Structural Transformation and Inequality Dynamics'. WIDER Working Paper 35/2020. Helsinki: UNU-WIDER.

Baker, C., and P. Phongpaichit (2014). *A History of Thailand*, 3rd edn. Cambridge: Cambridge University Press.

Feenstra, R.C., R. Inklaar and M.P. Timmer (2015). 'The Next Generation of the Penn World Table, *American Economic Review*, 105: 3150–3182.

Ingram, J. (1971). *Economic Change in Thailand, 1850-1970*. Stanford, CA: Stanford University Press.

Kuznets, S. (1955). 'Economic Growth and Income Inequality', *American Economic Review*, 45: 1–28.

Nidhiprabha, Bhanupong (2018). *Macroeconomic Policy for Emerging Markets: Lessons from Thailand*. London: Routledge.

Ravallion, M., and G. Datt (1996). 'How Important to India's Poor Is the Sectoral Composition of Economic Growth?', *World Bank Economic Review*, 10: 1–25.

Timmer, C.P. (2009). *A World without Agriculture: The Structural Transformation in Historical Perspective*. Washington, DC: AEI Press.

Timmer, C.P. (2014). 'Managing Structural Transformation: A Political Economy Approach'. WIDER Annual Lecture 18. Helsinki: UNU-WIDER.

Timmer, M., G.J. de Vries, and K. de Vries (2015). 'Patterns of Structural Change in Developing Countries'. In J. Weiss and M. Tribe (eds), *Routledge Handbook of Industry and Development*. London: Routledge, 65–83.

UNU-WIDER (2019). Standardized dataset based on World Income Inequality Database, WIID 4, version 22 February 2019. Helsinki: UNU-WIDER.

Vines, D., and P. Warr (2003). 'Thailand's Investment-Driven Boom and Crisis', *Oxford Economic Papers*, 55: 440–464.

Warr, P. (1999). 'What Happened to Thailand?', *The World Economy*, 22: 631–650.

Warr, P. (2005). 'Pro-Poor Growth', *Asia Pacific Economic Literature*, 19: 1–17.

Warr, P. (2013). 'Thailand's Development Strategy and Growth Performance'. In A.K. Fosu (ed.), *Achieving Development Success: Strategies and Lessons from the Developing World*. Oxford: Oxford University Press, 72–98.

Warr, P. (2014a). 'The Drivers of Poverty Reduction'. In I.A. Coxhead (ed.), *Handbook of Southeast Asian Economics*. London: Routledge, 303–326.

Warr, P. (2014b). 'Thailand: Economic Progress and the Move to Populism'. In R.E. Looney (ed.), *Handbook of Emerging Economies*. London: Routledge, 416–439.

Warr, P. (2020). 'Economic Development of Post-War Thailand'. In P. Chachavalpongpun (ed.), *Handbook of Contemporary Thailand*. London: Routledge, 36–51.

Warr, P. and B. Nidhiprabha (1996). *Thailand's Macroeconomic Miracle: Stable Adjustment and Sustained Growth, 1979 to 1995,* World Bank, Washington, DC and Oxford University Press, Kuala Lumpur, 1996.

Warr, P., and W. Suphannachart (2020). 'Benign Growth: Structural Transformation and Inclusive Growth in Thailand'. WIDER Working Paper 2020/46. Helsinki: UNU-WIDER.

Webster, D. (2005). 'Urbanisation'. In P. Warr (ed.), *Thailand beyond the Crisis*. London: Routledge, 124–151.

World Bank (n.d.). 'PovcalNet'. Online analysis tool for global poverty monitoring. Washington, DC: World Bank.

World Bank (1993). *The East Asian Miracle*. Washington, DC: World Bank.

PART II
SOUTH ASIA

6

Inclusive Structural Transformation in India

Past Episodes and Future Trajectories

Saon Ray and Sabyasachi Kar

1. Introduction

The Indian development experience has been a unique one. One the one hand, India is one of the fastest growing economies in the world today, and its growth has completely transformed the life of billions of its citizens. On the other hand, it is the world's largest democracy. Surely, there has been some tension between these twin objectives—transforming the economy in order to achieve high growth, and ensuring equity, which is demanded in a democratic system. How did the Indian state handle this Kuznetsian tension, which we call the 'developer's dilemma'? This chapter attempts to answer this question. We start by analysing the trends in structural transformation and inclusiveness that define the Indian development trajectory. Looking beyond these broad trends, we next identify the economic regimes that have attempted to resolve this dilemma in different ways. We then attempt to understand the political factors affecting each of these episodes. Finally, we draw conclusions about the lessons that can be learnt from the Indian experience.[1]

In terms of broad trends, we find that India, which started with a largely agricultural and stagnant economy at the time of her independence, achieved significant structural change during this period. However, the extent of industrialization, particularly in the manufacturing sector, was limited. Most of the transformation was in the business and non-business services sectors and to a certain extent in utilities and construction. These structural changes and the resultant growth helped the economy bring down poverty rates, making it somewhat more inclusive.

---

[1] See Ray and Kar (2020) for a more detailed version of this chapter.

Saon Ray and Sabyasachi Kar, *Inclusive Structural Transformation in India*. In: *The Developer's Dilemma*.
Edited by Armida Salsiah Alisjahbana, Kunal Sen, Andy Sumner, and Arief Anshory Yusuf, Oxford University Press.
© UNU-WIDER (2022). DOI: 10.1093/oso/9780192855299.003.0006

The extent of inclusiveness was, however, limited to poverty reduction, with inequality rates going up significantly over time.

We find that there are two distinct episodes of the developer's dilemma in post-independence India. The first episode (1960–1980) represents a period of dirigisme when the state intervened aggressively to keep inequality from rising, at the cost of any structural transformation. Thus, the Kuznetsian dilemma was resolved in this period by focusing completely on equity at the cost of prosperity. The growth rates during this episode were very low as a result of these interventions. It was a period of 'inclusion without growth'. The second episode (1980–2010) saw a gradual move towards liberalization and globalization. The objective of the state during this episode was to achieve structural transformation and growth; hence, the focus shifted from equity to prosperity. The resultant transformation spread to some of the more productive sectors of the economy—particularly business services—and, in line with Kuznets's hypothesis, this led to higher and rising levels of inequality. This resulted in what may be termed 'growth without inclusion'. However, given the democratic set-up, inclusiveness could not be ignored completely, and the regime attempted to achieve a balance by bringing down poverty through aggressive anti-poverty programmes.

In the political space, the first episode witnessed increasing political competition, with the ruling political party looking for a new political narrative to regain its popularity. The economic ideology for most of this episode was strongly influenced by theories of export pessimism and import substitution. A combination of these two factors—the search for a new political narrative and an ideology that was suspicious of privatization and globalization—led to an extremely dirigiste economic policy paradigm. The objective of policy was to achieve greater inclusiveness through a regulated process of industrialization. As mentioned earlier, this policy paradigm was very successful in stabilizing inequality but completely unsuccessful in bringing about any significant structural transformation in the economy.

The politics during the second episode became even more competitive with the emergence of regional political parties, clientelist politics, and money power. These changes forced the political parties to become much more pro-business during this episode. The economic ideology also underwent significant changes during this episode; cutting across parties, politicians became much more market-friendly. These political changes turned the economic policy paradigm towards liberalization and globalization. The result was significant structural transformation and growth in the economy. Intense political competition, however, prevented any reforms of the factor markets and this limited growth in the manufacturing sector.

This chapter presents each of these discussions in some detail in the subsequent sections. The structure of the chapter follows from this. Section 2 analyses the trends in structural transformation and inclusiveness, particularly during the period 1960–2010. Section 3 identifies and analyses the features of the developer's dilemma in the two episodes described above. Section 4 describes the politics and the resultant policy paradigms during these episodes. Section 5 concludes by drawing lessons about the Indian experience and suggesting possible future trajectories of structural transformation and inclusiveness in India.

2. Trends in structural transformation and inclusiveness in the Indian economy

During the colonial period, the Indian economy was largely based on land-intensive agriculture. Other sources of employment included labour-intensive small-scale industry and natural resource-intensive plantations. There were some modern industries, but they made up only a small part of total industrial output and national income. The rest of the economy consisted of government administration, commerce, transport, and real estate—what could be termed the services sector. India was an open economy during this period and exports comprised mostly of agricultural raw materials and products.

Under British rule, there was some industrialization and tertiarization in the economy in terms of national income. In terms of employment shares, 74.9 per cent of the workforce in 1900 was in agriculture, which increased to 76.5 per cent in 1925 and fell back to 74.8 per cent in 1946. The share of industry in the workforce was 10.6 per cent in 1900, fell to 9 per cent in 1925, and increased slightly to 9.6 per cent in 1946. The services sector's share in employment was 14.5 per cent in 1900; it remained the same in 1925 and rose slightly to 15.6 per cent by 1947. All these trends clearly highlight the limited structural transformation that took place in pre-independence India. Industry and services attained higher labour productivity during this period but were unable to absorb a higher share of labour from the agricultural sector.[2]

The Indian economy has experienced a remarkable transformation since independence. The average growth rate of gross domestic product (GDP) between 1960 and 2010 was about 5.1 per cent. Agricultural growth was about 2.8 per cent and industry and services grew at around 5.9 per cent and 6.6 per cent, respectively, during the same period. Figure 6.1 shows the decomposition of growth rates during this period by major sectors of the economy. Clearly, the contribution of the agricultural sector in the growth of output diminished remarkably over this period. The shares of non-business services and business services both went up. Manufacturing and utilities and construction maintained their shares, while the contribution of mining diminished. Overall, there is a clear indication of a tertiarization of the economy in terms of value added.

---

[2] Roy (2000) provides detailed analysis of the Indian economy in the pre-independence period.

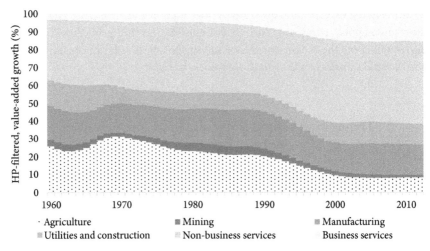

Fig. 6.1 Growth decomposition by sector, India, 1960–2012 (% of Hodrick–Prescott (HP)-filtered, value-added growth)

Note: Business services: financial intermediation, renting, business activities; non-business services: (a) wholesale and retail trade, repair of motor vehicles and motorcycles, personal and household goods, hotels and restaurants; (b) transport, storage, communications; (c) public administration, defence, education, health, social work; and (d) other community activities, social and personal service activities, activities of private households.
Source: authors' construction based on the Groningen Growth and Development Centre (GGDC) 10-Sector Database Version 2015 (Timmer et al. 2015).

Figures 6.2 and 6.3 show the effect of the different sectoral growth rates on the structure of the economy. Figure 6.2 gives the composition of value added in the economy. The continuous fall in the contribution of agriculture to overall growth led to the share of this sector falling from 52.7 per cent in 1960 to 15.3 per cent in 2010. The non-business services sector was the biggest gainer from this transformation, going up from 21.9 per cent in 1960 to 41.8 per cent in 2010. Business services also gained considerably, although from a very small base (from 4.0 per cent in 1960 to 11.1 per cent in 2010). The share of mining remained stagnant at around 2.4 per cent. Manufacturing increased from 11.6 per cent to 17.7 per cent and utilities and construction increased from 7.4 per cent to 10.7 per cent. This figure again highlights the strong tertiarization that was indicated in Figure 6.1. Although there is evidence of some industrialization, the increase in share over a fifty-year period is very small. This is true for both the manufacturing sector and the utilities and construction sector.

Figure 6.3 shows the composition of employment in the various sectors. As we found earlier, the sectoral share of employment in pre-independence India had always been disproportionately monopolized by agriculture. We find here that between 1960 and 2010, the share of agricultural employment fell from 71.8 per cent

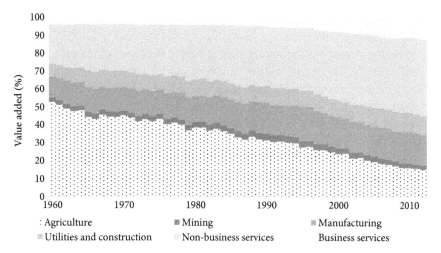

Fig. 6.2 Value-added composition, India, 1960–2012 (% of value added)

Source: authors' construction based on the GGDC 10-Sector Database Version 2015 (Timmer et al. 2015).

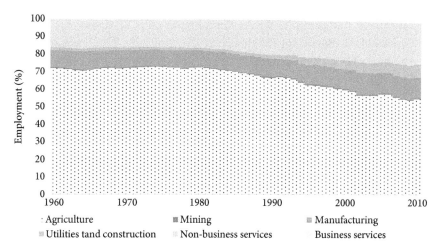

Fig. 6.3 Employment composition, India, 1960–2010 (% of employment)

Source: authors' construction based on the GGDC 10-Sector Database Version 2015 (Timmer et al. 2015).

to 54.6 per cent. This fall is significant, but less than that of value added from this sector. The shares of employment in mining and in business services were very small, although the latter showed significant growth from a very small base (0.2 per cent in 1960 to 2.2 per cent in 2010). The share of manufacturing employment increased very slightly from 9.6 per cent in 1960 to 11.5 per cent in 2010. The two sectors that showed a significant increase in employment share were utilities and construction and non-business services. The former grew from 1.6 per cent in

1960 to 7.4 per cent in 2010, while the latter grew from 16.1 per cent in 1960 to 23.6 per cent in 2010.

These trends highlight a number of points. First, structural transformation was more successful in terms of value-added share and less successful in terms of employment share. Second, industrialization was limited in terms of employment in manufacturing, but this was compensated by employment in the utilities and construction sector. Finally, the tertiarization that was found in value added is also reflected in employment.

The trends in structural transformation in India discussed above are confirmed by other studies. Rodrik et al. (2016) argue that, while structural change has contributed to growth in India, the economy has not undergone the rapid structural change that has been achieved in other countries, such as China or Vietnam. Amirapu and Subramanian (2015) have found that India has achieved only partial success in attaining multidimensional structural transformation. Kochhar et al. (2006) focus on the nature of the manufacturing sector in India, which has been skill-intensive rather than labour-intensive. According to them, together with the low scale of production compared with world averages, this has led to manufacturing absorbing less labour than in other countries.

Kotwal et al. (2011) studied the dominance of the services sector as the distinctive feature of the Indian growth experience. They argue that this is because India's growth has not been state-driven like that of other Asian countries, but occurred as a result of the coincidence of new technology and skilled manpower that could take advantage of the technology. Diao et al. (2017) find that in the Indian context, rapid productivity growth in the modern services sector outpaced the shifts in employment, primarily because the modern sector employs relatively few workers; hence, employment shares in the modern sector have changed very little. All of these contributions highlight the services-led nature of growth in the Indian economy.

We now turn to trends in inclusive growth in the Indian economy for the period up to 2010. Figure 6.4 presents the gross and net income Gini for India for the period under study. We find that inequality had a downward trend for the first part of this period, followed by a long upward trend during the second part. Overall, there is an increase in income inequality in India during this period. Chancel and Piketty (2017) also document this reduction in inequality up to the 1970s and a large increase since the mid-1980s.

3. Developer's dilemma: two episodes

In section 2, we studied the trends in structural transformation and inclusiveness in India for most of the post-independence period as two independent economic

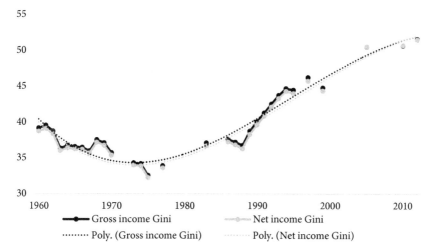

Fig. 6.4 Gross and net income Gini, India, 1960–2012

Source: authors' calculations based on UNU-WIDER World Income Inequality Database (WIID).

phenomena. However, the developer's dilemma highlights the trade-off that is usually faced by developing countries when they attempt to achieve both structural transformation and inclusive growth. How has this dilemma manifested itself in the Indian context and how has it been addressed by the Indian state?

If we focus on the value-added share of the different sectors of the Indian economy, we do not get a clear indication of the dilemma. Consider manufacturing and non-business services, two of the major non-agricultural sectors in the Indian economy. In both sectors, we find periods where inequality remains stable despite significant increases in the sectoral share of value added (roughly before 1980) and periods when inequality clearly rises with increases in the sectoral share. Thus, in terms of output, it seems that the dilemma is absent in the first period (1960–1980) but manifests itself in the second period (1980–2010).[3]

The developer's dilemma becomes much more clearly apparent when we focus on the employment shares of the different sectors of the Indian economy. Figures 6.5 and 6.6 present the employment share of manufacturing and non-business services, respectively. In both sectors we find that for most of the period before 1980, there is a fall in sectoral share and stability in inequality rates. In the period after 1980, both the sectoral shares of employment and inequality rates go up. Thus, in terms of employment shares, we find two distinct episodes of the developer's dilemma manifesting themselves in the post-independence period of the Indian economy. In the first episode (1960–1980), economic inequality is stabilized, while there is negligible structural transformation of the economy.

---

[3] See Figures 7 and 8 in Ray and Kar (2020).

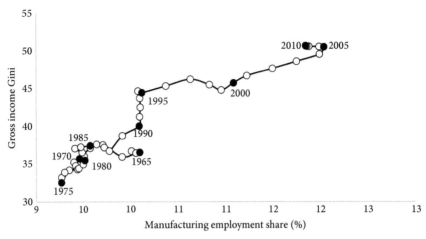

Fig. 6.5 Gross income Gini and manufacturing employment share, India, 1964–2010

Note: (i) the missing Gini coefficients were calculated using linear interpolation. See Figure 6.4 for the original data. (ii) Manufacturing value added and employment shares are five-year moving averages. For example, the data for 1975 are an average of data for 1971–1975. See Figures 6.2 and 6.3 for the original data. These notes apply to Figures 6.5 and 6.6.
Source: authors' construction based on the GGDC 10-Sector Database Version 2015 (Timmer et al. 2015) and UNU-WIDER World Income Inequality Database (WIID).

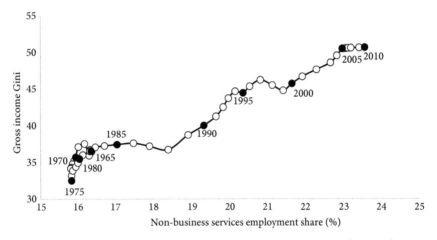

Fig. 6.6 Gross income Gini and non-business services employment share, India, 1964–2010

Source: authors' construction based on the GGDC 10-Sector Database Version 2015 (Timmer et al. 2015) and UNU-WIDER World Income Inequality Database (WIID).

In the second episode (1980–2010), there is significant structural transformation together with large increases in inequality. As we shall discuss in detail in subsequent sections, these two episodes roughly correspond to the two distinct

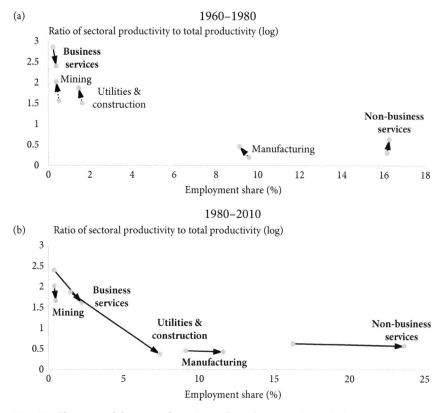

Fig. 6.7 Changes in labour productivity and employment share, India, 1960–2010

Note: Sectors with higher than economy-wide average labour productivity that experienced an increase in employment share are in bold.
Source: authors' construction based on the GGDC 10-Sector Database Version 2015 (Timmer et al. 2015).

economic regimes that were adopted in the Indian economy. The first was an economic regime characterized by dirigisme that resulted in a period of very low growth rates. The second regime was characterized by a gradual liberalization and globalization of the economy, with rising growth rates during this period.

So, what explains the trade-off highlighted in the developer's dilemma in the Indian context? Figure 6.7 gives some answers to this question in terms of the Kuznets hypothesis. This figure focuses on the changes in labour productivity and employment share in each of the major non-agricultural sectors during these two episodes.

The upper panel represents the first episode. Here, consistent with our previous discussion, we find that there are very small increases or decreases in employment share in any of the five non-agricultural sectors, indicating negligible structural transformation during this period. Since there is very little increase in the employment share of the higher productivity sectors, the Kuznetsian channel to higher inequality is restricted, allowing this episode to resolve the dilemma by stabilizing inequality in the economy.

The lower panel represents the second episode. Here, structural transformation is significant in all sectors except mining. It is notable that with significant structural transformation taking place in this period within the higher productivity sectors, particularly business services and, to a certain extent, also utilities and construction, the Kuznetsian channels of increasing inequality play an important role during this period. This explains the rising inequality in this episode.

What was the impact of the two distinctly different approaches to the developer's dilemma in each of these episodes, especially in terms of growth? Figure 6.8 throws light on this question by presenting the labour productivity growth for the whole period and the two episodes separately. It also gives the decomposition of this growth into two parts: (i) labour productivity growth within sectors ('Within'); and (ii) labour productivity growth due to movement of labour to other sectors ('Between'). The first point to note is that, while productivity growth was reasonable for the whole period, it was mostly due to much higher growth in the second episode, which made up for the lower growth in the first episode. Second, productivity growth in the first episode was completely within sectors, and structural transformation has a negative effect on 'Within' growth by moving labour into less productive sectors. In contrast, in the second episode, more than one-third of the productivity growth was due to structural transformation, that is, between sectors. Thus, structural transformation enabled higher overall growth in the second episode.[4]

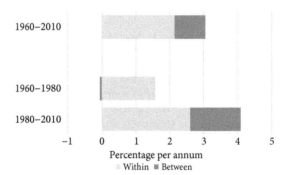

Fig. 6.8 Decomposition of labour productivity growth, India, 1960–2010

Note: Decomposition uses the methodology of McMillan and Rodrik (2011).
Source: authors' construction based on the GGDC 10-Sector Database Version 2015 (Timmer et al. 2015).

---

[4] This episodic nature of structural transformation has also been indicated in Ahsan and Mitra (2017).

4. Structural transformation and inclusive growth: politics and policies

The developer's dilemma is really about policy choices that developing countries make in order to achieve a balance between structural transformation and inclusiveness. These policy choices are, in turn, strongly influenced by two factors. The first is the extent of political competition in these countries. The more intense the political competition among political groups or parties, the lesser the possibility of the state adopting policies that bring about long-term development and wellbeing (Khan 2010) and the greater the possibility of the policies being short-sighted, avoiding any policies that are politically fraught. The second factor is the global trade possibilities available to developing countries. The greater the opportunities for participating in global trade and gaining from it, the stronger the possibility that the economic ideology of the policymakers will be pro-privatization and pro-globalization. In this section, we focus on these two factors and discuss how they influenced the policy paradigm during the two episodes defined above and the effect they had on structural transformation and inclusiveness during these episodes.

4.1 Politics and economic ideology: 1960–1980

Politics in India was completely dominated by the Indian National Congress (INC) party for most of this episode. However, it gradually lost its dominant power and was finally defeated in the election of 1977. Together with the numerous economic shocks that India faced in this period, the INC's objective of maintaining popularity and remaining in power ensured that it gradually turned away from the public-sector-led industrialization strategy that was initiated by Nehru during the 1960s to a very short-sighted, pro-poor, and anti-business economic regime under Indira Gandhi during this episode. The nationalization of domestically owned commercial banks in 1969 and the adoption of the Monopolies and Restrictive Trade Practices (MRTP) Act were part of this policy regime.

In terms of the global economy and global trade outlook, this first episode covered a period when the participation of developing countries in trade was largely restricted to the export of primary products to developed countries. Since the terms of trade were perceived to be very strongly against primary product exports, there was a strong feeling of export pessimism amongst developing country policymakers during this period. India was no exception to this and the economic ideology during this period was one of anti-globalization and import substitution. This economic ideology was further strengthened by two more factors. The first of these was the adverse experience of free trade in the pre-independence period under colonial oppression. The second was the highly successful Soviet experience at that time, which was also very statist, with a focus on the public sector.

4.2 Policies and outcomes: 1960–1980

Initially, the emphasis of this statist approach was on industrialization through massive investment in the public sector. Roy (2000) argues that this industrial policy followed from the Mahalanobis model (based on an adaptation of the Harrod–Domar model) and focused on the capital-intensive industries. The Industrial Policy Resolution of 1948 set out the goals of this industrial policy and the Industries (Development and Regulation) Act of 1951 created the instruments of implementation of the policy, namely, industrial licensing, tariffs on imports, and public investment. The Industrial Policy Resolution of 1948 emphasized the role of the state in the development of industry. The 1948 Resolution also underlined the role of small-scale and cottage industry in the development of the country. The Industrial Policy Resolution of 1956 laid emphasis on reducing disparities in income and wealth, regional disparities, and the concentration of monopoly power and private monopolies. It also emphasized the role of the state in setting up new industrial units and developing transport facilities.

Over time, a combination of two factors—the search for a new political narrative due to increasing political competition and an ideology that was suspicious of privatization and globalization—led to an increasingly dirigiste economic policy paradigm. The thrust towards industrialization weakened in the 1970s, as the country faced multiple shocks, including wars, severe droughts, and the global oil-price hikes. All of these put the ruling party under pressure, and it turned to more short-sighted policies focused on controlling inequality rather than on encouraging industrialization and growth. The Industrial Policy Resolution of 1973 highlighted the structural distortions that had crept in, and sought to remove these. Emphasis was laid on the interaction between the agricultural and industrial sectors. It introduced legislation to protect cottage industry. The investment limits for tiny and small-scale units were increased in the Industrial Policy Resolution of 1977, which also aimed at optimum utilization of energy supplies and alternative sources of energy. The Industrial Policy Resolution of 1980 (based on the Industrial Policy Resolution of 1956) had four main objectives: optimum use of installed capacity, maximization of production and increased productivity, employment generation, and promotion of export-orientated industries.

As we have seen in the previous sections, the policies for structural transformation were a complete failure in achieving this objective. As a result, they kept growth rates pegged at very low levels (leading to the term 'Hindu rate of growth'). Ahluwalia (1985, 1991) argues that the key elements of the policy framework that constrained economic growth in India are the Industries (Development and

Regulation) Act of 1951 and the Industrial Policy Resolution of 1956. The first piece of legislation introduced the system of licensing for private industry that governed almost all aspects of firm behaviour in the industrial sector, controlling not only entry into an industry and expansion of capacity, but also technology, output mix, capacity location, and import content. The principal aim of this Act was to channel investments in the industrial sector in 'socially desirable directions'. The system of controls was reinforced in the 1970s with the introduction of the Monopolies and Restrictive Trade Practices (MRTP) Act in 1970 and the Foreign Exchange Regulation Act (FERA) in 1973.

The combination of an industrial licensing system and an import licensing regime led to the elimination of the possibility of competition, both foreign and domestic, 'in any meaningful sense of the term' (Bhagwati and Desai 1970: 272). As the systems became increasingly complex over time, they resulted in 'a wasteful misallocation of investible resources among alternative industries and also accentuated the under-utilization of resources within these industries' (Bhagwati and Srinivasan 1975: 191), thus contributing to high levels of inefficiency in the industrial sector. The three main elements of this policy—extensive bureaucratic control over production, investment, and trade; inward-looking trade and investment policy; and the extension of the public sector beyond public utilities and infrastructure (Bhagwati 1993)—led to an increase in capital intensity and a falling output-to-capital ratio in almost all industries (Ahluwalia 1985).

The policies specifically targeting inclusive growth during this period focused on poverty, rural backwardness, and food sufficiency. The slogan 'Garibi Hatao' ('Remove poverty') was coined in the late 1960s for this purpose by Indira Gandhi. Schemes included the extension of rural roads, the building of schools, the opening of bank branches, and the installation of electricity connections in villages (Roy 2000). Another development was the introduction of the Public Distribution System (PDS). Food distributed through the PDS was initially meant to serve the poor, when food prices increased. India's agricultural policy was targeted to achieve food security, which for years after independence was mainly done by expanding the area under cultivation.[5] The focus shifted to productivity in the 1950s, as uncertainties linked to international political developments brought changes in import flows. The Green Revolution in agriculture was a continuation of the focus on agriculture productivity and the most notable active policy for inclusiveness adopted in the first episode. This policy introduced high-yielding varieties of wheat and greater application of chemical fertilizers to Indian farmers. Other measures introduced to boost this policy included credit to farmers from nationalized banks, subsidized electricity for the extraction of water, and subsidized fertilizers from nationalized producers. These were highly successful, and agricultural

---

[5] The agrarian reforms between 1950 and 1965 included the imposition of a 'land ceiling act', abolition of intermediary landlordship, and strengthening of cooperative credit institutions.

production increased by between 2 and 4 per cent per year between the 1970s and the 1990s.

Overall, the policy paradigm of the first episode was extremely harmful to the structural transformation of the economy. Specifically, industrialization in the manufacturing sector and in the utilities and construction sector remained concentrated in highly capital-intensive, public-sector undertakings. This led to negative growth of employment in these sectors. Overall, the lack of structural transformation during this episode kept inequality from increasing, but at the cost of very low growth rates. It was a case of 'inclusion without growth'.

4.3 Politics and economic ideology: 1980–2010

There were a variety of national-level political experiments to form a non-Congress government as a substitute for the old Congress Party during this episode. As a consequence, the country moved to a competitive political environment, with two or more political groups jockeying for power, a decreasing share of seats held by the majority party, and no single party assured of victory in national elections. The level of political fractionalization increased sharply in the late 1990s with the rise of regional parties, and it remained high in the 2000s. There were frequent changes of ruling party, the Bharatiya Janata Party (BJP) and the Congress alternately holding power in the period 2002–2010. The regional parties became important components of the ruling coalition and exerted a significant influence on what the main ruling party (whether the Congress or the BJP) could or could not do. Thus, whereas the political systems in many parts of the world (such as Bangladesh and Ghana) are characterized by classic competitive political settlements, India's political system became multipolar, rather than bipolar (Varshney 1999).

These changes in the political space had two distinct effects. First, the regional parties mostly used clientelist strategies in order to maintain their popularity and, given their importance in the new political space, the political environment became much more vulnerable to money power. This was accentuated by the rapid turnover of governments and closely contested elections, at both the national and regional levels, which led to a shortening of the time horizon of political parties. Second, again due to the increased fractionalization, election campaigns became increasingly expensive as political parties tried to attract voters with various inducements. Both of these effects led to an increasing pro-business economic ideology as political parties realized that their ability to fund their political activities depended on the growth of the economy and good relationships with the business class.

A significant change was also taking place in the economic ideology of the political parties during this period. In the international trade arena, a number of countries from East Asia had started gaining tremendously from exporting manufactured products to the West. When China joined this bandwagon, it soon became clear that the global economy and international trade gave a rare opportunity to developing countries to transform their economy through industrialization and exports. This led to a shift in the ideas and beliefs of Indian political leaders from a deep suspicion of the market and the private sector to a more pro-business orientation. This shift occurred across the political divide. Among the two dominant political parties, the right-of-centre BJP was more pro-market than the Congress but, with its nationalist leanings, was still suspicious of foreign investors, and therefore resistant to the easing of restrictions on foreign direct and portfolio investment. The left-of-centre Congress had been historically anti-business, but had become markedly pro-market under the leadership of Narasimha Rao. As Mehta and Walton (2014: 30) note, 'the policy changes on de-licensing and trade liberalization can be seen as a product of the confluence of a changing cognitive map of state elites, and an evolving, rather than a radical, shift in the relationship with business interests'.

Rodrik and Subramanian (2004), on the other hand, argue that rather than ideological factors, there were significant political economy factors underlying the change to a pro-business approach during this period. There was a realization that India's democracy was deepening and, as a result, the dominance of a single party was threatened by new opposition parties. At the same time, India saw the emergence of a business class that had the required capital to provide the political parties with funds to effectively fight their opposition. While the business class was getting stronger both economically and politically, other political elites that had been dominant in the past (e.g. the rich farmers and white-collar professionals described by Bardhan 1984) gradually receded into the background. It was clearly in the interest of Indira Gandhi to garner political support from the new business class rather than to go against them by opening up the economy with policies that fostered competitiveness. Thus, the institutional changes brought about during this period were driven mainly by a political bargain between the Congress Party and the business class, rather than for reasons of enhancing the productivity of the economy. This pro-business approach was further strengthened by Rajiv Gandhi after he came to power in 1984. This pro-business political approach and pro-market economic ideology came together to bring about a gradual process of liberalization and globalization in the Indian economy, in terms of both policy and economic outcomes, during this episode (Kar and Sen 2016).

The rising political competition during this episode, however, also acted as a restraint on certain aspects of liberalization. The business class had been articulating for some time that manufacturing growth in India was running into land constraints, labour market rigidities, and other supply-side issues. It was clear that in order to achieve manufacturing-led transition, there was a need for crucial supply-side reforms, including land reforms and labour reforms. However, this was a politically fraught issue, and reforms could only be pushed through if there was some consensus on the details of those reforms across the political parties—and the intense political competition during this period did not allow such a consensus to evolve. Thus, this episode threw up a political consensus for product market reforms without a corresponding consensus on factor market reforms.

4.4 Policies and outcomes: 1980–2010

The policies that brought about structural transformation in this episode were those that enabled a gradual process of liberalization and globalization of the Indian economy. In the mid-1980s, under the government of Rajiv Gandhi, there was liberalization of industrial controls when some industries were taken out of the purview of industrial licensing. Modernization of equipment was also allowed in a limited manner, and expansion of capacity up to a mandated efficient scale was permitted in industries where economies of scale were considered to be significant. Finally, the coverage of industrial licensing was also relaxed to allow not only small firms but also medium-sized firms to fall outside its purview. On trade policies, there was a gradual shift from quotas to tariffs, as well as a renewed emphasis by the new administration on export promotion.

The services sector also underwent reforms in the 1990s and 2000s. With liberalization, greater freedom of establishment was possible for both domestic and foreign service providers. The pace of reforms varied from sector to sector, with slower reforms in sectors in which restructuring would lead to large lay-offs, and sectors where reform could reduce access to services by rural or poor communities (Arnold et al. 2016).

As discussed previously, however, the policies of liberalization and reform could not include crucial-factor market reforms, particularly land and labour reforms, due to the increasing political competition during this episode. This had a dampening effect on the growth of the manufacturing sector and shaped the trajectory of both structural transformation and inclusiveness in India during these decades. Structurally, the lack of significant manufacturing growth led to a strong tertiarization of the economy, which also became more unequal and less inclusive, as a large part of the increase in employment share went to high-productivity sectors such as business services and utilities and construction.

As inequality increased in India during the second episode, particularly following the adoption of the reforms of the 1990s, it was felt that policies focusing on inclusion would have to be adopted, albeit within the liberalized framework of the economy. This gave rise to the anti-poverty Mahatma Gandhi National Rural Employment Guarantee Act (MGNREGA) programme, which guarantees 100 days of unskilled manual work to all rural households in India. Launched in 2006, it is the largest social security scheme in the world. The scheme gives an opportunity to rural households to earn a minimum income by getting the 100 days' work, once a job card has been issued to their family. Despite this programme, inequality continued to be high and continued to rise during this episode.

To sum up, the change in the global trade outlook for developing countries during this episode brought about a change in the economic ideology in India. The change in the ideology in turn brought about changes to the policy paradigm. These led to significant structural transformation in the economy, with a diminishing role for agriculture. Rising political competition, however, limited the extent of manufacturing industrialization. The lack of a significant rise in manufacturing sector employment and a corresponding rise in the non-manufacturing sectors with much higher labour productivity (utilities and construction and business services) also led to a rise in inequality during this episode. This may be termed 'growth without inclusion', and it brought back the Kuznetsian tension. Facing increasing political pressure, the state attempted to manage this tension through anti-poverty programmes.

5. Conclusion

The structural transformation of an economy is a complex process and its relationship with inequality depends on the relative growth of productivity, employment, and value added in different sectors. It takes very different paths in different countries, depending on how exogenous factors like the global economic outlook, local politics, or technological changes shape up in different periods. In short, the Kuznetsian tension and the developer's dilemma plays out very differently across countries and over time. What do we learn about these phenomena from the Indian experience?

We find that structural transformation does not necessarily lead to a Lewis-type manufacturing-based industrialization. For the fifty-year period that we study here, we find that India moved towards a significantly smaller agricultural sector, both in terms of value added and, to a lesser extent, in employment. This was mainly due to a strong trend towards tertiarization during this period. This mostly took place in non-business services, but also in the business services sector, which was becoming increasingly significant, particularly in terms of its share in value added. Industrialization, specifically in terms of value added, remained rather slow, both in manufacturing as well as in utilities and construction. In terms of employment share, the experience of these two sectors were very different. Manufacturing saw only limited growth in employment share. In the utilities and construction sector, however, particularly in construction, there was a large increase in employment share. Figure 6.9 characterizes the type of industrialization discussed in the introductory chapter of this book in terms of high or low

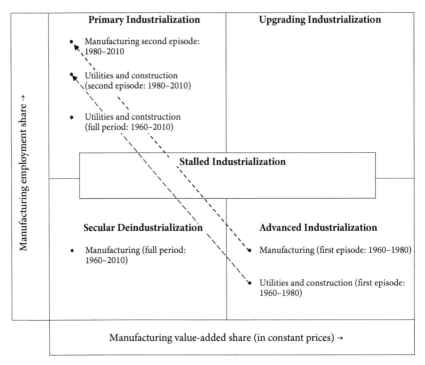

Fig. 6.9 Varieties of structural transformation in India, 1960–2010
Source: authors' illustration.

share of value added and employment. We find that for the full period (1960–2010) the transformation in the manufacturing sector is 'secular deindustrialization' or the lower-left box in Figure 6.9. For the same period however, over this long post-independence period, the utilities and construction sector exhibited 'primary industrialization', that is, the upper-left box in Figure 6.9. This characterization of the industrialization process for the full period is somewhat misleading, however, as the process can be very different over different episodes of development. In the Indian case, both the manufacturing sector and the utilities and construction sector experienced 'advanced industrialization' during the first episode (1960–1980). The corresponding characterization for both the sectors during the second episode (1980–2010) is 'primary industrialization'. In Figure 6.9, this represents a jump from the lower-right box to the upper-left box.

If the two episodes had distinctly different experience of industrialization, how did this impact the Kuznetsian tension in each of them? Figure 6.10 characterizes this tension for the Indian economy. As we have discussed, the first episode is defined by the global trade environment and local politics focused on stabilizing inequality; as a result, structural transformation and growth were low. This kept a check on the Kuznetsian tension during this episode, pacing it in the lower-left

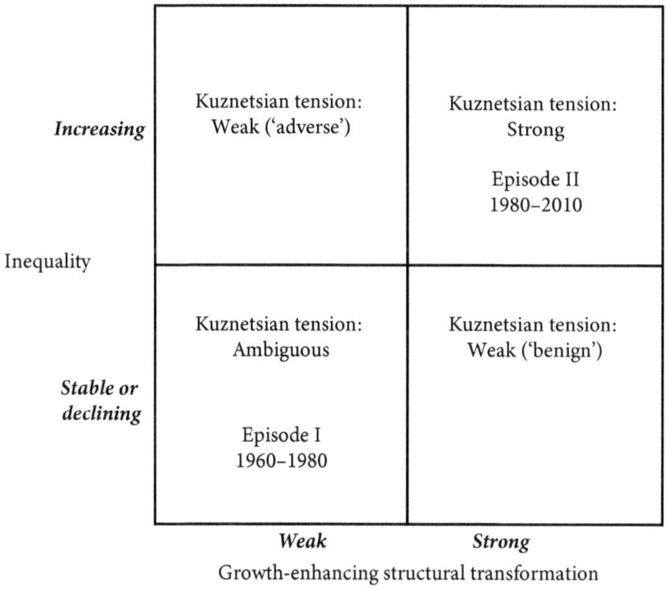

	Weak	**Strong**
Increasing	Kuznetsian tension: Weak ('adverse')	Kuznetsian tension: Strong Episode II 1980–2010
Stable or declining	Kuznetsian tension: Ambiguous Episode I 1960–1980	Kuznetsian tension: Weak ('benign')

Inequality (left axis) — Increasing / Stable or declining

Growth-enhancing structural transformation — Weak / Strong

Fig. 6.10 Patterns of Kuznetsian tension in India, 1960–2010
Source: authors' illustration.

box in Figure 6.10. In the second episode, global trade conditions changed and so did the economic ideology, favouring policies that resulted in significant structural transformation. However, rising political competition prevented the supply-side reforms that were needed for the growth of the manufacturing sector. As a result, the share in employment rose sharply in relatively high-productivity sectors such as business services and utilities and construction, and this, in turn, led to higher inequality. This brought back the Kuznetsian tension during this episode. The second episode thus belongs to the upper-right box of Figure 6.10.

Based on the Indian experience in these fifty years, what can we speculate about the future trajectory of structural transformation and inclusiveness in the Indian economy? Falling back on the previous discussion, there are two factors that significantly influenced the policy regimes that have thus far determined the trajectories of structural transformation and inclusiveness in India. The first of these was global trade opportunities for developing countries and their influence on the economic ideology of those countries. The second factor was the nature of the political competition in the country. Based on this analysis, there are three possible future trajectories that structural transformation and inclusiveness could take in India.

Suppose the world trade environment in future is characterized by low global growth and protectionist policies towards developing countries. Together with this, if political competition remains intense in India, then—much as in the first episode—the economic policy paradigm might turn anti-globalization, protectionist, and focused on controlling inequality. As in that episode, this would give rise to very little structural transformation and growth, although inequality might remain under control. On the other hand, consider a situation where world trade becomes favourable to developing countries, but political competition remains intense in India, with no consensus on supply-side reforms. This would enable India to continue the kind of transformation that was experienced in the second episode. This means achieving higher levels of de-agriculturalization, but with limited manufacturing industrialization. Since the manufacturing sector usually absorbs low-skilled workers, slower rates of manufacturing growth would also lead to higher levels of inequality. In such a case, the government would have to manage this Kuznetsian tension by increasing anti-poverty policies. Finally, we can hope for a future where world trade is favourable to developing countries and political competition does not derail a consensus on supply-side reforms. This will enable India not only to achieve significant structural transformation, but also to enjoy significantly increasing shares of manufacturing industrialization. The higher levels of manufacturing growth will also ensure higher levels of inclusiveness, keeping down the Kuznetsian tension in this case. Needless to add, this is the kind of structural transformation that would enable India to achieve truly inclusive growth.

References

Ahluwalia, I.J. (1985). *Industrial Growth in India: Stagnation since the Mid Sixties*. New Delhi: Oxford University Press.

Ahluwalia, I.J. (1991). *Productivity and Growth in Indian Manufacturing*. New Delhi: Oxford University Press.

Ahsan, R.N., and D. Mitra (2017). 'Can the Whole Actually Be Greater Than the Sum of Its Parts? Lessons from India's Growing Economy and Its Evolving Structure'. In M. McMillan, D. Rodrik, and C. Sepulveda (eds), *Structural Change, Fundamentals, and Growth: A Framework and Case Studies*. Washington, DC: IFPRI, 39–77.

Amirapu, A., and A. Subramanian (2015). 'Manufacturing or Services? An Indian Illustration of a Development Dilemma'. Working Paper 409. Washington, DC: Center for Global Development.

Arnold, J.M., B. Javorcik, M. Lipscomb, and A. Mattoo (2016). 'Services Reform and Manufacturing Performance: Evidence from India', *Economic Journal*, 126: 1–39. doi: https://doi.org/10.1111/ecoj.12206.

Bardhan, P. (1984). *The Political Economy of Development in India*. Oxford: Basil Blackwell.

Bhagwati, J. (1993). *India in Transition: Freeing the Economy*. Oxford: Oxford University Press.

Bhagwati, J., and P. Desai (1970). *Planning for Industrialization*. London: Oxford University Press.

Bhagwati, J.N., and T.N. Srinivasan (1975). *Foreign Trade Regimes and Economic Development: India*. New York: Columbia University Press.

Chancel, L., and T. Piketty (2017). 'Indian Income Inequality, 1922–2015: From British Raj to Billionaire Raj?' WID World Working Paper 2017/11. World Inequality Database. Paris.

Diao, X., M. McMillan, and D. Rodrik (2017). 'The Recent Growth Boom in Developing Economies: A Structural Change Perspective'. NBER Working Paper 23132. Cambridge, MA: National Bureau of Economic Research.

Kar, S., and K. Sen (2016). *The Political Economy of India's Growth Episodes*. London: Palgrave Pivot. doi: https://doi.org/10.1057/978-1-352-00026-9.

Khan, M. (2010). 'Political Settlements and the Governance of Growth-Enhancing Institutions'. Unpublished manuscript.

Kochhar, K., U. Kumar, R. Rajan, A. Subramanian, and I. Tokatlidis (2006). 'India's Pattern of Development: What Happened, What Follows?', *Journal of Monetary Economics*, 53: 981–1019. doi: https://doi.org/10.1016/j.jmoneco.2006.05.007.

Kotwal, A., B. Ramaswami, and W. Wadhwa (2011). 'Economic Liberalization and Indian Economic Growth: What's the Evidence?', *Journal of Economic Literature*, 49(4): 1152–1199. doi: https://doi.org/10.1257/jel.49.4.1152.

McMillan, M., and D. Rodrik (2011). 'Globalization, Structural Change and Productivity Growth.' In M. Bacchetta and M. Jansen (eds), *Making Globalization Socially Sustainable* Geneva: International Labour Organization and World Trade Organization, 49–84.

Mehta, P.B., and M. Walton (2014). 'Ideas, Interests and the Politics of Development Change in India: Capitalism, Inclusion and the State'. ESID Working Paper 36. Manchester: University of Manchester.

Ray, S., and S. Kar (2020). 'Kuznets' Tension in India: Two Episodes'. WIDER Working Paper 2020/24. Helsinki: UNU-WIDER.

Rodrik, D., and Subramanian, A. (2004). 'From Hindu Growth to Productivity Surge: The Myth of the Indian Growth Transition'. NBER Working Paper W10376. Cambridge, MA: National Bureau of Economic Research.

Rodrik, D., M. McMillan, and C. Sepulveda (2016). 'Structural Change, Fundamentals and Growth'. In M. McMillan, D. Rodrik, and C. Sepulveda (eds), *Structural Change, Fundamentals, and Growth: A Framework and Case Studies*. Washington, DC: IFPRI, 1–38.

Roy, T. (2000). *The Economic History of India: 1857–1947*, 3rd edn. New Delhi: Oxford University Press.

Timmer, M.P., G.J. de Vries, and K. de Vries (2015). 'Patterns of Structural Change in Developing Countries'. In J. Weiss and M. Tribe (eds), *Routledge Handbook of Industry and Development*. Abingdon: Routledge, 65–83.

UNU-WIDER (2019). Standardized dataset based on World Income Inequality Database, WIID 4, version 22 February 2019. Helsinki: UNU-WIDER.

Varshney, A. (1999). 'Mass Politics or Elite Politics: India's Reforms in Comparative Perspective'. In J.D. Sachs, A. Varshney, and N. Bajpai (eds), *India in the Era of Economic Reforms*. Delhi: Oxford University Press.

7

The Challenges of Structural Transformation, Inequality Dynamics, and Inclusive Growth in Bangladesh

Selim Raihan and Sunera Saba Khan

1. Introduction

This chapter, in the context of Bangladesh, focuses on the 'developer's dilemma'—the distributional tension that Kuznets (1955) hypothesized between structural transformation and inequality. The chapter examines the evolution, over time, of structural transformation and inclusive growth in Bangladesh. In particular, it explores the changes in the pattern and the role of the manufacturing sector contributing to structural transformation during the 1990s and the 2010s and their implications for the changes in poverty and inequality scenarios. The analysis of this chapter suggests that Bangladesh experienced 'strong' Kuznetsian tension during the 2000s and 2010s, and this has been associated with the growth of the manufacturing sector's value-added and employment shares, or 'upgrading industrialization', during the 2000s and 2010s.

Bangladesh's long-term trend in gross domestic product (GDP) growth rate shows that the country has continued to gradually boost its growth rate over the past forty-six years, following independence in 1971. Starting with a highly volatile growth rate in the 1970s, the rate of GDP growth in the 2000s and 2010s grew higher and much steadier. The growth rate has risen steadily since the early 1990s, rising to over 5 per cent a year, just reaching the 6 per cent mark for a number of years over the 2000s, and then hitting the 7 per cent mark over the past few years. The average growth rate of GDP rose from 3.7 per cent in the 1970s to 6.7 per cent in the 2010s. For every decade since the 1990s, Bangladesh has been able to raise the average GDP growth rate by one percentage point. In 2015, as per the World Bank's classification, the country made the graduation from low-income to lower-middle-income country status. In 2018, the country met the conditions of the first review to graduate from least-developed country (LDC) status, and it is expected to graduate from this status by 2024.

Selim Raihan and Sunera Saba Khan, *The Challenges of Structural Transformation, Inequality Dynamics, and Inclusive Growth in Bangladesh*. In: *The Developer's Dilemma*. Edited by Armida Salsiah Alisjahbana, Kunal Sen, Andy Sumner, and Arief Anshory Yusuf, Oxford University Press. © UNU-WIDER (2022). DOI: 10.1093/oso/9780192855299.003.0007

The composition of GDP between the early 1970s and the late 2010s changed quite significantly. During this period, the share of agriculture in GDP declined from as high as over 50 per cent to less than 15 per cent, the share of the services sector increased from around 35 per cent to more than 55 per cent, and that of industry increased from as low as 15 per cent to 30 per cent. As industry includes manufacturing, mining, and construction, if we look at the share of the manufacturing sector in GDP, it appears that the share increased from as low as 5 per cent to 18 per cent during the same period and the share in recent years has been on the rise. This suggests that, contrary to many developing countries of a similar level of development, where the manufacturing shares in GDP have been either very low or on a declining trend, Bangladesh has been successful in increasing the manufacturing share in GDP. However, despite the aforementioned success, over the years, the concentration in the manufacturing sector in Bangladesh increased in favour of the ready-made garments (RMG) sector, while the non-RMG manufacturing sectors performed rather poorly.

With accelerated economic growth, there have been important structural changes in the economy of Bangladesh over the past four decades. Strong economic growth in Bangladesh led to some positive economic and social changes in the country. However, there are also important challenges in the form of lack of economic and export diversification, slow employment generation, poor working conditions, and a high prevalence of informality in the labour market. The country aspires to be become an upper-middle-income country by 2031. In this context, there is a need for a significant departure from the current pattern of structural transformation in the economy. Also, as the incidence of poverty is still high in a country with a population of more than 160 million and inequality is on the rise, the issue of inclusive growth is extremely important to achieving the desired pattern of structural transformation of the economy. Against this backdrop, this chapter analyses the nature of structural transformation in Bangladesh with an emphasis on inequality dynamics and inclusive growth.

2. Economic history before the 1971 war of independence

Bangladesh became an independent state and was separated from Pakistan in 1971 through a nine-month war of independence. Pakistan emerged when the 200 years of British rule came to an end in 1947 and two countries were created on the Indian subcontinent—India and Pakistan. Pakistan comprised two non-contiguous halves—East Pakistan and West Pakistan. These two wings had a number of structural differences in terms of land/population ratio and development strategy. At the time of independence in 1947, both wings of Pakistan were agrarian economies.

During the 1950s and 1960s, Pakistan adopted an import substitution trade strategy that imposed import tariffs to protect domestic industries and taxed agricultural exports (Anjum and Sgro 2017). The lion's share of export earnings was from jute, which was from the East Pakistan. During those years, the economy of West Pakistan experienced notable progress in the form of industrial and agricultural development and business expansion (Bose 1983). The planning commission was formed to help devise the five-year plans. The plans focused strongly on industrial development in West Pakistan, which resulted in inequality in regional income. While this form of industrialization largely benefited the western wing, East Pakistan was highly agrarian; as a result, it did not receive priority and had low per capita income gains. Per capita income disparity between East and West Pakistan was on the rise from the early 1950s onwards. According to East Pakistani economists, East and West Pakistan were individual regions with their own distinctive economies. As a result of the immobility of labour between the two regions and the high cost of intra-regional transportation of commodities, they stressed the need for regional autonomy for economic development in Pakistan. The issues put forward by East Pakistan resulted in an increase in the sense of mistrust between the two regions which lasted throughout the next decade. During this time. economic growth in East Pakistan was sluggish, resource allocation from the central government was inefficient, and there was a lack of effective political representation (Islam 2003).

Eventually, the discrepancies between East and West Pakistanis led to the need for restructuring the rules that governed the Pakistani state. The Six Point Programme in 1966 initiated the restructuring process, which stressed the need for a higher level of autonomy for East Pakistan. The Six Point Programme was aimed at reducing the disparity between the two wings of Pakistan (Islam 2003). This programme, eventually, acted as a stepping-stone for the liberation war in 1971 and the ending of the rule of West Pakistan in East Pakistan. The war in 1971 resulted in the splitting up of Pakistan and the birth of Bangladesh.

3. Structural transformation in Bangladesh

Raihan (2018a)[1] explored the future prospects of Bangladesh's structural transformation by applying an analysis of Bangladesh's past economic growth in a comparative perspective. Bangladesh's real GDP growth rate over the past ten years (2007–2016) was also one of the least volatile growth rates. Figure 7.1 presents thirty countries in the world to have registered an annual average GDP growth rate of 6 per cent or more over a period of ten years from 2007 to 2016. In Figure 7.1, these countries' growth rates are plotted against the standard deviation of growth

---

[1] On which this section draws heavily.

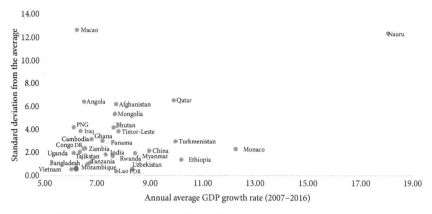

Fig. 7.1 GDP growth rate and volatility of Bangladesh in a comparative perspective (average of 2007–2016)

Note: The darker dot represents Bangladesh.

Source: authors' construction based on World Development Indicators (World Bank n.d.-b).

rates from their respective averages. The low standard deviation, in this case, would suggest low volatility of growth rate during the period under consideration. Figure 7.1 shows that Bangladesh was among these thirty countries and also that its GDP growth rate had been one of the least volatile during this period. Among these thirty countries, Bangladesh ranked third in terms of least volatility of growth rate, and only Lao Peoples' Democratic Republic and Vietnam were ahead of Bangladesh in this regard. Though countries like China and India had average growth rates higher than that of Bangladesh, they experienced much larger volatility than Bangladesh experienced.

However, there are some apparent contradictions that are revealed by analysing Bangladesh's past growth experience. Bangladesh is among the top five out of those thirty countries, with a very high share of manufacturing exports in total merchandise exports. In 2016, among these top five countries, Bangladesh, Cambodia, and China had shares of more than 90 per cent, while India and Vietnam had shares of 73 per cent and 82 per cent, respectively. Interestingly, from 66 per cent in 1980, Bangladesh was able to increase this share to as high as 96 per cent by 2016. Bangladesh's progress in manufacturing exports is comparable only to that of China and Vietnam.

The aforementioned apparent contradiction, however, lies in the fact that Bangladesh made such progress without any rapid structural transformation of the economy. Despite a very high share of manufacturing exports in total merchandise exports, the export basket of Bangladesh remained highly concentrated around low value-added and low-complexity products. A measure of the complexity of the economy is the economic complexity index (ECI) of the Center for International Development at Harvard University. The ECI measures the knowledge intensity of an economy by considering the knowledge intensity of the products it exports. Among the aforementioned top five countries, Bangladesh performed poorly in the ECI. Between 1972 and 2016, Bangladesh never had a positive ECI value and the country's ECI deteriorated over time. In contrast, China, India, and Vietnam have observed positive and growing ECI over the past two-and-a-half decades. Furthermore, Bangladesh also performed very poorly in terms of cost of doing business: the country ranked 168th out of 190 countries, according to the World Bank's 2020 Doing Business index.

The structural transformation that has taken place up until now in Bangladesh is heavily linked to the pattern of imports and exports of the country. In 1972, exports and imports as shares of GDP were 5.7 per cent and 13.7 per cent, respectively. In 2019, exports and imports as shares of GDP stood at 15.3 per cent and 21.4 per cent, respectively (World Bank n.d.-b). Over the years, Bangladesh has been successful in shifting from an aid-dependent to a trade-orientated economy. In 1973, net official development assistance (ODA) received as share of gross national income (GNI) was 5.2 per cent and throughout the 1970s and 1980s, this ratio remained between 4 and 8 per cent. However, by 2018, the ratio had come down to 1.1 per cent (World Bank n.d.-b). Accelerated exports and remittance flow during the 1990s and onwards helped to reduce the dependence on external assistance. However, aid continues to play an important role in Bangladesh's development. Aid funds have also been diverted to finance the budget deficit and development projects in the country. External debt stock as a percentage of GDP in Bangladesh, compared with other countries, is still low. However, for further infrastructural development and structural transformation the country will need an increased flow of foreign loans. Therefore, in the near future external debt is likely to increase.

The evolution of the composition of imports suggests that importing of agriculture raw materials was high in the initial years, but over time this dependency has reduced (Figure 7.2). Over the years, Bangladesh has become self-sufficient in agriculture and has made progress in terms of attaining food security. Over time, manufacturing raw material imports for use in export-orientated industries have increased. Unlike many other developing countries, which are dependent on food imports, a large component of imports is manufacturing raw materials, linked to the country's export composition. Bangladesh has experienced changes in export composition too. The country has shifted from raw jute export in the early 1970s to the ready-made garmet (RMG) industry in recent decades. Figure 7.3 depicts that a large chunk of Bangladesh's exports is now dominated by manufactures, which is the RMG. The high dependence on the RMG sector is a matter of concern. Therefore, with respect to structural transformation, an important question for Bangladesh is how to diversify the export basket.

If we focus on the manufacturing sector, despite some fluctuations, the share of manufacturing in GDP increased from as low as 4 per cent in 1972 to around

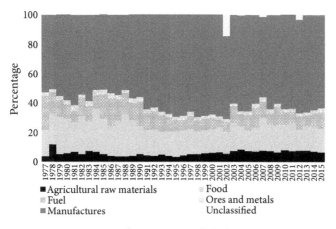

Fig. 7.2 Composition of imports, Bangladesh, 1977–2015

Source: authors' construction based on World Development Indicators
(World Bank n.d.-b).

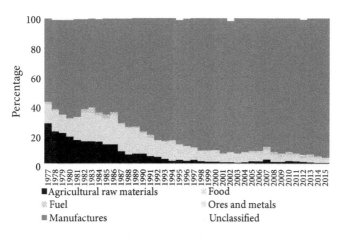

Fig. 7.3 Composition of exports, Bangladesh, 1977–2015

Source: authors' construction based on World Development Indicators
(World Bank n.d.-b).

15 per cent in 1984. But, between 1984 and 2016, this share increased by only 3
percentage points, from 15 per cent to 18 per cent (World Bank n.d.-b). Though
there has been a consistent but slow upward trend in the share of manufacturing
in GDP between 1990 and 2016, the trend in the share of manufacturing in the
country's employment has been rather uneven during the same period. From a
share of 12.4 per cent manufacturing employment in 1990, the share declined to 7.6
per cent in 2000. However, the manufacturing employment share has seen a steep
rise since 2000, and in recent years, the share stood at around 14 per cent (ILO
2019). Figure 7.4 suggests that while the phase of industrialization in Bangladesh

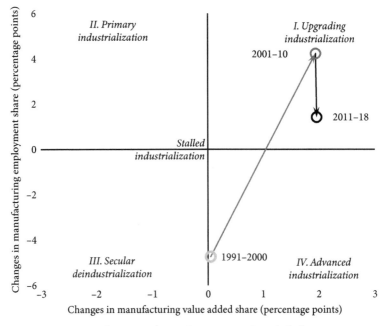

Fig. 7.4 Varieties of structural transformation in Bangladesh, 1991–2018

Source: authors' construction based on Kim and Sumner (2019), World Development Indicators (World Bank n.d.-b), and ILOSTAT (ILO n.d.).

during the 1990s was very close to a secular deindustrialization, during the 2000s and 2010s Bangladesh moved to the phase of upgrading industrialization.

Despite the aforementioned progress in industrialization over the past two decades, one major concern is that the manufacturing sector in Bangladesh is highly concentrated around low value-added RMG. The country has not been yet able to move successfully to the next generation of manufacturing, especially to high value-added manufacturing.

4. Income inequality, employment, and inclusive growth in Bangladesh

While it is apparent that Bangladesh has been able to reduce poverty based on the US$1.90 poverty line income to around 14 per cent in 2016 from as high as around 40 per cent in 2000, the poverty rates based on other poverty line incomes were very high in 2016. With respect to the US$3.20 poverty line income in 2016, the poverty rate was more than 55 per cent. In the case of the US$5.50 poverty line income, the poverty rate in 2016 was around 85 per cent and for the US$10 poverty line income the poverty rate is close to 97 per cent (World Bank n.d.-a). For the last two poverty line incomes, the reduction in poverty rates has been very slow over the past three decades.

Major economic policies in Bangladesh highlight the importance of accelerated economic growth, along with the reduction in poverty and improvement in the inequality scenario. However, over the past decade since 2010, despite high economic growth, the country has witnessed a rise in the inequality index. According to the Household Income and Expenditure Survey (HIES) of the Bangladesh Bureau of Statistics (BBS 2016), the Gini coefficient of income, which is a popular measure of income inequality, rose from 0.458 in 2010 to 0.482 in 2016. The actual inequality picture is thought to be worse than the BBS's survey estimate, as these household surveys mostly fail to capture information from ultra-rich households. However, despite the data limitations, the growing inequality index suggests that the richer segment of society has been benefited more by economic growth during the aforementioned period, and the economic growth process has been far from inclusive. Figure 7.5 presents the 2 × 2 matrix depicting the Kuznetsian tension of inequality. During the period between 1991 and 2000 there was weak ('adverse') Kuznetsian tension, as inequality was on the rise while the growth-enhancing structural transformation was weak. However, during both the periods of the

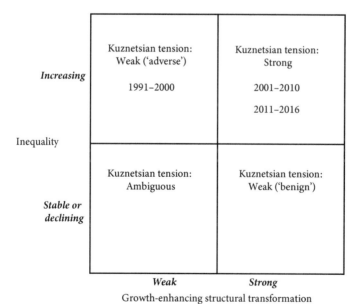

Fig. 7.5 Patterns of Kuznetsian tension in Bangladesh, 1991–2016

Source: authors' construction based on World Development Indicators (World Bank n.d.-b).

2000s and 2010s, the Kuznetsian tension appeared to be strong, as inequality was still on the rise and at the same time growth-enhancing structural transformation was strong.

One of the factors affecting structural transformation and inequality dynamics in Bangladesh is the country's ability to use the benefits of the demographic dividend. Raihan (2018b) argued that although the economy of Bangladesh has steadily grown over the past two decades, utilizing the potential of the youth population remains a big challenge. The country, being at the middle of the period of demographic transition, is yet to reap the benefits of the demographic dividend. As the window of opportunity of demographic dividend is only open until 2040, the composition of the workforce is highly dominated by low-skilled workers, which is a major concern in terms of receiving the true benefit of the demographic dividend. The Labour Force Survey 2016/17 of the BBS (2018) reveals that, although as high as 31.6 per cent of the total labour force are aged between fifteen and twenty-nine years, the youth unemployment rate of 10.6 per cent is much higher than the national average of 4.2 per cent—with the female unemployment rate much higher than that of men. There is a high degree of unemployment among educated youth too, as 13.4 per cent of unemployed youths have tertiary education and another 22.3 per cent have higher secondary education. Furthermore, the rate for youth not in education, employment, or training (NEET) is found to be 29.8 per cent, with this rate for female youths as high as 49.4 per cent. Raihan (2018b) further argued that the dominance of informal sector employment and lack of decent work are among the notable predicaments of the youth employment scenario, where, in addition, young women are lagging behind their male counterparts. Though there are several youth-focused policies, for example, the National Youth Policy (2017), the National Skill Development Policy (2011), and the Seventh Five-Year Plan, most of these policies are argued to lack detailed work plans for implementation as well as any effective financing strategy.

In relation to ensuring decent jobs, there are concerns about a high degree of informal employment in Bangladesh. In 2016/17, as much as 85 per cent of employment was informal. Women are more likely than men to be in informal employment. Also, though over the past three decades, the labour force participation (LFP) rate of women has increased, the LFP rate of women remained stagnant, between 33 per cent and 36 per cent, from 2010 to 2016/17 (BBS 2018). Raihan and Bidisha (2018) explored both the supply- and demand-side factors affecting female LFP in Bangladesh. Their analysis suggests that issues such as child marriage and early pregnancy, coupled with reproductive and domestic responsibilities, have not changed much with the economic progress of the country, and these factors constrict female LFP.

There has been a significant rise in the share of urban population in the total population over the years, and in recent years the pace of urbanization has been rather rapid. This has been promoted by a high rate of migration from the rural areas to urban areas due to both push and pull factors. Push factors include land-lessness triggered by various economic (i.e. impoverishment) and environmental (i.e. various natural disasters) factors, and pull factors include better income op-portunities in the urban areas. In 2017, around 37 per cent of the total population of Bangladesh lived in urban areas (World Bank n.d.-b). Despite the growing share of urban population, the quality of services for citizens in urban areas remains poor.

5. Policies shaped structural transformation, inequality, and inclusive growth in Bangladesh

In Bangladesh, three broad regimes of trade policy reforms can be defined: 1972–1980, the regime of restricted trade; 1980–1991, the regime of moderate trade liberalization; and from 1991 onwards, the regime of rapid trade liberaliza-tion (Raihan, 2007). During the first regime, trade, industrial, and other associated policies were targeted at developing an inward-looking economy. The broad ob-jective of the policy regime was to develop a public-sector-oriented economy, with the major emphasis placed on the leading and dominating role of the state. The expansion of the private sector was limited. On the other hand, the second policy regime is characterized by moderate reforms in all major aspects of eco-nomic policies and programmes ((Sobhan 1990; Rahman 1994). The restrictions on trade were relaxed and different industrial policies were put in place to move the economy from an inward-looking to an outward-looking one. Significant privati-zation took place during this period (World Bank 1989; Bhuyan and Rashid 1993). During the third trade policy regime, the speed of reforms intensified. The trade regime became significantly more open compared with the previous two regimes, while industrial and other policies continued to uphold the broad objective of private-sector development.

After 1991, considerable rationalization of tariff rates took place in the form of lowering high tariff rates, reducing the number of rates, and compressing tariff bands. As a result, average nominal rates of protection for all tradables fell from 88.6 per cent in 1991 to 22.2 per cent in 1999. The import-weighted tariff also declined significantly during this period. Also, the dispersion in tariff rates was re-duced. As a result of the continued liberalization of the import regime, the number of tariff rates was reduced from eight in 1993 to five in 2003, and the maximum tariff rate was brought down from 350 per cent to 32.5 per cent during the same period (Raihan 2007).

Until the mid-1980s, Bangladesh followed a strategy of import substitution. That regime was also characterized by a high degree of anti-export bias. However, since 1985, several export policy reforms have been implemented, which have included trade, exchange rate, monetary, and fiscal policy incentives, aimed at increasing effective assistance to exports. A few sectors, especially RMGs, have been major beneficiaries of these reforms. Reforms have provided exporters with unrestricted and duty-free access to imported inputs, financial incentives in the form of easy access to credit and credit subsidies, and various forms of fiscal incentives, such as rebates on income taxes and concessionary duties on imported capital machinery (Raihan and Razzaque 2007).

The growth of Bangladesh's RMG exports is largely attributable to the international trade regime in textiles and clothing, which, until 2004, was governed by the Multi-Fibre Arrangement (MFA) quota system. This system restricted competition in the global market by providing reserved markets for a number of developing countries, including Bangladesh, where textiles and clothing items had not been traditional exports. The duty-free access for Bangladesh's RMG products in the European Union (EU) has also greatly supported the growth of the sector. It then follows that despite the impressive growth record, the export base and the export markets have remained rather narrow for Bangladesh, which is a matter of great concern. Undiversified exports, in terms of both product range and markets, are likely to be much more vulnerable to various shocks than well-diversified exports. Despite the policy reforms and various incentives offered, it seems that Bangladesh has failed to develop a diversified export structure. It is also important to note that export markets for Bangladesh have been highly concentrated, with North America and the EU being the major destinations. In 2018/19, around 62 per cent of the country's total exports went to the EU, while another 22 per cent was destined for North America.[2]

Though all of the country's successive governments since independence have announced policies and strategies to accelerate economic growth through industrial sector development and diversification, industrial sector's diversification remained unsuccessful. This lack of diversification can be associated with factors such as energy shortages, reduced bank credit availability, weak foreign direct investment (FDI) inflow, labour unrest, poor law and order conditions, etc. Also, no less to blame are the contradictory policies that vitiated the overall business climate, discouraged investors, and hindered the country's industrial activity. Such industrial policies were not successful because they lacked a strategic vision or a clear path for the growth of industry. The policies barely tackled the major concerns that hampered economic development, making the policy measures ineffective. The supply-side constraints, both systemic and policy-induced, that were the major impediments to the expansion of private-sector manufacturing industries were virtually not recognized in the policies.

For structural transformation, an important contributor is FDI. However, even compared with the LDC norm, Bangladesh has still not been able to attract much FDI. In 2016, the ratio of FDI to GDP in Bangladesh was less than 1 per cent,

---

[2] See http://www.bgmea.com.bd/page/Export_Performance (accessed 7 October 2021).

whereas the LDC average was 3.3 per cent and the lower-middle-country average was 2.1 per cent (World Bank n.d.-b). Bangladesh's weak infrastructure and poor business climate are critical issues in attracting both domestic and foreign investment. As in the 2020 Doing Business index of the World Bank, Bangladesh ranked 168th among 190 countries, the country's worst performance is observed in the areas of 'enforcing contracts', 'getting electricity', and 'registering property'.

Agriculture still constitutes a major sector in the economy. Over the years, trade liberalization has led to a reduction of tariffs on imports of agriculture. With the tariff reduction on imports of agricultural inputs, there were steep reductions in the prices of inputs, leading to a more efficient distribution of inputs and reductions in marketing margins (World Bank 2016). The agriculture sector received a boost as result of the reduction in prices of pumps and tube well equipment brought about by liberalization of imports. Input market reforms led to the cultivation of irrigated rice (boro crop) even in the winter season. Reforms increased the use of technology in agriculture production. Reforms in the 1980s helped to increase government savings by reducing subsidies on inputs. The reforms led to the 'Green Revolution' as new varieties of rice were introduced by farmers and cropping land was put to use more than once a year. As a result, rice production expanded during this period, allowing the country to reach close to self-sufficiency in the early 2000s.

Social protection programmes have always been at the core of the anti-poverty strategy of governments. They mainly address two issues in Bangladesh: risk and vulnerability. Social protection programmes in Bangladesh can be categorized into the following groups: cash transfer (mainly targeting poor individuals or families directly); income support to poor households; conditional transfer to poor households (conditional on these households sending their children to school); access to or possession of income-generating assets and households for the ultra-poor; and the creation of job opportunities for the ultra-poor by providing free collateral loans, programmes for public works, and various rural development programmes (Khatun and Saadat 2018). However, the erosion of informal safety nets, rapid urbanization, economic integration worldwide, and democratization of the political system have led to the demand for more strategic social protection programmes, which Bangladesh is still lacking. Also, the country spends less than 2 per cent on social protection, which is much lower than what is required. Hence, a total restructuring of the social protection policies and programmes is needed.

While Bangladesh has made significant progress in gross enrolment in both male and female primary education, the country is seriously lagging behind in securing quality education for all. If we take average years of schooling as an indicator of any country's educational status, in 2017, according to World Bank (n.d.-b), Bangladesh's average was just 5.8 years—higher than Pakistan (5.2) but lower than India (6.4). But Bangladesh was well behind Sri Lanka (10.9) and some of the leading countries in South-East Asia, such as Malaysia (10.2), Thailand (7.6), and Vietnam (8.2). Disappointingly, with around 2 per cent of GDP allocated to public expenditure on education in 2016, Bangladesh was among the countries in the world with the lowest ratio. The average ratio was 3.3 per cent for LDCs, 4.3 per cent for lower-middle-income countries, 4.1 per cent for upper-middle-income countries, and 5.2 per cent for high-income countries. Bangladesh's ratio of public expenditure on education to GDP was even lower than the South Asian average. This is one of the reasons why private spending on education as a share of monthly household spending in Bangladesh is much higher than that of other South Asian nations. According to the latest household income and expenditure surveys available from five South Asian countries, the share of private expenditure on education in average monthly household expenditure in Bangladesh is about 5.5 per cent, compared with 2.6 per cent in India, 4.8 per cent in Nepal, 2.5 per cent in Pakistan, and 1.9 per cent in Sri Lanka (Raihan 2017). This indicates that responsibility for educational expenditure falls heavily on private households in Bangladesh, and the position of the government is not yet ideal.

It should be mentioned here that there are huge inequalities in the education sector in Bangladesh too. Differences are observed between regions and between rich and poor. Poorer people and people in remote rural areas have more restricted access than other groups to higher education and to better-quality educational services. Also, the current education system is not helpful in building a strong education sector because quality, access, and opportunities differ considerably across the different mediums of education—namely English medium, Bangla medium, and Madrasa system—and also among educational institutions in the public and private sectors.

Public health spending as a percentage of GDP in Bangladesh is just 0.4 per cent—one of the lowest in the world. For this reason, Bangladesh's share of out-of-pocket health spending in overall health spending is one of the highest in the world. In 2017, it was as high as 74 per cent, compared with the 51.65 per cent LDC average or the 57.3 per cent lower-middle world average (World Bank n.d.-b). This indicates that the burden of health spending falls heavily on Bangladeshi households, while the government contributes a far smaller share.

In the context of the labour market dynamics of Bangladesh, international labour migration has been performing a substantial role since the early 1990s. A densely populated country mostly comprising unskilled and semi-skilled labours, Bangladesh has sent more than 10 million migrant workers to more than 140 countries across the globe over a period of four decades since the late 1970s. A substantial part of the employment of the labour force has been generated by the international labour market, which comprises more than 12 per cent of the total labour force. About 1.8 million new labourers enter the market each year, while the current labour market mechanism only generates about 200,000 new formal sector jobs each year. Since the early millennium, remittance has been translated into one of the growth drivers of Bangladesh and has contributed significantly in terms of poverty reduction and improving household welfare for a mass population. Workers' remittances accounted for around 6 per cent of GDP in 2017. Studies show that the households of migrant workers benefit from remittances by having better education outcomes and better access to health care, water, sanitation, and nutrition. In the case of Bangladesh, remittance earnings are considered a vital source of foreign exchange, and short-term overseas employment helps to reduce unemployment (Raihan et al. 2009).

Over the past two decades, Bangladesh has shown progress on a number of social indicators, mostly due to a multifaceted service provision regime. With the expansion of services provided by non-governmental organizations (NGOs) during this period, the possibility of scaling up innovative anti-poverty experiments into nationwide programmes has become evident. Innovations in providing access to credit to the previously 'unbanked' poor, the development of a non-formal education system for poor children, particularly girls, and door-to-door health services through thousands of village-based community health workers are some of the notable examples. Despite a strong patriarchal society, the large proportion of NGO beneficiaries comprising poor women is evidence of the institutionalization of a large segment of NGO beneficiaries.

6. The political economy of structural transformation, inequality, and employment in Bangladesh

Hassan and Raihan (2018) applied the 'deals' framework to explore the politics of development in Bangladesh. In contrast to 'rules' (formal law-based governance), 'deals' are characterized by informal arrangements and personalized transaction. Deals can be further categorized as open versus closed deals and ordered versus disordered deals. If the deals, once negotiated between business actors and state officials, are honoured, they are considered ordered; if they are not, they are disordered. If deals are widely available, they are open; if they are limited to a few elites, they are closed.

Bangladesh has been generally pro-business, except during a few years after independence. But it manifested big 'soft state' syndromes and was hesitant on enforcing regulatory reforms, especially related to privatization and relaxing the bureaucratic regulation of industry. The convergence of international pressure (by the World Bank and the International Monetary Fund (IMF)) and national politics since the late 1970s, dominated by pro-market elites (politicians and bureaucrats) provided room for the state to devise and implement business-friendly regulatory and economic policies. These features of the political settlement of elites at the macro level broadly dominated the deals mechanism at the meso level and organized state–business relationships during the earlier growth acceleration phases.

A distinctly noticeable change in the deals landscape emerged in the late 1970s—from a mostly closed and disordered one to an increasingly open and ordered one (governing industrial nationalization procedures, the distribution of licences and permits, ambiguity about land reform, the granting of property rights, etc.). In its bid to establish new entrepreneurs and improve the industrial development driven by the private sector, the state adopted a de facto highly lax form of regulatory environment, sanctioning loans for industries from specialized state-owned banks that culminated in a high level of defaulting on bank loans. This policy of so-called 'primitive accumulation' was usually focused on cronyism to a lesser degree (for a few politically aligned and partisan business people), and mostly focused on open deals (for the majority of business people without political identity). The latter category created a constructive form of market-led corruption (bribing of government officials by business people) as well as large-scale rent-seeking, primarily by bank officials but also by officials of the ministries concerned, and the mechanism was largely regulated by an organized system of deals. This form of rent management contributed to the emergence of the RMG sector in the late 1970s and to the development of local entrepreneurs, specifically in the RMG sector. Many of these entrepreneurs, too, were created by the privatization of some state-owned industries.

Closed but organized deals during the 1980s can be found to cover a range of economic activities—licensing, export and import, and large-scale development ventures, though not specifically developing industries. The management of sanctioning industrial loans and the restructuring of the nationalized sectors remained marked by a mixture of cronyism and open-ordered deals. These forms of state–business relations led to the development of a significant number of local entrepreneurs (in particular, an escalation of owners of RMG factories) and private-sector capital accumulation, which may explain, to some degree, the acceleration of growth, although low in nature, that one sees during that decade.

During the competitive democratic political period (1991–2013), a major transformation of the deals mechanism occurred, primarily as a result of comparatively newer methods of rent management—a complex combination of monopolistic and especially duopolistic rent distributions (sharing rents around the political divide). In line with the process of de facto rent management, direct access to state resources/privileges (permits, licences, leases, etc.) tended to be largely closed and ordered and, critically, depended on the political identity of the person. Yet market players with the wrong political identity (or no political attachment, as was the case for most business people) were still able to work with government elites to gain state resources, under the environment of closed deals. These business practices, in essence, effectively turned closed deals into open deals.

In Bangladesh, the competitive political process ended in 2013. What evolved after that can be considered the dominant-party phase in the political realm. During this dominant-party phase, earlier rent management (i.e. rent distribution across the political divide) changed considerably. Crony capitalist practices have seen a sharp rise since the emergence of dominant-party politics. Cases of crony capitalism in the banking industry have become prevalent, as reported widely in the print media. Private bank licensing was also the result of an apparent type of crony capitalism. Except in a few important sectors of the economy, such as electricity (in particular, related to large ventures) and very large infrastructure projects, state–business activities are now subject to growing numbers of rent-seekers (more politicians, government officials, police, regulatory officers, etc.), which has increased the cost of doing business. The rent-seeking model has also changed from the earlier fairly centralized one to an increasingly decentralized one. However, important economic sectors—large power plants, for example, or infrastructure—are still largely dominated by centralized rent allocation processes. This has resulted in a large rise in the number of actors involved in rent-seeking activities. Businesses now have to deal with veto-empowered rent-seekers at different levels of the hierarchies of the bureaucracy.

7. The future trajectory of the structural transformation, inequality, and inclusive growth in Bangladesh

The aforementioned analysis suggests that despite slow progress in structural transformation, poor business environment, and weak institutions, Bangladesh has been so far able to keep the momentum of economic growth. One political economy explanation for this apparent contradiction could be that Bangladesh has so far used its 'youth bulge' of demographic dividend quite efficiently and also has tapped in quite remarkably to its comparative advantage in low-skilled labour on two major fronts: RMG exports and exports of low-skilled labour. According to the United Nations Population Fund (UNFPA), a 'demographic dividend' is the economic growth potential that can result from shifts in a population's age structure, mainly when the working-age share of the population (fifteen to sixty-four) is larger than the non-working-age share of the population (fourteen and younger, and sixty-five and older). One problem with UNFPA's definition is that the age span (fifteen to sixty-four) is quite long and it doesn't capture the youth bulge aspect of the demographic dividend. In this case, the share of the youth population (fifteen to twenty-four) in the total population would be a more relevant indicator. It appears that among the aforementioned five countries, the youth bulge share of the population, between 1980 and 2015, increased for Bangladesh while for Cambodia, China, India, and Vietnam it declined. In 2015, Bangladesh's youth bulge share (19.5 per cent) was much higher than those of China (13 per cent), India (18.4 per cent), or Vietnam (16.9 per cent).

With this high youth bulge as part of the demographic dividend, Bangladesh also managed to maintain a labour regime for a long time characterized by an equilibrium trap of low-skilled labour and low wages, poor working conditions, and relaxed execution of labour laws in defiance of workers' rights. Despite over-all weak governance and weak institutions, there have been supportive, efficient, non-conventional economic and political institutions in place in maintaining this labour regime. The returns from such a labour regime in the form of economic and political rents are so high that they act as a disincentive for further economic and export diversification, and in turn the production and export of high value-added and sophisticated products, investment in workers' skill development, improve-ment in working conditions, and better execution of labour laws to ensure workers' rights. Apparently, such high rents have also been able to offset much of the loss arising from the poor business environment.

Can Bangladesh sustain the current momentum of economic growth? From a political economy perspective, the ongoing economic growth momentum is likely to persist as long as Bangladesh can continue to manage the labour regime riding on the youth bulge and comparative advantage in low-skilled labour. However, there are concerns that the challenges in the future are likely to be very differ-ent from those that Bangladesh encountered in the past. In the coming years, if proper investments are not made on human capital development, Bangladesh will lose much of the larger prospective productive returns from the youth bulge and demographic dividend. The country is also in the process of graduating from LDC status, aims to achieve the Sustainable Development Goals (SDGs) by 2030, and wants to move up to upper-middle-income country status. The economic growth strategies thus need to be revisited to negotiate the coming challenges.

8. Conclusion

Bangladesh's economic growth and development performance over the past two decades have been impressive. With the poor quality of institutions, such perfor-mance has often been termed a 'development surprise' or the 'Bangladesh paradox'. Despite the aforementioned achievements, the fundamental question is whether Bangladesh can continue its success and achieve larger development goals with business-as-usual processes. There are concerns that the weak institutional capac-ity of the country may work as a binding constraint as the country seeks to meet the stiff targets of the SDGs by 2030, aspires to become an upper-middle-income country by 2031, and aspires to becoming a developed country by 2041.

The trends in the quality of formal institutions between 1996 and 2016, as man-ifested by the movements on world governance indicators, suggest that, with some fluctuations, there are deteriorations in the areas of 'voice and accountability', 'po-litical stability', and 'government effectiveness', and some trivial improvements in the areas of 'regulatory quality', 'rule of law', and 'ccontrol of corruption'. As the country is plunged into a number of challenges related to slow progress in structural transformation, lack of economic diversification, a high degree of informality in the labour market, the slow pace of job creation, the poor status of social and physical infrastructure, the slow reduction in poverty, and rising inequality, such poor improvements in formal institutions could lead to a situation where Bangladesh is trapped in the lower-middle-income country category.

References

Anjum, M.I., and P.M. Sgro (2017). 'A Brief History of Pakistan's Economic Development', *Real World Economics Review*, 80: 171–178.

BBS (Bangladesh Bureau of Statistics) (2016). *Report of the Household Income and Expenditure Survey 2016*. Dhaka: BBS, Statistics Division, Ministry of Planning.

BBS (2018). *Report on Labour Force Survey (LFS) 2016–17*. Dhaka: BBS, Statistics Division, Ministry of Planning.

Bhuyan, A.R., and M.A. Rashid (1993). *Trade Regimes and Industrial Growth: A Case Study of Bangladesh*. Dhaka: Bureau of Economic Research, University of Dhaka.

Bose, S.R. (1983). 'The Pakistan Economy since Independence (1947–70)'. In D. Kumar and M. Desai (eds), *The Cambridge Economic History of India*. Cambridge: Cambridge University Press, 995–1026.

Hassan, M., and S. Raihan (2018). 'Navigating the Deals World: The Politics of Economic Growth in Bangladesh'. In L. Pritchett, K. Sen, and E. Werker (eds), *Deals and Development*. Oxford: Oxford University Press, 96–128

ILO (International Labour Organization) (n.d.). 'ILOSTAT', ILO, https://ilostat.ilo.org/ (accessed 15 March 2019).

Islam, N. (2003). *Making of a Nation. Bangladesh: An Economist's Tale*. Dhaka: University Press Ltd.

Khatun, F., and S.Y. Saadat (2018). 'Towards a Social Protection Strategy for Bangladesh'. CPD Working Paper 117. Dhaka: Centre for Policy Dialogue (CPD), https://cpd.org.bd/wp-content/uploads/2018/08/Working-Paper-117-Towards-a-Social-Protection-Strategy-for-Bangladesh.pdf (accessed 20 December 2019).

Kim, K., and A. Sumner (2019). 'The Five Varieties of Industrialisation: A New Typology of Diverse Empirical Experience in the Developing World.' ESRC GPID Research Network Working Paper 18. London: ESRC Global Poverty and Inequality Dynamics Research Network (GPID).

Kuznets, S. (1955). 'Economic Growth and Income Inequality', *American Economic Review*, 45(1): 1–28.

Rahman, S.H. (1994). 'Trade and Industrialization in Bangladesh'. In G.K. Helliner (ed.), *Trade Policy and Industrialisation in Turbulent Times*. London: Routledge, 259–291

Raihan, S. (2007). *Dynamics of Trade Liberalisation in Bangladesh: Analyses of Policies and Practices*. Dhaka: Pathak Samabesh.

Raihan, S. (2017). 'Is Our Education Sector Ready for the Future Challenges?', The Daily Star, 5 November 2017, www.thedailystar.net/opinion/society/our-education-sector-ready-the-future-challenges-1486282 (accessed 30 March 2020).

Raihan, S. (2018a). 'Can Bangladesh Sustain Its Growth Momentum?', The Daily Star, 3 June 2019, www.thedailystar.net/opinion/economics/can-bangladesh-sustain-its-growth-momentum-1585306 (accessed 30 March 2020).

Raihan, S. (2018b). 'Structural Change in Bangladesh: Challenges for Growth and Employment Creation'. In S. Raihan (ed.), *Structural Change and Dynamics of Labor Markets in Bangladesh*. Singapore: Springer, 1–18

Raihan, S., and S.H. Bidisha (2018). 'Female Employment Stagnation in Bangladesh'. Economic Dialogue on Inclusive Growth in Bangladesh (EDIG) Research Paper. London: ODI (Overseas Development Institute), The Asia Foundation, and UKaid.

Raihan, S., and M.A. Razzaque (2007). 'A Review of the Evolution of Trade and Industrial Policies in Bangladesh'. In A. Razzaque and S. Raihan (eds), *Trade and Industrial Policy Environment in Bangladesh with Special Emphasis on Some Non-Traditional Export Sectors*. Dhaka: Pathak Samabesh, 26–42

Raihan, S., G. Sugiyarto, H.K. Bazlul, and S. Jha (2009). 'Remittances and Household Welfare: A Case Study of Bangladesh'. Economics Working Paper 189. Mandaluyong City, Manila: Asian Development Bank.

Sobhan, R. (1990). 'The Political Economy of South Asian Economic Cooperation', *Bangladesh Journal of Political Economy*, 10(1): 26–48.

World Bank (1989). 'Bangladesh: Manufacturing Public Enterprise Reform'. Report 7654-BD. Washington, DC: World Bank.

World Bank (2016). 'Bangladesh: Growing the Economy through Advances in Agriculture'. World Bank, 9 October, www.worldbank.org/en/results/2016/10/07/bangladesh-growing-economy-through-advances-in-agriculture (accessed 19 January 2019).

World Bank (n.d.-a). 'PovcalNet'. Online analysis tool for global poverty monitoring. Washington, DC: World Bank. http://iresearch.worldbank.org/PovcalNet/povOnDemand.aspx (accessed 15 February 2019).

World Bank (n.d.-b). 'World Development Indicators' (data base). Washington, DC: World Bank. http://databank.worldbank.org/data/source/world-development-indicators (accessed 15 February 2019).

PART III
SUB-SAHARAN AFRICA

8

Adverse Political Settlements

An Impediment to Structural Transformation and Inclusive Growth in Ghana

Robert Darko Osei, Richmond Atta-Ankomah, and Monica Lambon-Quayefio

1. Introduction

The desire for a transformative change in the structure of the Ghanaian economy dates back to the immediate post-independence period.[1] Unfortunately, the pace of structural transformation has been rather slow, and largely characterized by fairly stagnant manufacturing value-added and employment shares. In the past two decades, there seems to have been renewed hope that the country can get on to a path of higher growth and transformation, and in a way that is inclusive. Inclusive growth here is used to refer to a situation where economic growth is beneficial to all, including the poor. This renewed optimism is based on the fact that, generally, economic growth in Ghana over the past two decades has been good, averaging over 6 per cent annually. Also, the start of oil production in 2010 gave added hope that the country will have increased resources to support the structural transformation efforts.

Ghana's growth and poverty reduction success has been well documented (see Osei and Jedwab 2017; Aryeetey and Baah-Boateng 2015). However, inequality in Ghana remains a challenge and has been increasing since the early 1990s (Cooke et al. 2016; Atta-Ankomah et al. 2020). On the one hand, this could actually be consistent with Kuznets's hypothesis, where, in the early years of a country's development, growth is associated with increased inequality (Huang et al. 2012). On the other hand, this may suggest that structural transformation of the economy may have been rather weak, and characterized by growth that is not inclusive. The

---

[1] We acknowledge very useful comments from Andrew Sumner and participants at the September 2020 workshop, The Development Dilemma: Structural Transformation, Inequality and Inclusive Growth, in Bangkok. All errors are those of the authors.

Robert Darko Osei, et al., *Adverse political settlements*. In: *The Developer's Dilemma*.
Edited by Armida Salsiah Alisjahbana, Kunal Sen, Andy Sumner, and Arief Anshory Yusuf, Oxford University Press.
© UNU-WIDER (2022). DOI: 10.1093/oso/9780192855299.003.0008

key, though, is to understand the nature of the industrialization path that has been associated with structural transformation in Ghana. Indeed, the new debates around inclusive structural transformation relate to the type of industrialization pathway embarked upon, as that dictates the policy choices available to a country (Kim and Sumner 2019).

This study provides an analysis of structural transformation and inclusive growth in Ghana. It does this by interrogating the policies pursued, and the political imperatives driving the policies and how they are implemented and also discusses how all these have influenced the pathway of structural transformation and inclusive growth in the past six decades after independence.

2. Structural transformation and inclusive growth from 1960 to the 1980s

2.1 Trends in structural transformation: a period of secular deindustrialization

The transformation of Ghana's economy in the immediate post-independence period can be described as a short-lived primary industrialization. The economy in the first half of the 1960s was largely characterized by high shares of agriculture in aggregate value added and modest gains in the shares for the burgeoning manufacturing sector. The manufacturing sector share (that is, manufacturing output as a percentage of gross domestic product (GDP)), for instance, recorded modest increases from 13.7 per cent in 1960 to about 19 per cent in the mid-1970s—growing at an average rate of 6 per cent per year. The increasing share for the manufacturing sector was due to the industrialization drive of the Kwame Nkrumah-led government, which focused on expanding Ghana's manufacturing base as part of the import substitution industrialization (ISI) policies.

After the early 1960s and until the mid-1980s, estimates from Timmer et al. (2015) indicate that the economy experienced a stagnation in all major sectors, affecting the overall growth trajectory of the country. The manufacturing sub-sector, which was particularly affected, recorded double-digit negative growth rates in the early 1980s and was the least contributor to economic growth. The downturn in the economy in the early 1970s and mid-1980s coincided with high instability in Ghana's politics, with four episodes of *coup d'états* in this period (Osei 2001).

The structure of the economy also reflected in the employment patterns for the various sectors, as suggested by Aryeetey and Baah-Boateng (2015). Looking at this period, the employment shares for the agricultural sector declined marginally from 61 per cent in 1960 to about 58 per cent by the 1980s (see Figure 8.1). At the same time, the employment shares for the manufacturing sector, although stagnated between 1964 and 1967, continued to rise, averaging about 2 per cent per year until the end of that decade. The employment shares for the non-business services subsector increased from 22 per cent in the early 1960s to 27 per cent

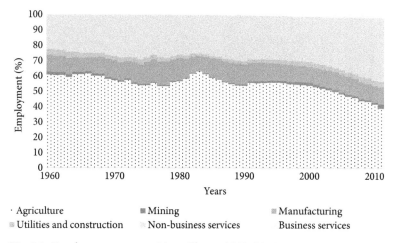

Fig. 8.1 Employment composition, Ghana, 1960–2011

Notes: Business services: financial intermediation, renting, business activities; non-business services: (a) wholesale and retail trade, repair of motor vehicles and motorcycles, personal and household goods, hotels and restaurants; (b) transport, storage, communications; (c) public administration, defence, education, health, social work; and (d) other community activities, social and personal service activities, activities of private households. These notes apply to Figs 8.1, 8.4, 8.6, 8.7, 8.12, and 8.13.
Source: authors' compilation based on World Bank (2019) and (UNU-WIDER 2019).

by the end of the decade, and remained so until the end of the 1980s. This non-business services sub-sector was characterized by low productivity and low skills, and included activities such as wholesale and retail activities and repair of motor vehicles. The employment shares for the high-productivity business services sub-sector, on the other hand, remained constant throughout the period at 0.3 per cent annually. We will characterize the economy over this period as being on a secular deindustrialization path where overall employment shares for manufacturing remained stagnant and the manufacturing value added shares decreased (Figure 8.2).

From about the mid-1980s, the country shifted away from the import substitution development strategy to a more liberalized trade regime, as recommended under the structural adjustment programme (SAP). This led to increased trade, but with little emphasis on the manufacturing sector.

Figures 8.3 and 8.4 tell a compelling story about the growth of the manufacturing sector and its role in the structural transformation path for Ghana. We note that the period between 1960 and 1983 recorded the lowest growth in labour productivity in the history of the country. Productivity growth for both within and between sectors recorded negative growth rates. This trend has been attributed to the political and economic instability that characterized this period (Osei and Jedwab 2017).

Between 1960 and 1983, the high labour productivity sectors included business services, mining, and utilities and construction sectors. However, these high-productivity sectors accounted for low employment shares. On the other hand,

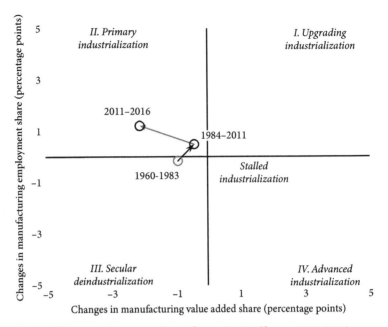

Fig. 8.2 Varieties of structural transformation in Ghana, 1960–2016
Source: authors' construct based on Kim and Sumner (2019).

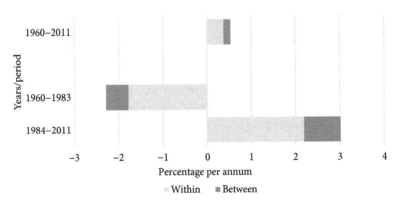

Fig. 8.3 Decomposition of labour productivity growth, Ghana, 1960–2011
Note: Decomposition uses the methodology of McMillan and Rodrik (2011).
Source: authors' compilation based on Timmer et al. (2015) and the Groningen Growth and
Development Centre (GGDC) (2015).

the non-business sector, dominated by informal activities, employed large shares
of the labour force but was characterized by low labour productivity. Meanwhile,
the declining manufacturing sector during this period also showed low levels
of productivity and employment shares (see Figure 8.4). Contrary to the classical structural adjustment trajectory, although the employment shares for the

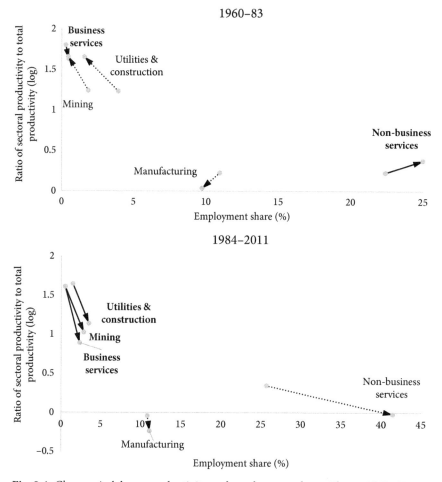

Fig. 8.4 Changes in labour productivity and employment share, Ghana, 1960–2011

Note: Sectors with higher than economy-wide average labour productivity that experienced an increase in employment shares are in bold.

Source: authors' compilation based on Timmer et al. (2015) and the GGDC (2015).

low-productivity agricultural sector declined, there was neither a corresponding increase in employment shares for the manufacturing sector nor an increase in labour productivity. This, perhaps, was an early indication of the country's pattern of transformation in which the manufacturing sector was leapfrogged.

In summary, the nature of Ghana's structural transformation started off as primary industrialization in the early-to-mid-1960s. The industrialization agenda which began in this period focused on light manufacturing for the domestic market, as part of the ISI policies that were implemented. However, the industrialization drive stalled from the mid-1960s, when the economy began to stagnate amid political and macroeconomic instability, resulting in secular deindustrialization.

2.2 Policies and politics that shaped structural transformation and inclusive growth

Policies of this period started with significant accumulation of physical capital as part of the industrialization strategy. However, this was not sustained. The worsening macroeconomic environment, which manifested in a deteriorating balance-of-payments and credit ratings, eventually led to the overthrow of the Nkrumah government, and with it an end to the socialist's policies on economic and structural transformation.

The two short-lived successive governments after Nkrumah implemented policies that were sharply opposed to the socialist's policies of industrialization pursued before. The ideologies of the National Liberation Council and the Progress Party governments focused more on pro-private capital (Fosu and Aryeetey 2008). Policies during these regimes aimed at achieving reduced inflation, reduced public investment, a tighter control over import licences, and a devaluation of the cedi (Killick 1978). Fosu and Aryeetey (2008) note that both total factor productivity and physical capital's contribution to overall growth continued to decline, although some positive results with respect to the macroeconomy was achieved. The period was also characterized by high levels of inequality which, some argue, was inherited from periods during colonization (Aboagye and Bolt 2018).

The decade-long decline in Ghana's economic performance from the early 1970s to the early 1980s was characterized by political instability, with five different regimes during this short span (Fosu and Aryeetey 2008). While these governments pursued different and uncoordinated economic policies, total factor productivity continued to decline. Fosu and Aryeetey (2008) argue that the policies pursued in this period focused fundamentally on import substitution, restrictive foreign exchange regime, quantitative restrictions on imports, and price controls. Again, the extreme economic difficulties of the time led to another *coup d'etat* in 1981, with the hope of changing the course of the Ghanaian economy. The Provisional National Defence Council (PNDC) regime was radical in its policies, similar to Nkrumah's socialist ideology of state control. Initially, the policies implemented focused on reducing the role of the private sector (particularly due to the rising inequality), while increasing the role of the state in the provision of essential services. The aim was to protect the poor from both local and foreign capitalists that had dominated the private sector. The weak growth-enhancing structural transformation, coupled with rising inequality, produced a weak and adverse Kuznetsian tension during this period (see Figure 8.5).

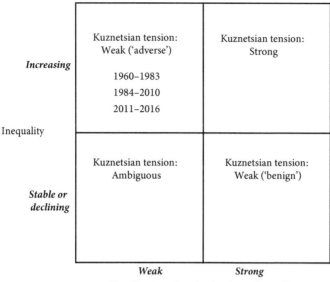

Fig. 8.5 Patterns of Kuznetsian tension in Ghana, 1960–2016
Source: authors' construct based on Kim and Sumner (2019).

The continued hardship, despite the radical interventions by the PNDC government, compelled the government to reconsider its earlier stance on policy prescriptions from international financial institutions. This led the then government to sign up for the Economic Recovery Programme (ERP) in 1983. The medium-term objective of the ERP was to generate sustainable growth and development, while increasing the capacity of the economy to adjust to shocks (Aryeetey and Harrigan 2000).

The ERP consisted of two categories of policies, intended, first, to achieve economic stabilization and, second, to restore economic growth through improved efficiency and productive capacities. Policies related to macroeconomic stabilization included a set of fiscal and monetary, as well as trade and payment policies. Ghana's success in implementing the adjustment programmes was hailed by the World Bank (1993) and some researchers (see, e.g. Corbo and Fisher 1995; Osei 2001; Killick 2000). Despite the growth spurts however, progress was not as strong as expected (Aryeetey and Tarp 2000). Questions began to surface as to why the growth rates were slower than those of economies in East Asia. Aryeetey and Tarp (2000) have argued that the packages of macroeconomic and institutional policies implemented as part of Ghana's ERP were not based on a unified framework of economic theory.

In the early years of the reform (ERP), specific policies that focused on achieving fiscal balance were implemented. Government expenditure was expected to reduce significantly by restricting increases in public-sector wages and salaries, while increasing government revenue. By 1983, the government had raised tax rates on rental income and on consumables such as beer, cigarettes, and gasoline, while new taxes on wealth, including property and non-commercial vehicles, were introduced. The government also introduced simplified tax schedules that capped the import tariff at a maximum of 30 per cent. This was complemented with a strengthening of the government's tax collection system. The policies on revenue mobilization yielded positive results and government revenue increased significantly (Aryeetey and Tarp 2000).

During this period, although investment in public infrastructure provided the required social infrastructure, the level of macroeconomic instability, and political instability in particular, did not create the required environment for the transformation of the economy. In the absence of data on inclusive growth indicators during this period, Gyimah-Boadi and Jeffries (2000) suggest that growth from the early 1960s to the mid-1960s was not inclusive. They explain that the government's highly ambitious strategy of import substitution created pay-offs for the most active political constituency of the Convention People's Party, as well as a large number of educated and semi-educated graduates.

Similarly, under the leadership of Busia whose ideology on liberalization focused on the rural population, particularly cocoa farmers, it is reported that the levels of investment was biased in favour of the Ashanti and Brong-Ahafo regions, which were seen as the main political constituency of the regime (see Gyimah-Boadi and Jeffries 2000; Resnick 2016). General Ignatius Acheampong's tenure (1972–1978) was also characterized by policies that catered to the needs of the urban population, who were thought to have been negatively affected by the policies implemented under the previous regime. Therefore, it has been argued that in large part economic policy during this period was largely driven by 'political rationality' (Gyimah-Boadi and Jeffries 2000). It is based on this line of thinking that Frimpong-Ansah (1991) characterized the political elite at the time as 'vampire elements' who had remained even after the overthrow of Nkrumah (see Osei 2001). The high inequality associated with this time period reflects aspects of the adverse Kuznetsian tension as per the characterization in Figure 8.5.

3. Structural transformation and inclusive growth, 1984–2010

3.1 Trends in structural transformation: a period of stalled industrialization amid a changing policy and political space

Following the start of the implementation of the ERP/SAP in 1983, overall economic growth and that of all the economic sectors, including manufacturing, started to respond in a positive way. However, by the end of the 1980s, these bullish growth trends had become sluggish, declining continuously until 1995. It then became relatively more stable and indeed started showing signs of an acceleration from the middle of the 2000s.

Between 1989 and 2010, the manufacturing sector's contribution to overall economic growth declined continuously, while that of the utilities and construction sector, and later, mining grew (Figure 8.6). The result was a less important manufacturing sub-sector relative to industry as a whole. Following an initial expansion in the second half of the 1980s, the manufacturing sector's share in total output declined from 13.3 per cent in 1989 to 8.8 per cent in 2010 (Figure 8.7). The services sector's contribution[2] to total output gained ten percentage points over the period and had reached 48.3 per cent by 2010. The agricultural sector also declined continuously from 41 per cent in 1984 to 29.5 per cent by 2010 (Figure 8.7). The trends in value-added shares across the sectors were generally reflected in sectoral employment shares over the period. A key standout feature of the trends in employment shares is that the manufacturing sector average for the 1989–2010 period was similar to that for the 1960–1983 period.

The period was also characterized by a high and growing trade deficit that was largely associated with unfavourable balance of trade in manufactures. Overall economic growth in this period was, therefore, largely driven by expansion in

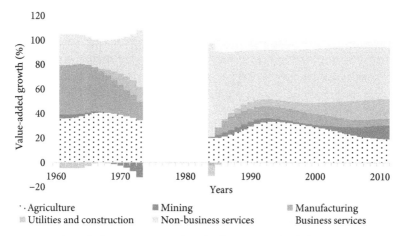

Fig. 8.6 Growth decomposition of Hodrick–Prescott (HP)-filtered value added by sector, Ghana, 1960–2011

Note: Excludes years in which any of the sectors' values of contribution to value-added growth was smaller than −15.0 per cent.
Source: authors' compilation based on Timmer et al. (2015) and the GGDC (2015).

---

[2] The services sector's contribution to valued added is made up of business services and non-business services.

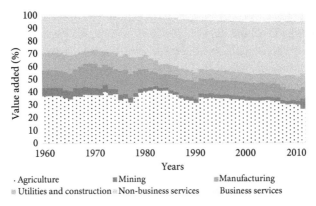

Fig. 8.7 Value-added composition, Ghana, 1960–2011

Source: authors' compilation based on Timmer et al. (2015) and the GGDC (2015).

the services sector, and to some extent the non-manufacturing sub-sectors of industry. The manufacturing sub-sector, however, remained generally stymied, even though overall economic growth was stable. Based on these trends, we argue that the structure of Ghana's economy responded to the ERP/SAP but in a way that rather promoted the services sector, as well as the non-manufacturing sub-sectors of industry. Unfortunately, the efficacy of the policies for the manufacturing sector was largely muted.

In spite of the unfavourable trade performance, growth in aggregate labour productivity between 1984 and 2010 averaged 3 per cent per annum, compared with an abysmal average of negative 2.3 per cent for the period 1960–1983 (Figure 8.3). However, the growth in labour productivity in the period 1984–2010 was largely driven by within-sector differences in productivity, just as observed for the period 1960–1983. This could suggest one of two things. First, it could be the case that differences in labour productivity across the sectors may not have changed significantly between the two periods. Second, inelastic supply of labour could have accounted for the lack of mobility of labour between sectors. As noted earlier, the manufacturing sector's share in value added experienced a gradual decline in the 1984–2010 period while its share in employment largely remained unchanged, moving Ghana towards stalled primary industrialization (Figure 8.2). Indeed, the share of manufacturing in total labour productivity continued with its downward trend from the 1960–1983 period and went into negatives by 2011. Meanwhile, other sectors, particularly the non-business services sector, experienced a high increase of their shares in total labour productivity.

So why did the rebound in industry and manufacturing after the adoption of ERP/SAP fade so quickly? The ERP/SAP came with the implementation of a number of policy reforms, including trade and market liberalization policies, privatization of state-owned enterprises, tax reforms, and a shift from ISI to an export-led industrialization strategy (Ackah et al. 2014). To complement the new outward-looking, export-led strategy, there were efforts made to restructure the industrial sector by addressing constraints that emerged from the ISI strategy, enhancing capacity utilization and strengthening institutional support to manufacturing firms. Ackah et al. (2014) argue that while these policy reforms are credited with the initial rebound in the manufacturing and industrial sector, the same are to blame for the loss in growth momentum by the late 1980s. This is because the manufacturing firms were exposed to intense competition from imports, high-interest cost and currency depreciation (Ackah et al. 2014). This led to efforts in the 1990s to deepen institutional support to the manufacturing and industrial sector, with the implementation of sector-specific programmes while enhancing business support services.

The early 2000s, which saw political power change hands for the first time in the fourth republic, came with a slight redirection of Ghana's industrialization strategy, with emphasis on private-sector-led industrial production through the application of science and technology. This was part of a series of broad development programmes—the Ghana Poverty Reduction Strategy (GPRS I) and Growth and Poverty Reduction Strategy (GPRS II)—supported by the World Bank and the International Monetary Fund (IMF) and implemented during the 2000s with the aim of achieving inclusive growth.

3.2   Trends in inclusive growth, policy, and political environment

In the 1980s and 1990s, when the SAP was in vogue, it was generally believed that the country needed to endure the short-run social cost, as the long-run benefits were going to be enormous (Sowa 2002). Hence, there was no explicit policy emphasis on inclusive growth until the late 1990s, when the calls to put a human face on the adjustment measures were heeded. These calls culminated in the worldwide adoption of the Millennium Development Goals (MDGs) in the early 2000s (Sowa 2002). Data from the World Bank (n.d.-a) shows that in Ghana, for example, the incidence of poverty, based on the US$3.2 poverty line, increased from 75.6 per cent in 1987 to 78.6 per cent in 1991.

The promulgation of the MDGs coincided with the adoption of GPRS I and GPRS II, which emphasized inclusive growth. GPRS I provided direct support for human development, with special programmes for the vulnerable and excluded in society, as well as the active involvement of the private sector as the main engine of growth. By 2005, the incidence of poverty, based on US$3.2 poverty line, had reduced to 50.1 per cent (World Bank n.d.-a). GPRS II was implemented between 2006 and 2009 to consolidate and enhance the progress made under GPRS

I by placing more emphasis on accelerated economic growth, sustained poverty reduction, and the attainment of middle-income status.

The government benefited from a wide range of financial assistance, including funds from the Heavily Indebted Poor Countries Initiative, the Multilateral Debt Relief Initiative, Multi-Donor Budget Support, and the United States Millennium Challenge Corporation support (UNDP 2015). Commitment to the MDGs translated into increased expenditure on the education and health sectors and other social protection policies/programmes, such as the elimination of school fees at the primary level, capitation grant, national health insurance scheme, and the Livelihood Empowerment Against Poverty (LEAP) programme (a cash grant programme). These efforts yielded some results and Ghana saw a reduction in the incidence of poverty to 32.5 per cent by 2012, based on US$3.2 poverty line (World Bank n.d.-a). However, it appears that non-poor households benefited more from the sustained high growth compared with poor households. An analysis from various waves of the Ghana Living Standards Survey (GLSS) between 1991 and 2005 shows that households in the upper deciles experienced higher growth in consumption expenditure than households in the lower deciles (GSS 2007).

The last three decades have witnessed an increase in economic inequality, particularly during the 1990s and 2000s (Figure 8.8). An important factor that has contributed to this trend is the nature of structural change that Ghana experienced over this period. Osei and Jedwab (2017) argue that structural change in Ghana was characterized by a decline in the agricultural sector's share in employment but the released labour were absorbed into the relatively low-productivity end of the informal sector. Manufacturing's share in value added was on a downward trend, as mentioned in section 3.1, and associated with this was an increase in income inequality between 1990 and 2010 (Figure 8.8). The relationship between inequality and growth-enhancing transformation remained 'adverse' in the 1984–2010 period (Figure 8.5). Linked to the weak growth-enhancing structural transformation in this period is that the employment–growth elasticity (estimated at 0.47) remained low (Baah-Boateng 2013; Aryeetey and Baah-Boateng 2015), with a large proportion of available jobs being vulnerable and/or falling short of being decent jobs (Baah-Boateng and Ewusi 2013). The weak response of employment to economic growth has been attributed to the fact that much of the growth was driven by low employment-generating sectors (Aryeetey and Baah-Boateng 2015) rather than by a transformative restructuring of the economy (Osei and Jedwab 2017).

Inclusive growth policies and outcomes over this period occurred within a changing political environment, which was particularly important with respect to its conditioning effects on the policies, processes, and outcomes. From the early 1980s to 1992, when the ERP/SAP was implemented, Ghana was under Rawlings' military dictatorship. This political environment allowed Rawlings to stay committed to economic reform, relying on a careful balancing act between technocratic implementation and authoritarian practices (Resnick 2016). This approach,

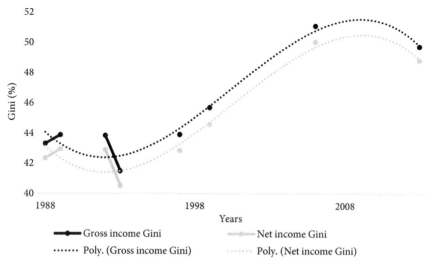

Fig. 8.8 Gross and net income Gini, Ghana, 1988–2013

Source: authors' compilation based on UNU-WIDER (2019).

according to Rothchild (1991), Jeffries (1992) and MacLean (2010), crippled the political power of interest groups, hence they were unable to influence the government's reform agenda. The transition to democracy, however, was characterized by a shift in the incentive structure and interest group dynamics (Resnick 2016). The bid to win elections every four years created the avenue for resistance by interest groups and the incentive for politicians to respond (Resnick 2016). For example, the move by the government to introduce a 17 per cent value-added tax in 1995 was opposed by a coalition of interest groups who demonstrated in Accra and Kumasi to register their displeasure, and eventually led to the reversal of the policy (Osei 2000). Similarly, urban interest groups capitalized on the 'political business cycle' to agitate for the reversal of increases in utility prices, as noted by Hutchful (2002). According to Resnick (2016), a large proportion of the gains from the ERP had been eroded by the end of the first decade following the democratic transition.

Aryeetey (forthcoming) argues that the electoral cycle in most democratic countries in sub-Saharan Africa often dictates the nature of plans and policies, as well as their implementation. With the nature of Ghana's political settlement increasingly becoming a competitive clientelist type (Oduro et al. 2014), the two dominant political parties—the National Democratic Congress (NDC) and the New Patriotic Party (NPP)—have continued to 'impress' the voting public with policies in the bid to win the next election. The NPP government, for instance, reversed some of the ERP policies by increasing the public and civil service wages, as well as subsidies in the energy sector just as the 2008 election drew closer (Gyimah-Boadi 2009; Whitfield 2010). More recently, successive governments have had to continue with and, in some cases, scale up a host of social protection programmes implemented in the 2000s, partly due to the political importance of these programmes and the fears of political backlash and of losing votes in the next elections (Aryeetey, forthcoming).

4. Structural transformation and inclusive growth after 2010

4.1 Policies and trends in structural transformation

The post-2010 period marks a watershed moment in Ghana's industrialization agenda as a result of the discovery and production of oil in commercial quantities in this period. Oil production began in December 2010, and in that year real GDP grew by 7.9 per cent—3 percentage points higher than the growth achieved in the previous year. Overall economic growth hit 14 per cent in 2011, when oil production took place all year round. However, growth declined continuously after 2011 and reached 3.7 per cent in 2016. Part of the reason for the decline in growth experienced over that period was a massive and sustained power crisis between 2012 and 2016. This affected the economy badly, particularly the manufacturing sector (Abeberese et al. 2017). However, data from the 2020 World Development Indicators (WDI) (World Bank n.d.-b) show that the share of manufacturing in value added trended upwards between 2011 and 2018, even though the increases in the shares of non-manufacturing industrial sector (particularly oil and mining) were much higher. Interestingly, growth in the value added share for manufacturing declined while growth in manufacturing's share in employment increased in this period (Figure 8.2) suggesting a shift towards primary industrialization trajectory.

Between 2010 and 2013, the government pursued the Ghana Shared Growth and Development Agenda (GSGDA I), which coincided with the beginning of oil production in Ghana. In addition to ensuring continued macroeconomic stability and enhancing the competitiveness of the private sector, GSGDA I aimed to change the structure of the economy to favour the services and industrial sectors. Some of the specific strategies under GSGDA I included the development of infrastructure, as well as the salt and petrochemical-based industries to support oil and gas production. GSGDA I was succeeded by GSGDA II in 2014. GSGDA II aimed to sustain the shared growth while the economy continued on the path of transformation and was to be implemented up to 2017. The administration that took over in 2017 has emphasized agricultural mechanization, productivity enhancement, and industrial transformation. Some of the key programmes and policies through which the goals of industrialization is to be achieved include 'Planting for Food and Jobs', 'Rearing for Food and Jobs', the 'One District, One Factory', and 'One Village One Dam' initiatives.

4.2 Policies and trends in inclusive growth

Between 2012/13 and 2016/17, the incidence of poverty in Ghana fell by only 0.8 of a percentage point. Of this, economic growth effects was 2.2 percentage points, while redistribution effect was 1.4 percentage points (GSS 2018). Thus, the incidence of poverty would have fallen by 2.2 percentage points if the redistribution effect had been zero. This suggests that growing economic inequality in Ghana has negatively affected Ghana's growth–poverty elasticity. Indeed, analysis from the last four waves of the GLSS showed that Ghana's growth–poverty elasticity declined from 0.17 in the 2005/06–2012/13 period to 0.07 in the 2012/13–2016/17 period (GSS 2018). This means that the level of poverty reduction associated with a percentage increase in growth has declined, implying that economic growth has become less pro-poor after 2010. It needs to be noted that as inequality increased between 2012 and 2017, the manufacturing sector's share in value added trended upwards. We will argue, however, that the Kuznetsian tension remained weak or 'adverse' even though the country seemed to be moving towards the region of strong Kuznetsian tension—where increasing inequality is associated with stronger growth-enhancing structural transformation.

It must be noted that at the onset of oil production in 2010 there was concern about the need to ensure that the growth process was inclusive so that the already growing regional or spatial inequalities could be mitigated (Osei 2012). These concerns, in part, informed the policy direction of GSGDA I and GSGDA II. However, the period was associated with a large reduction in Ghana's growth–poverty elasticity. Also, largely due to the capital-intensive nature of the oil and mining sector, growth did not translate into increased job creation and decent work for the growing labour force. Instead, labour moved from rural agriculture into low-productivity areas within the services sector—characterized by wholesale and retail activities. Consequently, we will argue that 'structural transformation' in this period has been superficial and non-inclusive (see, e.g. Rodrik 2013; McMillan et al. 2014).

In addition to the ambitious interventions in agriculture and industry by the government since 2017, there has also been an expanded access to senior high education in another intervention dubbed the 'Free Senior High School' policy, which began in September 2017. Financed mainly by government proceeds from oil production, figures touted by government officials indicate that enrolment increased by 69 per cent between 2017 and 2019, although significant infrastructural (both hard and soft) constraints remain (Ghana Business News 2019). This clearly has implications for the medium-to-long-term link between structural transformation and inclusive growth.

5. The future trajectory of the structural transformation–inequality–inclusive growth nexus

The future trajectory of the structural transformation–inequality–inclusive growth nexus is one that is difficult to predict with a high degree of accuracy, given the importance of the evolving nature of political settlements and its implication for the deals environment (see Osei et al. 2017). In particular, one notes that an increasingly important feature of the politics in Ghana is that when there is a change in the party in power, some programmes of the previous government are discontinued. This means that the trajectory of the structural transformation–inclusive growth nexus is also dependent on whether there will be a change in the ruling party. However, we will still argue that the expected trajectory will take one of two forms—one associated with the medium term and the other with the long term.

In the medium term, one expects the relationship to be inelastic—where some amount of structural transformation will occur, but with limited positive changes to inequality. We premise this argument on a number of related points. First, the changing structure of the economy is bound to continue, with growth in the services sector remaining strong and dominant. Second, even though we expect the growth in employment share in services to increase, this is likely to be dominated by the low-productivity sub-sectors, such as retail trade. We base this medium-term projection on two complementary factors. First, as noted in Osei et al. (2017), political patronage remains rife even though political settlement is becoming more competitive in Ghana. This means that the deals space is still dominated by elites so that growth favours sectors that are not too inclusive—particularly the extractive sectors. A second related point is that low-skilled labour from agriculture cannot move easily to the high-productivity end of the services sector. This is in large part a result of the generally low human capital associated with labour in the agricultural sector. This makes the movement of labour to the higher productivity end of the services sector (associated with higher skill sets) more difficult. It is for these reasons that we expect the medium-term elasticity of structural change with respect to inclusive growth to be limited.

In the long term, one expects changes to favour a trajectory where structural transformation impacts more positively on inclusive growth and, as a result, reduces inequality. We base our long-term projection on the following complementary factors. First, the current educational policies of the government have the potential to increase the average human capital of the populace as a whole and also increase the emphasis on technical and vocational skills. This will potentially reduce the rigidities associated with vertical movement along the skills ladder of the labour force. Second, and as argued by Osei et al. (2017), the power of the growing middle class is bound to put increasing pressure on the political elite and force political settlements to become more competitive. This, coupled with increasing oil resources, will eventually engender investments in sectors that are pro-inclusive growth. For this reason, one expects a more favourable structural transformation–inclusive growth nexus in the long term.

These projections are not without risks, however. A key downside risk that may affect this long-term projection could come from the very nature of competitive elections in Ghana. Increasingly, this has the potential of compromising political settlements in Ghana in a way that is not conducive to inclusive growth. Our reasoning is premised on the fact that competitive elections are increasingly demanding more resources for the running of political parties. Additionally, the winner-takes-all politics in Ghana (see Gyampo 2015) means that individuals are increasingly investing a lot more in political parties, with the objective of gaining better leverage when their party wins elections. Unfortunately, the increasing demand for resources from party financiers is intensifying rent-seeking behaviour. Rents, as we know, are typically highest in the extractive sectors and so there is increasing leverage for policy to favour activities in this sector. This 'political settlement–economic rent-seeking' trap that the country finds itself in, is not easy to break out of and has the potential of working against policies that seek to maximize the speed and benefits of structural transformation for inclusive growth.

6. Conclusion

In this chapter, we have examined the nature of the link between structural transformation and inclusive growth in Ghana by discussing policies as well as the pathways of structural transformation since independence. We further juxtapose this with key outcomes in the form of growth, poverty, and inequality over time. In particular, we assessed how the nature of structural transformation helped to shape shared growth outcomes for Ghana. Our main findings are summarized as follows.

First, the structure of the Ghanaian economy has changed, with services having become the dominant sector. However, the evidence suggests that this change has not been of the transformative type. Whereas the changing structure has been associated with changing employment shares from agriculture to the services sector, we note that the productivity differentials between these sub-sectors have not been very large. This finding, which is consistent with Osei et al. (2017), suggests that labour movement in Ghana over the years has been from low-productivity agriculture to the low-productivity end of the services sector. Indeed, productivity has remained highest in the non-manufacturing industrial sector (extractive sector), and this sector has not attracted a significant share of labour. Unsurprisingly, therefore, the link between productivity growth and employment in Ghana is found to be weak.

Second, Ghana's overall growth has improved markedly since the mid-1980s. This has in large part been driven by market-friendly policies, within a more stable macroeconomic and political environment. Additionally, and in more recent times, the start of oil production has reinforced this growth of the economy.

Third, we find that while the incidence of poverty has declined over the years, inequality has persisted. Part of the challenge, we argue, is the fact that employment growth has lagged behind economic growth. This muted employment response to growth is in part due to the nature of structural change that is occurring, and also to the low skill set of the labour force, which makes labour supply inelastic.

We conclude by noting that structural transformation in Ghana can be characterized as having generally remained around stalled primary industrialization. Indeed, associated with this has been an increasing inequality, suggesting adverse Kuznet tension. In spite of this muted structural transformation in Ghana, there is potential for it to be more impactful on inclusive growth, particularly in the long term. However, even this potential transformation in the long run is not certain and is threatened by the nature of competitive elections in Ghana.

References

Abeberese, A., C. Ackah, and P. Asuming (2017). 'How Did the 2012–2015 Power Crisis Affect Small and Medium Manufacturing Firms in Ghana?'. IGC Policy Brief 33305. Ghana: International Growth Centre, https://www.theigc.org/wp-content/uploads/2017/08/Asuming-et-al-2017-policy-brief.pdf (accessed March 2020).

Aboagye, P. Y., &Bolt, J. (2018). Economic Inequality in Ghana, 1891-1960. (African Economic History Network Working Paper Series No.38/2018). https://www.aehnetwork.org/working-papers/economic-inequality-in-ghana-1891-1960

Ackah, C., C. Adjasi, and F. Turkson (2014). 'Scoping Study on the Evolution of Industry in Ghana'. WIDER Working Paper 75/2014. Helsinki: UNU-WIDER.

Aryeetey, E. (forthcoming). 'The Political Economy of Structural Transformation: Has Democracy Failed African Economies?'. Helsinki: UNU-WIDER.

Aryeetey, E., and W. Baah-Boateng (2015). 'Understanding Ghana's Growth Success Story and Job Creation Challenges'. WIDER Working Paper 140/2015. Helsinki: UNU-WIDER.

Aryeetey, E. and Harrigan, J. (2000) "Macroeconomic and Sectoral Developments since 1970", in Ernest Aryeetey, Jane Harrigan, and Machiko Nissanke (eds), *Economic Reforms in Ghana: the Miracle and the Mirage* (Oxford: James Currey and Woeli Publishers), 5–31.

Aryeetey, E., and F. Tarp (2000). 'Structural Adjustment and After: Which Way Forward?'. In E. Aryeetey, J. Harrigan, and M. Nissanke (eds), *Economic Reforms in Ghana: The Miracle and Mirage.* Trenton, NJ: Africa World Press.

Atta-Ankomah, R. Osei, R. D., Osei-Akoto, I., Asante, F. A., Oduro, A. D., Owoo, N. . . . Afranie, S. (2020). *Inequality Diagnostics for Ghana.* African Center of Excellence for Inequality Research (ACEIR).

Atta-Ankomah, R. & Osei, R. D. (2021). Structural Change and Welfare: A Micro Panel Data Evidence from Ghana. *The Journal of Development Studies, 57(11),* 1927–1944.

Baah-Boateng, W. (2013). 'Unemployment in Ghana: A Cross-Sectional Analysis from Demand and Supply Perspectives', *African Journal of Economic and Management Studies*, 6(4): 402–415.

Baah-Boateng, W. and Ewusi K. (2013) 'Employment: Policies and Options' in Ewusi K. (ed.) *Policies and Options for Ghana's Economic Development* 3rd Edition, 190–221; Institute of Statistical Social and Economic Research (ISSER), University of Ghana, Legon Publication

Cooke, E., S. Hague, and A. McKay (2016). *The Ghana Poverty and Inequality Report Using the Sixth Ghana Living Standard Survey*. Accra: UNICEF.

Corbo, V., and S. Fisher (1995). 'Structural Adjustment: Stabilisation and Policy Reform-Domestic and International Finance'. In J. Behrman and T. Srinivasan (eds), *Handbook of Development Economics*, Vol. 3B. Amsterdam: North Holland, 2845–2924.

Fosu, A. (2001). *Emerging Africa: The Case of Ghana*. Nairobi: African Economic Research Consortium.

Fosu, A., and E. Aryeetey (2008). 'Economic Growth in Ghana, 1960–2000'. In B. Ndulu, S. O'Connell, J. Azam, R. Bates, A. Fosu, J. Gunning, and D. Nijinkeu (eds), *The Political Economy of Economic Growth in Africa, 1960–2000. Volume 2: Country Case Studies*. New York: Cambridge University Press, 68–94

Frimpong-Ansah, J. (1991). *The Vampire State in Africa: The Political Economy of Decline in Ghana*. London: James Currey.

GGDC (2015). 'GGDC 10-Sector Database, Version 2015'. Groningen Growth and Development Centre (GGDC), Groningen University, https://www.rug.nl/ggdc/productivity/10-sector/ (accessed March 2020).

Ghana Business News (2019). 'Free SHS Has Increased Enrolment by 69%—Bawumia', 30 December, https://www.ghanabusinessnews.com/2019/12/30/free-shs-has-increased-enrolment-by-69-bawumia/ (accessed 5 February 2020).

GSS (2007). *Pattern and Trends of Poverty in Ghana, 1991–2006*. Accra: Ghana Statistical Service (GSS).

GSS (2018). *Ghana Living Standard Survey 7(GLSS7): Poverty Trends in Ghana, 2005–2017*. Accra: Ghana Statistical Service (GSS).

Gyampo, R.E.V. (2015). 'Winner-Takes-All Politics in Ghana: The Case for Effective Council of State', *Journal of Politics & Governance*, 4(1): 20–28.

Gyimah-Boadi, E. (2009). 'A "Liberal" Development State in Ghana: An Emerging Paradigm for Democracy and Economic Growth'. Paper presented at the conference 'From Asymmetry to Symmetry? The West, Non-West and the Idea of Development as Conceptual Flow', 13–16 July. Heidelberg: University of Heidelberg.

Gyimah-Boadi, E., and R. Jeffries (2000). 'The Political Economy of Reform'. In E. Aryeetey, J. Harrigan, and M. Nissanke (eds), *Economic Reforms in Ghana: The Miracle and the Mirage*. Trenton, NJ: Africa World Press, 32–50.

Huang, H.C., Y.C. Lin, and C.C. Yeh (2012). 'An Appropriate Test of the Kuznets Hypothesis', *Applied Economics Letters*, 19(1): 47–51.

Hutchful, E. (2002). *Ghana's Adjustment Experience: The Paradox of Reform*. Geneva: United Nations Research Institute for Social Development.

Jeffries, R. (1992). 'Urban Popular Attitudes Towards the Economic Recovery Programme and the PNDC Government in Ghana', *African Affairs*, 91(363): 207–226.

Killick, T. (1978). *Development Economics in Action: A Study of Economic Policies in Ghana*. London: Heinemann.

Killick, T. (2000). 'Fragile Still: The Structure of Ghana's Economy 1960–94'. In E. Aryeetey, J. Harrigan, and M. Nissanke (eds), *Economic Reforms in Ghana: The Miracle and the Mirage*. Trenton, NJ: Africa World Press, 51–67.

Kim, K., and A Sumner (2019). 'The Five Varieties of Industrialisation: A New Typology of Diverse Empirical Experience in the Developing World'. ESRC GPID Research Network Working Paper, 18. London: ESRC Global Poverty and Inequality Dynamics Research Network (GPID).

Maclean, L. (2010). *Informal Institutions and Citizenship in Rural Africa: Risk and Reciprocity in Ghana and Côte d'Ivoire*. New York: Cambridge University Press.

McMillan, M., and D. Rodrik (2011). 'Globalisation, Structural Change and Productivity Growth'. In M.B. Jansen (ed.), *Making Globalisation Socially Sustainable*. Geneva: International Labour Organisation and World Trade Organisation, 49–84.

McMillan, M., D. Rodrik, and I. Verduzco-Gallo (2014). 'Globalization, Structural Change, and Productivity Growth, with an Update on Africa'. *World Development*, 63(1): 11–32.

Oduro, F., M. Awal, and M. Ashon (2014). 'A Dynamic Mapping of the Political Settlement in Ghana'. ESID Working Paper 28. Manchester: Effective States and Inclusive Development Research Centre, University of Manchester.

Osei, P. (2000). 'Political Liberalisation and the Implementation of Value Added Tax in Ghana', *Journal of Modern African Studies*, 38: 255–278.

Osei, R. (2001). 'A Growth Collapse with Diffuse Resource: Ghana'. In R. Auty (ed.), *Resource Abundance and Economic Development*. Oxford: Oxford University Press, 165–178.

Osei, R. D. (2012). 'Aid, Growth and Private Capital Flows to Ghana'. WIDER Working Paper 22/2012. Helsinki: UNU-WIDER.

Osei, R.D., and R. Jedwab (2017). 'Structural Change in a Poor African Country: New Historical Evidence from Ghana'. In M. McMillan, D. Rodrik, and C. Sepúlveda (eds), *Structural Change, Fundamentals and Growth: A Framework and Case Studies*. Washington, DC: International Food Policy Research Institute, 161–96.

Osei, R.D., C. Ackah, G. Domfe, and M. Danquah (2017). 'Political Settlements and Structural Change: Why Growth Has Not Been Transformational in Ghana'. In L. Pritchett, K. Sen, and E. Werker (2018). *Deals and Development: The Political Dynamics of Growth Episodes*. Oxford: Oxford University Press, 159–162. DOI: https://doi.org/10.1093/oso/9780198801641.001.0001

Osei, R.D., and R. Jedwab (2017). 'Structural Change in a Poor African Country: New Historical Evidence from Ghana'. In M. McMillan, D. Rodrik, and C. Sepúlveda (eds), *Structural Change, Fundamentals and Growth: A Framework and Case Studies* (161–96). Washington DC: International Food Policy Research Institute.

Oteng-Ababio, M., G. Owusu, C. Wrigley-Asante, and A. Owusu (2016). 'Longitudinal Analysis of Trends and Patterns of Crime in Ghana (1980–2010): A New Perspective'., *African Geographical Review*, 35(3): 193–211. DOI: https://doi.org/10.2499/9780896292147_ch4

Resnick, D. (2016). 'Strong Democracy, Weak State: The Political Economy of Ghana's Stalled Structural Transformation'. IFPRI Discussion Paper 01574. Washington, DC: International Food Policy Research Institute.

Rodrik, D. (2013). 'Africa's Structural Transformation Challenge', *Project Syndicate*, 12 December, https://www.project-syndicate.org/commentary/dani-rodrik-shows-why-sub-saharan-africa-s-impressive-economic-performance-is-not-sustainable?barrier=accesspaylog (accessed June 2019).

Rothchild, D. (1991). *Ghana: The Political Economy of Recovery*. Boulder, CO: Lynne Rienner.

Sowa, N. (2002). 'An Assessment of Poverty Reducing Policies and Programmes in Ghana'. A paper prepared for presentation at a MIMAP Workshop on Assessing Poverty Policies, Raba, Morocco, 25–31 January. Ottawa: IDRC.

Timmer, M.P., G.J. de Vries, and K. de Vries (2015). 'Patterns of Structural Change in Developing Countries'. In J. Weiss and M. Tribe (eds), *Routledge Handbook of Industry and Development*. Abingdon: Routledge, 65–83.

UNDP (2015). 'Ghana Millennium Development Goals'. New York: United Nations Development Programme (UNDP), https://www.gh.undp.org/content/ghana/en/home/library/poverty/2015-ghana-millennium-development-goals-report.html (accessed March 2020).

UNU-WIDER (2019). Standardized dataset based on World Income Inequality Database, WIID 4, version 22 February 2019. Helsinki: UNU-WIDER.

Whitfield, L. (2010). 'The State Elite, PRSPs, and Policy Implementation in Aid-dependent Ghana', *Third World Quarterly*, 31(5): 721–737.

World Bank (n.d.-a). 'PovcalNet'. Online analysis tool for global poverty monitoring. Washington, DC: World Bank.

World Bank (n.d.-b). 'World Development Indicators' (data base). Washington, DC: World Bank.

World Bank (1993). *Ghana 2000 and Beyond: Setting the Stage for Accelerated Growth and Poverty Reduction*. Africa Regional Office, Western Africa Department. Washington, DC: World Bank

9

Economic Growth, Rising Inequality, and Deindustrialization

South Africa's Kuznetsian Tension

Haroon Bhorat, Kezia Lilenstein, Morné Oosthuizen, François Steenkamp, and Amy Thornton

1 Introduction

In South Africa, we have an interesting case for contextualizing the 'developer's dilemma'. In 1994, on the eve of South Africa's transition to democracy, we have a semi-industrialized economy re-entering the global economy after a period of economic isolation and political turmoil. Further, we have a country with one of the most unequal societies in the world, ridden with widespread poverty, and plagued by high open unemployment.[1] Thus, we have a developing country that needs to undergo a pattern of structural transformation which drives inclusive economic growth. The South African economy did generate moderate economic growth in the post-apartheid period—certainly prior to the financial crisis in 2009. However, while the economy grew, inequality also rose, poverty decreased slightly but remained endemic, and unemployment swelled.[2] The structure of the economy transformed as it shifted toward services—tertiarization—and underwent secular deindustrialization. As such, we are presented with a Kuznetsian tension where a period of growth-inducing structural transformation has been accompanied by rising inequality (Kuznets 1955).

Further, we have a country that differentiates itself from the rest of the region within which it is located—sub-Saharan Africa. Applying the taxonomy used in Alisjahbana et al. (2020), South Africa can be described as 'structurally developing'

---

[1] In Figure 9.7, we observe a net income Gini of 68.7 in 1993. Kingdon and Knight (2007) measure narrow unemployment at 17 per cent in 1995. Bhorat et al. (2020a) measure the headcount poverty at the US$1.90 line as 29.3 per cent in 1993.

[2] In Figure 9.7, we observe a net income Gini of 73.4 in 2010. The narrow unemployment rate is estimated at 29.1 per cent in 2019 (Statistics South Africa 2020). Bhorat et al. (2020a) measure the headcount poverty at the US$1.90 line as 18.8 per cent in 2014.

Haroon Bhorat, et al., *Economic Growth, Rising Inequality, and Deindustrialization*. In: *The Developer's Dilemma*.
Edited by Armida Salsiah Alisjahbana, Kunal Sen, Andy Sumner, and Arief Anshory Yusuf,
Oxford University Press. © UNU-WIDER (2022). DOI: 10.1093/oso/9780192855299.003.0009

rather than 'structurally underdeveloped'. Further, its pattern of structural transformation for the period 1980–2010 categorizes it as a 'mature transformer' as opposed to the region which is categorized as a 'struggling transformer'. Indeed, it is the most industrialized country within the region, and unlike other countries in the region, it has fully undergone 'de-agriculturalization' and is one of the most urbanized in Africa.

This chapter evaluates structural transformation and inequality dynamics in the South African context. In section 2, we discuss trends in structural transformation from the 1960s onwards. The discussion centres around three analytical periods: (i) 1960–1980, the period of industrialization; (ii) 1981–1993, the period of decline; and (iii) 1994–present, the post-apartheid period. Section 3 provides an examination of the growth and distributive outcomes, in terms of inequality, employment, and inclusive growth, in each period. In section 4, we consider the political economy and policies shaping structural transformation, inequality, and inclusive growth for each period. Section 5 concludes.

2. Trends in structural transformation

Leading into the 1960s, the South African economy was moving along the path of industrialization, while the race-based policies and institutions, which first emerged during the colonial period, and later accelerated under apartheid rule, entrenched a race-based inequality.[3] The early part of the twentieth century saw an agrarian economy shift towards industry, mining at first, followed by manufacturing. Government regulations, such as the Natives Land Act of 1913, effectively eliminated the Black agricultural peasantry and created a mass of workers whose only option in terms of livelihood was to labour on White farms or mines (Bundy 1979). In terms of urbanization, a slew of policies were legislated to facilitate racially segregated urban development, which reflected the economic need for cheap migrant labour to support rapid industrialization, and the political concern of permanent rural–urban migration (Turok 2012). The discovery of diamonds, and later gold, shifted an agrarian economy towards a mineral driven one (Nattrass and Seekings 2010). Gold mining, in particular, was characterized by costly capital-intensive, deep-level mining activity and to ensure the profitability of mines, labour costs had to be kept low. This was achieved by adjusting the labour mix towards the increased employment of Black African labour at the expense of costly White workers. Due to the industry's economic importance, the state wanted to maintain the profitability of mines, but was also concerned with the living standards of the White population, which demanded a 'living' or 'civilized'

---

[3] A more detailed discussion on the pattern of structural transformation and its distributional outcomes in the pre-1960 period can be found in Bhorat et al. (2020a).

wage (Nattrass and Seekings 2010). To balance these two priorities, the state sought to find other sectors of the economy in which to employ White workers at high wages. Thus, the state sought to incentivize the development of the manufacturing sector, which set South Africa's path towards an increasingly industrialized economy leading into the 1960s. However, while the economy was industrializing, Blacks were systematically excluded from, first, land and water, then minerals, capital for investment, and finally human capital, all of which drove a widening inequality between Blacks and Whites, and the economy overall (Wilson 2011).

The post-1960 period is known as the 'winds of change' period, when the process of decolonization and the separation of the UK from its Southern African colonies was formalized. However, this process stalled at the South African borders as separate development took over in the form of formal apartheid systems. Overall, the post-1960 period has been turbulent both politically and economically in South Africa. Considering growth trends and economic structure, the period can be divided into three. The first period was characterized by relatively high economic growth and an expanding manufacturing sector, ending in 1981. The second period was characterized by a combination of challenges—including the after-effects of the oil crisis, the gold boom and bust, and increasing internal and external opposition to apartheid—and culminated in the 1994 democratic elections. The third period, the post-apartheid era, has seen South Africa's reintegration into the global economy and a recovery in economic growth. In the remainder of this section, we detail the patterns of structural transformation in each of these periods.

2.1 Period I: industrialization (pre-1981)

Often referred to as the 'golden age of growth' in South Africa, real gross domestic product (GDP) growth was at its highest since the Second World War during the 1960s, averaging 6.3 and 5.1 per cent per annum over the 1960–1965 and 1965–1970 periods, respectively. Growth lost momentum in the 1970s, with real GDP growth averaging 3.4 per cent over the period 1970–1980, as manufacturing growth stalled and the effects of the oil crisis were felt. This period of growth was driven by the expansion of the services sector, but most importantly, the expansion of the manufacturing sector, and hence the process of industrialization (Figure 9.2).

Leading into the 1960s, industrialization had gained full momentum, culminating in peak industrialization being reached at the start of the 1980s, and hence the period 1960–1980 is marked by what Kim and Sumner (2019) term 'upgrading industrialization' (Figure 9.2). Over this period of manufacturing-led industrialization, the manufacturing share of value-added increased from 15.3 per cent in 1960 to 23.7 per cent in 1980 (Figure 9.1), and thus accounted for just over one-fifth of annual value-added growth (Figure 9.3). In addition, the manufacturing share

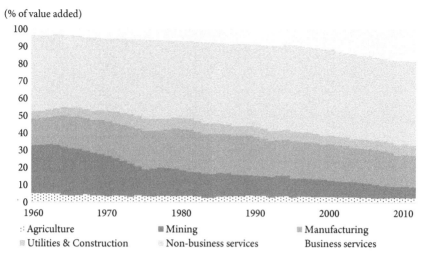

(% of value added)

Agriculture · Mining · Manufacturing · Utilities & Construction · Non-business services · Business services

Fig. 9.1 Composition of value added, South Africa, 1960–2011

Notes: Business services are financial intermediation, renting, business activities; non-business services are: (a) wholesale and retail trade, repair of motor vehicles and motorcycles, personal and household goods, hotels and restaurants; (b) transport, storage, communications; (c) public administration, defence, education, health, social work; and (d) other community activities, social and personal service activities, activities of private households.
Source: authors' calculations based on the Groningen Growth and Development Centre (GGDC) 10-Sector Database Version 2015 (Timmer et al. 2015).

of employment increased from 15.3 to 16.5 per cent over the corresponding period (Figure 9.4). We thus observe a movement of labour towards a high productivity sector. Bhorat et al. (2020a) show that labour productivity almost doubled in the sector over the period.

In tandem with this process of manufacturing-led industrialization, the relative importance of the agricultural sector continued to decline. While value added in the agricultural sector declined from a low base of 5.2 per cent in 1960 to 3.7 per cent in 1980 (Figure 9.1), the effects of de-agriculturalization were most keenly felt in employment. While in 1960 agriculture dominated employment, constituting 48.8 per cent of employment, the sector's share of employment almost halved over the period to 26.0 per cent in 1980 (Figure 9.4). Bhorat et al. (2020a) show that labour productivity in the sector almost tripled over the period. This productivity growth may be partly explained by capital intensification in the sector, since the relative cost of capital fell by approximately 50 per cent over the corresponding period—through a combination of investment subsidies, tax breaks, and negative real interest rates (Nattrass and Seekings 2010).

Further, we observe a marked shift towards the services sector over this period. It is evident in Figure 9.1 that value added in the services sector (business services plus non-business services) increased from 47.4 per cent in 1960 to 51.6 per cent in 1980. The corresponding expansion in employment was much starker, increasing

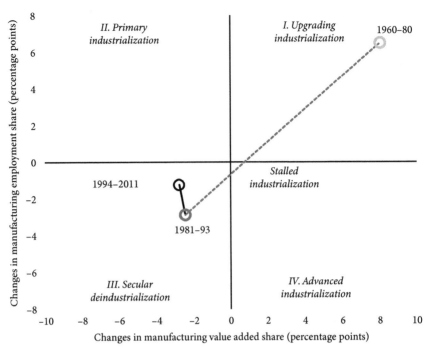

Fig. 9.2 Varieties of structural transformation in South Africa, 1960–2011

Source: authors' illustration based on Kim and Sumner (2019).

by 13.4 percentage points to 42.0 per cent in 1980. This pattern of tertiarization would continue in subsequent decades.

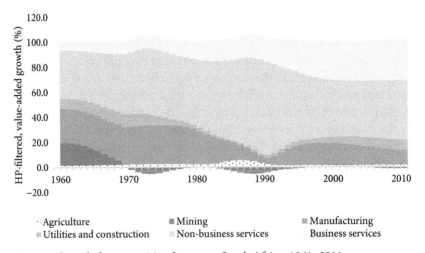

Fig. 9.3 Growth decomposition by sector, South Africa, 1961–2011

Source: authors' calculations based on the GGDC 10-Sector Database Version 2015 (Timmer et al. 2015).

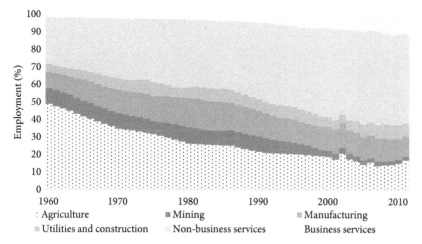

Fig. 9.4 Composition of employment, South Africa, 1960–2011

Source: authors' calculations based on the GGDC 10-Sector Database Version 2015 (Timmer et al. 2015).

Period I (1960–1980) is one marked by substantial labour productivity growth and hence growth-inducing structural transformation. Bhorat et al. (2020a) show that aggregate labour productivity more than doubled over the period, equivalent to an average annual growth rate of 3.6 per cent. Applying the methodology of McMillan and Rodrik (2011), which decomposes labour productivity growth into within-sector and between-sector elements, it is evident that between-sector productivity growth, and hence structural transformation, played a key role in driving productivity growth over the period (Figure 9.5). As alluded to above, and evident in Figure 9.6a, this productivity growth was driven by a movement of labour towards the relatively high productivity manufacturing and services sectors.

Consistent with the region within which it lies, South Africa started the period as, what Alisjahbana, et al. (2020) term, 'structurally underdeveloped'. However, over a comparable period, South Africa outperformed the region, and ended the period as 'structurally developing'. In fact, South Africa's pattern of structural transformation over this period was more in line with that experienced in developing East Asia. Given South Africa's pattern of structural transformation over this period, using the taxonomy developed by Alisjahbana et al. (2020), South Africa is termed a 'catching-up reformer', while its home region is termed a 'struggling transformer'.

2.2 Period II: decline (1981–1993)

Moving from the 1970s to the 1980s, economic growth decelerated to such an extent that real GDP per capita growth contracted between 1980 and 1995. Both internal and external factors played a role in this contractionary period. Slow

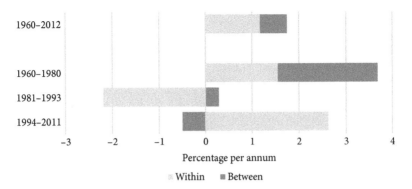

Fig. 9.5 Decomposition of labour productivity growth, South Africa, 1960–2011

Note: decomposition uses the methodology of McMillan and Rodrik (2011).
Source: authors' calculations based on the GGDC 10-Sector Database Version 2015 (Timmer et al. 2015).

growth was not unique to South Africa, with the Western world only just emerging from the recession of the early 1970s, which was at least partially driven by the Organization of the Petroleum Exporting Countries (OPEC) oil crises. The mid-1980s also saw a decline in gold exports and the depreciation of the exchange rate after the collapse of the 1970s commodity price boom, which resulted directly in a declining level of output (Bell and Madula 2001). At the same time, there was growing international opposition to apartheid and rising political instability. This contributed to a substantial increase in debt, and a sharp fall in foreign direct investment (FDI) inflows.

Period II is characterized by the onset of a pattern of 'secular deindustrialization' and the increasing tertiarization of the economy, both of which continued into the twenty-first century. It is evident in Figures 9.1 and 9.4 that both manufacturing's value-added share and employment share declined over the period. Drawing on Kim and Sumner (2019), South Africa's industrialization path, which shifts from 'upgrading industrialization' in period I, to 'secular deindustrialization' in period II, is consistent with a 'premature deindustrialization path' (Figure 9.2). Agriculture's share of employment declines from constituting one-quarter of all jobs in 1981 to one-fifth in 1993, while its share of value added remains constant. The services sector continued to expand, with its employment share growing from 41.3 per cent in 1981 to 51.9 per cent in 1993. Similarly, the sector's share of value added increased from 44.5 to 49.1 per cent. Thus, this sector grew to constitute one-half of the South African economy.

The decline in manufacturing, and the general collapse of the economy, is related to the deterioration of economy-wide investment, as downstream manufacturing goods are particularly sensitive to levels of investment in the economy (Bell and Madula 2001). Manufacturing, in general, is an import-intensive industry and was particularly badly hit by the rising price of imports resulting from the

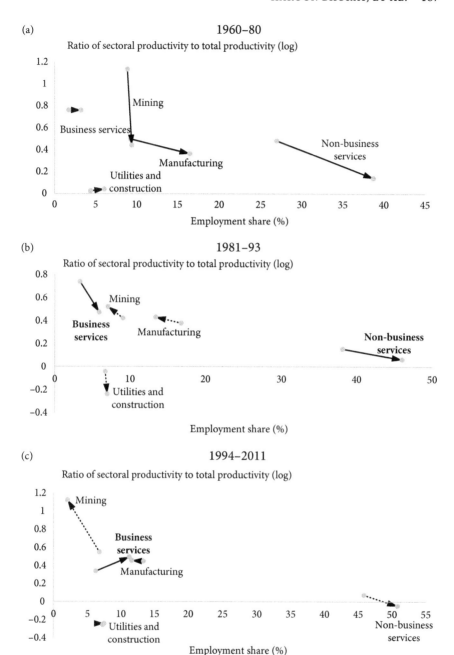

Fig. 9.6 Changes in labour productivity and employment share, South Africa, 1960–2011

Note: Sectors with higher than economy-wide average labour productivity that experienced an increase in employment share are in bold.
Source: authors' calculations based on the GGDC 10-Sector Database Version 2015 (Timmer et al. 2015).

depreciation of the exchange rate (Bell and Madula 2001). The regression of the manufacturing sector corresponds with the sector's weak export performance. The decline in manufacturing exports can also be linked to increased competition coming from the intrusion of Asian Newly Industrialized Countries (NICs) into the world market. Furthermore, South Africa had become increasingly isolated in the face of stringent economic sanctions put in place in opposition to the apartheid government.

In comparison to period I, period II is marked by declining labour productivity growth, and hence growth-reducing structural transformation. Figure 9.5 shows that labour productivity declined, on average, 1.9 per cent per annum over the period, and that this decline was driven by within-sector variation. We observe in Figure 9.6b that labour resources moved away from the relatively high productivity mining and manufacturing sectors towards the services sector, however, primarily towards the relatively lower productivity non-business services sector. The pattern of structural transformation arising in this period, driven by tertiarization, especially in non-business services, is consistent with that experienced by the Latin American region over the period 1980 to 2010. Alisjahbana et al. (2020) categorize this pattern of structural transformation as being consistent with a 'mature transformer'.

2.3   Period III: the post-apartheid period (1994–present)

With the end of apartheid in 1994, economic growth reignited as economic sanctions were removed, FDI surged, and trade policy was liberalized in the late 1990s. This growth was relatively robust, at least until the global financial crisis. From a low of 0.9 per cent per annum in the 1990–1995 period, growth averaged above 3 per cent per annum in the 2000–2005 and 2005–2010 periods, before moderating during the 2010s (see Figure 1 in Bhorat et al. 2020a).

The pattern of premature deindustrialization, which took root in the 1980s, continued into the twenty-first century. As evident in Figures 9.1 and 9.4, the share of manufacturing in both value added and employment declined in the post-apartheid period, which Kim and Sumner (2019) would label 'secular deindustrialization'.

Overall, there has been a general inability of the manufacturing sector to drive substantial increases in output and employment. The reasons for this are numerous. Bell and Madula (2001) argue that the manufacturing sector's general inability to recover as a key driver of growth in South Africa is driven by the 'external constraint', increased global competition, and generally adverse conditions for investment over the period. Furthermore, South Africa is experiencing a scarcity of high-skilled workers. Bhorat (2001) shows that there have been substantial increases in the demand for highly skilled workers in the manufacturing sector, coupled with a decline in demand for skilled and unskilled workers. With the growing services sector also demanding highly skilled workers, the manufacturing sector is struggling to compete with these skills-intensive industries for workers. This has contributed to an inability to penetrate skills-intensive, high-tech manufacturing subsectors.

Correspondingly, the services sector continued to expand to such an extent that by the 2000s, South Africa had become a de facto services-based economy (Bhorat et al. 2018). By 1999, non-business services accounted for one in every two workers, while the sector's share of value added averaged approximately 49 per cent over the post-apartheid period (Figures 9.1 and 9.4). It was during this period that business services started to expand more rapidly. The sector's share of value added more than doubled from 8.7 per cent in 1994 to 18.4 per cent in 2011, with the sector accounting for close to one-third of annual value-added growth in the 2000s (Figure 9.3). The business services employment share almost doubled from 6.2 per cent in 1994 to 11.3 per cent in 2011. However, employment growth in this high-productivity services sector needs to be tempered by the fact that a large share of employment in this sector is through the use by employers of temporary employment services (TES) firms[4] (Bhorat et al. 2018). Bhorat et al. (2018) show that low-skill, low-wage TES employment has risen substantially in the post-apartheid period—TES employment made up 61 per cent of total business services employment in 2014.

The post-apartheid period again sees labour productivity growth (2.1 per cent per annum) and thus growth-inducing structural transformation. However, unlike the growth experienced in period I, where productivity growth was driven by between sector changes, in period III, productivity growth was driven by within-sector changes (Figure 9.5). Interestingly, as labour moves to the services sector over this period, the movement is either to relatively high-productivity business services or to relatively low-productivity non-business services (Figure 9.6c). This pattern is consistent with that observed in Latin America—a 'mature transformer' (Alisjahbana et al. 2020).

3. Income inequality, employment, and inclusive growth

3.1 Period I: industrialization (pre-1981)

Unsurprisingly given the unequal economic access legislated along racial lines, the 1960s and 1970s is a period characterized by high levels of income inequality. Looking at Figure 9.7, the net income Gini coefficient began the period at 54, rose to a high of 63.5 in 1975, and dropped to 51.3 in 1980.

---

[4] TES workers are employed through third-party companies and perform activities such as cleaning or security services at formal sector firms.

However, it is likely that the Gini coefficient estimates, taken from a standard-ized dataset (UNU-WIDER 2019) based on the World Income Inequality Database (WIID), for this period and going into the 1980s, are underestimated. Wittenberg (2015) critiques a comparable dataset with similar Gini coefficient levels for this period—the Standardized World Income Inequality Database (SWIID) developed by Frederick Solt—and argues that the estimates are too low.[5] Wittenberg (2015) noted four potential sources of error: measurement error, model error, imputa-tion error, and sampling error. The WIID is likely to suffer from similar sources of error. Wittenberg (2015) notes that the Simkins (1979) Gini coefficient estimate of 0.71 for 1970 is more in line with the political and social realities of the time. Sim-ilar sentiments are expressed by Seekings and Nattrass (2005), who cite McGrath's (1983) estimate of 0.68 for 1975. As such, the Net income Gini estimate at 63.5 in Figure 9.7, rather than being an outlier, is likely to be a more realistic estimate.

Regarding the trend in income inequality over this period, Seekings and Nat-trass (2005: 303) contend that overall, inequality levels changed little during the second half of the twentieth century. This is evident when the authors cite Gini coefficient estimates from Whiteford and van Seventer (2000) of 0.68, 0.68 and 0.69, for the years 1975, 1991, and 1996, respectively. Returning to the estimates in Figure 9.7, apart from the data point in 1975, the trends in inequality levels do seem to remain relatively stable over period I. However, as discussed above, in level terms, it is more likely that the Gini coefficient estimates were closer to that estimated for 1975. The estimates in Figure 9.7 also show that inequality started to

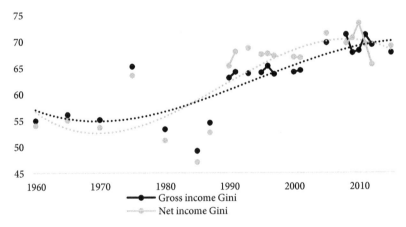

Fig. 9.7 Gross and net income Gini, South Africa, 1960–2015

Source: UNU-WIDER World Income Inequality Database (WIID).

---

[5] Wittenberg (2015) also notes that the WIID (Version 3A), while having higher Gini estimates than the SWIID, also underestimates the level of income inequality during this period.

decline slightly towards the end of the 1970s, going into the 1980s, the reasons for which we discuss in the next subsection.

As such, period I is characterized by upgrading industrialization and thus growth-inducing structural transformation, coupled with very high, yet stable (slightly declining into the 1980s) levels of income inequality. Therefore, applying the taxonomy of Alisjahbana et al. (2020), depicted in Figure 9.8, South Africa experienced a weak and benign Kuznets tension over this period.

Baymul and Sen (2020), find that contrary to the Kuznets (1955) hypothesis, the movement of workers to manufacturing unambiguously decreases income inequality. Taking their findings into account, arguably this period of upgrading industrialization played a role in keeping inequality levels stable, while the potential inequality-decreasing effects that they speak of are likely to have been tempered by apartheid legislation. Race-based policies, such as the 'civilised labour' policy, exclusion of Blacks from the industrial relations system, and legislation in the form of the 1953 Bantu Education Act that undermined Black accumulation of human capital, were designed to keep Black workers out of relatively higher-paying skill-intensive occupations, which suppressed occupational mobility and wage growth. Ultimately, the potential for this economic boom period to lower inequality levels, which at this stage were driven by inter-racial inequality, was curtailed by political-economy considerations.

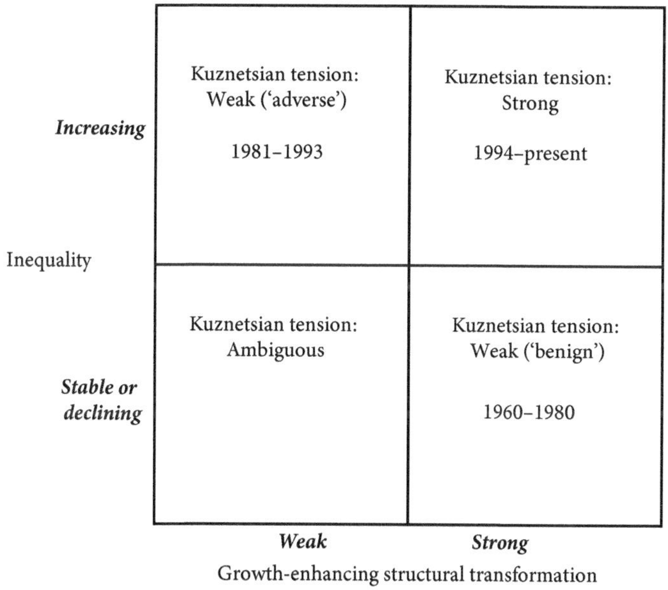

	Weak	Strong
Increasing	Kuznetsian tension: Weak ('adverse') 1981–1993	Kuznetsian tension: Strong 1994–present
Stable or declining	Kuznetsian tension: Ambiguous	Kuznetsian tension: Weak ('benign') 1960–1980

Inequality (vertical axis label); Growth-enhancing structural transformation (horizontal axis label)

Fig. 9.8 Patterns of Kuznetsian tension in South Africa, 1960–present

Source: authors' illustration based on Alisjahbana et al. (2020).

3.2 Period II: decline (1981–1993)

While inequality rose on aggregate during this period, we observe a slight decline in inequality levels in the 1980s, and then rising inequality towards the end of the apartheid period (Figure 9.7). van der Berg and Bhorat (1999) assert that the declining inequality of the 1980s is a result of the racial wage gap narrowing over the period. They note that higher levels of education, increased occupational mobility of Black Africans, and the rise of powerful Black trade unions, are contributing factors to the narrowing racial wage gap.

The shifting dynamics of the labour market contributed to the structure of inequality changing over time, certainly as it began to rise in the post-apartheid period. Employment growth lagged labour market growth, leading to rising unemployment in the period. By 1994, about one-half of all economically active South Africans were unable to find formal-sector employment (van der Berg and Bhorat 1999). Whiteford and van Seventer (2000) show that the driver of income inequality in South Africa shifted over the period from inter-racial inequality to intra-racial inequality.

Although we observe some inequality-reducing effects in the 1980s, that may be a result of the manufacturing-led industrialization in period I; this period marks the initiation of premature deindustrialization accompanied by the increased tertiarization of the economy, which is accompanied by rising inequality. This period of deindustrialization and tertiarization aligns with Baymul and Sen (2020), who find that the movement of labour into services has an increasing effect on inequality for countries at an early stage of structural transformation—they categorize South Africa as structurally developing. Applying the taxonomy of Alisjahbana et al. (2020), the combination of rising inequality and weak growth-enhancing structural transformation meant that South Africa experienced a weak and adverse Kuznetsian tension over this period (Figure 9.8).

3.3 Period III: the post-apartheid period (1994–present)

The high levels of inequality faced by South Africans during apartheid persisted into the post-apartheid era. Looking at Figure 9.7, it appears that inequality levels were slightly higher in the 2000s (mean gross income Gini of 68.2) relative to the 1990s (mean gross income Gini of 64.0). Indeed, the consensus is that inequality has either not changed or has increased since 1994, despite the dismantling of discriminatory legislation (Wittenberg 2017). This increase comes mainly from a rise in within-race inequality among Black Africans, as some members of the population have succeeded in advancing economically (Wittenberg 2017).

The manner in which the economy has structurally transformed in the post-apartheid period provides insight into these persistently high and rising inequality levels. As mentioned earlier, the economy has continued along the path of prema-ture deindustrialization, and the continued tertiarization of the economy resulted in services-led growth. This pattern of structural transformation coupled with ris-ing inequality is consistent with Baymul and Sen (2020), who find that services-led structural transformation for countries at the early stages of structural transfor-mation, such as South Africa, is inequality-enhancing. They also find that this inequality-enhancing effect may be stronger for business relative to non-business services, which is consistent with South Africa's experience where business ser-vices growth was particularly strong in period III. Drawing on Alisjahbana et al. (2020), this structural transformation-inequality pattern has a strong Kuznetsian tension—see Figure 9.8.

The relationship between structural transformation and inequality can also be viewed in terms of changes in wage income across the distribution (Bhorat et al. 2020b). Plotting the average annualized growth rate of real monthly earnings for the period 2000–2015 against wage percentiles, shows a u-shaped pattern con-sistent with wage polarization (see Figure 15 in Bhorat et al. 2020a). Wages at the bottom and top of the distribution increase, with the magnitude substantially greater for the latter, while wages in the middle of the distribution remain stag-nant or decrease. Inequality-decreasing growth at the bottom of the distribution can be linked to the implementation of and increases in minimum wages over the period. There has also been a proliferation of low-paid jobs associated with the burgeoning services sector, such as TES workers in the business services sector, and other low-skilled service-sector workers (Bhorat et al. 2020b). The stagnation of wages in the middle of the distribution can be attributed, at least partially, to the changing structure of the economy, such as the decline of manufacturing under premature deindustrialization. Further, increases in the general level of education and the rapid increase in medium-skilled workers meant that a large pool of sim-ilarly educated people were competing for jobs, particularly manufacturing jobs, that were easy to offshore and substitute with technology. Inequality-increasing wage growth at the top of the distribution is associated with increasing returns to high-skilled work as well as more analytical, decision-making, and creative tasks being required by the high-skilled business and finance services sector (Bhorat et al. 2020b).

The failure of the education system to provide quality education to the majority of the population has led to a severe skills shortage in the economy, which ham-pers the country's ability to drive inclusive economic growth.[6] The combination of the sluggish transformation of the education system and increasing demand for high-skilled workers associated with services-led structural transformation has

---

[6] Spaull (2013) shows that South Africa still has the worst education system of all middle-income countries that participate in cross-national assessments of educational achievement, and also performs worse than many low-income countries.

only exacerbated South Africa's unemployment problem, with the unemployment rate estimated at 29.1 per cent in 2019 (Statistics South Africa 2020). The overall result is a shortage of highly educated, high-skilled workers and insufficient demand for low-skilled workers.

In summary, South Africa entered the post-apartheid period with a socially engineered high level of inequality established along racial lines, and this has changed little. Despite intra-racial inequality becoming increasingly important over the period, inter-racial inequality is still key to understanding inequality in South Africa. The inability to substantially shift inequality levels is linked to a failure of the economy to generate inclusive pro-poor growth, in part due to the generally tepid performance of the economy. As growth has continued to be weak, the economy has failed to create jobs even close to the rate needed to employ all active labour market participants.

4. Political economy and policies shaping structural transformation, inequality, and inclusive growth

4.1 Period I: industrialization (pre-1981)

The origin and character of inequality in South Africa can be traced back to its colonial roots, which were further entrenched after the discovery of gold at the end of the nineteenth century. Keeping labour costs low was a critical way in which the profit of the mines was sustained. A series of sophisticated labour market institutions were set up between 1910 and 1930 to preserve a 'civilized' standard of living for the White population group. Thus, the ratio of earnings of White to Black African workers was about 10:1 during the inter-war period. The government also set up a White welfare state, including the introduction of a state non-contributory pension and other social assistance, as well as generous state investment in White public education (Nattrass and Seekings 2010).

In order to establish a Black African labour base to supply the White urban economic centres with labour, the apartheid government spatially segregated the country, establishing ten 'nominally self-governing territories (homelands') where Black African people were expected to live, and regulated urbanization through policy such as 'influx control'. Black Africans living in the cities were evicted and forcibly relocated to the homelands, which were rural and marginalized from economic opportunities. However, urbanization of Black Africans did increase over this period as townships started to emerge and authorization to live in this urban setting was based on whether a person had employment in the city or was born there. Apartheid policies served to keep the Black African population landless, largely unskilled, and, while concentrated far from work opportunities, dependent on wage labour (Nattrass and Seekings 2010).

A key factor contributing to South Africa's period of industrialization was the import-substituting policies pursued by the government between 1925 and 1973, the aim of which was to stimulate domestic manufacturing and state investment (Schneider 2000). This, as well as the development of a 'mineral energy complex'— the extraction of raw materials coupled with state support, including low-cost energy—was a driving factor in the growth of the manufacturing industry (Black et al. 2016). Indeed, the period was one of direct and indirect state support for industry, in the form of cheap energy and other incentives, with the state-owned Industrial Development Corporation (IDC) playing a central role in promoting the development of heavy industry (Black et al. 2016). Other large, state-owned corporations were run with the aim of stimulating domestic manufacturing and providing cheap imports for the mining industry.

The rapid expansion of the economy, driven by manufacturing-led industrialization, necessitated at least the partial weakening of some of South Africa's race-based labour market policies. The ongoing need to promote economic growth eventually led to shifts in occupational mobility and increased wages for Black workers. With industry booming, it was increasingly difficult to rely solely on White employees (van der Berg et al. 2001). This resulted in a reclassification of jobs, which allowed for restricted movement of Black workers into jobs which were previously demarcated for White workers. This increase in bargaining power was mirrored in the marked increase in unionization after Black unions were legalized in 1979 (van der Berg et al. 2001). Thus, the political landscape was inextricably linked to the movements of structural transformation and inequality at the time.

4.2 Period II: decline (1981–1993)

While the growth in the manufacturing sector in period I has been attributed to the government's policy of import substitution, its continued pursuit of this and other protectionist policies contributed to the decline in period II. These policies weakened the efficiency of South African producers, and the manufacturing sector's competitiveness vis-à-vis foreign manufacturers was undermined (Hausman 2008). This led to a shift towards a policy of export-orientated industrialization in what were essentially the conditions of an economic crisis. In 1983, a deliberate process of import liberalization was instituted, and in 1989 systems of duty-free imports-for-exports were instilled in downstream manufacturing subsectors, such as textiles and clothing (Bell and Madula 2001). Between 1990 and 1995, export subsidies were introduced and import surcharges were removed. However, Edwards and Lawrence (2008) argue that, overall, there was a strong shift towards protectionism in the mid-to-late 1980s. Regardless, the outcome was that the economy did not recover, and growth in real GDP per capita was negative over the period.

While the economy struggled due to poor economic conditions globally, South Africa's specific history also exacerbated this period of poor growth and deindustrialization. This was a period of growing opposition to the apartheid government, and South Africa became increasingly economically isolated. Political turmoil was increasing in the form of both violent and non-violent active resistance such as mass strikes, boycotts, and protests. This culminated in the government declaring a state of emergency in 1986 and detaining thousands of its political opponents without trial. In the same year, the Comprehensive Anti-Apartheid Act was passed by the US Congress, imposing sanctions on South Africa and bolstering an ongoing disinvestment campaign.

Thus, a combination of factors external and internal to South Africa contributed to the economic decline in this period.

4.3 Period III: the post-apartheid period (1994–present)

The post-apartheid government was faced with severe structural complexities and the triad of high open unemployment, severe income inequality, and widespread poverty. In order to address the apartheid-era policies, which led to these conditions, the post-apartheid period has seen a myriad of macro-economic policies emerge and then fade—starting with the Reconstruction and Development Programme, followed by the Growth, Employment and Redistribution plan, the Accelerated and Shared Growth Initiative, and most recently the National Development Plan (NDP), which was implemented in 2013. The NDP lays out a panoptical, long-term vision for South Africa. It includes a comprehensive range of development goals for 2030, including growing the economy at 5 per cent per annum, universal access to broadband internet, the elimination of poverty, a reduction of inequality, and an almost doubling of the number of people in employment in order to achieve an economy at virtually full employment (National Planning Commission 2012).

In order to address the racial inequalities specifically, the African National Congress (ANC) implemented broad-based Black economic empowerment (B-BBEE) in 2003 as a key component of dismantling the White stranglehold on the South African economy. B-BBEE is a direct intervention aimed at redistributing assets and opportunities in order to pursue an economy representative of the racial demographics in the country. However, twenty-five years after the end of apartheid, corporate South Africa continues to be managed and owned primarily by the minority White population, and the distribution of B-BBEE-related benefits has led to the personal enrichment of prominent, well-connected figures. Overall, both the scope of the policy and its outcomes remain unclear, and controversy surrounding the effectiveness of the policy is growing.

The post-apartheid growth strategy sought to promote international competitiveness, trade liberalization, and support for non-mineral-based subsectors with high value-added activities (Black and Roberts 2009). The Industrial Policy Action Plan (IPAP) outlines a number of policy interventions aiming to achieve structural change by encouraging the growth of the manufacturing sector. Despite this, South Africa has experienced continued deindustrialization with concurrent tertiarization. In recent years, trade liberalization has hit import-competing industries hard and there has been a striking collapse in exports in a number of subsectors of the manufacturing industry, particularly downstream durable goods.

Given that the sectors currently driving growth are skills-intensive, this has contributed to the phenomenon of 'job-poor growth'. In other words, economic growth has generated an insufficient number of jobs relative to the large increase in labour market entrants. Persistently high unemployment rates have therefore necessitated the design of appropriate labour market policies to increase labour market access for marginalized South Africans. To this end, South Africa has implemented active labour market policies in the form of a job retraining scheme, two variants of a public employment scheme, and a firm-based wage subsidy intervention. While these schemes have seen some success, they have had limited impact on the pervasive unemployment levels in the economy (Bhorat et al. 2019).

One of the more prominent pro-poor policies has been the widening and deepening of social security in the post-apartheid period. In 2018, 18 million people were covered by social security (National Treasury 2019), up from 4 million in 1994. There are seven government grants available, including the old age grant, the child support grant, and the disability grant. The expansion of government grants has been a crucial component of the promotion of sustainable livelihoods for the poor. Leibbrandt et al. (2012) find that in 1993, government grants comprised 15 per cent of income in the poorest income decile. By 2008, this had increased to 73 per cent.

The labour market continues to be a major driver of overall inequality. Lack of access to labour market income, and inequality of income earned, accounts for more than 80 per cent of total inequality in 1993 and 2008 (Leibbrandt et al. 2012). In order to combat wage inequality, the government introduced the first minimum wage in the contract cleaning sector in 1999. By 2015, there were nine sectoral minimum wages which covered 31 per cent of the formal sector (ILO 2015). Most of these sectors experienced annual real increases in their wages with the onset of a minimum wage (Bhorat et al. 2016). Further, in January 2019, the government implemented a national minimum wage (NMW) of ZAR20 an hour.

This discussion highlights the fact that the government is committed to the idea of South Africa becoming a 'developmental state'. Overall, however, the country's turbulent and complex history has had a long-lasting effect on its ability to actualize pro-poor and inclusive growth. The alignment of the colonial and apartheid state with the business sector and the centrality of the labour movement in mobilizing resistance to apartheid have resulted in deep-seated antipathy between labour and business that persists today. This has meant that it has been extremely difficult to generate a national consensus on the country's future development path. At the same time, a rising public-sector wage bill, corruption, and weak economic and employment growth have considerably limited the state's ability to make the appropriate investments required to direct or facilitate economic transformation.

5. Conclusion

Over the period 1960–1980, South Africa enjoyed growth-enhancing structural transformation, driven by 'upgrading industrialization'. Productivity growth was driven by a shift of labour resources from the low-productivity agricultural sector towards the high-productivity manufacturing sector. Consequently, the South African economy shifted from being 'structurally underdeveloped', as was the case with the majority of countries in the region, to being 'structurally developing'. Relating this pattern of structural change to inequality, which remained high but stable over the period, we observe a weak and benign Kuznetsian tension.

However, if a movement of labour to manufacturing decreases inequality, which Baymul and Sen (2020) find to be the case, then ultimately, South Africa missed an opportunity to undergo a period of inequality-decreasing growth. Undoubtedly, the oppressive race-based apartheid laws of the time hindered the economic advancement of Black Africans, which in turn limited these inequality decreasing effects. These laws, hindering the economic advancement of Black Africans; regulated the extent to which they could urbanize and work in city factories; limited the accumulation of human capital among Black Africans, and thus their ability to advance in the labour market; curtailed job mobility and the bargaining power among Black Africans; excluded Black Africans from certain skilled occupations; and ultimately limited the supply of skilled labour needed by a growing manufacturing sector.

What followed in the 1980s was a period of decline, with sluggish GDP growth rates, and the onset of premature deindustrialization. This was driven by both poor global conditions and growing economic isolation due to South Africa's ongoing political system of legalized racial oppression. Overall, inequality increased over this period, and combined with growth-reducing structural transformation, we observe a weak and adverse Kuznetsian tension. Ultimately, the apartheid edifice unravelled, and South Africa transitioned into the post-apartheid period.

It is within the post-apartheid period that the developer's dilemma becomes apparent in the South African context, for during this period a strong Kuznetsian tension emerges. Structural transformation is characterized by continued secular deindustrialization and accelerated tertiarization. The growth-inducing structural transformation over this period is driven by the expansion of the services sector, particularly business services. Furthermore, inequality continues to rise in a society with the highest level of inequality in the world. This structural transformation–inequality pattern is consistent with Baymul and Sen (2020), who find that the movement of labour to services, particularly business services, at the early stages of structural transformation, increases inequality. South Africa's pattern of structural transformation over this period is consistent with that of a 'mature transformer', which aligns more with Latin American countries than with the 'struggling transformers' in its own region. Further, in contrast to South Africa's strong Kuznetsian tension, the sub-Saharan Africa region is characterized by weak structural transformation and stable inequality, thus experiencing an ambiguous Kuznetsian tension over this period.

The structural transformation pathway laid out in this chapter has left South Africa in a similar position to that of many African countries—where the inclusive growth path is not straightforward, and the historical road map of industrialization as the growth and employment driver in the economy is no longer applicable. South Africa will therefore need to strategize around attempting to revitalize a flagging manufacturing sector, which has thus far failed to be competitive, or attempt a services-led growth path, with the aim of absorbing the country's large supply of low-skilled unemployed into employment. Establishing a successful pro-poor growth path is essential to combat the persistently high levels of inequality in the economy and to create sustainable livelihoods for those previously excluded from economic opportunities.

References

Alisjahbana, A.S., K. Kim, K. Sen, A. Sumner, and A. Yusuf (2020). 'The Developer's Dilemma: A Survey of Structural Transformation and Inequality Dynamics'. WIDER Working Paper 35/2020. Helsinki: UNU-WIDER.

Baymul, C., and K. Sen (2020). 'Was Kuznets Right? New Evidence on the Relationship between Structural Transformation and Inequality', *Journal of Development Studies*, 56(9): 1643–1662.

Bell, T., and N. Madula (2001). 'Where Has All the Growth Gone? South African Manufacturing Industry 1970–2000'. Trade and Industrial Policy Strategies Annual Forum, Misty Hills, Muldersdrift, South Africa, August.

Bhorat, H. (2001). 'Employment Trends in South Africa'. Occasional Paper 2. Johannesburg: Friedrich Ebert Stiftung.

Bhorat, H., T. Caetano, B. Jourdan, R. Kanbur, C. Rooney, B. Stanwix, and I. Woolard (2016). 'Investigating the Feasibility of a National Minimum Wage for South Africa'. Working Paper 2016/01. Cape Town: DPRU, University of Cape Town.

Bhorat, H., C. Rooney, and F. Steenkamp (2018). 'Understanding and Characterizing the Services Sector in South Africa: An Overview'. In R. Newfarmer, J. Page, and F.

Tarp (eds), *Industries without Smokestacks: Industrialization in Africa Reconsidered*. Chapter 14, pp. 275–295 Oxford: Oxford University Press.

Bhorat, H., K. Lilenstein and F. Steenkamp. (2019). 'Labour Market Policy Responses Amid Globalization: The Case of South Africa. In M. Bacchetta, E. Milet, and J. Monteiro (eds), *Making Globalization More Inclusive: Lessons from Experience with Adjustment Policies*. Chapter 7, pp.163–182 Geneva: WTO Publications.

Bhorat, H., K. Lilenstein, M. Oosthuizen, and A. Thornton (2020a). 'Structural Transformation, Inequality, and Inclusive Growth in South Africa'. WIDER Working Paper 50/2020. Helsinki: UNU-WIDER.

Bhorat, H., K. Lilenstein, M. Oosthuizen, and A. Thornton (2020b). 'Wage Polarisation in a High Inequality Emerging Economy: The Case of South Africa'. WIDER Working Paper 55/2020. Helsinki: UNU-WIDER.

Black, A., and S. Roberts (2009). 'The Evolution and Impact of Industrial and Competition Policies'. In J. Aron, S.B. Kahn, and G. Kingdon (eds), *South African Economic Policy since Democracy*. Chapter 8, pp. 211–243 Cape Town: Oxford University Press.

Black, A., S. Craig, and P. Dunne (2016). 'Capital Intensity, Industrial Policy and Employment in the South African Manufacturing Sector'. REDI3x3 Working paper 23. Cape Town: REDI (Research Project on Employment, Income Distribution and Inclusive Growth).

Bundy, C. (1979). *The Rise and Fall of the South African Peasantry*. Berkeley and Los Angeles, CA: University of California Press.

Edwards, L., and R. Lawrence (2008). 'South African Trade Policy Matters: Trade Performance and Trade Policy', *Economics of Transition*, 16(4): 585–608.

Hausmann, R. (2008). 'Final Recommendations of the International Panel on ASGISA'. Pretoria: National Treasury, http://www.treasury.gov.za/comm_media/press/2008/Final%20Recommendations%20of%20the%20International%20Panel.pdf (accessed 31 July 2019).

ILO (2015). *Towards a South African National Minimum Wage: National Minimum Wage Booklet*. Geneva: International Labour Organization and Labour Research Service.

Kim, K., and A. Sumner (2019). 'The Five Varieties of Industrialization: A New Typology of Diverse Empirical Experience in the Developing World'. ESRC GPID Research Network Working Paper 18. London: ESRC Global Poverty and Inequality Dynamics Research Network (GPID).

Kingdon, G. and J. Knight. (2007). 'Unemployment in South Africa, 1995–2003: Causes, Problems and Policies', *Journal of African Economies*, 16(5): 813–848.

Kuznets, S. (1955). 'Economic Growth and Income Inequality', *American Economic Review*, 45(1): 1–28.

Leibbrandt, M., A. Finn, and I. Woolard (2012). 'Describing and Decomposing Post-Apartheid Income Inequality in South Africa', *Development Southern Africa*, 29(1): 19–34.

McGrath, M. (1983). 'The Distribution of Personal Income in South Africa in Selected Years over the Period from 1945 to 1980'. Ph.D. Dissertation. Durban: University of Natal.

McMillan, M.S., and D. Rodrik (2011). 'Globalization, Structural Change and Productivity Growth'. NBER Working Paper 17143. Cambridge, MA: National Bureau of Economic Research.

National Planning Commission (2012). *Our Future—Make It Work: National Development Plan 2030*. Cape Town: Department of The Presidency, South Africa.

National Treasury (2019). *Budget Review 2019*. Pretoria: National Treasury, http://www.treasury.gov.za/documents/national%20budget/2019/review/FullBR.pdf (accessed 31 July 2019).

Nattrass, N., and J. Seekings (2010) 'The Economy and Poverty in the Twentieth Century in South Africa'. Centre for Social Science Research Working Paper 276. Cape Town: University of Cape Town.

Schneider, G.E. (2000). 'The Development of the Manufacturing Sector in South Africa', *Journal of Economic Issues*, 34(2): 413–424.

Seekings, J. and N. Nattrass (2005). *Class, Race and Inequality in South Africa*. New Haven, CT and London: Yale University Press.

Simkins, C. (1979). 'The Distribution of Personal Income among Income Recipients, 1970 and 1976'. DSRG Working Paper 9. Pietermaritzburg: Development Studies Research Group, University of Natal, http://opendocs.ids.ac.uk/opendocs/ (accessed 7 October 2021).

Spaull, N. (2013). *South Africa's Education Crisis: The Quality of Education in South Africa 1994–2011*. Johannesburg: Centre for Development and Enterprise.

Statistics South Africa (2020). 'Statistical Release P0211. Quarterly Labour Force Survey: Quarter 2, 2019'. Pretoria: Statistics South Africa.

Timmer, M., G. de Vries, and K. de Vries (2015). 'Patterns of Structural Change in Developing Countries'. In J. Weiss, and M. Tribe (eds), *Routledge Handbook of Industry and Development*. London: Routledge, 65–83.

Turok, I. (2012). 'Urbanisation and Development in South Africa: Economic Imperatives. Spatial Distortions and Strategic Responses'. Urbanization and Emerging Population Issues Working Paper 8. London: Human Settlements Group.

UNU-WIDER (2019). Standardized dataset based on World Income Inequality Database, WIID 4, version 22 February 2019. Helsinki: UNU-WIDER.

van der Berg, S., and H. Bhorat (1999). 'The Present as a Legacy of the Past: The Labour Market, Inequality and Poverty in South Africa'. Working Paper 99/29. Cape Town: DPRU, University of Cape Town.

van der Berg, S., H. Bhorat, and M. Leibbrandt (2001). 'Introduction'. In H. Bhorat, M. Leibbrandt, M. Maziya, S. van der Berg, and I. Woolard (eds), *Fighting Poverty: Labour Markets and Inequality in South Africa*. pp. 1–20. Cape Town: University of Cape Town Press.

Whiteford, A.C. and D.E. van Seventer (2000). 'South Africa's Changing Income Distribution in the 1990s', *Journal of Studies in Economics and Econometrics*, 24(3): 7–30.

Wilson, F. (2011). 'Historical Roots of Inequality in South Africa', *Economic History of Developing Regions*. 26(1): 1–15.

Wittenberg, M. (2015). 'Problems with SWIID: The Case of South Africa'. A Southern Africa Labour and Development Research Unit Working Paper Number 148 and DataFirst Technical Paper 30. Cape Town: SALDRU, University of Cape Town.

Wittenberg, M. (2017). 'Wages and Wage Inequality in South Africa 1994–2011: Part 2—Inequality Measurement and Trends', *South African Journal of Economics*, 85(2): 298–318.

PART IV
LATIN AMERICA

10

Inclusive Growth without Structural Transformation?

The Case of Brazil

Sergio Firpo, Renan Pieri, and Rafaela Nogueira

1 Introduction

In this chapter, we discuss the developer's dilemma in Brazil. The dilemma faced by middle-income countries, as defined by Kim, Sumner, and Yusuf (2019), is between promoting economic growth through structural transformation and productivity growth or promoting inclusive growth. This developer's dilemma is not new in economics. In a seminal paper of 1955, Simon Kuznets, despite a lack of data, pointed out that economic growth could promote the reduction of income inequality for developed countries, but could have the opposite effect for developing countries.

For developing countries, Kuznets (1955) described the drop in income inequality in the first half of the twentieth century as a 'puzzle'. That interpretation is explained by the fact that in this period there were strong industrialization and urbanization processes, which, according to the author, should have increased inequality because agricultural societies faced lower inequality at that time. Urbanization, however, led to a fall in inequality because it increased the incomes of low-income workers in urban areas. At the same time, the burden of rural households fell on the national economy. Therefore, inequality decreased even though urban workers had higher incomes than rural households.

Kuznets (1955) also argued that inequality would usually be lower in developing countries. This was because even the rich would be poor compared with high-income citizens in developed countries, while the poorest would have to have enough to survive. However, this was not the case for many countries. Brazil, for example, had a very rich elite during its pre-industrial era, despite its low average income per capita.

Sergio Firpo, Renan Pieri, and Rafaela Nogueira, *Inclusive Growth without Structural Transformation?*. In: *The Developer's Dilemma*. Edited by Armida Salsiah Alisjahbana, Kunal Sen, Andy Sumner, and Arief Anshory Yusuf, Oxford University Press. © UNU-WIDER (2022). DOI: 10.1093/oso/9780192855299.003.0010

Industrialization and urbanization do not necessarily reduce inequality in developing countries. According to Sen (2014), at times of accelerated growth formal institutions are created to stabilize the relationship between politicians (and bureaucrats) and the firms (investors) that promote growth. This might explain the high level of income inequality in Brazilian society during the urbanization process. Naturally, accelerating growth creates inequality. In periods of growth maintenance, there is room to create institutions that promote inclusive growth.

For the Brazilian economy, the dilemma is that structural transformation led to a significant increase in labour productivity, especially between the 1950s and the 1980s. The Brazilian experience shows that the lack of certain factors during the process of structural transformation is fundamental with regard to the shift to sustainable inclusive growth. In particular, these factors included a lack of investment in basic human capital or the creation of an institutional setting that would secure market transactions. Thus, if we follow the framework of Kim and Sumner (2019), Brazil experienced an incomplete structural transformation: its secular deindustrialization was marked by a decline in the value-added and employment shares of the manufacturing sector during the 1990s and the 2000s.

In section 2 of this chapter, we present a general assessment of the developer's dilemma in Brazil. Next, we divide recent Brazilian economic history into three periods. The period before 1964 (the year of the beginning of the Brazilian military regime) is explored in section 3. The period from 1964 to 1994 (the year of monetary stabilization) is discussed in section 4. Section 5 discusses the period from 1994 to 2011, when there was a significant drop in economic inequality. Section 6 deals with the evolution of the economy after 2011—a period when the country experienced a severe economic crisis—and Brazil's economic prospects for the future. In section 7, the main conclusions are presented.

2. The developer's dilemma in Brazil: an overview

Herrendorf et al. (2013) define structural transformation as a process of the reallocation of economic activity across sectors. The process of structural transformation moved Brazil from a rural economy to an urban and more complex economy, and was the main driver of the labour productivity growth that occurred between the 1950s and the 1970s. In 1940, 68 per cent of the population lived in rural areas. By 2010, this figure had fallen to 15 per cent (IBGE 2020).

The structural transformation of Brazil was directly related to its industrialization process. The combination of rapid urbanization with an active import substitution policy created the basis for the growth of the manufacturing sector. Initially, a base industry with strong state investment in the 1930s, and with a growing consumer goods industry from the 1950s onwards, the manufacturing sector started to play a more relevant role in economic growth, even in an economy that was still predominantly agricultural. However, the progress of the structural transformation process did not appear to be related to a reduction in economic inequality in these first decades of industrialization.

Following Kim and Sumner (2019) terminology, Figure 10.9 presents the different periods of industrialization on Brazilian history. From 1950 to 1964, employment share and value added for manufacturing sector both increased and Brazil lived a period of upgrading industrialization. In the next two periods analysed in this chapter (1964–94 and 1994–2011), the employment share of the manufacturing sector declined, and Brazil experienced a moment of secular deindustrialization. This secular deindustrialization was not uniform over time and Brazil combined moments of increase of employment share (in the second half of the 1980s) or increase of value-added share (in the second half of the 1990s and first half of the 2000s). This slight growth of value-added share from 1994 to the mid-2000s suggests a short period of advanced industrialization.

Figure 10.1 presents Gini indices between 1960 and 2016. Economic inequality grew between the 1960s and the beginning of the 1970s, a period when the process of structural transformation had greater weight in the growth of labour productivity. After this, between the mid-1970s and the end of the twentieth century, inequality remained stable. It would only fall again with the new cycle of economic growth in the 2000s, which will be described in section 5. Firpo and

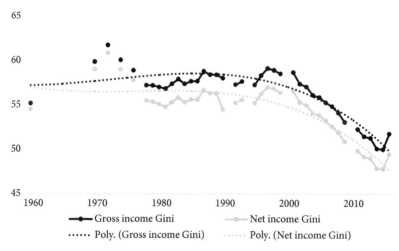

Fig. 10.1 Gross and net income Gini, Brazil, 1960–2016

Note: There are some data concerns over inequality data in the 1970s (notably, poor coverage of household surveys, missing or imputed years, high inflation, and discrepancy among nominal values of labour income).
Source: authors' calculations based UNU-WIDER World Income Inequality Database (WIID).

Pieri (2017) investigated how structural transformation drove Brazilian productivity between 1950 and 2005. They concluded that it was an important force until the mid-1970s. After that period, labour productivity did not increase, and the sparse episodes of productivity gain were mostly associated with within-sector changes, such as during the mid-1990s, when the country faced an intense process of trade liberalization.

The long stability of income inequality between 1964 (more after 1980) and 1994 and the important role of structural transformation promoting economic growth allows us to classify the Kuznetsian tension in this period was most of the time weak (benign). After 1994, the drop of inequality and the loss of relevance of structural transformation made the Kuznetsian tension ambiguous.[1]

Following the end of the hyperinflation era in 1994, Brazil struggled with low economic growth and stagnant labour productivity. However, the combination of social policies focused on the poor, the boom in commodity prices, and the rise of consumer credit promoted a wave of the creation of formal contract jobs, which successfully reduced poverty and income inequality. Also, Brazil increased access to education in such a way that average schooling rose from 4.7 years in 1980 to 8.1 years in 2010. Firpo, Pieri and Nogueira (2020) present the evolution of average schooling years in Brazil. Despite the facts that school quality was still a troubling problem, and that a large share of students did not have access to higher education, advances in the amount of schooling contributed to a fall in the returns to education over the period.

Unlike many other (mostly developed) countries that promoted openness in their trade flows with the rest of the world economy, Brazil did not experience a subsequent increase in inequality. Indeed, inequality has fallen since the 2000s. Historical data comparing the evolution of the Gini during the 1970s—the period of annual ten-percentage-point increases in gross domestic product (GDP)—with more recent years reveals that the Brazilian 'golden age' of structural transformation and rapid economic gains was also the period when inequality dramatically increased. By contrast, in more recent periods, especially the 2000s, productivity was stagnant, but nevertheless the economy grew and inequality fell. The growth of the Brazilian domestic consumer market and changes in the demographic profile of workers caused a massive reduction in inequality, despite some recent setbacks due to the economic crisis of 2014.

The developer's dilemma in Brazil is about how to reconcile a new cycle of structural transformation with inclusive growth. In the following sections, we detail the political economy and the process of structural transformation for the periods before 1964 (the year of the military coup), from 1964–1994 (the years of dictatorship and hyperinflation), and from 1994–2011 (the years after monetary stabilization).

---

[1] We cannot classify Kuznetsian tension before 1964 for lack of data on income inequality.

3. A brief economic history of Brazil up to 1964

Brazil started the twentieth century with a rural economy based on the production and export of coffee. Only in 1888 did the country abolish slavery. The end
of slavery still did not mean the economic inclusion of the Black population, and
Brazil entered the twentieth century with an illiterate and essentially poor population. Until 1930, political power was shared by the rural elites of the states of São
Paulo and Minas Gerais, representing the interests of coffee and milk producers.
There was no electricity in most cities, and there were very few manufacturers in
the country.

The political environment began to change in 1930, with a revolution organized
by states from outside the centre of power. The dictatorship of Getúlio Vargas,
following nationalist movements of the time, created the first-base industries,
focusing on state companies in steel and oil. Over the next two decades, a non-
durable goods industry flourished in Brazil, mainly due to the policy of import
substitution. A trade policy with high tariffs and various forms of non-tariff barrier
(NTB) has featured in several periods of Brazilian history. In addition to being a
conscious strategy of development through the domestic production of goods that
had previously been imported, for most of the long period between the 1880s and
the 1980s Brazilian protectionism was due mainly to problems with the balance of
payments (de Paiva Abreu 2004a). The import substitution system, as it is known
nowadays, was created because of government difficulties in dealing with debts in
foreign currency after the 1929 crash, but over time Brazilian policymakers came
to see it as a strategy to develop the manufacturing sector in Brazil.

According to de Paiva Abreu (2004a), the average import tariff in the 1880s was
38 per cent in Brazil, a situation shared with other Latin American countries such
as Mexico (39.7 per cent) and Colombia (45.7 per cent). The highest rates were set
mainly for consumer goods, while tariffs for capital goods were also high. For de
Paiva Abreu, the reasons for Brazil's development of a protectionist trade policy
were the size of the territory and the inelasticity of demand for coffee, which allowed farmers to pass on most of the enhancement of production inputs due to
high tariffs. Another relevant factor was the dependence of government revenues
on import taxes.

In the 1950s, the durable goods industry also grew in Brazil, and there was a
rapid process of urbanization, with people migrating from poorer regions in the
north and north-east to the south-eastern region, where most manufacturers were
concentrated. This movement would last until the end of the 1980s, and this was
the most important period of structural transformation in Brazil. Thus, structural
transformation in Brazil has been directly related to urbanization and the inter-
regional migration process. Following Kim and Sumner (2019) terminology, this
was the upgrading industrialization period for Brazil.

As the urban population grew, unions became more important in political life. At the end of the 1950s, Brazil was a very different country than it had been at the beginning of the century: most people now lived in cities, and new political actors had emerged. In the context of the Cold War, moreover, Brazilian political groups started to question democracy and its results. There followed some years of growing inflation and political turbulence, with the resignation of President Jânio Quadros in 1961; three years later, in March 1964, the military took political power, and it ruled the country for twenty-five years.

Along with this industrialization process, there was a strong growth of labour productivity. Figure 10.2 shows the growth rate of labour productivity in each of the three periods analysed. Between 1950 and 1964, average labour productivity grew by 3.8 per cent per year.

Structural change is closely linked to the migration of people from less productive sectors to more productive sectors. In decompositions of productivity development, this component is called the 'Between' component. Labour productivity changes may also include 'Within' components, related to improvements in the companies themselves, their processes, or their employment of more productive workers. In the case of Brazil, Figure 10.2 shows that most of the productivity growth between 1950 and 2011 was due to 'Within' changes, possibly related to an increase in the capital stock of the economy over time and significant improvements in access to education. Figure 10.2 also shows that productivity grew significantly more between 1950 and 1964 than in subsequent periods. For the

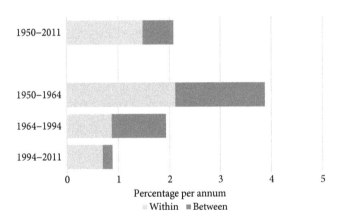

Fig. 10.2 Decomposition of labour productivity growth, Brazil, 1950–2011

Note: Decomposition uses the methodology of McMillan and Rodrik (2011).
Source: authors' calculations based on the Groningen Growth and Development Centre (GGDC) 10-Sector Database Version 2015 (Timmer et al. 2015).

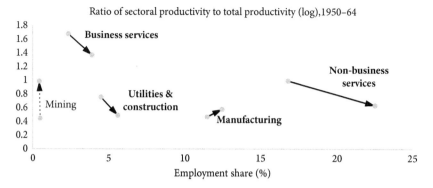

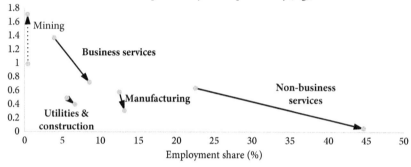

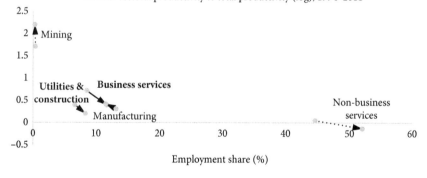

Fig. 10.3 Changes in labour productivity and employment share by sector, Brazil, 1950–2011

Note: Sectors with higher than economy-wide average labour productivity that experienced an increase in employment share are in bold.
Source: authors' calculations based on the GGDC 10-Sector Database Version 2015 (Timmer et al. 2015).

years between 1950 and 1964, around 45 per cent of productivity growth can be explained by the structural transformation component.

Figure 10.3 shows the variation of the log of the ratio between sectoral productivity and the average productivity of the economy. For values above zero, the sector had productivity above the economy average. In the first panel, it is observed that between 1950 and 1964 the productivity of all sectors presented is higher than the economy average because agriculture is excluded. Between 1950 and 1964, the share of agricultural employment in total employment fell from 64 per cent to 55 per cent; thus, agriculture was still the sector that employed the greatest number. At the same time, its share in GDP fell from 13.3 per cent to 9.5 per cent.

It is also observed that the service sectors (business and non-business) and the utilities and construction sector underwent a relative fall in productivity, as they began to have a greater employment share (the employment share of non-business services grew from 16.8 per cent to 22.5 per cent). This highlights the phenomenon of structural transformation, since these sectors incorporated workers from agriculture during the industrialization process. The average product per worker in the period increased by 70 per cent. In the opposite direction, the mining and manufacturing sectors had an increase in productivity in relation to other sectors, with the average product per worker in the manufacturing sector growing by around 90 per cent.

4. Trends in structural transformation, 1964–c. 1994

From 1964 to 1994 is the beginning of the secular deindustrialization of Brazil. After General Castelo Branco assumed the presidency of Brazil, the government's first economic plan (*Programa de ação econômica do governo*) dealt with high inflation by reducing the money supply and controlling the labour unions. The plan also regulated the financial system, establishing the rules that continue to organize financial activity in Brazil today. At this time, the Brazilian Central Bank was created.

Maintaining the nationalist ideology that had been followed by Getúlio Vargas, the military presidents continued to use an import substitution system with high tariffs on imports, and they increased the state's participation in the economy. The military governments of the 1960s and 1970s invested heavily in manufacturing, expanding Brazilian production of non-durable consumer goods and capital goods. During these years, there were also numerous infrastructure projects such as roads and hydroelectric plants. From 1967 to 1973, Brazil experienced very high GDP growth rates. This period is known as the 'economic miracle' in Brazil.

Brazilian GDP per capita grew by 108 per cent between 1964 and 1994. In the period from 1967 to1973 alone, GDP per capita grew by 52 per cent (Bolt and van Zanden 2015). However, the rapid GDP growth was accompanied by a growth in income inequality.

The Gini index went from 54.5 in 1960 to 61.7 in 1972, the latter being the historical maximum of this indicator for Brazil. After this, Gini fell, and it was stable until 1994 to a similar level from 1960. With stability of inequality and a high relevance of structural transformation, the Kuznetsian tension was benign in this period. This economic performance was based on the accumulation of physical capital; Brazil did not put the same energy into human capital accumulation. In 1970, the average duration of schooling in Brazil was 3.77 years, significantly below Chile (6.45) and Argentina (6.82) (Firpo et al. 2020).

The two oil shocks and unruly government expenditure led the Brazilian federal government to default on its foreign debt in 1982. The closure of the financial markets and the political pressure to maintain the tax burden left the Brazilian government with inflation as the only mechanism to finance government expenditure. In the 1980s, Brazil faced a period of incredible hyperinflation, comparable only to that seen in certain countries during the 1930s. The redemocratization process after 1985 brought a number of social demands that it had not been possible to voice under the military regime. This made the battle against inflation even harder. Various economic plans tried to reduce price levels, but all of them failed to deal with the government deficit. As is common during hyperinflation, economic activity was very disorganized. As poor people had less access to financial market products, they suffered most of the consequences of inflation, and income inequality grew faster in this decade.

Firpo et al. (2020) presents the annual inflation rates between 1950 and 2010. From 1981, the inflation rate remained above 100 per cent per year, and it maintained an increasing trend throughout the 1980s. In 1989, inflation was 1,430 per cent; in 1990, it reached 2,947 per cent, the highest rate in the Brazilian historical inflation series. The hyperinflation period lasted until 1994, a year that ended with 2,079 per cent inflation. With the success of the Real Plan in 1994, inflation suddenly dropped to 66 per cent in 1995, and it has converged at less than one digit since 1997. To fight hyperinflation, the Real Plan acted on several fronts: it promoted a privatization programme for some state companies, which increased the economy's competitiveness; it promoted fiscal reform; and above all, it introduced a fixed exchange rate regime at a very appreciated level. Hyperinflation ended, but the manufacturing sector's share of GDP fell due to the economic liberalization (as will be described further below). The manufacturing sector's share of job creation fell from 15.3 per cent in 1989 (pre-liberalization) to 11.6 per cent in 1998 (Firpo et al. 2020).

Between 1964 and 1994, the growth in the share of the services sectors in employment, especially non-business services, accelerated: this sector went from 22 per cent of workers to 44 per cent. Conversely, the agricultural sector went from 55 per cent of workers to 26.5 per cent. This movement was accompanied by a relative fall in productivity in the non-business service sector, which converged with the average productivity of the economy. Mining was the only sector that once again showed relative productivity growth, although it was not relevant in terms of the number of job openings. The average product per worker in the economy grew by about 70 per cent during the period.

4.1 Trade liberalization

As mentioned in section 3. A brief economic history of Brazil up to 1964, the import substitution system was one of the main drivers of the manufacturing sector's growth in Brazil.[2] However, from the late 1970s, the process began to run down: Brazil faced serious constraints in the balance of payments, and it was not possible to further expand the range of imported products that could be substituted with similar domestic products. A debate emerged about the possibility of greater openness to foreign trade in order to mitigate the economic crisis.

According to Kume et al. (2003), in the years that preceded Brazil's opening up to trade, the country's foreign trade policy consisted of the following: a widespread presence of tariffs with redundant parts; the collection of additional taxes, such as taxes on credit, exchange, and insurance (IOF), the rate of port improvement (TMP), and additional freight for merchant marine renewal; the existence of forty-two special regimes allowing exemption from or reductions of taxes; and the use of NTBs, such as lists of products on which the issuance of import licenses was suspended, specific authorizations for some products, and annual import quotas for companies.

Thus, an effective process of trade liberalization would depend not only on tariff reductions, but also on the elimination of NTBs and special arrangements. In Brazil, the first phase of the liberalization process occurred between 1988 and 1989. It consisted of the fixing of lower tariffs and the elimination of IOF and TMP charges, but it did not eliminate special schemes or other NTBs, which were the major effective forms of protection for domestic production (de Paiva Abreu 2004b; Kume et al. 2003).

Some studies have measured the effects of liberalization on Brazil's labour market. Dix-Carneiro and Kovak (2015) analyse the impact of liberalization on migration and wages in local markets. They conclude that locations where the tariff reduction was 10 per cent higher than average saw a 9.4 per cent greater fall in wages than other regions. In addition, the states most affected by liberalization lost approximately 0.5 per cent of their populations because of trade liberalization.

Ferreira, Leite, and Wai-Po (2007) test the impact of liberalization on the distribution of hourly wages. They find that liberalization did not particularly affect the manufacturing sector, but its overall impact on the economy contributed to a reduction of inequality. Krishna et al. (2011) find a positive effect of liberalization on wages in export sectors compared with non-importing sectors.

Gonzaga et al. (2006) obtain other evidence on inequality. They show that liberalization affected skilled-labour-intensive sectors more than unskilled-labour-intensive sectors. As a result, there was a reduction in income differences between the two groups in the post-liberalization period.

---

[2] The discussion in this section draws on Pieri (2015).

Also exploring the labour channel, Dix-Carneiro et al. (2018) exploit the shocks due to trade liberalization on labour demand to estimate its impact on crime rates. They find a negative relationship between labour demand and crime rates.

In the second phase, 1991–1993, there was a strong reduction of tariffs such that the modal tariff was 20 per cent. Tariffs on virtually all products suffered drastic reductions, except in industries such as computing, chemicals, automobiles, and other innovative technologies. However, it was the elimination of NTBs that caused the greatest impact on liberalization. de Paiva Abreu (2004b) and Kume et al. (2003) explain that this period saw the elimination of import licence suspensions, special import regimes, and company import quotas. Thus, the end of NTBs led prices to become the main instrument of trade protection, directly reflecting the degree of protection of each industry.

The third stage of the process occurred in 1994 with the need for monetary stabilization. Import tariffs of zero or two per cent on products with greater weightings in the price index were established, and the Mercosur common external tariff was anticipated to begin in 1995. Brazilian tariffs are now 10.2 per cent on average, a level comparable to other developing economies that are more open to international trade (de Paiva Abreu 2004b; Kume et al. 2003).

4.2 Structural transformation and inclusive growth

The manufacturing sector in Brazil experienced a period of growth until the end of the 1980s, and a process of retraction from the 1990s with economic liberalization. Thus, between 1964 and 1994, there was an intense structural transformation of the Brazilian economy. Firpo, Pieri and Nogueira (2020) present the historical evolution of value added by sector. Notably, agriculture's share of GDP lost ground, falling from 10.2 per cent in 1960 to 6.3 per cent in 2011, although the most critical period seems to have been in the late 1970s, when it reached 4.5 per cent. The share of the manufacturing sector also fell, from 22 per cent to 17.6 per cent. The sector that has the greatest share throughout the historical series is non-business services, which includes trade, restaurants, hotels, transport, storage and communications, government and community services, and social and personal services. This sector has a historical average of 44 per cent of GDP.

As in other countries, the structural transformation of Brazil was associated with workers' transition from the agricultural sector to the service sector, as shown in Figure 10.4. This was a direct consequence of the urbanization process. Although manufacturing had a relevant role in the economy in the 1960s and 1970s, it is less labour-intensive, so the share of workers in the manufacturing sector has been almost stable over time.

The Brazilian export composition shows the country's transition from a well-defined role as exporter of food and raw materials to a model with a greater share of

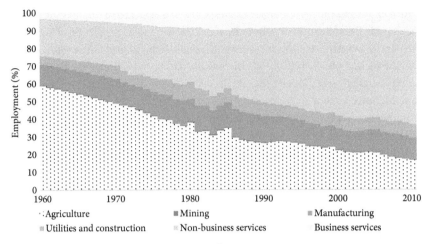

Fig. 10.4 Employment composition, Brazil, 1960–2011

Notes: (i) Business services: financial intermediation, renting, business activities; (ii) non-business services: (a) wholesale and retail trade, repair of motor vehicles and motorcycles, personal and household goods, hotels and restaurants; (b) transport, storage, communications; (c) public administration, defence, education, health, social work; (d) other community activities, social and personal service activities, activities of private households.
Source: authors' calculations based on the GGDC 10-Sector Database Version 2015 (Timmer et al. 2015).

manufacturing. The share of manufacturing in Brazilian exports peaked in the late 1980s and early 1990s, with a subsequent decline alongside the deindustrialization of the country (Firpo et al. 2020).

Firpo et al. (2020) shows the breakdown of the growth in value added by sector between 1960 and 2011 using the Hodrick–Prescott filter. There was a reversal in the trends for most sectors around 1991. From then on, the share of non-business services began to drop, and the share of utilities and construction, agriculture, and especially manufacturing increased. It is possible that this reversal in the trends was related to the strong economic liberalization that occurred under Fernando Collor's government, which suddenly changed the economic sectors' relative prices, causing a shock of competition with foreign companies.

For most of the period between 1964 and the early 2000s, the gross income Gini fell very little. In the same period, the manufacturing sector's share of total value added in the economy fell, although there were some fluctuations. This is shown in Figure 10.5. Graphically, there is no clear relationship between the evolution of the Gini and the share of the industry in value added. For most of the period, the Gini was almost stable, while the industry share fell from 22 per cent in 1964 to 18.3 per cent in 2011. After the mid-2000s, the figure suggests that the fall in Gini was associated with a slight decline in manufacturing's share, although it is not possible to confirm the statistical significance here.

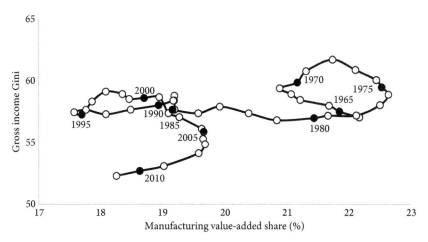

Fig. 10.5 Gross income Gini and manufacturing value-added share, Brazil, 1964–2011

Notes: Missing Gini coefficients calculated using linear interpolation. Manufacturing value-added and employment shares are five-year moving averages. For example, the data for 1975 is an average of data for 1971–1975.
Source: authors' calculations based on the GGDC 10-Sector Database Version 2015 (Timmer et al. 2015) and UNU-WIDER World Income Inequality Database (WIID).

Figure 10.6 shows the relationship between the Gini index and the non-business services sector's share of GDP. Between 1965 and 2000, the Gini remained practically unchanged, despite the fluctuation in the share of the non-business services sector. The exception is the period from 1965 to 1978, when the Gini oscillated. There was initially a drop in the non-business services sector's share of GDP between 1978 and 1986, followed by a significant increase until 2000. Thereafter, a new trend is noted, with a slight drop in the sector's share of GDP accompanied by a reduction in inequality, at least until 2011.

Figure 10.7 shows two relevant findings about the recent evolution of the Gini index in Brazil. First, there has been a steady increase in the share of non-business services in total employment, which more than doubled between 1964 and 2012. In 1965, 22.2 per cent of employed people were in the non-business services sector; in 2012, the figure was 51.5 per cent. Second, at least until the end of the twentieth century, there seems to have been no relationship between the non-business services sector's increased share of employment and income inequality, as measured here by the Gini. The exception occurs at the beginning of the series, between the 1960s and 1970s, when there is an abrupt increase in the Gini. From the 2000s onwards, the Gini declines at the same time as the share of the non-business services sector. The main hypothesis to explain this is that during this period, labour income increased because there was an increase in the number of formal contract jobs generated, which contributed to a reduction in inequality. In addition, the

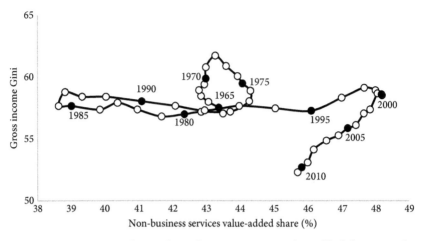

Fig. 10.6 Gross income Gini and non-business services value-added share, Brazil, 1964–2011

Notes: Missing Gini coefficients calculated using linear interpolation. Manufacturing value-added and employment shares are five-year moving averages. For example, the data for 1975 is an average of data for 1971–1975.
Source: authors' calculations based on the GGDC 10-Sector Database Version 2015 (Timmer et al. 2015) and UNU-WIDER World Income Inequality Database (WIID).

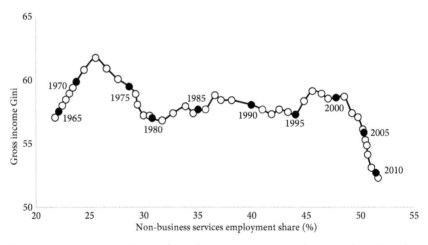

Fig. 10.7 Gross income Gini and non-business services employment share, Brazil, 1964–2011

Notes: Missing Gini coefficients calculated using linear interpolation. Manufacturing value-added and employment shares are five-year moving averages. For example, the data for 1975 is an average of data for 1971–1975.
Source: authors' calculations based on the GGDC 10-Sector Database Version 2015 (Timmer et al. 2015) and UNU-WIDER World Income Inequality Database (WIID).

facts that average schooling has increased and there has been a consequent drop in the schooling premium contributed to the reduction of income differentials.

5. Trends in inclusive growth, 1994–c.2011

From 1994 to the mid-2000s, the pattern of structural transformation of secular deindustrialization is less intense because although employment share in the manufacturing sector is still declining, the value-added share is slightly higher, putting Brazil closer to an advanced industrialization period. But since the second half of the 2000s, the value-added of the manufacturing sector dropped and employment share was stable.

The Real Plan stabilized prices, and the country was free of hyperinflation after fifteen years. Income inequality then decreased at a faster pace from the 2000s onwards. In the first years following the Real Plan, economic growth was slow. To fight inflation, the Central Bank fixed the exchange rate at a level that made it very difficult to export goods or compete with foreign goods. Moreover, the 1990s was a decade of economic crises that reduced demand for Brazilian products in some countries, including Mexico (1994), Russia (1997), the 'Asian Tigers' (1998), Brazil itself, (1999), and Argentina at the beginning of the next decade (2001).

In the 2000s, Brazil's economic performance started to rise. The boom in commodity prices and the stability of the currency after 1994 led to years of reduction in unemployment rates, an increase in the percentage of formal contract workers, an increase in labour earnings, and a reduction of income inequality. The growth of Chinese demand for grain boosted commodity exports, and the consumer credit expansion allowed the generation of jobs in regions outside the industrial centre, especially in north-eastern Brazil.

In 2004, the federal government introduced social programmes for income and goods distribution, and it created the Bolsa Família, a large conditional cash transfer programme that almost eradicated extreme poverty. Income inequality then decreased not because the rich were losing income, but due to the increase in labour earnings among the poorest.

Firpo et al. (2020) shows the evolution of the number of Bolsa Família participants between 2004 and 2016. The number of beneficiary families grew from 6.5 million in 2004 to 13.5 million in 2016. These numbers indicate that the programme contributed to a significant fall in income inequality. In addition, the conditions of the programme included the requirement that children should attend school, which also contributed to the increase in schooling in the period. The figures after 2014 coincide with a period of more inclusive growth: there was a rapid fall in the Gini index following the introduction of the Bolsa Família, from 57.07 in 2003 to 50.04 in 2015.

The Bolsa Família programme has been very successful in fighting poverty in Brazil. Using the poverty line of US$10 a day, 79 per cent of Brazil's population was poor in 1980, and this dropped to 42 per cent in 2015. Using the poverty line of US$1.9 dollars a day, extreme poverty dropped from 28 per cent in 1983 to three per cent in 2015. Although the decreasing tendency of poverty rates started in the 1980s, it was only after the macroeconomic stabilization of the 1990s, and the consequent growth of formal contract jobs combined with social programmes, that Brazil speeded up its poverty reduction (see Figure 10.8).

Coincidentally or not, these movements in inequality were correlated with the intensity of structural transformation. With the decrease of both income inequality and the role of structural transformation, Kuznetsian tension was ambiguous. The structural transformation was greater when inequality rose, and when it fell, inequality also decreased. But does this imply that structural change affects inequality negatively? Ferreira et al. (2017) provide some evidence that the reduction in inequality during this period was related to changes in how observable individual characteristics were rewarded in the labour market. A reduction in the gaps on those returns is the main explanation for the reduction of inequality in Brazil.

This inclusive growth in the labour market is evident when we analyse the evolution of formal contract jobs. Informal workers are employees without a formal contract or self-employed workers, who in Brazil usually do not enjoy social protection. The percentage of informal contract workers fell from 56.2 per cent in 1998 to 45 per cent in 2014. Even so, the percentage of informal contract workers is quite high and contributes to the inequality of earnings in the labour market, since this type of employment pays less on average (Firpo et al. 2020).

In addition to the Bolsa Família, another important public policy of the 1990s and 2000s was the growth of the minimum wage. Between 1990 and 2000, the

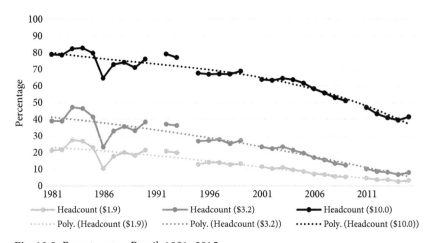

Fig. 10.8 Poverty rates, Brazil, 1981–2015

Source: authors' calculations based on PovcalNet, version March 2019 (World Bank 2019).

minimum wage saw a real increase of 35 per cent. Between 2000 and 2010, the gain was greater, around 82 per cent (Firpo et al. 2020).

The combination of monetary stabilization (which benefited all social strata), real increases in the minimum wage (which benefited the middle class), and the Bolsa Família programme (which focused on the poorest) led to a significant fall in economic inequality, promoting more inclusive growth. However, there was a significant drop in the growth of labour productivity, leading to stagnation. As shown in Figure 10.2, productivity growth between 1994 and 2011 was only 0.44 per cent per year. Of this change, 78 per cent was due to 'Within' changes: workers within each sector of economic activity became more productive, and structural transformation played a less relevant role in the period. This increase in the 'Within' component was possibly due to the large increase in average schooling in the period. Between 1990 and 2010, average schooling increased from 6.6 to 8.1 years (an increase of 22.5 per cent) (Firpo et al. 2020).

The period 1994–2011 saw a drop in product per worker in some sectors, such as utilities and construction, business services, and non-business services. The latter started to see productivity below the economy average. In the opposite direction, the mining and agriculture sectors saw an increase in productivity during the period, with output per worker growing by 89 per cent and 123 per cent, respectively. Average productivity grew by about 16 per cent in the period.

6. Trends after 2011, and future trajectory

Brazil ended the first decade of the new millennium with a positive outlook. Poverty had never been so low. The boom in commodity prices had increased exports and boosted the agricultural sector. The services sector had benefited from more credit in the market and generated millions of jobs. Brazil seemed finally to have left behind the years of bad economic performance.

But the country had only postponed some important problems that would generate the worst economic crisis in Brazilian history. In 2015 and 2016, GDP dropped by nine per cent and the unemployment rate reached 13 per cent, with more than 28 million workers working fewer hours than they wished. Since then, the economy has stagnated and productivity growth has been very slow. What has happened to the Brazilian economy?

There has been a severe fiscal crisis. Government expenditure (at all three levels: federal, state, and municipality) has increased continuously since the last Constitution of 1988. The Constitution includes some groups in the social security system that do not contribute to their future pensions. Additionally, there has been a growth in the public worker pension deficit, and the government has substantially increased the number of public workers over time. If the government were a private company, it could reduce its expenditure by firing some workers. But in Brazil it is illegal for the government to do so.

At the end of 2014, the prediction of a collapse in public finances reduced private investment, and consequently labour demand fell abruptly. Many companies went bankrupt, and the government decreased its purchases, pushing unemployment even higher.

So, the developer's dilemma in Brazil today is about how to organize public finances through a reform of the Constitution that will allow the government to reduce the fiscal deficit. Only after this, and with the confidence of economic agents, can there be a return to the path of policies that promote inclusive growth.

7. Conclusions and policy implications

This chapter has analysed the evolution of the structural transformation of the Brazilian economy in recent decades from a historical point of view. In doing so, it has evaluated the role played by different economic sectors in the historic reduction of economic inequality that occurred over the period.

For comparison with other chapters in this volume, Figure 10.9 shows the patterns of structural transformation in Brazil. In Brazil, structural transformation

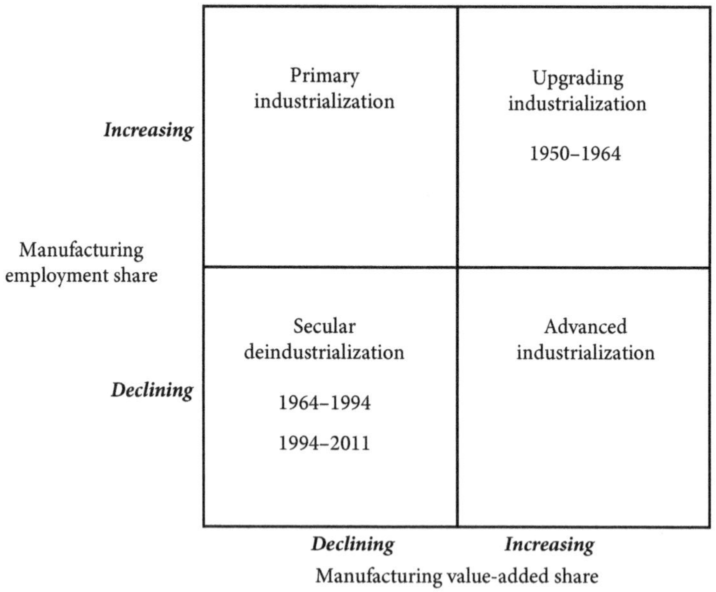

Fig. 10.9 Varieties of structural transformation in Brazil, 1950–2011

Note: There are some data concerns over inequality data in the 1970s (notably, poor coverage of household surveys, missing or imputed years, high inflation, and discrepancy among nominal values of labour income).
Source: authors' calculations based on the GGDC 10-Sector Database Version 2015 (Timmer et al. 2015).

was associated with a strong displacement of workers from less productive sectors (in this case, agriculture) to more productive sectors (manufacturing and services). This structural transformation was the main driver of the upgrading industrialization period (1950–1964). Even between 1964–1994, a period of secular deindustrialization, when there was smaller growth in productivity and declining manufacturing employment share and manufacturing value added share, structural transformation still played an important role.

In this chapter, there have been two outstanding issues. First, as the structural transformation process diminished, the growth of labour productivity decreased, as did GDP growth. Second, economic growth only became inclusive—that is, reduced economic inequality—at the beginning of this century, when productivity was practically stagnant and average schooling increased substantially.

What the Brazilian experience seems to suggest is that structural transformation affects labour productivity, but inclusive growth is not an obvious consequence of this process. It seems to depend on the causes behind the structural transformation. In the Brazilian case, as with most Latin American countries (Chile as an exception), the industrialization process was not accompanied by an accumulation

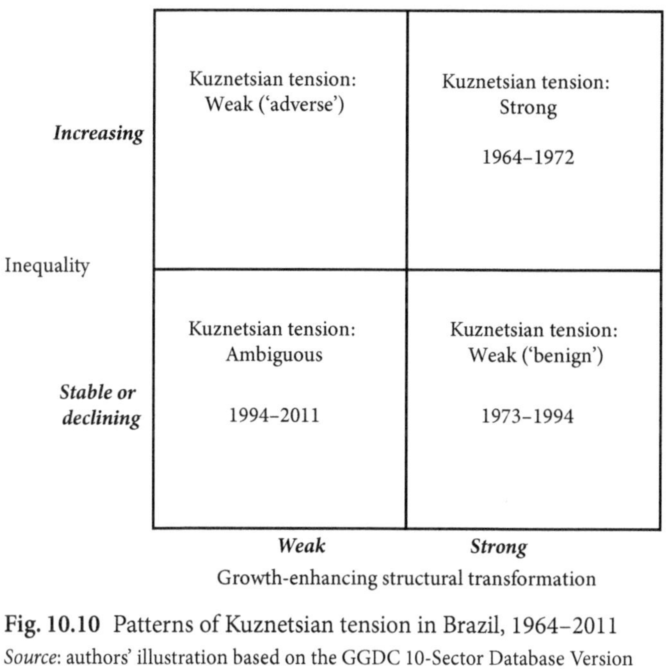

	Weak	Strong
Increasing	Kuznetsian tension: Weak ('adverse')	Kuznetsian tension: Strong 1964–1972
Stable or declining	Kuznetsian tension: Ambiguous 1994–2011	Kuznetsian tension: Weak ('benign') 1973–1994

Inequality

Weak   **Strong**
Growth-enhancing structural transformation

Fig. 10.10 Patterns of Kuznetsian tension in Brazil, 1964–2011

Source: authors' illustration based on the GGDC 10-Sector Database Version 2015 (Timmer et al. 2015) and UNU-WIDER World Income Inequality Database (WIID).

of human capital and was mainly due to the import substitution system, which created opportunities for the manufacturing sector by making foreign products more expensive for consumers, thereby concentrating income.

Another conclusion of this chapter is about the change of the Kuznetsian tension overtime. We don't have data on inequality for the period before 1964, so it is not classifiable. But over the period 1964–1994 the Brazilian economy experienced different periods of inequality growth and growth-enhancing structural transformation. Structural transformation played an important role between 1964 and 1994, although the process was strong in the first half of these three decades. Inequality grew during 1964–1972, but since 1978 it converged for the average level of the period and remained constant until 1994. So, we conclude that Kuznetsian tension was weak (benign) in most of the period.

For the period 1964–1994, Brazil experienced a strong structural transformation process but inequality increased or remained stable in this period. As we pointed out in the chapter, the import substitution system, urbanization, and industrial policy seems to explain most of the structural transformation and they are not related themselves with the persistent high inequality. However, Brazilian government managed inflation poorly and the price level increased significantly in the 1970s, reaching a hyperinflation level in the 1980s. The high inflation affected mostly the low-income population. This, combined with the low attendance to school in the same period, helps to explain the persistence of income inequality.

From 1994–2011, the structural transformation was less growth-enhancing. Also, Brazil presented an unprecedented decline in inequality in the beginning of this century due to the increase of formal contract jobs, price stability, and the increase of average schooling years of the population. So, the Kuznetsian tension was ambiguous in this period.

Given the stagnation of labour productivity in Brazil over the past few decades, a new cycle of structural change should be followed by social policies that focus on the most vulnerable, as has been the practice since the late 1990s.

References

Bolt, J., and J. van Zanden (2015). 'GDP per Capita: IISH Data Collection, V1', https://hdl.handle.net/10622/8FCYOX (accessed 5 March 2020).

de Paiva Abreu, M. (2004a). 'The Political Economy of High Protection in Brazil before 1987'. Special Initiative on Trade and Integration Working Paper SITI-08a. New York: Inter-American Development Bank.

de Paiva Abreu, M. (2004b). 'Trade Liberalization and the Political Economy of Protection in Brazil since 1987'. Special Initiative on Trade and Integration Working Paper SITI-08b. New York: Inter-American Development Bank.

de Zwart, P. (2015). 'Inflation: IISH Data Collection, V1', https://hdl.handle.net/10622/UJ3H1Q (accessed 5 March 2020).

Dix-Carneiro, R., and B. Kovak (2015). 'Trade Liberalization and the Skill Premium: A Local Labor Markets Approach', *American Economic Review Papers and Proceedings*, 105(5): 551–557.

Dix-Carneiro, R., R.R. Soares, and G. Ulyssea (2018). 'Economic Shocks and Crime: Evidence from the Brazilian Trade Liberalization', *American Economic Journal: Applied Economics*, 10(4): 158–195.

Ferreira, F., P.G. Leite, and M. Wai-Poi (2007). 'Trade Liberalization, Employment Flows, and Wage Inequality in Brazil'. Policy Research Working Paper 4108. Washington, DC: World Bank Group.

Ferreira, F., S. Firpo, and J. Messina (2017). 'Ageing Poorly? Accounting for the Decline in Earnings Inequality in Brazil, 1995–2012'. Policy Research Working Paper 8018. Washington, DC: World Bank Group.

Firpo, S., and R. Pieri. (2017). 'Structural Change, Productivity Growth, and Trade Policy in Brazil'. In M.S. McMillan, D. Rodrik, and C. Sepúlveda (eds), *Structural Change, Fundamentals, and Growth: A Framework and Case Studies*. Washington, DC: IFPRI, 267–92.

Firpo, S., R. Pieri, and R. Nogueira (2020). 'Inclusive Growth without Structural Transformation? The Case Of Brazil'. WIDER Working Paper 2020/58. Helsinki: UNU-WIDER.

Gonzaga, G., N.M. Filho, and C. Terra (2006). 'Trade Liberalization and the Evolution of Skill Earnings Differentials in Brazil', *Journal of International Economics*, 68(2): 345–367.

Herrendorf, B., R. Rogerson, and A. Valentinyi (2013). 'Growth and Structural Transformation'. Working Paper 18996. Cambridge, MA: NBER.

IBGE (2020). '2010 Census', http://www.ibge.gov.br/ (accessed 10 February 2020).

Kim, K., and A. Sumner (2019). 'The Five Varieties of Industrialization: A New Typology of Diverse Empirical Experience in the Developing World'. Working Paper 18. London: ESRC Global Poverty and Inequality Dynamics Research Network (GPID).

Kim, K., A. Sumner, and A. Yusuf (2019). 'Is Structural Transformation-Led Economic Growth Immiserizing or Inclusive? The Case of Indonesia'. In P. Shaffer, R. Kanbur, and R. Sandbrook (eds), *Immiserizing Growth: When Growth Fails the Poor*. Oxford: Oxford University Press, 226–49.

Krishna, P., J.P. Poole, and M.Z. Senses (2011). 'Wage Effects of Trade Reform with Endogenous Worker Mobility'. Working Paper 17256. Cambridge, MA: NBER.

Kume, H., G. Piani, and C.F.B. de Souza (2003). 'A política brasileira de importação no período 1987–1998: Descrição e avaliação'. In C.H. Corseuil and H. Kume (eds), *A abertura comercial brasileira nos anos 1990: Impactos sobre emprego e salário*. Rio de Janeiro: MTE/IPEA, 9–37.

Kuznets, S. (1955). 'Economic Growth and Income Inequality', *American Economic Review*, 45(1): 1–28.

McMillan, M., and D. Rodrik (2011). 'Globalization, Structural Change and Productivity Growth'. In M. Bacchetta and M. Jansen (eds), *Making Globalization Socially Sustainable*. Geneva: ILO and WTO, 39–84.

Pieri, R.G.D. (2015). 'Ensaios em economia política aplicada'. Ph.D. thesis. São Paulo: Getulio Vargas Foundation.

Sen, K. (2014). 'Inclusive Growth: When May We Expect It? When May We Not?', *Asian Development Review*, 31(1): 136–162.

Timmer, M.P., G.J. de Vries, and K. de Vries (2015). 'Patterns of Structural Change in Developing Countries'. In J. Weiss and M. Tribe (eds), *Routledge Handbook of Industry and Development*. London: Routledge, 65–83.

UNU-WIDER (2019). Standardized dataset based on World Income Inequality Database, WIID 4, version 22 February 2019. Helsinki: UNU-WIDER.

van Leeuwen, B., and J. van Leeuwen-Li (2015). 'Average Years of Education: IISH Data Collection, V1', http://hdl.handle.net/10622/KCBMKI (accessed 5 March 2020).

World Bank (2019). 'PovcalNet'. Version March 2019. Online analysis tool for global poverty monitoring. Washington, DC: World Bank., http://iresearch.worldbank.org/PovcalNet/povOnDemand.aspx (accessed 20 September 2019).

11

Structural Transformations and the Lack of Inclusive Growth

The Case of Chile

Andrés Solimano and Gabriela Zapata-Román

1 Introduction

The developer's dilemma describes the Kuznetsian tension between structural transformations and inclusive growth. Kuznets (1955) identified a process whereby inequality increased at initial stages of development and reversed later as development proceeds. A key component of structural transformation (ST) refers to the evolution of different productive sectors in the economy, measured by changes in sector shares of gross domestic product (GDP), labour, and exports. Particularly, we define ST as the reallocation of economic activity between and within sectors towards higher-productivity activities (Herrendorf et al. 2014). The movement of labour to more productive activities is a driver of economic development as it increases overall productivity and efficiency in the economy. However, policy-induced labour reallocations can also reduce growth when labour is transferred from higher-productivity to lower-productivity sectors (McMillan and Rodrik 2011), as it has been observed in some periods in Chile and Latin America.

Developed and developing countries have had different patterns of ST. Historically during the nineteenth and twentieth centuries, while developed countries shifted away from primary/agricultural goods production towards manufacturing industries and then to services industries, some developing countries have shifted from agriculture to services (retail and trade) without developing a strong manufacturing sector—a process known as premature deindustrialization (Rodrik 2016). The service sector is, in general, more productive than agriculture but is not, across the board, technology intensive.[1] On the contrary, a sizable manufacturing

---

[1] The pattern of premature deindustrialization is not always the case. Korea, Taiwan, Singapore, and Finland created strong technology-intensive sectors during their development processes.

Andrés Solimano and Gabriela Zapata-Román, *Structural Transformations and the Lack of Inclusive Growth. The Case of Chile*. In: *The Developer's Dilemma*. Edited by Armida Salsiah Alisjahbana, Kunal Sen, Andy Sumner, and Arief Anshory Yusuf, Oxford University Press. © UNU-WIDER (2022). DOI: 10.1093/oso/9780192855299.003.0011

sector is strongly associated with a high degree of industrialization and therefore, with more sustainable development.

The ST undertaken in Chile in the past five decades, which we analyse in this chapter, has been related to rapid trade liberalization and an absence of industrial policies, along with privatization and deregulation extended to both the productive and social sectors (education, health, pensions, social housing). Chilean economic growth relies, on the demand side, on the dynamism of exports, private investment, and private consumption; on the supply side, it relies, mainly, on the mining and services sectors. However, in spite of a rising GDP trajectory, the country has undergone a steady process of deindustrialization, with the share of manufacturing in GDP reaching a historic low of 10 per cent in 2018, a level resembling that of the early 1930s at the outset of the Great Depression. In contrast, in 1972 manufacturing was 26 per cent of GDP (Lüders et al. 2016).

Although the naked neoliberalism of the Pinochet era (1973–1989) has been somewhat tempered since the early 1990s by public investment in the social sectors, infrastructure, and regional development, the bulk of the economic model put in place in those years remains in place today and, lately, has provoked serious social resistance. In October 2019, an unexpected wave of acute social unrest developed that appears mostly associated with widespread dissatisfaction towards regressive features of the Chilean economic model, primarily inherited from the dictatorship period. Social indicators show a mix of declining poverty along with persistent inequality of income and wealth, with high asset concentration within powerful economic elites. The Gini coefficient for both monetary incomes (adjusting for transfers) and net wealth, places Chile as the second most unequal country among the Organisation for Economic Co-operation and Development (OECD) countries (OECD 2018a) and among the top ten–fifteen most unequal countries in the world (Solimano 2016). In turn, the income share of the richest 1 per cent of the population captures nearly one-third of national income (López et al. 2013). Chilean development patterns of the past few decades contain several features in need of substantive redirection to be suitable with the United Nations Sustainable Development Goals (UNSDGs) agenda for 2030, which stress ecological sustainability, social equity, participatory development, and productive diversification, among other goals.

This chapter describes the STs that Chile has experienced in the past fifty years and how they have contributed—or not—to inclusive growth. For this, we will analyse the indicators of sectoral production, employment, and productivity, together with data on poverty and inequality from a standardized dataset based on the World Income Inequality Database (WIID) (UNU-WIDER 2019). The second part of the chapter examines the political economy and public policies that have influenced those STs and the future trajectory of ST, employment, and inclusive growth.

2. The developer's dilemma in Chile: an overview

The developer's dilemma relates to how countries manage the tension between ST and inclusive growth. The former refers to shifts in employment between and within sectors to higher-productivity activities essential for economic development. The latter involves spreading the benefits of growth broadly. Economic growth led by ST is more likely to be sustained in the medium term in a way that commodity boom-led growth is not (Herrendorf et al. 2014). This is not least to avoid a growth slowdown or a contested 'middle-income trap' (Eichengreen and Gupta 2013).

The pattern that Chile has followed since the second half of the twentieth century does not seem to be guided by this type of ST. Growth has been mainly led by the strengthening of the services sector at the expense of the manufacturing sector. Services are labour-intensive but have low productivity, since they do not require significant investments in physical and human capital. On the contrary, the development of the manufacturing sector is linked to a more sustainable type of growth, high productivity, and job creation. In the early 1960s, the manufacturing sector contributed more than 30 per cent of economic growth, much like the contribution of non-financial services.

What followed was a very rapid decline in the role of the industrial, manufacturing, and non-manufacturing sectors, together with the scaling up of the impact of financial and non-financial services and mining. By the mid-1970s, the contribution of manufacturing to value-added growth was negative, while financial, non-financial, and mining services accounted for 90 per cent. After a gradual upturn of the contribution of the manufacturing sector to economic growth, it turned to a downward trend, reaching 15 per cent in 2011; see Figure 1 in Solimano and Zapata-Román (2019).

The second part of the developer's dilemma refers to the degree of inclusive growth. In Chile, economic growth has been linked to a sharp decrease in income poverty, particularly since the 1990s. Poverty measured by labour incomes is much higher; see Duran and Kremerman (2021). Inequality, on the other hand, has proved to be more structural and persistent. Since ST is strongly connected with changes in the manufacturing sector, we plot gross income Gini against the value-added manufacturing share in constant prices and the manufacturing employment share (Figure 11.1). We distinguish four periods, which are linked to historical and political developments in the economy and society. The first period, before the dictatorship (up to 1973), had the lowest inequality, along with a rising manufacturing share. The second period, during the dictatorship (1974–1989) that saw great social and economic changes in Chile coincide with the debt crisis of the 1980s and the subsequent recession. In this period, inequality increased strongly, and the decline of the manufacturing industry began. Although there was a small decline in the levels of inequality during the second half of the 1980s and until the end

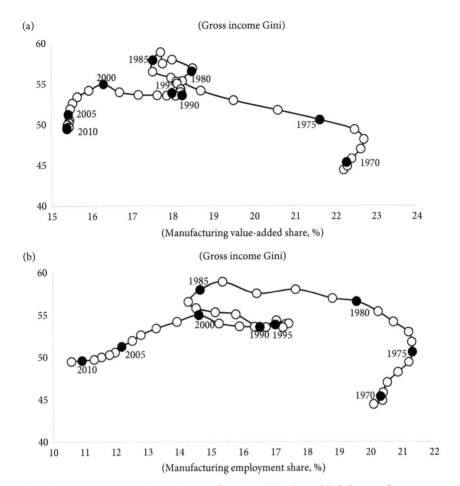

Fig. 11.1 Gross income Gini and manufacturing (a) value-added share and
(b) employment share, Chile, 1968–2011

Notes: (i) The missing Gini coefficients were calculated using linear interpolation. (ii) Manufacturing
value-added and employment shares are five-year moving averages. For example, the data for 1975 is
an average of data for 1971–1975.
Source: authors' illustration based on Timmer et al. (2015); Groningen Growth and Development
Centre (GGDC) 10-Sector Database Version 2015 (GGDC 2015); UNU-WIDER World Income
Inequality Database (WIID).

of the dictatorship, the first decade in the post-Pinochet democracy (1990–1999),
our third period, is marked by growing inequality and sustained economic growth
that extended until the Asian Financial Crisis. This external crisis hit Chile due to
its dependence on international trade with Asia. Lower growth rates and declining inequality accompanied the beginning of the new century (2000–2011), our
fourth period. During this time, the downward trajectory of the manufacturing
sector has remained steady, measured through both the share of value added and
employment.

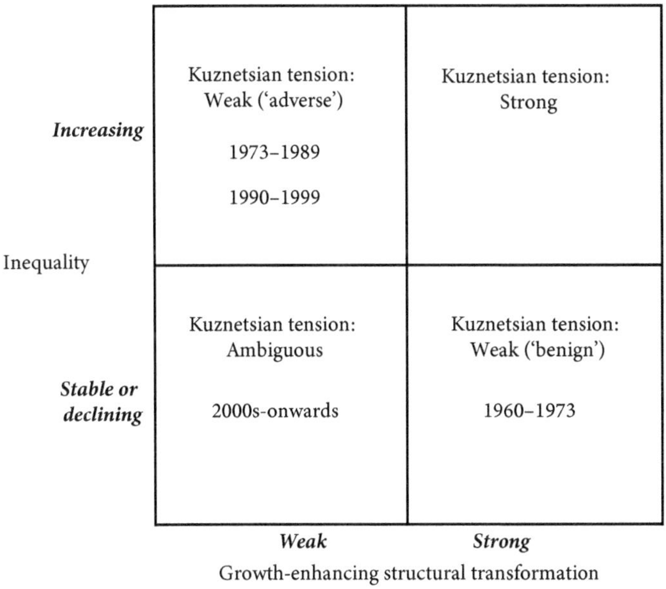

	Weak ('adverse')	Strong
Increasing	Kuznetsian tension: Weak ('adverse') 1973–1989 1990–1999	Kuznetsian tension: Strong
Inequality		
Stable or declining	Kuznetsian tension: Ambiguous 2000s-onwards	Kuznetsian tension: Weak ('benign') 1960–1973
	Weak	*Strong*

Growth-enhancing structural transformation

Fig. 11.2 Patterns of Kuznetsian tension in Chile, 1960–2011
Source: authors' illustration.

Therefore, we do not observe a time-period describing a strong Kuznets tension, that is, increasing inequality with growth-enhancing STs. We identify a weak tension in the first period (before 1973), with low inequality and a growing manufacturing sector. This turns to an adverse weak tension in the following periods 1973–1989 and 1990–1999, given a rising inequality and a shrinking manufacturing sector. Since the 2000s, we observe an ambiguous tension, due to declining inequality combined with an also declining manufacturing sector. For comparison with other chapters in this volume, Figure 11.2 presents the modalities of the Kuznets tension for Chile.

3. Trends in structural transformation

The types of STs that allowed differentiating between developed and developing countries were, according to Solow (1956), related to sectoral development, factors of production, characteristics of the financial system, and healthy dynamic influences, for example, a large proportion of workers who are highly qualified and employed in the formal sector and a diversified manufacturing industry that is larger than other sectors, such as agriculture or mining; also, strong public finances with low debt dependency that rely on direct taxes and provide social security, as well as diversified foreign trade in terms of products and recipient countries. Finally, low poverty and post-tax inequality, plus a well-developed financial system, high investment, and savings, are usually accompanied by slow population growth and high urbanization.

Sumner (2017), in a more contemporary understanding of STs, grouped these characteristics into three main areas. The first refers to sector aspects, or changes in the relative weight of the different productive sectors and their employment shares, towards higher productivity. Second, the factor aspects of ST are about the composition of the productive structure and productivity levels—drivers of economic growth. The third aspect relates to the characteristics of global integration in terms of trade and investment patterns. In the rest of this section, we will discuss the transitions Chile has experienced in relation to these three aspects.

3.1 Changes in the Chilean economic structure

Structural transformations are often described as the movement from agriculture to other, more productive activities. In Chile, this trend has been seen in the displacement of employment away from agriculture but not in value added. Agriculture represented about 4 per cent of value added from 1960 to 2000 and has been closer to 5 per cent of the country's value added since 2000 (see Figure 11.3).

The size of the manufacturing sector is strongly associated with the degree of industrialization and therefore with more sustainable development. In Chile, the sector was growing and reached a peak of about 24 per cent of the total value added in 1972. In September 1973, an authoritarian military government took power in the country and pursued several policies that affected the trajectory of ST. These

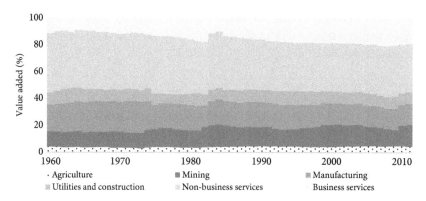

Fig. 11.3 Value-added composition for Chile, 1960–2011

Source: authors' illustration based on the GGDC 10-Sector Database Version 2015 (Timmer et al. 2015).

included exchange rate devaluation, privatization of public enterprises, opening up to international trade, and curtailment of labour unions. Of these neoliberal reforms, trade liberalization was perhaps the one that most dramatically affected the country's productive structure. Prior to 1974, the manufacturing industry enjoyed high tariff protection, which was gradually phased out, along with all import quotas, leaving flat import tariffs of 10 per cent in 1979. Trade liberalization induced a significant change in relative prices in favour of agriculture, mining, and non-tradable goods, affecting the allocation of resources within the economy (Alvarez and Fuentes 2006; Contreras and Ffrench-Davis 2012). By 1975, Chile's GDP had dropped nearly 12 per cent, with annual inflation exceeding 300 per cent. The military government adopted a shock treatment strategy to curb inflation, and also the terms of trade declined. This entailed contractionary fiscal and monetary policy, along with a significant devaluation of the Chilean peso (Ffrench-Davis 2018; Solimano 2012a). These measures did not have a substantial impact on sticky inflation, but led to a sharp contraction of economic activity and a reduction of real wages. By 1975, industrial production had fallen by 28 per cent (Jadresic 1986).

With the opening up to international trade and the Latin American debt crises at the beginning of the 1980s, the manufacturing sector reached the lowest point of the decade in 1982 at 15.7 per cent of total GDP. Manufacturing started to recover by the second half of the 1980s until 1994, when the second phase of contraction started. Since the beginning of the twenty-first century, the declining trend of the manufacturing sector's share of GDP has continued. The latest figures from the Chilean Central Bank show an even more pessimistic scenario, with the manufacturing sector falling to 10.3 per cent of GDP in 2018.

Mining is a key productive sector for the country. Chile is the world's largest copper producer and owns one-third of the world's copper reserves, which are mainly used for electrical conduction. The share of the mining sector has represented, on average, 15 per cent of the total economy since the mid-1970s. Fluctuations in the international price of copper have defined the trajectory of the sector, as this metal represents more than one-half of the country's total exports,[2] and the fall of the sector during the first half of the 1990s parallels the sharp drop in the international price of copper (SONAMI 2019). The boom in copper prices during the 2000s increased the profitability of the industry, attracting foreign investment, which helped to grow the sector (OECD and UN 2018).

The largest sector of the Chilean economy is services. To visualize the trends in this sector, we split it into two parts; the first comprises finance, insurance, real estate, and business services, and the second comprises non-business services. The latter includes trade, restaurants, and hotels; transport, storage, and

---

[2] During the period 1960–1974, copper accounted, on average, for 80 per cent of total exports. That figure dropped to about 60 per cent in the period 1975–1989 and fell to about 50 per cent from the 1990s, on average.

communication; and community, social, and personal services. The service sector, as a whole, has had rather stable participation in the total economy at 52–56 per cent of the total value added from 1960 onwards. However, its composition has changed over time: non-business services have reduced its share in total output, while the financial services sector has steadily increased its relevance, reaching 20 per cent of GDP by 2010. In other words, we observe a trend towards financialization of the economy that coincides with the deindustrialization process.

To summarize, the productive structure in Chile has experienced significant changes over the past fifty years. We can identify some trends in structural changes in sector shares. The first is the growth of the services and financial sector, as well as the mining sector. Services tend to be labour-intensive but not technology-intensive; and mining is technology-intensive but requires few workers, most of whom are highly qualified. The second trend is deindustrialization, shown by the shrinkage of the relative position of the manufacturing sector in aggregate output. For comparison with other chapters in this volume, the varieties of ST in Chile over the period are presented in Figure 11.4.

Industries such as textile, metal-mechanic, and shoe production contracted sharply with trade liberalization in the mid-1970s and, later, with enhanced price competition from China and other East Asian markets. The ownership

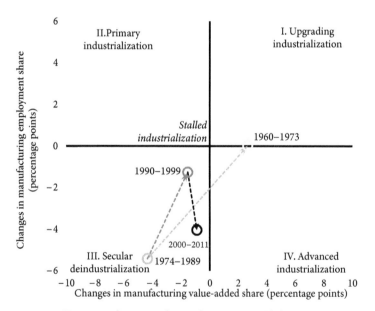

Fig. 11.4 Varieties of structural transformation in Chile, 1960–2011

Source: authors' calculations based on the GGDC 10-Sector Database Version 2015 (Timmer et al. 2015).

structure of productive assets strongly tilted towards the private sector due to the wave of privatization following the free market revolution of the mid-1970s. This trend of deindustrialization is worrisome and could negatively affect Chile's ability to achieve STs towards higher and more sophisticated levels of productive development and technological advance.

3.2 Changes in employment structure

Following changes in its productive structure, Chile's employment structure has undergone drastic changes since 1960. In most sectors, we can distinguish inflexion points in the employment trajectories that coincide with both political and economic crises.

In 1960, three sectors represented 87 per cent of total employment: non-business services, agriculture, and manufacturing. Between 1960 and the mid-1970s, the employment share in agriculture fell steadily, and was absorbed mainly by the manufacturing and non-business service sectors. The period after the military coup (1973–1975) marks a turning point for the manufacturing sector, which fell from 22 to 14 per cent of total employment between 1973 and 1982. The declining trend in agriculture remained, and the non-business services sector offset both shrinkages. With the economic crisis of 1981–1982, GDP per capita fell by 17 per cent and the unemployment rate doubled, reaching 20 per cent in 1982 (Cowan et al. 2004).

After the debt crises, the economy recovered slowly until the end of the military government in 1989. The financial sector became more regulated and received substantial public resources after the crash, doubling its employment share during the 1980s. In 1990, the occupation structure was dominated by non-business services, which represented 48 per cent of total employment, while agriculture and manufacturing represented 18 per cent each.

The rapid growth of the 1990s once again impacted the labour participation of various economic sectors. The share of agricultural employment fell by almost one-half in this decade, accounting for only 10 per cent of total jobs in 2000. The employment shares of mining and manufacturing also declined considerably. The service sector absorbed the decrease in employment in agriculture, mining, and manufacturing, becoming the largest sector by employment, with 67 per cent of the workforce. The 1990s saw accelerated GDP growth and a decline in the relative contribution of manufacturing to overall job creation, along with a consolidation of financialization. The first decade of the twenty-first century accentuated the upward trend in the service sector, which reached 70 per cent of total employment in 2012, with employment in the agriculture and manufacturing sectors falling to 8 and 10 per cent, respectively—see Figure 4 in Solimano and Zapata-Román (2019).

In summary, in this period we observe even more drastic changes in the distribution of employment than we saw in the productive structure. These are related to the flow of workers from agriculture and manufacturing to the services sector. Within services, the absorption of employment is mainly in the subsectors of commerce, restaurants, and personal and social services. There is a tendency towards financialization, given the high growth of employment in the financial sector. The latter requires more qualified workers and concentrates a greater use of technology than other services, but only accounts for one-quarter of all services, which in turn represent almost 70 per cent of total employment in Chile. More recent figures for sectoral GDP indicate that the manufacturing sector continues to shrink, as does the number of jobs, deepening the deindustrialization of the country.

The path followed by the manufacturing sector in Chile is called premature deindustrialization. According to Rodrik (2016), countries experiencing premature deindustrialization observe a sustained decline in both manufacturing value added and employment shares (secular deindustrialization) before reaching the phase of advanced industrialization, or even the stage of upgrading industrialization.

3.3 Changes in labour productivity

According to McMillan and Rodrik (2011), total labour productivity can grow only for two reasons: first, when productivity rises within a sector through capital accumulation, technological development, or a reduction of plant misallocation; second, when there is reallocation of labour across sectors with different productivity levels, from low-productivity to high-productivity sectors. The first type of productivity growth is called a 'within-sector' component, and the second is called 'structural change' because it enhances economy-wide productivity growth.

In developing countries, labour productivity gaps are usually very large between sectors. This is particularly the case when these countries have mining enclaves, which are technologically intensive but employ a small share of the labour force, as is the case in Africa and Latin America. It was expected that after long dictatorships in the 1980s in many Latin American countries, a new economic environment would yield significantly enhanced productivity performance. However, the intensified competition caused by trade liberalization left fewer manufacturing firms in the market, and displaced workers from closed firms ended up in less productive activities, such as services. Thus, the decline in the manufacturing sector translated into growth-reducing structural change (McMillan and Rodrik 2011).

Chile did not depart from this regional trend. The entire increase in labour productivity from 1960 to 2011 was due to the within-sector component, with a negative structural growth (see Figure 11.5). The highest productivity increase occurred with the return to democracy in the 1990s, which coincides with a strong economic boost in the country. During this decade, Chile's GDP grew on average 6 per cent annually, although the structural change in labour productivity was negative due to the expansion of the services sector in terms of both value added and employment.

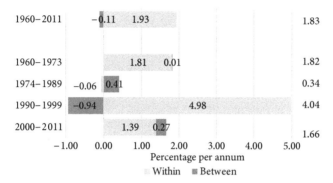

Fig. 11.5 Decomposition of labour productivity growth in Chile, 1960–2011

Note: The decomposition uses the methodology of McMillan and Rodrik (2011).
Source: authors' illustration based on the GGDC 10-Sector Database Version 2015 (Timmer et al. 2015).

Comparing average labour productivity can be misleading if labour shares vary significantly across sectors. For instance, the reason that the labour productivity of the mining sector is so high might simply be because the labour share of this highly capital-intensive sector is small. For that reason, we need to analyse together the changes in productivity and changes in employment shares, for the different sub-periods—see Figure 6 in Solimano and Zapata-Román (2019).

We do not observe significant simultaneous rises in relative productivity and employment in any of the periods. The above-average productivity sectors that increase their employment shares from 1960 to 1973 are manufacturing and non-business services; however, the relative productivity in both cases declined in the period. During the dictatorship, relative productivity worsened in most sectors. This was accompanied by escalations in the employment shares of all services, particularly in non-business services. On the contrary, the employment share in manufacturing fell more than 4 percentage points. In the 1990s, the generation of employment in the services sector was intensified, although at lower levels of relative productivity. The turn of the century came with a slowdown of the economy and minor changes in productivity and employment.

3.4 Trade structure (exports, imports)

Another important factor in ST is the diversification of the economy in terms of activities and markets. The Chilean export structure is very constrained in both. Currently, China, the United States, Japan, and South Korea are its main trading partners; together, they receive 57 per cent of Chile's total exports (Simoes and Hidalgo 2011). Copper and its by-products account for almost one-half of total exports; the remaining half is still very concentrated in natural resources, with limited value added. A major weakness of this trade structure is that it makes the country very vulnerable to external shocks. A contraction in demand by any of these four countries, as well as changes in the international prices of the commodities, can affect the entire economy (OECD and UN 2018).

Despite these weaknesses, there is progress in terms of mineral dependency. From 1962 to 1974, copper and other metals represented on average 87 per cent of total exports, a share that was consistently reduced until the beginning of the new century. The boom in copper's price from the 2000s attracted foreign investment in the sector, which again increased the proportion of this metal in total exports. Still, the upsurge in the production of other metals, such as lithium, allows some degree of diversification. Besides mining exports, Chile has developed an important agroindustry export sector in winery, fruit, fishmeal, and forestry-related products.

However, Chile's imports map out the limitations of the country's productive structure. From the mid-1980s, on average, 70 per cent of the country's imports have been manufactured products. Little progress has been made to revert this tendency, since there has not been a clear decrease in these imports in the past decade. There has also been a rise in fuel consumption, particularly from the 2000s, directly related to the mining industry, which uses energy-intensive production processes.

4. Trends in income inequality, employment, and inclusive growth

Inclusive growth is defined in terms of who benefits from economic growth and by how much, in other words, to what extent growth leads to a reduction in poverty and a decline in inequality.[3] The concept can be extended to include the direct participation of the poor in growth processes via employment and/or reduction in the inequality of opportunity through capability expansion (e.g. health and education access) (Sen 2014).

---

[3] Some versions of the concept of 'inclusive growth' only define inclusive growth as leading to a reduction in poverty, without also requiring a decline in inequality.

4.1 Growth, poverty, and inequality

After 1973, during the military dictatorship, overall inequality increased, although some specific social indicators improved. For example, the number of students in secondary education increased from 51 per cent in 1973 to 75 per cent in 1989, and infant mortality fell from 66 per 1,000 live births to 33 between 1973 and 1980.[4] However, economic, tax, and labour reforms have strongly affected employment and salaries in rather regressive ways. By 1989, the average real wage was eight percentage points below its 1970 level, with 45 per cent of the population living in poverty (MIDEPLAN 1998).[5]

The return of democracy to Chile in the 1990s came with a steady decrease in its poverty. Income poverty was reduced to 36 per cent by 2000 and to 8.6 per cent by 2017 (World Bank 2019). A large proportion of this reduction during the period 1990–1996 can be attributed to sustained economic growth and increasing employment and wages (Contreras 2003). In addition, rising private investment and job creation helped to revert the increase in unemployment and depression of real wages from the dictatorship period (Contreras and Ffrench-Davis 2012). A growth in social spending (targeted cash transfers and subsidies) also contributed to poverty reduction (Gammage et al. 2014).

To reduce income poverty, Chile has relied on aggregate economic growth complemented by subsidies targeted at the poor. However, this strategy has not been as successful in improving other dimensions of well-being. At the national level, the measure of multidimensional poverty (which tracks access to education, health, housing, and other social services) is twice as high as income poverty, at 20.9 per cent in 2015 (CASEN 2015). Indices of educational attainment are systematically lower for the poor. At the same time, open unemployment and labour market informality are systematically higher for the poor (CASEN 2017; Solimano 2018).

Chile has one of the highest levels of inequality in Latin America, with a gross Gini coefficient of 49.36 in 2015. An important source of inequality in Chile is high-income shares at the top of the distribution. According to Gammage et al. (2014), the richest decile had 35.6 times the wealth of the poorest decile in 2011. Additionally, the income share of the wealthiest 1 per cent of the population was, on average, 32.8 per cent of the entire country's income during the period 2005–2010; the share of the top 0.1 per cent was 19.9 per cent; and the top 0.01 per cent got 11.5 per cent of the country's wealth (López et al. 2013).[6] When analysing the

---

[4] See https://childmortality.org/data/Chile; data provided by the Instituto Nacional de Estadísticas (accessed 7 October 2021).

[5] According to other international benchmarks, in 1987 almost 75 per cent of the population was below the US$10 per day threshold and almost 12 per cent under the US$1.9 dollars per day threshold.

[6] These numbers are high by global standards. In 2007, in the United States, the income share of the top 1 per cent was 23 per cent, in the UK it was 14 per cent, and in France it was 8 per cent, based on income data from the respective internal revenue services (Atkinson et al. 2011).

trajectories of income inequality before and after taxes and subsidies, we notice very small differences between them, suggesting that tax redistribution is very limited in Chile.

Between 2000 and 2015, the Gini coefficient fell by almost six points. This is certainly a positive development, although in the same period, the income of the bottom decile (the poorest) grew 145 per cent in real terms, while that of the richest decile grew 30 per cent. However, in absolute terms, the wealthiest decile increased its income by a factor of 9, while the poorest did it only by a factor of 2.5. It is not surprising, then, that although the least advantaged more than doubled their real income, their perception of the income gap not shortening persists (PNUD 2017).

Despite the trend of declining inequality since the 2000s, it is hard to conclude that Chilean economic growth in recent decades has been inclusive, given these high indices of inequality. Although 'all boats have been lifted on the rising tide', the main winners of this period of prosperity and growth are located at the top of the distribution. The causes of this bias towards the very rich in the Chilean growth process needs to be analysed in more detail, which goes beyond the scope of this chapter. Part of the story is likely to be related to the concentration of wealth that emerged after the privatization of public assets undertaken in the 1970s, 1980s, and some in the 1990s. Tax policies that are not progressive, a steady deterioration in public education since the 1980s, and weak labour unions are all factors that have conspired against more inclusive growth (Solimano 2012a, 2012b).

5. Public policies and political economy aspects of Chilean ST and development

Structural transformation and the pattern of overall economic development are shaped, jointly, by public policies and political economy conditions. The former refers to areas such as international trade, industrial policy, credit, macroeconomic management, and others. The second set of variables refers to factors such as relative power of labour, influence of economic elites, degree of social mobilization, distributive conflicts, and institutional frameworks.

5.1 Before dictatorship

The import substitution industrialization (ISI) strategy followed by Chile from the early 1940s to the early 1970s—before industrialists supported the military coup of September 1973—created productive activities that enjoyed import protection from tariffs and other devices (quotas and preferential import arrangements for intermediate parts and capital equipment). The ISI strategy also came with expanded labour union membership in the public and industrial sectors. Labour unions were particularly active in the 1950s and 1960s as inflation eroded the purchasing power of wages. In the early 1970s, although inflation skyrocketed in 1972–1973, the labour union movement, in general, supported the Allende government (1970–1973) and the head of the Nationwide Labour Confederation became the minister of labour and social security in the Popular Unity government. The agrarian elite of landholders benefited from the ownership of large areas of land, which started to change with the launch of agrarian reform from the mid-1960s until 1973. In the social area, public policies were advancing towards increasing degrees of universality in the provision of social services within a general trend of rising inclusion of the middle and working classes through access to public education, public health, housing, and social security schemes. Social rights were promoted through progressive legislation and labour codes improving universality, but faced difficulties in reaching the very poor in rural areas and the marginalized in urban centres.

The political economy of the 1960s was characterized by higher demands for democratization, reflected in the growing participation of various groups in national decisions and the acceleration of agrarian reform. The Allende period of transition to democratic socialism was more polarized. Economic elites opposed nationalization policies and agrarian reform. They resented the attempt to change the economic and political structure of Chile away from the traditional power elites and towards the working classes. On the foreign front, US copper corporations, dissatisfied with nationalization terms, managed to mobilize the US government—headed at the time by President Richard Nixon and Secretary of State Henry Kissinger—to cut multilateral funding to Chile from the International Monetary Fund and the World Bank. The Church Report of the US Congress later confirmed that the Nixon administration also engaged in political and economic destabilization of the Allende government and favoured the military coup of September 1973 (Solimano 2012a, 2012b).

The Allende government had active support from labour unions, peasant organizations, left-wing political parties, intellectuals, and progressive middle-class organizations. However, the economic crisis that erupted in 1972, resulting in high inflation, food shortages, strikes, and the stalling of growth, turned upper-middle-income groups and well-to-do households against the government, and even mobilized some labour unions in the copper sector. This climate of internal division eventually also reached the armed forces, traditionally respectful of civilian democratic rule (see Solimano 2012a, 2012b).

5.2 The Pinochet era

After the military coup, basic democratic procedures were suspended for nearly two decades: parliament remained closed from the day of the coup (11 September 1973); labour union activity was severely restricted, if not banned; civil rights were suspended; left-wing parties were prohibited; the press was tightly censored by military delegates; and political opponents and labour leaders were persecuted and imprisoned, with serious violations of human rights recorded.

The free-market economic agenda of the military regime affected traditional industrialists who had flourished in the ISI period. Neoliberal policies had the support of a class of new owners who acquired public enterprises at low cost, and also of financial intermediaries that reaped big benefits from banking deregulation. Workers could not effectively oppose privatization policies and massive lay-offs occurred in the public sector as unions were severely restricted in their activities. A new dynamic sector was the agroindustry for export, which created additional support groups for trade opening. This sector benefited from more competitive real exchange rates and lower tariffs, and from policies adopted in the 1960s to promote forestry, fishing, and fruit planting.

Since the mid-1970s, policies that have shaped ST have included—tariff reductions and elimination of non-tariff trade barriers, exchange rate policies with alternating objectives in various periods (e.g. anti-inflation between 1979 and 1982 versus export promotion post-1985), the absence of explicit industrial policies, and policies of selling public enterprises created by the Chilean state from the 1940s to the 1970s (the ISI period). Regarding social policy, the approach changed markedly in the late 1970s and early 1980s, when the Pinochet regime launched a set of so-called 'market-orientated social policies'. In the new scheme, the supply of social services traditionally provided by the state started to be delivered by the private sector, often through for-profit companies. In fact, the military regime passed new laws that allowed for-profit providers to operate in the education, health, housing, and pension-fund management sectors. These commercial providers could start charging fees at 'market prices' for social services. Pricing was not the only critical dimension. Given the complex nature of education and health services, along with the fact that the privatized social security system was based on risk–return combinations hardly understood by the population, issues of highly imperfect information and insufficient regulation under oligopolistic market structures also became very relevant. Although more regulation and expansion of social services were introduced after the return of democracy, the overall market orientation of social policies undertaken in the Pinochet era was largely preserved afterwards.

Market-orientated social policies shifted the cost of accessing social services to beneficiaries, reducing state financial burden and increasing it for households. According to the OECD and the World Bank, Chilean families pay—relative to their budgets—the highest proportion for the education of their children (nearly 28 per cent) out of all OECD economies (see OECD 2018b, 2019; Solimano 2012a, 2012b, 2018).

In the market-based social policy model, the recipient's ability to pay determines the quantity and quality of education, health services, and housing. The income level of students and their families becomes a critical determinant of access to education. In this context, talented students from low-income families often cannot afford to attend good schools, creating an adverse selection system that is both detrimental to long-run growth (due to the loss of human capital accumulation) and also exacerbates pre-existing inequality (Bourguignon 2018; Corak 2013; Gaentzsch and Zapata Román 2018; Torche 2014).

The strategy of several governments for dealing with the lack of access to university education due to insufficient income has been to offer student loans administered by commercial banks (charging significant real interest rates that later were reduced through a government subsidy to commercial banks). As expected, there has been an increase in the level of student debt. The rate of return to university education is not guaranteed, as certain university careers, offered by less prestigious private universities, do not always ensure good job market access (Gaentzsch and Zapata-Román 2020). Resistance to policies of privatization, high fees, and the proliferation of student debt, have given rise to an active student movement mobilizing around an agenda of 'quality and free education for all'. The current president of the country is Gabriel Boric, 36 years old and a former leader of the student movement.

Over 80 per cent of the population uses the public health system, which tends to be chronically undercapitalized; there are significant waiting periods for surgeries and other complex medical services. The remaining 20 per cent avoid queuing by going to expensive private clinics. The scheme is financially managed through a private health insurance system called ISAPRES.

An important piece of market-orientated social policy was the privatization of the pension system for the civilian population in 1981 (Solimano 2021). This system is still in operation. Currently, more than 10 million people hold individual pension-savings accounts (of which 5.5 million regularly contribute to the system) managed by for-profit private pension-fund management companies—the AFPs by its Spanish acronym. Under this scheme, the state is barred by law from offering pension-fund management services to the population that could compete with the AFPs (Solimano 2021). New entrants to the workforce have been obliged to contribute on this pay-as-you-go, private-funding modality since 1981. The accumulated pension funds of wage earners in the hands of the AFP system (managed by six private firms) is US$220 billion in 2019, equivalent to 70 per cent of Chilean GDP. These funds, in turn, are the main source of low-cost capital for large Chilean corporations, commercial banks, and foreign corporations. Fund management companies charge a fee to every pension account and earn an average rate of return of 25–30 per cent of the invested capital (Solimano 2017, 2021).

In contrast to the high profit rate of the pension management companies, the average monthly pension received by the pensioners is close to US$300, certainly a modest amount in a country with a per capita income per month slightly above US$2,000.[7] To ensure a minimum pension to low-income people, the state finances out of general tax revenues a basic pension pillar. This pillar reaches about 1.5 million people and provides a pension of US$150 per month to the poorest 60 per cent of the population; the state also provides a subsidy (Aporte Previsional Solidario (APS)) to a range of people in receipt of low pensions.

5.3 The return to democracy

After the restoration of democracy in 1990, civilian governments abstained from progressive redistribution and largely continued with the free-market, pro-business policies of Pinochet in a less ideological/more programmatic manner. New fiscal resources were also devoted to increasing public investment and social sector spending, two neglected areas during the military regime.

Post-Pinochet civilian governments did not revise the obscure privatizations of public enterprises of the 1980s. Economic conglomerates expanded their command of resources, consolidating their political influence over public policies adopted by new governments. Further privatization took place during the post-Pinochet democratic period. Water provision to large cities was transferred to private companies during the government of President Frei Ruiz-Tagle (1994–2000), along with the closing of coal mining in the historic Lota area in the south of the country.

Civilian governments also maintained the private provision of education, health, and the capitalization pension systems instituted by the military regime in the early 1980s. However, in the early 2000s some new programmes in the health sector were put in place, such as the AUGE[8] plan that provided financial resources to patients for the treatment of a list of medical illnesses. In 2008, under the first Bachelet government, a partial reform of the pension system was carried out that created a pillar of minimum pensions and supplementary subsidies for people with small pensions. However, the Bachelet reforms fell short of posing any challenge to the monopoly of the dominant AFP system, which remained virtually intact after these reforms (Solimano 2021). The big pension saving surpluses (on the order of 70 per cent of GDP) continued to be channelled to large corporations, shaping the savings-investment process in a pro-capital fashion. In turn, labour legislation encouraging 'job flexibility' has been functional in maintaining a modest labour share in national income (around 35 per cent).

---

[7] The state also funds pensions of the old pension system and provides the bulk of funding for the pension system of retired personnel of the armed forces, who receive average pensions that can be up to four times higher than the average pensions paid to the civilian population.

[8] The AUGE plan was renamed to Explicit Health Guarantees (GES), they constitute a set of benefits guaranteed by law for people enrolled in both public and private health.

Employment generation benefited, in a quantitative sense, from economy-wide growth, and free-market labour legislation has enabled ample control of the labour process by capital owners. The main source of employment creation has been the services sector, in particular trade, hotels and restaurants, and the financial sector. However, job stability and labour rights have been diminished by the weak bargaining power of labour due to de-unionization, outsourcing, and fragmentation of labour unions, affecting the quality and pay conditions of new jobs.

In the second government of Bachelet (2014–2018), the tax system underwent changes whose net distributional effects are ambiguous. On the one hand, the tax reform of 2014 moderately increased corporation income taxes and reduced deductions from corporation taxation to personal taxes for firm owners (pro-equality changes). On the other hand, it reduced top marginal income tax rates from 40 per cent to 30 per cent. This policy goes against reducing the income share of top earners (the upper 1 or 0.1 per cent), which in Chile, as shown in section 1. Introduction, is exceedingly high.

6. The future trajectories of ST, inequality, and inclusive growth

The Chilean economy faces several challenges in the years ahead, the resolution of which will affect future trajectories of ST, inequality, and growth. In the 2000s, a series of macroeconomic reforms was introduced to reduce the effects of external shocks and consolidate macroeconomic stability. A rule to increase fiscal spending according to expected long-term growth and terms of trade was put in place, and in 2008 an economic and social stability fund was created, along with a pension reserve fund. An (orthodox) independent central bank holding only an inflationary objective complemented the macro framework with a flexible exchange rate regime and a precautionary policy of holding relatively large international reserves. As of 2022 annual inflation accelerated to near 7 percent due to the effects of COVID-related supply shocks with the Ukraine conflict leading to further increases in energy and food prices.

There are, nevertheless, important remaining challenges on the real side of the economy such as sustainability of growth, diversification of the country's economic structure, faster productivity growth, and ecological protection. As the country approaches higher levels of per capita income, convergence to the high growth rates of the mid-1980s and 1990s (6–7 per cent per year) is highly unlikely as overall productivity growth has stalled for more than a decade. Further acceleration in the rate of economic growth will depend more on productivity growth and technical improvements than on factor accumulation because of diminishing returns to capital. In addition, natural resources will be severely strained with an attempt to achieve higher growth based on the consumption of natural capital that the current practice follows. In turn, the current *composition* of growth, as discussed in section 3, is tilted to mining and services, with a diminished manufacturing sector. A reversal of these trends may not be easy; currently, Chile spends less than 0.4 per cent of its GDP on research and development (R&D) (well below the average OECD level of around 2.5 per cent of GDP) and successive governments have been reluctant to adopt more active industrial policies. Also, the value-added intensity of the export bundle remains moderate, as the country still relies on the export of commodities (copper) with relatively low value added, although agroindustry exports are more labour-intensive. In the last OECD 'Productive Transformation Policy Review', the need for an 'update' of the development strategy in Chile was highlighted. The review stresses the importance of increasing factor productivity growth, lowering the territorial concentration of production, raising value addition in services, and reducing over-reliance on mining, among other deficiencies. The report proposed exploiting opportunities in green production, developing solar energy, increasing digitalization, and investing in big data and broader internet connections. The emphasis and recommendations of the report seem reasonable, although it is probably over-optimistic in its assessment of the willingness and ability of governments, inspired by a hands-off approach to development, to carry out this 'update' of the Chilean development strategy (OECD and UN 2018). This can change with the new Boric administration.

Future trends in inequality and the prospect of more inclusive growth also remain uncertain. A Kuznets dynamic may be operating (in which at certain GDP per capita the economy becomes less unequal) as the gross and net income Gini coefficients have declined by five or six percentage points over the past fifteen to twenty years. The expansion of higher education from nearly 200,000 students to close to one million over this period has reduced the education premium and lessened labour income inequality. In the future, the earnings capacities of low-income workers will depend on their access to quality public education at primary, secondary, and tertiary levels—a goal hampered by the current deterioration of public education at primary and secondary levels. Capital incomes, in turn, depend on interest earned on financial assets, dividend flows from physical assets, and profits from current production. Chile exhibits high levels of wealth inequality, which may be difficult to reduce through taxes on the very rich or other means because of political resistance to redistributive policies by powerful economic elites.

7. Conclusion

The Chilean development strategy of the past three or four decades has given priority to aggregate economic growth, orthodox macroeconomic management, and high profitability for foreign direct investment and big domestic business. There has been a pay-off in GDP growth, higher GDP per capita, and higher living standards. However, this prosperity may have been, to an extent, borrowed, as it has relied on the intensive exploitation of non-reproducible natural resources. In addition, from the 2000s, observed rates of GDP growth started to slow down. At the sector level, the economy has specialized in mining, finance, and services, with a diminished share of the manufacturing sector in output that reached a historical low of 10 per cent of GDP in 2017. In October-December 2019, the country faced a period of serious social unrest and protests, the 'estallido social', with their roots in dissatisfaction with the neoliberal economic model and its features of low wages, expensive social services, and overall social inequality giving rise to a constitutional convention drafting a new constitution that overcomes the one inherited from the Pinochet regime that has supported the neoliberal economic model.

The empirical analysis of this chapter shows a decline in the value-added shares of manufacturing and agriculture, and a rise in services, particularly finance, trade, and hotels and restaurants, with ups and downs in mining shares in the transition from the ISI strategy to the outward-orientated neoliberal model. These trends are more strongly accentuated for employment shares, with the decline in relative employment generation in agriculture and manufacturing going directly to the services sector, which accounts now for two-thirds of total employment in the economy. Trade liberalization led to severe reductions in the value-added shares of textiles, metal-mechanic, and shoe factories within manufacturing.

Social indicators for the past three decades display a mixed story: while total income-based poverty declined from 45 per cent in the late 1980s to less than 10 per cent in 2017, multidimensional poverty measured as gaps in access to education, health, good jobs, and housing was nearly 20 per cent in 2017 although these social indicators worsened during the pandemic of COVID-19 in 2020 and 2021. Inequality of income has dropped in the past twenty years, but it remains at high levels by international standards of countries with a similar level of per capita income. In turn, the Gini coefficients for total net wealth (around 70 per cent) and financial wealth (close to 90 per cent) are substantially higher than the net income Gini (nearly 50 per cent), adding a very relevant dimension (i.e. wealth inequality) to the issue of economic inequality. Income and wealth concentration at the top (richest 1 and 0.1 per cent) are very high in Chile.

A more balanced and sustainable development strategy for Chile, in line with the UNSDGs and climate warming trends, for example, would require significant changes in its production structure. Policy improvement will require moving away from the intensive use of natural resources and towards knowledge-intensive sectors, a revival of manufacturing, and clean production lines supported by a more environmentally conscious tax system. The reduction of high inequality and deconcentration of wealth, again to be aligned with the UNSDGs, requires important reforms in the tax system and the structure of markets, effective anti-trust legislation, and the rebalancing of bargaining capacities between labour and capital that revert the enormous economic surplus currently appropriated by wealthy elites, enabling more inclusive growth.

References

Alvarez, R., and J.R. Fuentes (2006). 'Trade Reforms and Manufacturing Industry in Chile'. In P.A. Aroca and G.J.D. Hewings (eds), *Structure and Structural Change in the Chilean Economy*. London: Palgrave Macmillan, 71–94.

Atkinson, A.B., T. Piketty, and E. Saez (2011). 'Top Incomes in the Long Run of History', *Journal of Economic Literature*, 49(1): 3–71.

Bourguignon, F. (2018). 'Measuring the Inequality of Opportunities'. In J. Stiglitz, J. Fitoussi, and M. Durand (eds), *For Good Measure: Advancing Research on Well-Being Metrics Beyond GDP*. Paris: OECD Publishing, Chapter 5, 101–142.

CASEN (2015) *Ampliando al Mirada sobre la pobreza y la desigualdad*. Santiago: Observatorio Social, Gobierno de Chile.

CASEN (2017). *Síntesis de Resultados. Ministerio de Desarrollo*. Santiago: Gobierno de Chile.

Contreras, D. (2003). 'Poverty and Inequality in a Rapid Growth Economy: Chile 1990–96', *Journal of Development Studies*, 39: 181–200.

Contreras, D., and R. Ffrench-Davis (2012). 'Policy Regimes, Inequality, Poverty and Growth: The Chilean Experience, 1973–2010'. WIDER Working Paper 04/2012. Helsinki: UNU-WIDER.

Corak, M. (2013). 'Income Inequality, Equality of Opportunity, and Intergenerational Mobility', *Journal of Economic Perspectives*, 27: 79–102.

Cowan, K.N., A. Micco, A. Mizala, C.P. Pagés, and P. Romaguera (2004). *Un diagnóstico del desempleo en Chile*. Washington, DC: Inter-American Development Bank.

Duran, G. and M. Kremerman (2021). 'La pobreza del "modelo" chileno: La insuficiencia de los ingresos del trabajo y las pensiones' Documento de Trabajo, Fundacion Sol, ISSN0719-6695; Santiago, Chile.

Eichengreen, B., and P. Gupta (2013). 'The Two Waves of Service-Sector Growth', *Oxford Economics Papers*, 65: 96–123.

Ffrench-Davis, R. (2018). *Reformas económicas en Chile 1973–2017*. Santiago: Penguin Random House Grupo Editorial Chile.

Gaentzsch, A., and G. Zapata Román (2018). 'More Educated, Less Mobile? Diverging Trends in Income and Education Mobility in Chile and Peru', *Journal of Income Distribution*, 27: 66–105.

Gaentzsch, A. and G. Zapata Román (2020). 'Climbing the Ladder: Determinants of Access to Higher Education in Chile and Peru'. UNRISD Working Paper WP-2020-2. UNRISD. https://www.unrisd.org/unrisd/website/document.nsf/(httpPublications)/904B2706D3EEBF7D8025854A00556683?OpenDocument

Gammage, S., T. Alburquerque, and G. Durán (2014). *Inclusive Labour Markets, Labour Relations and Working Conditions Branch*. Geneva: International Labour Office.

Herrendorf, B., R. Rogerson, and Á. Valentinyi (2014). 'Growth and Structural Transformation'. In P. Aghion and S.N. Durlauf (eds), *Handbook of Economic Growth*. New York: Elsevier, 147–193.

Jadresic, E. (1986). *Evolución del empleo y desempleo en Chile, 1970–85*. Santiago: Colección estudios CIEPLAN.

Kim, K., and A. Sumner (2019). 'The Five Varieties of Industrialisation: A New Typology of Diverse Empirical Experience in the Developing World'. ESRC GPID Research Network Working Paper 18. London: Global Poverty and Inequality Dynamics Research Network (GPID).

Kuznets, S. (1955). 'Economic Growth and Income Inequality', *American Economic Review*, 45(1): 1–28.

López, R., E. Figueroa, and P. Gutiérrez (2013). 'La "Parte del León": Nuevas estimaciones de la participación de los super ricos en el ingreso de Chile'. Working Paper 32. Santiago: Departamento de Economia, Universidad de Chile.

Lüders, R., J. Díaz, and G. Wagner (2016). *La República en cifras: Historical Statistics*. Santiago: Ediciones UC.

McMillan, M.S., and D. Rodrik (2011). 'Globalization, Structural Change and Productivity Growth'. Working Paper 17143. Cambridge, MA: National Bureau of Economic Research.

MIDEPLAN (1998). *Evolución de la Pobreza e Indigencia en Chile 1987–1996*. Santiago: Gobierno de Chile.

OECD (2016). *Chile: Policy Priorities for Stronger and More Equitable Growth*. Paris: OECD Publishing.

OECD (2018a). 'Income Distribution and Poverty: Overview', www.oecd.org/social /inequality.htm#income (accessed 25 July 2018).

OECD (2018b). 'Chile'. In *Education at a Glance 2018: OECD Indicators*. Paris: OECD Publishing.

OECD (2019). 'Education GPS', http://gpseducation.oecd.org (accessed 4 January 2019).

OECD and UN (2018). *Production Transformation Policy Review of Chile: Reaping the Benefits of New Frontiers, OECD Development Pathways*. Paris: OECD Publishing.

PNUD (2017). *Desiguales. Orígenes, cambios y desafíos de la brecha social en Chile*. Santiago: Programa de las Naciones Unidas Para el Desarrollo.

Rodrik, D. (2016). 'Premature Deindustrialization', *Journal of Economic Growth*, 21: 1–33.

Sen, K. (2014). 'Inclusive Growth: When May We Expect It? When May We Not?', *Asian Development Review*, 31: 136–162.

Simoes, A.J.G., and C.A. Hidalgo (2011). 'The Economic Complexity Observatory: An Analytical Tool for Understanding the Dynamics of Economic Development'. Workshops at the Twenty-Fifth AAAI Conference on Artificial Intelligence, 7–11 August, San Francisco, CA.

Solimano, A. (2012a). *Chile and the Neoliberal Trap: The Post-Pinochet Era*. Cambridge: Cambridge University Press.

Solimano, A. (2012b). *Capitalismo a la chilena: Y la prosperidad de las elites*. Santiago: Editorial Catalonia.

Solimano, A. (2016). *Global Capitalism in Disarray: Inequality, Debt, and Austerity*. Oxford: Oxford University Press.

Solimano, A. (2017). *Pensiones a la chilena*. Santiago: Editorial Catalonia.

Solimano, A. (2018). 'Estrategia de Desarrollo Economico en Chile: Crecimiento, Pobreza Estructural y Desigualdad de iIngresos y Riqueza'. In *Chile Del Siglo XXI: Propuestas Desde La Economia*. Berlin: Heinrich Böll Stiftung and Estudios Nueva Economia.

Solimano, A. (2021). The Rise and Fall of the Privatized Pension System in Chile. An International Perspective. London and New York: Anthem Press.

Solimano, A., and D. Calderón Guajardo (2015). *Economic Inequality and Macroeconomic Cycles: Evidence for Latin America*. Santiago: UN-ECLAC.

Solimano, A., and D. Calderón Guajardo (2017). 'The Copper Sector, Fiscal Rules and Stabilization Funds in Chile@ Scope and Limits'. UNU-WIDER Working Paper 2017/53. Helsinki: UNU-WIDER.

Solimano, A. and G. Zapata-Román (2019). 'Structural Transformations and the Lack of Inclusive Growth: The Case of Chile'. WIDER Working Paper 2019/118. Helsinki: UNU-WIDER.

Solow, R.M. (1956). 'A Contribution to the Theory of Economic Growth', *Quarterly Journal of Economics*, 70: 65–94.

SONAMI (2019). *Estadisticas de precios*. Santiago: Sociedad Nacional de Mineria.

Sumner, A. (2017). 'The Developer's Dilemma: The Inequality Dynamics of Structural Transformations and Inclusive Growth'. Paper presented at the Global Poverty and Inequality Dynamics Research Network Workshop, Bangkok, 10 September 2019. London: Global Poverty and Inequality Dynamics Research Network.

Timmer, M.P., G.J. de Vries, and K. de Vries (2015). 'Patterns of Structural Change in Developing Countries'. In J. Weiss and M. Tribe (eds), *Routledge Handbook of Industry and Development*. London: Routledge, 65–83.

Torche, F. (2014). 'Intergenerational Mobility and Inequality: The Latin American Case', *Annual Review of Sociology*, 40: 619–642.

UNU-WIDER (2019). Standardized dataset based on World Income Inequality Database, WIID 4, version 22 February 2019. Helsinki: UNU-WIDER.

World Bank (2019). 'Poverty Headcount Ratio at National Poverty Lines (% of Population): Chile', https://data.worldbank.org/indicator/SI.POV.NAHC?locations=CL (accessed 8 July 2018).

PART V
LOOKING AHEAD

12

Leapfrogging into the Unknown

The Future of Structural Change in the Developing World

Lukas Schlogl

1 Introduction

What will the future of structural transformation look like in the developing world?[1]

This chapter discusses and extrapolates a set of trends in the structure of employment and value added, global trade, and technological upgrading that is likely to shape developing economies going forward. Across each of these domains, the chapter reviews assessments in current empirical and theoretical literature. Further, it offers a conceptual framework for understanding the opportunities and challenges around structural transformation posed for developing countries in the face of contemporary technological change.

The chapter posits that a defining issue for the future of structural change is that of new 'asynchronies' in the sequencing of development pathways—echoing themes of prematurity, economic catch-up, and technological imitation. The notion of 'leapfrogging' (i.e. of adopting frontier technologies and skipping intermediate stages in technological development) has recently gained traction and is critically assessed here. It is argued that emerging development challenges across different domains of economic activity centre around understanding and managing the risks and opportunities offered by novel constellations of maturity and prematurity of development. A key risk is that the decreasing relative capacity of the industrial sector to generate mass employment in an age of high technology will make it harder to achieve the downswing in inequality promised by economic maturity (per Kuznets 1955).

---

[1] The author would like to thank Jostein Hauge, Kyunghoon Kim and Andy Sumner, as well as participants at the 2019 United Nations University-World Institute for Development Economics Research (UNU-WIDER) workshop 'The Developer's Dilemma' in Bangkok, for valuable comments. The usual disclaimers apply.

Lukas Schlogl, *Leapfrogging into the Unknown*. In: *The Developer's Dilemma*.
Edited by Armida Salsiah Alisjahbana, Kunal Sen, Andy Sumner, and Arief Anshory Yusuf, Oxford University Press.

The chapter is structured as follows. Section 2 offers a framework for understanding scenarios of catch-up structural transformation in a context of technological borrowing. It argues that novel constellations of earliness and lateness in economic and technological development are key to this understanding. Section 3 sketches and extrapolates long-term trends of structural change in employment and value added. The novel constellations here are a trend towards premature tertiarization, new forms of global structural convergence, and the 'hybridization' of economic sectors. Section 4 explores the issue of trade and globalization in times of automation, with a focus on the debated threat of 'reshoring' of previously offshored activities. Late-developing countries now face competition from labour-saving technology up the stream of global values chains. Finally, Section 5 analyses technological leapfrogging in the service sector, drawing on empirical trends and examples from South-East Asia that could be considered typical for modernizing middle-income countries. Section 6 concludes.

2. Catch-up in the age of automation: an analytical framework

In the 1950s, economic historian Alexander Gerschenkron (1951) posited that a country's 'economic backwardness' (i.e. its relative lack of industrialization) could, in some respects, be considered an advantage. By importing modern technologies from leading industrialized countries and by investing in cutting-edge machinery and equipment, 'latecomers' to the development process could skip stages of modernization that previous scholars such as Walt Rostow had deemed necessary in any successful path towards economic development. Skipping, in Gerschenkron's view, would enable late-developing economies to generate faster and more capital-intensive industrial growth, unhindered by societal constraints and orchestrated by a strong, dirigiste state (for a more recent discussion, see Mathews (2006); see Nayyar (2013) for a history of the catch-up paradigm and Lin (2016) for a discussion of latecomer advantages and disadvantages).

Arguments in the vein of Gerschenkron are currently seeing a revival in the flourishing discourse of technological 'leapfrogging' (e.g. Lee 2019). The idea that less-developed countries could reap the benefits of skipping intermediate stages in technological progress—for example, jumping straight into mobile-phone-based e-payment systems without first building an automated teller machine (ATM) infrastructure—can also be heard across the board of international development organizations. There are, however, critical voices. Pritchett (2020) argues that technological research and development (R&D) in high-income countries reflects distorted price signals due to immigration barriers, among other things. This makes technology economize on factors of production such as routine manual labour that are in fact abundant in low-income countries. In the view of Pritchett

(2020: 132), 'this pattern of innovation is a massive negative externality to the global economy as what is needed, (…) is jobs for low to medium skill labor' in developing countries. Pritchett's view implies that the adoption of technology developed *in* and *for* high-income countries is not necessarily advantageous in other circumstances.

In a simplified overview, one could conceptualize the possible configurations of economic development and technology adoption along a two-by-two matrix of earliness and lateness in each dimension (see Table 12.1 and Figure 12.1). A conventional 'lining-up' pathway would envisage late-developing countries adopting a new technology later than high-income countries—in the strictest sense, adoption would take place only at a time when the adopting countries have reached a comparable level of economic development to that of developed countries at the time of adoption.[2] Examples for lining up of that kind can be found across a whole range of economic activities, most notably in agriculture, that are often carried out manually in developing countries yet are automated in Organisation for Economic Co-operation and Development (OECD) countries. Technology adoption might happen only after prices have dropped, after patents have expired, after goods are sold in a second-hand, used state (e.g. machinery, vehicles), etc. However, as the overall structure of the economy in late-developing countries is characterized by numerous forms of lateness, a lining-up approach should be distinguished from

Table 12.1 Constellations along the technology–development nexus

| | | Economic development | |
		Late	Early
Technology adoption	Late	*Lining up* A conventional pathway of following step-by-step historical patterns without 'jumping the queue' of technological development	*Lagging* A conservative pathway of delaying overdue technological steps and of late borrowing from innovators
	Early	*Leaping* A disruptive pathway defying historical patterns by skipping steps in technological development	*Leading* An innovative pathway of pushing the technological frontier and of taking new or rapid steps in technological development

Source: author's illustration.

[2] Within the class of 'lining up' developing countries, one could potentially further differentiate between earlier and later adoption given a comparable level of development, that is, lagging within lining up.

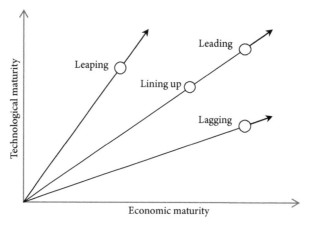

Fig. 12.1 Development pathways with reference to economic and technological maturity
Source: author's illustration.

the notion of lagging behind. Technology adoption depends on complementarities of skill, infrastructure, regulation, and of other factors, and would thus not typically be expected in the absence thereof.

In contrast, 'lagging' would mean late adoption of technology despite economic maturity and the presence of relevant complementarities. Consider, for instance, the current lack of high-speed rail networks in the United States and the UK, while such infrastructure has long been present in high-income countries (HICs) such as Japan, France, or Spain, and even in some middle-income countries (MICs) such as China. The United States is similarly lagging in some aspects of airport infrastructure compared to other HICs. Several countries in continental Europe could be considered to be lagging in innovation in the digital and engineering sector compared to the United States or Scandinavia, in the adoption of self-checkout technology in the retail sector, or in the availability of high-speed internet.

From California's Silicon Valley to Berlin's Silicon Allee, technological 'leading' is almost by definition predominantly found across the high-income OECD world but also increasingly so in China. Finally, cases of 'leaping' (or 'leapfrogging'), meaning early adoption of technologies despite late development, can be found across the developing world. The mobile-phone-based financial service *M-Pesa* in Kenya and Tanzania is often mentioned under this rubric. Automated train and subway systems exist in many MICs, notably in Asia, and self-checkout and e-kiosk systems in retail and food services are currently being rolled out in some countries in these regions. All of these are cases of 'early adoption during late development'.

Section 5 of this chapter will discuss in more detail the introduction of automated toll booth technology in South-East Asia as an example of leap(frogg)ing.

A view of development as sequenced adoption of technology along a stepwise pathway serves as no more than a point of orientation and comparison. Empirical evidence on the benefits and downsides of developmental asynchronicity is relatively scarce. Empirically, Gerschenkron's original research focused on newly industrialized countries in Eastern Europe and Russia, which the data of the time fitted. Later research on economic convergence, in contrast, has long struggled to find much evidence in support of economic convergence, which should follow from latecomer advantages (e.g. Pritchett 1997; Nayyar 2013). China's rapid industrial catch-up, thanks in part to an aggressive strategy of borrowing and copying foreign technologies, on the other hand, would appear to lend some credibility to Gerschenkron's optimistic thesis. The neoclassical standard model of growth, the Solow–Swan model, also suggests higher growth potentials during catch-up than at the technological frontier.

There is some evidence that developing countries 'import' OECD-type challenges such as skills-biased technological change and labour market polarization via technology transfers in global value chains (GVCs) (see Ugur and Mitra (2017), who provide a systematic review of technology adoption and employment in least-developed countries (LDCs) finding both skills bias and challenges of employment creation; see also Yasara and Rejesus (2020); Pahl and Timmer (2019)). Chang and Andreoni (2020: 7) further point out that 'the debate around digitalization is dominated by the idea of a leap into a post-industrial age, without the realization that manufacturing processes and the materiality of production will still matter in such an economy'. Even if one rejects Gerschenkron's optimism, though, it seems sensible to concede that optimal structural change is a moving target that depends on changing conditions such as relative factor prices, technological frontiers, and a changing landscape of international competition. Policies of structural change will thus have to be adaptive and staying 'in line' with development conventions is by no means always advisable.

Table 12.2 sketches an indicative list of opportunities and risks with a view to the leaping approach. Disadvantageous leaps are referred to here as 'technology creeps', capturing the idea that technology is creeping into domains without a plausible development rationale. Unquestionably, though, the dividing line between 'leap' and 'creep' is fuzzy and the same phenomena might well be labelled differently by different scholarly camps. The present chapter explores the debate of prematurity with a focus on the first three domains on which Table 12.2 provides examples, while the bottom three are mentioned for indicative purposes only. The list is not exhaustive.

Table 12.2 Early adoption during late development: opportunities and risks

	Technology leap Early adoption of technologies conducive to catch-up development (Gerschenkron's 'advantages of backwardness')	**Technology creep** Early adoption of technologies disadvantageous to catch-up development (Pritchett's 'distorted patterns of innovation')
Structural change	Sector hybridization and upgrading, convergence of industrial activity	Premature deindustrialization ('Disrupted Development' per Schlögl and Sumner 2020)
Labour market	Automation displacing scarce or augmenting abundant labour	Automation displacing abundant labour; jobless growth
Trade	Offshoring with technology transfers	'Value-added erosion' due to GVC participation (Caraballo and Jiang 2016)
Governance	Free access to information, distant learning, e-participation	Mass surveillance, manipulation of online discourse, misinformation
Global power relations	Technological independence due to early-mover advantages	Technological dependency due to patents or lock-in effects, 'data colonies'
Environment	Efficiency gains, green technology, carbon decoupling	Growing energy consumption, electronic waste, rise in emissions

Source: author's illustration.

3. Towards structural convergence and hybridization

What do earliness and lateness imply for the realm of structural change? Historically, the trend over the past decades has largely been for sectoral employment shares to gradually decline in agriculture from already low levels and to grow in the service sector. Industrial employment shares have declined in all but the very lowest-income countries. This general pattern of structural change tends to be visible across different geographical regions and country-income groups; see Sen (2019), who discusses the standard model and deviations from it in low-income economies.

Extrapolating this historical trend, sometimes referred to as 'Petty's Law', into the future would suggest a continued increase of service-sector work at the expense of both industrial and agricultural work. Farmers would be increasingly concentrated in the LDCs, where they are already concentrated today, while farming everywhere else would become ever more capital-intensive. Even if there are calls for more decentralized, organic forms of agriculture, it is hard to imagine a reversal of the declining employment trend in agriculture, given rapid technological advances in this field from drones to automated crop-picking to satellite-assisted 'precision agriculture'. As the world continues to reduce human labour input to farming and manufacturing, the 'post-industrial' revolution, which took off in mid-twentieth-century Europe, will keep unfolding until it reaches a point where the vast majority of human labour is pursued in some variety of service sector. Most potential for structural change of this conventional, cross-sector, kind is left in low-income countries (LICs) and it is in in these countries where it is already showing the fastest pace (Merotto et al. 2018).

It is noteworthy that the country-level share of industrial employment (currently at around roughly one-fifth to one-quarter of the labour force on average) has, over time, increasingly become detached from the level of economic development of a country. LICs like Benin or the Republic of Congo, lower-middle-income countries (LMICs) like Bangladesh or India, upper-middle-income countries (UMICs) like Mexico or Paraguay and high-income countries (HICs) like Finland or Switzerland employ around 20–25 per cent of their labour force in the industrial sector (World Bank n.d.). The countries with the lowest gross domestic product (GDP) per capita are still dominated by agricultural employment, while the richest ones are strongly service-sector-based economies, yet the global trend appears to be towards increasing homogeneity in terms of industrial employment shares.

There is thus a trend of structural convergence as LICs have expanded their industrial employment shares (from low levels) while HICs show declining shares from moderate levels, on a population-weighted account. Projecting this past trend into the future would imply that the developing world will overtake high-income economies in terms of country-level industrial employment shares; see Schlogl (2020) for a visual depiction based on International Labour Organization-modelled estimates provided by World Bank (n.d.). If the historical inverse-U-shaped pattern, which suggests that industrial employment first expands and then contracts during economic development, continues to hold, the share of employment in industry will at some point go into reverse: from industrialization to deindustrialization. This turning point—which would adequately be called the 'Clark turning point' after Clark (1940), who first noted these sector dynamics[3]—lies, at least on average, in the future.[4] Since the developing world has larger labour

---

[3] Clark (1940) was the first to note that 'the proportion of the working population engaged in secondary industry appears in every country to rise to a maximum and then to begin falling, apparently indicating that each country reaches a stage of maximum industrialization beyond which industry begins to decline relative to tertiary production'.

[4] The narrower category of employment in *manufacturing* as opposed to industry seems to have gone into reverse earlier in developing countries, as pointed out by Rodrik (2016) and others under the thesis of 'premature deindustrialization'.

forces than the developed world, industrial employment convergence is compatible with the world having gone through a rise, in absolute terms, in the global number of workers employed in industry.

Employment in agriculture has declined across all countries over the past fifty years. The change has been most dramatic in East and South-East Asia and least dramatic in sub-Saharan Africa. The value-added share of agriculture (has also declined in all but the richest developing countries (Brazil, Chile, and South Africa) where it had already fallen to a low level decades ago. The only other sectoral trend which has been equally geographically universal is the rise in service-sector-based employment, which is visible in all major developing economies. Other shifts in the economic structure appear to be more country- or region-specific. East Asia, for instance, has seen an expansion of manufacturing employment not present in other regions. What does this mean for the future? Most potential for conventional structural change lies in Africa, which currently still employs around 60 per cent of its labour force in agriculture—a share roughly equal to that of developing East Asia (excluding China) around 1970. Moreover, it is worth noting that once labour has exited the agricultural sector, the dynamics of structural change become more static.

Is the expansion of the service sector, tertiarization, likely to stay with us? The trend will arguably continue even if countries place some weight on a degree of agricultural and industrial self-sufficiency and if the international division of labour thus remains partial—as Keynes (1933) advocated for and as modern defenders of industrial policy keep promoting today. Technological advances mean that a growing 'robot reserve army' is pushing the human labour force into non-automatable tasks, creating a technological 'dual economy' with new dynamics of labour surplus exchange (Schlogl and Sumner 2020). This is a new development constellation which late-developing countries are facing.

Alonso-Soto (2020) shows that contemporary patterns of structural change are exposing emerging economies to labour-displacing technologies and thus reducing manual—though not always routine—work. Non-automatable tasks will be increasingly located in sectors like education, health care, or social services, which require human interaction, flexibility, creativity, human touch, empathy, and similar difficult-to-automate qualities (Autor et al. 2003; Goos and Manning 2007; Autor and Dorn 2013; Frey and Osborne 2013). Though the service sector contains an extent of automatable work (e.g. cognitively repetitive or highly structured tasks), which may become redundant thanks to digitization and artificial intelligence (Willcocks and Lacity 2016), most scholars expect that this sector will remain a refuge of human competitive advantage (Autor 2015).

Does this mean that the world is deindustrializing? In one sense, in terms of country-level employment shares, it does, albeit less so in LICs. Tech companies such as Google or Amazon, as the modern equivalents of past manufacturing giants, employ far fewer people than Ford or General Motors did, while ranking similarly on the Fortune 500 (Madrigal 2017). Similarly, one could point to a modern mobile network operator such as Safaricom, catering to over 20 million users of the earlier mentioned *M-Pesa*, which directly employs just over 6,000 staff, though it is one of the most profitable companies in all of Africa (Safaricom 2019). Factories will surely continue to be built in developing countries, but should also be expected to depend on less labour input relative to other sectors. Labour-intensive cut–mend–trim or assembly-type activities might become obsolete in light of rapid advances in garment and manufacturing technology (see, e.g. Nayak and Padhye 2018).

In another sense, however, in terms of the absolute number of workers employed in industry, the world may not deindustrialize given growing labour forces in developing countries. Haraguchi et al. (2017: 293) argue that, from a global perspective, 'the manufacturing sector's value added and employment contribution to world GDP and employment, respectively, have not changed significantly since 1970'. Rather, they argue, manufacturing has shifted to a handful of populous developing countries. One could contend, of course, that manufacturing remaining constant throughout decades of structural change (largely in the form of agriculture-to-services shifts), means a *relative displacement* of manufacturing.

In yet another sense, in terms of industrial value added to GDP, this is a more open question. Globally, the population-weighted average value added of industry (including construction, mining, and utilities) has been on a declining trajectory, driven by the continued value-added tertiarization of high-income economies followed by MICs. A majority of LICs, on the other hand, have seen value-added shares in industry expand, albeit from a low level. Put differently, employment deindustrialization means that relatively fewer workers will be required to produce a unit of industrial output, but not that less industrial output is produced. Generally, value addition and employment are, though, on similar trajectories.

In yet another sense, though, what may be more likely than deindustrialization in a strict sense is an increasing conceptual blurring of economic sectors—an argument also made by Gollin (2018). On the one hand, services are already increasingly industrial, meaning scaled up for mass consumption and assisted by technologies. Medical care or education, for better or worse, belong to a 'service industry' in the sense that they are capital-intensive, characterized by economies of scale and agglomeration, and that their business processes tend to be increasingly highly structured, standardized, and have a highly developed division of labour. Increasingly, services are also tradable nowadays. Computing and information and communication technology (ICT) is a hybrid of industrial and service-sector-based business, sometimes classified into the 'quarternary sector'. As ICT gets injected into ever more economic activities, the boundaries between services and industry get blurry and services become 'industries without smokestacks' (Newfarmer et al. 2018).

Industrial manufacturing, on the other hand, depends on service inputs and partly creates or incorporate these, for example, financial and business services. Advances such as 3D-printing and digitization also mean a higher degree of personalization and customizability in industrial production. There are thus 'industrial services' emerging. Farming, of course, is already an industrial enterprise in many places, operating with considerable machinery to turn agricultural raw materials into processed outputs for mass markets. 'Industrial agriculture' is the dominant form of food production in HICs. More recently, agri-tech start-ups have also ventured into domains such as 'farming as a service', blending these sectors as well. Perhaps, the future of structural transformation is thus less one of deindustrialization in a conventional sense and rather one of sectoral *hybridization*.

If so, would this be a problematic development? Gollin (2018) argues that 'growth theory and empirics are relatively agnostic as to the sectoral pathways of development'—a dollar added to the economy is a dollar added, regardless of what activity generated it. This is the sector-agnostic, neoclassical view (Schlogl and Sumner 2020). This view chimes with findings that productivity growth increasingly 'tends to come more from gains *within sectors* than from the movement of labor between sectors' (Merotto et al. 2018, my emphasis; see also McMillan et al. 2014; Timmer et al. 2014). Gollin (2018) argues that the knowledge-related externalities traditionally associated with manufacturing are likely to also be present in the service sector.

Much will, of course, depend on what activities emerge in the heterogeneous service sector. It is hard to picture a successful economic development model based on the kind of informal, low-skilled, low-productivity services—from street vending to transport to security services—which are still prevalent in the low-to-middle-income developing world today. Advocates of industrial-led development argue that sustained economic and productivity growth without manufacturing is empirically rare, that the service sector is still less tradable than manufacturing, that service expansion depends on manufacturing development, and that technology might not erode manufacturing jobs after all (for a recent discussion, see Hauge and Chang 2019). The key issue for the future of structural change nevertheless is arguably about the quality and value-adding capacity of specific economic activities, rather than one about broad (and to some degree arbitrary) sectoral categories. Not only that, the long-standing debate of whether industry is the key to development is increasingly being superseded by a new debate: is *technology adoption* key to development?

4. Peak globalization?

Questions about the future of structural change and technology adoption and are intricately linked to questions about the future of globalization. In their seminal book, *The Second Machine Age*, Brynjolfsson and McAfee (2014: 184) argued that the 'biggest effect of automation is likely to be on workers not in America (…) but rather in developing nations that currently rely on low-cost labor for their competitive advantage'. They argued that 'off-shoring is often only a way station on the road to automation' (Brynjolfsson and McAfee 2014: 184). In a recent talk on the future of work, the economic historian Robert Skidelsky flat out speculated that we may have reached 'peak globalization' because of automation.[5] The impact of robotics, Skidelsky argued, would be a substantial reduction in supply chain trade and an overall falling trade share. Avent (2017) is similarly concerned with the risk of 'reshoring', meaning the return of offshored processes to OECD countries. One could cite examples like Adidas's speed factory, which is now producing millions of 3D-printed shoes in the United States and Germany, rather than in Vietnam or India.

To what extent reshoring is a real threat to developing countries remains controversial. UNCTAD (2017: x) sees 'relatively little evidence for such reshoring'. In a forward-looking view, Baldwin (2016: 283) even argues that the future of globalization allows people from LICs 'to offer their labor services in advanced economies without actually being there' and that the negative impact on jobs in developed, rather than developing, countries 'could be shocking'. He argues that the costs of ICT and of international trade will continue to fall, enabling communication and face-to-face interaction across a distance, and thus fostering tele-presence and tele-robotics. Further drops in separation costs will mean that offshoring in international production networks continues rather than coming to a halt, with rising wages in developing countries only acting as a mild counterforce, if we are to believe Baldwin's account.

Baldwin thus expects the global division of labour to deepen, rather than GVCs to disintegrate, and he sees East Africa among the main beneficiaries. If the 'GVC revolution' continues, developing nations beyond the Asian tigers 'could join the rapid-industrialization parade' (Baldwin 2016). In his most recent book, Baldwin follows this argument, positing that global tele-migration and 'remote intelligence' will disrupt labour markets *in favour of* low-skilled work in the Global South (one could call that the 'Mechanical Turk Model'). Rather than a collapse of low-cost arbitration, Baldwin (2019) sees the future trade of developing countries based on qualitative specialization and fractionalization akin to intra-European Union trade today. One could contend that Baldwin's account seems to best fit ICT-driven business process outsourcing (e.g. call centres in the Philippines), which constitutes a minor part of overall GVC trade in terms of value added. There are also various barriers to globally scaling up this kind of tradable services, among them being language.

---

[5] In a public lecture on 'Technology and Utopia' given by Skidelsky on 12 June 2019 at the Institute for Advanced Studies, Vienna.

Empirically, there is some evidence to suggest that automation technologies could benefit developing countries. Banga (2019) argues for India that manufacturing firms, by expanding their digital capabilities, managed to upgrade their product portfolio, making it more sophisticated and thus more internationally competitive. Hallward-Driemeier and Nayyar (2019) find that robotization in HICs has generally been associated with growing green-field foreign direct investment (FDI) to developing countries. Artuc et al. (2018) argue, based on a task-based Ricardian model that an increase in the adoption of robots in HICs leads to a rise of imports in intermediate goods from developing countries and a rise of exports of manufactured final goods to developing countries. The robots, in their model, are deployed in the Global North due to higher labour costs there—initially depressing labour demand and wages in this region and thus making Northern producers more competitive. This technology-driven structural change continues until all labour has moved into sectors where automation is difficult, and the North has reached a frontier in the feasibility of further robotization. The effect is then reversed, and wages start bouncing back. For the South, Artuc et al. (2018) predict moderate gains in real wages and welfare as consumer prices of final goods drop and demand for exports from developing country rises.

The model of Artuc et al. (2018) is, arguably, based on optimistic assumptions. First, the 'initial' slump in real wages is significant and will only be offset in the long run (when, as Keynes' saying goes, 'we are all dead'). In the meantime, the political fallout from continued wage stagnation, rapid creative destruction, and labour displacement could be significant (see Frey 2019). While real wages in the South do improve somewhat, they will be outpaced at a later point by wage growth in the North, if the model holds true. We would then experience a drop in developing-country real wages at a point where further drops in robot costs may be ever harder to achieve (consider also that robots themselves are final products manufactured in HICs and thus their cost is not exogenous).

Second, is this kind of trade specialization favourable to the South? As was pointed out, sectors do not matter from a neoclassical point of view. Surely, though, a pattern whereby developing countries import disproportionately larger amounts of final goods while exporting a somewhat larger quantity of raw materials or intermediate goods, will worsen the terms of trade. Artuc et al. (2018) view developing countries as providers of intermediate goods, but that assumption might be questionable. The key development challenge of today's developing countries is that they import large amounts of intermediate goods (refined/processed commodities, high value-added components etc.) and then export final goods after only low-value-added assembly. This GVC structure harms developing countries' terms of trade. Introducing automation here will then lead to advanced countries continuing to produce intermediate goods, but they will now increasingly assemble them onshore (i.e. consuming intermediate goods domestically). Therefore, advanced countries will end up exporting final goods, but unlike developing countries of today, with large domestic value added. In this case, the developing countries will end up specializing in raw materials.

Even if developing countries do provide intermediate goods, a world in which a set of economic 'centres' are running robotized industrial clusters that add large economic value while developing-country 'peripheries' provide the material inputs, may raise new questions of structural dependency. More than thirty years ago, Ernst (1985) warned that automation technologies in electronics manufacturing would likely only penetrate 'into a very select group of Third World industrial growth poles' and would be 'largely controlled by the OECD-based multinationals'. He advocated appropriate 'countervailing strategies' by governments of LDCs.

Third, Artuc et al. (2018) predict that the adoption of robots will depress labour demand mainly in the North. In a GVC world, however, robots in the North compete with low-skilled labour downstream in the South—notwithstanding this labour being cheap. The sheer potential of automation could thus act as an increasingly forceful break on developing-country wage growth. It is questionable whether an increase in the demand for primary and intermediate goods by the North will create labour demand (and thus broadly shared wage gains) in developing countries, given that extractive and heavy industries as well as manufacturing and assembly of intermediate goods are becoming ever less labour-intensive. Finally, there seems to be some evidence of a premature spread of automation technologies into developing economies via leapfrogging, likely facilitated by technological subsidies and the public-good nature of technology. The spread of automated payment systems in the South, for instance, is hardly reflective of relative labour costs (see Section 4). It may mean that workers in developing countries will be increasingly competing against machines at lower levels of development than used to be the case for workers in the North.

A more pessimistic view is taken by Rodrik (2018: 14) who argues that 'new technologies present a double whammy to low-income countries': first, they are biased towards high skills and thus reduce the low-cost and low-skill labour advantage of developing countries; second, developing countries are integrated into GVCs, which make it harder to compete via a low-skill advantage. Rodrik argues that, on balance, the disadvantages offset the advantages for developing economies. Caraballo and Jiang (2016) find empirically that there is a 'value-added erosion' for countries getting integrated into the lower-stream parts of GVCs, while high value-adding activities are completed by foreign-led firms upstream in the GVC. Further, in a later empirical paper, Artuc et al. (2019) find that robotization in the United States lowers growth in exports from Mexico to the United States, challenging the somewhat more optimistic modelled predictions of Artuc et al. (2018). Empirically, Guerriero (2019) also finds a global trend for the labour share of income to have fallen since the mid-1980s—a trend, which has been associated with automation (IMF 2017: 121f.; Schwellnus et al. 2018). Taken together, such findings seem to spell some trouble for the future of structural change.

If the automation sceptics are proven correct, the future of structural change will bring about policy challenges around global economic distribution: The 'developer's dilemma' (Sumner 2017, 2018) of promoting structural transformation while sharing economic benefits widely could become harder. While industrial mass employment had guaranteed a decline in inequality with economic maturity, as per Kuznets's (1955) famous curve, this trajectory is doubtful in an age of concentrated capital-intensification and widespread declines in the labour share. On top of 'value-added erosion' of the previous globalization period, we may find 'value-added absorption' as multinational companies 'take back' the activities currently conducted by developing countries at the middle part of the GVC smile curve with the help of automation technologies. The policy-prescriptive literature in international development has been foregrounding measures such as 'upskilling' of developing countries' labour forces or Danish-style 'flexicurity' (World Bank 2009; World Economic Forum 2017; Baldwin 2019). These measures are largely borrowed from HIC contexts and it remains questionable whether they can be transferred to developing countries, where high-quality tertiary education is typically rare and social safety nets are rudimentary. Technological catch-up also tends to be faster than convergence in social and educational policy—the tensions created by this configuration will remain a challenge for future structural policy.

5. A glimpse of the future: South-East Asia between technological catch-up and 'automation creep'

South-East Asia is a region which exemplifies, in a nutshell, several broader trends and challenges of structural change during late industrialization/early deindustrialization. The region comprises a number of populous semi-industrializing MICs which are integrated into GVCs, are fairly vulnerable to automation, face a much-debated 'middle-income trap', and have adopted a path of unequalizing tertiarization. The following section briefly describes the structural context of this region and then discusses a new trajectory of structural change, so-called leapfrogging, which is likely to become salient in the wider developing world.

To begin with, the movement of labour across economic sectors in South-East Asia has followed a similar pattern, as outlined in section 3. Throughout the past twenty years, employment in agriculture has generally contracted while it has expanded in the service sector. Industrial employment shows a more chequered pattern, with most countries still increasing their employment but some—the richer ones: Malaysia, Singapore, Brunei—on the declining slope of employment. The available country-comparable data suggests that Malaysia reached the 'Clark turning point' of industrial employment transitioning into decline in the late

1990s; Brunei likely in the early 1990s; and Singapore's turning lies further back in the past. The remaining region is still on the upwards slope of job industrialization.

Singapore had the region's highest level of service-sector employment at 83 per cent in 2018, surpassing even US and UK peak levels. Consequently, the share of work considered in current estimates to be susceptible to robotization is the lowest in the region (see Schlogl 2020 for a depiction of the share of the automatable labour force in South-East Asia vis-á-vis the level of development). According to McKinsey (2017), as much as half of the labour force in countries like Malaysia and Indonesia is, in principle, automatable using existing technology. Similar estimates by the World Bank (2016, n.d.) estimates are even more pessimistic.

With the exception of Singapore, South-East Asia has relatively large populations in low-skilled manual occupations like agriculture, leaving much potential for robotization in the future. In line with this, the productivity gap, measured as output per worker in constant purchasing power parity (PPP)-adjusted dollars, of Association of Southeast Asian Nations (ASEAN) countries with OECD countries is still wide (World Bank n.d.). Notwithstanding continuous increases in productivity since the 1990s, the region has only converged by a few percentage points since the beginning of the 1990s, despite the dent in OECD output left by the 2008 Great Recession.

High automatability thus reflects a low degree of robotization on a per capita basis in South-East Asia. This would chime with a thesis that developing countries, including in South-East Asia, are 'under-robotized', which is, for instance, argued in UNCTAD (2017). From this perspective, robotization, paired with skills upgrading and employment tertiarization—technologically displaced agricultural and industrial labour moving into the service sector—will push countries up the productivity and development ladder (see Schlogl 2020 for a depiction of the incidence of industrial robots by level of human development based on UNDP (2020) and IFR (2018). The relationship of these variables follows a logarithmic function). Robotization would be especially pressing in the tradable sectors, where countries face international price competition.

'Under-robotization' is thus one way of interpreting the challenge of economic development in the age of automation. There are a few caveats. First, considering that Singapore has the world's second highest density of installed industrial robots per employee in the manufacturing sector, according to the International Federation of Robotics (IFR 2018), McKinsey's estimate of almost one-half of the labour force being technologically replaceable by existing technology is concerning. Even a country with superior technological upgrading faces the 'robot reserve army'. Second, while developing countries are under-robotized both on a per capita and GDP per capita level, the *growth* in robot density adjusted for wages is high in developing countries (Atkinson 2018). The region is thus on a path towards catch-up with automation.

Third, even if the 'direct' effects of robotization in developing countries, which UNCTAD (2017) refers to, may so far be negligible, indirect effects could well be significant. Among such indirect effects, the aforementioned phenomenon of reshoring would only be the most extreme case. Less extreme would be the mere potential, or threat, of reshoring—or offshoring into new robotized tech clusters located elsewhere—putting a brake on wage growth in the tradable sector of developing countries. Robots installed in countries with high labour costs are competing with workers elsewhere and thus have spill-over effects to countries with low robot density nonetheless, even if offshored activities are not actually reshored. Fourth, we are witnessing the adoption of cutting-edge labour-saving technology across South-East Asia even in non-tradable sectors, including the service sector. There is a new form of 'automation creep' beyond the expectable area of tradable industrial production, which is deserving of much greater scholarly attention. This form of 'automation creep' could potentially threaten the labour absorption capacity of the non-tradable sectors, which are driving structural transformation in countries experiencing slow industrialization or stuck in the low-value-adding section of GVCs.

Consider the recent spread of automatic tolling systems in a number of South and South-East Asian countries, including Thailand, Malaysia, the Philippines, Singapore, and Indonesia. Tollbooth operation (i.e. the handling and checking of toll payment on toll roads) is a prototypical example of the labour-intensive, manually repetitive, and low-skilled professions which tend to be at high risk of technological disruption. The spread of technologies such as electronic payment systems, 'smart cards', and near-field communication, object detection sensors, and automatic boom barriers will continue to make human workers in this sector redundant.

Indonesia is one example where an automated tollbooth system was recently rolled out on a nationwide scale. The state-owned toll road service provider Jasa Marga introduced an e-payment system with contactless charge cards in 2017. While formerly each toll gate had required five employees working in shifts to ensure that vehicles had paid the road toll, the cashless system now runs essentially without human operators. On the upside, this speeds up the transaction process and reduces traffic congestion in a country plagued by traffic jams. However, it has placed a question over 20,000 jobs, according to media reports, coinciding with an announcement by the Indonesian Minister of Finance at the annual meeting of the International Monetary Fund and the World Bank that automation might create a case for a future universal basic income in Indonesia. There have been no reports of mass lay-offs in Indonesia so far, albeit these could unfold in a gradual manner over time or take the form of a reduced intake of new employees in the future. In a detailed investor report on Jasa Marga, the Korean consulting firm Mirae Asset (2018) argued that the new e-toll system was 'needed to suppress rising personnel expenses' in the company and would lead to reduced recruitment in the future.

What is the reason for this 'runaway' automation in non-tradable sectors in South-East Asia? First, it could be the result of a deliberate development strategy. Cost competition does not end at the doors of a factory hall, where goods for international supply chains are produced. For instance, workers commute to factories and, if an e-toll system reduces transport costs and time, such cost reductions will indirectly lower the cost of labour and thus of factory production. The same would hold for other domains like public infrastructure, food, housing, and so on. The wider domestic economy is thus not insulated from international trade (as OECD countries know well from debates about the feasibility of the welfare state under conditions of global competition). The fact that in Indonesia it was the government which mandated cashless toll road transactions in 2017 (Mirae Asset 2018) would speak for the thesis that this is a part of an orchestrated developmental strategy. Atkinson (2018), who puzzles over why South-East Asia is ahead of other countries in terms of the growth in robot density, also cites 'national goals and strategies' and 'proactive tax policies' alongside a pro-robot 'culture'. Technological adoption is also actively promoted through international norms, for example, UN organizations pushing and subsidizing digitization, 'smart cities', and technological upgrading.

Second, technological leapfrogging of this kind could be due to the global *public-good nature* of technology. This view would hold that the spread of technology is hard to contain, whether or not macroeconomic benefits prevail. Even if contactless pay cards were not developed for use in toll gates in Indonesia, but rather for telephone and ATM cards in high-wage Europe, in line with the notion of 'directed technological change', such technology is today available for worldwide commercial adoption at falling costs. For instance, the fast-food chain McDonald's is currently rolling out its self-service kiosk system to countries in South-East Asia. Comin and Mestieri (2018) show that the lags in technological adoption between poor and rich countries have converged over time. Technological innovation receives substantial public subsidies in HICs in the form of higher education finance and R&D incentives, among other policies. Adding to that weak labour organization in the Global South, adoption of such labour-displacing technology might paradoxically be easier in countries where labour costs would otherwise provide a much smaller incentive for robotization.[6] Technological 'leapfrogging' of this kind presents a double-edged sword: rather than high labour costs incentivizing the development and adoption of labour-saving technology, developing countries adopt these technologies at comparatively low wage levels.

Service automation in developing countries suggests that the future of structural and technological change raises questions about the ideal sequencing of economic development and the right timing of technology transfer from advanced

---

[6] For instance, Cheng et al. (2019: 84) argue that in China the 'lack of strong and independent unions may partly contribute to their tolerance of robot adoption'.

nations. Further, it also raises questions about the social policy context in which the developer's dilemma is to be managed going forward.

6. Conclusion

This chapter discussed the future of structural change with a focus on new constellations of maturity and prematurity in technological and economic development. It sketched potential trajectories of catch-up structural change along the dimensions of early or late technology adoption and early or late economic development.

Going forward, a key configuration is that of 'early adoption during late development'. Advocates of this path speak of 'leapfrogging' and argue that skipping steps along the path to technological maturity constitutes, using the words of Gerschenkron (1951), an 'advantage of backwardness'. Critics contend that the adoption of technology developed in and for HICs may not always be advantageous in other places, notably in the absence of relevant complementarities. To illustrate this idea, the chapter introduced the notion of 'technology leap' versus 'technology creep'. It then analysed examples and reviewed assessments of new development constellations of particular relevance for the future of structural change: the changing composition of employment and value added, the changing landscape of global trade in an age of automation, and technological upgrading in services.

Extrapolating historical trends, a continued increase of service-sector work at the expense of both industrial and agricultural work is likely to unfold in the medium term. In historical comparison, country-level shares of industrial employment appear to be increasingly detached from the level of economic development of a country. A conceptual blurring, or 'hybridization', of economic sectors is taking place as mass agriculture, the service industry, and the skilled manufacturing industry begin to share structural similarities of tradability, economies of scale, or capital intensity, among others.

Whether automation and digitization pose a threat to developing countries in a GVC world is debated with arguments and evidence brought forward on both sides. The chapter argued that tensions about terms-of-trade deterioration and structural dependency might resurface in a situation in which a developing-country periphery provides simple inputs to highly robotized industrial clusters. In a similar vein, there are voices of concern about new forms of technological domination (e.g. Kwet 2019). The chapter discussed the notion that developing countries are 'under-robotized' and presented evidence pro and contra this view.

To exemplify challenges around leapfrogging, the chapter then explored the case of automation in late-industrializing South-East Asia. Despite regional heterogeneity, the region broadly fits the global picture of structural change but also provides examples of technological upgrading that are likely to become salient across the middle-income developing world going forward. The available country-comparable data suggests that the richest countries in this region have reached the 'Clark turning point' of industrial employment going into decline while the rest of the region is still on the upwards slope of industrialization. Automation is progressing, somewhat paradoxically, in non-tradable sectors like transport. Along with the worries of premature deindustrialization, the next challenge of structural transformation in middle-income regions like South-East Asia could be automation in routine services, currently a refuge of human comparative advantage over machines.

While a changing global division of labour in the age of automation thus raises questions about structural dependency, leapfrogging raises questions about the optimal sequencing of economic development.

References

Alonso-Soto, D. (2020). 'Technology and the Future of Work in Emerging Economies: What is Different?'. OECD Social, Employment and Migration Working Papers 236. Paris: OECD, https://www.oecd-ilibrary.org/social-issues-migration-health/oecd-social-employment-and-migration-working-papers_1815199x (accessed 1 February 2020).

Artuc, E., P. Bastos, and B. Rijkers (2018). 'Robots, Tasks and Trade'. Policy Research Working Paper 8674. Washington, DC: World Bank.

Artuc, E., L. Christiaensen, and H. Winkler (2019). 'Does Automation in Rich Countries Hurt Developing Ones? Evidence from the U.S. and Mexico'. doi: https://doi.org/10.1596/31425.

Atkinson, R.D. (2018). Which Nations Really Lead in Industrial Robot Adoption? Washington, DC: Information Technology & Innovation Foundation.

Autor, D.H. (2015). 'Why Are There Still So Many Jobs? The History and Future of Workplace Automation', Journal of Economic Perspectives, 29(3): 3–30. doi: https://doi.org/10.1257/jep.29.3.3.

Autor, D.H., and D. Dorn (2013). 'The Growth of Low-Skill Service Jobs and the Polarization of the US Labor Market', American Economic Review, 103(5): 1553–1597. doi: https://doi.org/10.1257/aer.103.5.1553.

Autor, D.H., F. Levy, and R.J. Murnane (2003). 'The Skill Content of Recent Technological Change: An Empirical Exploration', Quarterly Journal of Economics, 118(4): 1279–1333. doi: https://doi.org/10.1162/003355303322552801.

Avent, R. (2017). The Wealth of Humans: Work and Its Absence in the Twenty-First Century. London: Penguin Random House.

Baldwin, R. (2016). The Great Convergence: Information Technology and the New Globalization. Cambridge and London: Belknap Press.

Baldwin, R. (2019). The Globotics Upheaval: Globalization, Robotics, and the Future of Work. New York: Oxford University Press.

Banga, K. (2019). 'Digital Technologies and "Value" Capture in Global Value Chains Empirical Evidence from Indian Manufacturing Firms'. WIDER Working Paper 2019/43. Helsinki: UNU-WIDER.

Brynjolfsson, E., and A. McAfee, A. (2014). *The Second Machine Age: Work, Progress, and Prosperity in a Time of Brilliant Technologies*. New York, NY and London: W.W. Norton & Company.

Caraballo, J.G., and X. Jiang (2016). 'Value-Added Erosion in Global Value Chains: An Empirical Assessment', *Journal of Economic Issues*, 50(1): 288–296.

Chang, H., and A. Andreoni (2020). 'Industrial Policy in the 21st Century', *Development and Change*, 1–28. doi: https://doi.org/10.1111/dech.12570.

Cheng, H., R. Jia, D. Li, and H. Li (2019). 'The Rise of Robots in China', *Journal of Economic Perspectives*, 33(2): 71–88. doi: https://doi.org/10.1257/jep.33.2.71.

Clark, C. (1940). *The Conditions of Economic Progress*. London: MacMillan & Co.

Comin, D., and M. Mestieri (2018). 'If Technology Has Arrived Everywhere, Why Has Income Diverged?', *American Economic Journal: Macroeconomics*, 10(3): 137–178.

Ernst, D. (1985). 'Automation and the Worldwide Restructuring of the Electronics Industry: Strategic Implications for Developing Countries', *World Development*, 13(3): 333–352. doi: https://doi.org/10.1016/0305-750X(85)90134-2.

Frey, C.B. (2019). *The Technology Trap: Capital, Labor, and Power in the Age of Automation*. Princeton, NJ and Oxford: Princeton University Press.

Frey, C.B., and M.A. Osborne (2013). 'The Future of Employment: How Susceptible Are Jobs to Computerisation?', *Technological Forecasting and Social Change*, 114: 254–280. doi: https://doi.org/10.1016/j.techfore.2016.08.019.

Gerschenkron, A. (1951). *Economic Backwardness in Historical Perspective*. Cambridge, MA: Belknap Press.

Gollin, D. (2018). 'Structural Transformation and Growth without Industrialisation'. Background Paper 2. Oxford: Pathways for Prosperity Commission.

Goos, M., and A. Manning (2007). 'Lousy and Lovely Jobs: The Rising Polarization of Work in Britain', *Review of Economics and Statistics*, 89(1): 118–133. doi: https://doi.org/10.1162/rest.89.1.118.

Guerriero, M. (2019). 'The Labour Share of Income around the World: Evidence from a Panel Dataset'. ADBI Working Paper 920. Tokyo: Asian Development Bank Institute.

Hallward-Driemeier, M., and G. Nayyar (2019). 'Have Robots Grounded the Flying Geese?: Evidence from Greenfield FDI in Manufacturing'. Policy Research Working Paper 9097. Washington, DC: World Bank.

Haraguchi, N., C.F.C. Cheng, and E. Smeets (2017). 'The Importance of Manufacturing in Economic Development: Has This Changed?', *World Development*, 93: 293–315.

Hauge, J., and H.-J. Chang (2019). 'The Role of Manufacturing Versus Services in Economic Development'. In P. Bianchi, C.R. Durán, and S. Labory (eds), *Transforming Industrial Policy for the Digital Age*. Cheltenham and Northampton: Edward Elgar. doi: https://doi.org/10.4337/9781788976152.00007.

IFR (2018). 'Robot Density Rises Globally.' IFR Press Releases, 7 February, https://ifr.org/ifr-press-releases/news/robot-density-rises-globally (accessed 28 February 2020).

IMF (2017). *World Economic Outlook April 2017. Gaining Momentum?* Washington, DC: International Monetary Fund.

Keynes, J.M. (1933). 'National Self-Sufficiency', *The Yale Review*, 22(4): 755–769.

Kuznets, S. (1955). 'Economic Growth and Income Inequality', *American Economic Review*, 45(1): 1–28.

Kwet, M. (2019). 'Digital Colonialism: US Empire and the New Imperialism in the Global South', *Race and Class*, 60(4): 3–26. doi: https://doi.org/10.1177/0306396818823172.

Lee, K. (2019). *The Art of Economic Catch-Up: Barriers, Detours and Leapfrogging in Innovation Systems*. Cambridge, New York, Melbourne, Madrid, Cape Town, Singapore, Sao Paulo: Cambridge University Press.

Lin, J.Y. (2016). 'The Latecomer Advantages and Disadvantages: A New Structural Economics Perspective'. In M. Andersson and T. Axelsson (eds), *Diverse Development Paths and Structural Transformation in the Escape from Poverty*. Oxford: Oxford University Press, pp. 43–67.

Madrigal, A.C. (2017). 'Silicon Valley's Big Three vs. Detroit's Golden-Age Big Three', *The Atlantic*, 24 May, https://www.theatlantic.com/technology/archive/2017/05/silicon-valley-big-three/527838/ (accessed 1 March 2020).

Mathews, J.A. (2006). 'Catch-Up Strategies and the Latecomer Effect in Industrial Development', *New Political Economy*, 11(3): 313–335. doi: https://doi.org/10.1080/13563460600840142.

McKinsey Global Institute (2017). 'Where Machines Could Replace Humans—and Where They Can't (Yet)'. Tableau Public Dataset, https://public.tableau.com/en-us/s/gallery/where-machines-could-replace-humans (accessed 1 February 2020).

McMillan, M., D. Rodrik, and Í. Verduzco-Gallo (2014). 'Globalization, Structural Change, and Productivity Growth, with an Update on Africa', *World Development*, 63: 11–32. doi: https://doi.org/10.1016/j.worlddev.2013.10.012.

Merotto, D., M. Weber, and R. Aterido (2018). *Pathways to Better Jobs in IDA Countries: Findings from Jobs Diagnostics, Jobs Series*. Washington, DC: World Bank.

Mirae Asset (2018). *Jasa Marga Company Report*. Seoul: Mirae Asset.

Nayak, R., and R. Padhye (2018). *Automation in Garment Manufacturing*. Duxford, Cambridge, Kidlington: Woodhead Publishing.

Nayyar, D. (2013). *Catch Up: Developing Countries in the World Economy*. Oxford: Oxford University Press.

Newfarmer, R.S., J. Page, and F. Tarp (2018). *Industries without Smokestacks: Industrialization in Africa Reconsidered*. Oxford: Oxford University Press.

Pahl, S., and M.P. Timmer (2019). 'Do Global Value Chains Enhance Economic Upgrading? A Long View', *Journal of Development Studies*. doi: https://doi.org/10.1080/00220388.2019.1702159.

Pritchett, L. (1997). 'Divergence, Big Time', *Journal of Economic Perspectives*, 11(3): 3–17.

Pritchett, L. (2020). 'The Future of Jobs Is Facing One, Maybe Two, of the Biggest Price Distortions Ever', *Middle East Development Journal*, 12(1): 131–156.

Rodrik, D. (2016) 'Premature Deindustrialization', *Journal of Economic Growth*, 21(1): 1–33. doi: https://doi.org/10.1007/s10887-015-9122-3.

Rodrik, D. (2018). 'New Technologies, Global Value Chains, and the Developing Economies', Background Paper 1. Oxford: Pathways for Prosperity Commission.

Safaricom (2019). *Annual Report and Financial Statements*. Nairobi: Safaricom, https://www.safaricom.co.ke/images/Downloads/Safaricom_Annual_Report_2019.pdf (accessed 1 February 2020).

Schlogl, L. (2020). 'Leapfrogging into the Unknown: The Future of Structural Change in the Developing World'. Working Paper 2020/25. UNU-WIDER: Helsinki. doi: https://doi.org/10.35188/UNU-WIDER/2020/782-8.

Schlogl, L., and A. Sumner (2020). *Disrupted Development and the Future of Inequality in the Age of Automation*. Cham: Palgrave Macmillan.

Schwellnus, C., M. Pak, P.-A. Pionnier, and E. Crivellaro (2018). 'Labour Share Developments over the Past Two Decades: The Role of Technological Progress, Globalisation and 'Winner-Takes-Most' Dynamics'. Economics Department Working Papers 1503. Paris: OECD.

Sen, K. (2019). 'Structural Transformation around the World: Patterns and Drivers', *Asian Development Review*, 36(2): 1–31. doi: https://doi.org/10.1162/adev_a_00130.

Sumner, A. (2017). 'The Developer's Dilemma: The Inequality Dynamics of Structural Transformation and Inclusive Growth'. Working Paper 1. London: Global Poverty and Inequality Dynamics Research Network.

Sumner, A. (2018). *Development and Distribution: Structural Change in South East Asia*. Oxford: Oxford University Press.

Timmer, M. P., G. De Vries, and K. De Vries (2014). 'Growth and Patterns of Structural Change in Developing Countries'. *GGDC Research Memoranda*, Groningen: GGDC, GD–149.

Ugur, M., and A. Mitra (2017). 'Technology Adoption and Employment in Less Developed Countries: A Mixed-Method Systematic Review', *World Development*, 96: 1–18. doi: https://doi.org/10.1016/j.worlddev.2017.03.015.

UNCTAD (2017). *Trade and Development Report 2017—Beyond Austerity: Towards A Global New Deal*. New York and Geneva: UNCTAD, http://unctad.org/en/PublicationsLibrary/tdr2017_en.pdf (accessed 1 February 2020).

UNDP (2020). 'Human Development Index, Human Development Data', http://hdr.undp.org/en/composite/HDI (accessed 1 February 2020).

Willcocks, L.P., and M. Lacity (2016). *Service Automation: Robots and the Future of Work*. Stratford: Steve Brookes Publishing.

World Bank (n.d.). 'World Development Indicators' (data base). Washington, DC: World Bank. https://datacatalog.worldbank.org/dataset/world-development-indicators (accessed 1 January 2020).

World Bank (2009). *World Development Report: Changing Nature of Work*. doi: https://doi.org/10.1596/978-1-4648-1328-3.

World Bank (2016). *Digital Dividends, World Development Report*. Washington DC: World Bank. doi: https://doi.org/10.1017/CBO9781107415324.004.

World Economic Forum (2017). *Impact of the Fourth Industrial Revolution on Supply Chains*. Geneva: World Economic Forum, http://www3.weforum.org/docs/WEF_Impact_of_the_Fourth_Industrial_Revolution_on_Supply_Chains_.pdf (accessed 1 February 2020).

Yasara, M., and R.M. Rejesus (2020). 'International Linkages, Technology Transfer, and the Skilled Labor Wage Share: Evidence from Plant-Level Data in Indonesia', *World Development*, 128. doi: https://doi.org/10.1016/j.worlddev.2019.104847.

13

The Developer's Dilemma

Conclusions

Armida Salsiah Alisjahbana, Kunal Sen, Andy Sumner,
and Arief Anshory Yusuf

1 Introduction

The United Nations University-World Institute for Development Economics Research's (UNU-WIDER's) inaugural director—the Sri Lankan senior civil servant and Keynesian economist, Lal Jayawardena—was deeply committed to equity. He helped to create collective organizations to realize developing countries' demands and acted as advisor to the Brandt Commission. As Amartya Sen summed up, Lal 'wanted to build a society that would be foundationally more just' (cited in Singh 2005: 1221). This book has focused on one of the challenges of building a foundationally more just society, specifically, the concern formulated by Simon Kuznets and other pioneers of development economics such as W. Arthur Lewis that economic development would lead to an upswing in income inequality as a consequence of economic dualism and the shift of labour from low-productivity to higher-productivity sectors. This process of structural transformation—when production transitions from lower-productivity to higher-productivity activities—is the basis of economic development in the Classical School of economic development associated with Kuznets, Lewis, and others. Conventionally, this has been understood as a transformation from predominantly agricultural production to mostly manufacturing and is indicated by the large-scale movement of workers from low-productivity to high-productivity sectors of the economy.

While this process is crucial to generating sufficient wealth to improve human well-being, Kuznets and Lewis presumed that it would also lead to upward pressure on inequality, at least in the short term, because economic development processes start unevenly. Some areas and people benefit before others. This implies that government policies are essential to counteract upward pressure on inequality and spread the benefits of development wider, from dynamic, modern activities to

Armida Salsiah Alisjahbana, et al., *The Developer's Dilemma*. In: *The Developer's Dilemma*.
Edited by Armida Salsiah Alisjahbana, Kunal Sen, Andy Sumner, and Arief Anshory Yusuf, Oxford University Press.
© UNU-WIDER. (2022). DOI: 10.1093/oso/9780192855299.003.0013

other sectors of the economy. To echo Lewis, this means 'trickle-along' rather than trickle-down.

This tension between building a productive economy and the unequal distribution of the benefits in the earlier days is what we have called 'the developer's dilemma' in this book. We have focused on a set of questions. Specifically, at the outset we asked:

1. What are the types of structural transformation (ST) that have been experienced by developing countries?
2. What are the inequality dynamics that accompany each type of ST?
3. Which policies have been enacted to manage the tension between ST and income inequality?

The key findings from this project's multi-country examination of development trajectories through nine in-depth country case studies led by national research teams are as follows. In terms of Question 1, we identified multiple pathways of economic development and provided a typology of varieties of ST with empirical cases for each one. Second, in terms of Question 2, we found that there are differing inequality dynamics for each variety of ST and furthermore that rising inequality during economic development is not inevitable. Thus, development can, indeed, be inclusive in principle. Finally, in terms of Question 3, we conclude, based on our findings, that broad-based economic development requires public policies to address any upward pressure on inequality. This is exactly what Kuznets argued in his seminal paper, yet this has been mostly lost due to the excessive focus on the infamous, inverted-U curve (see Kanbur 2019). Public policies are needed to address the divergences in income that may arise. To echo Lal's thinking, building a society that is foundationally more just requires public policies to support those left behind.

This concluding chapter pulls together the case studies of our book to discuss each of the questions above. The conclusion is structured as follows. Section 2 outlines our conceptual framework. Section 3 then focuses on each of our case studies by region and discusses the types of ST, inequality dynamics, and policies in each country. Section 4 compares country episodes in order to discuss how countries that have managed the developer's dilemma have done so. Section 5 concludes.

2. Our conceptual framework

In our introductory chapter we presented five varieties of ST: *primary industrialization*, *upgrading industrialization*, *advanced industrialization*, *stalled industrialization*, and *secular deindustrialization* drawing on the approach of Kim and Sumner (2019). We also outlined, in our introductory chapter, four types of Kuznetsian tension based on a 2 × 2 matrix of trends in income inequality (i.e.

stable/declining inequality or increasing) versus the strength of growth-enhancing ST (i.e. weak or strong).

Each quadrant of the matrix tells a different story about the developer's dilemma. If we focus on the supply of labour from low-productivity sectors and the demand for labour in high-productivity sectors, the drivers of ST frame the patterns of ST through policies, as do the modern sector's demand for labour and the traditional sector's supply of the latter. For example, if participation in specific global value chains (GVCs) engenders high-skills-biased or routine-biased labour demand in the modern sector, this will have consequences for inequality (mediated by policies). On the other hand, if participation in certain GVCs generates high demand for low-skilled labour in the modern sector, the consequences for inequality will differ (mediated by policies).

Moreover, the resulting variety of ST will have further consequences for the inequality dynamics. For instance, primary industrialization can create much employment, particularly so for low-skilled workers in manufacturing, and thus potentially have an equalizing effect. On the other hand, stalled industrialization, upgrading industrialization, and deindustrialization could imply weaker job growth in manufacturing and an expanding modern and/or traditional service sector, which may be equalizing or unequalizing, depending on policies.

As is clear in the above, policies mediate between the drivers and varieties of ST, on the one hand, and their impacts on labour demand in the modern sector and labour supply from the traditional sector, on the other hand. Which policies have led to, or exacerbated, a strong Kuznetsian tension or have contributed to a benign one? To answer this question, we first need to clarify what we mean by 'ST' and 'inequality' policies. Following Lewis, ST policies are defined as those policies that increase the supply of and/or the demand for labour in the modern, higher-productivity sector. Policies to address inequality are defined as direct/indirect attempts to redistribute income downwards. It is important to note that there are (i) policies used to pursue ST, which may, as a consequence, contribute to up-ward or downward movements of inequality; and (ii) policies employed to address inequality, which may in turn weaken or strengthen ST or engender different intersectoral movements of labour. We next discuss each of the case studies by region in our framework.

3. The empirical experience of developing countries

3.1 East Asia

What can we draw from our case studies? In East Asia, we considered Indonesia, China, and Thailand. Indonesia experienced upgrading industrialization from 1975 through to 1996. Following the Asian Financial Crisis, stalled industrialization set in, with both manufacturing value-added and employment shares declining between 1999 and the 2010s, while the service sector shares expanded rapidly. The period from the mid-1960s to the mid-1970s and the period 1999–2012 were periods characterized by a weak (adverse) Kutznetsian tension and inequality rose alongside weak, growth-enhancing ST. In contrast, the period of 1975–1996 was one of a weak (benign) Kuznetsian tension, where there was strong growth-enhancing ST alongside stable inequality. While it is yet too early to identify a definite trend since the mid-2010s, industrialization appears to be struggling to accelerate, although the trend of increasing inequality seems to have stopped.

How about policies for ST? During the second half of the 1960s, the Indonesian government's main focus was to stabilize the economic conditions, rather than to actively search for methods to stimulate ST. Subsequently, between 1975 and 1985, import substitution policies were implemented to promote ST. The government used oil revenues and adopted protectionist measures to foster capital-intensive industries. Between 1985 and 1996, highly favourable exchange rate movements (due to the Plaza Accord) and economic liberalization was pursued, and export-orientated policies were implemented. Foreign direct investments (FDI) flowed into labour-intensive manufacturing sectors. While the whole of the second period between the mid-1970s and the mid-1990s was characterized by largely stable inequality, it is important to highlight that the expansion of the manufacturing employment share was more significant from 1985 to 1995. During the following period, 1999–2010s, efforts to invigorate ST were limited. Since the mid-2010s, the government has been strengthening its role to stimulate ST with a particular focus on infrastructure development.

How did Indonesia approach policies to address inequality? The Indonesian government used policies on rural development, education provision, and pro-poor spending to reduce poverty and address inequality between the 1970s and the 1990s. The concurrent implementation of these policies and the policies to promote ST led to a sustainable expansion of high-productivity activities. After the Asian Financial Crisis, poverty continued to decline, yet inequality increased significantly to the early 2010s. Social spending was constrained due to large fuel subsidies for most of this period, while most jobs were created in service sub-sectors with low productivity. From the mid-2010s, government expenditure on social assistance expanded notably, especially in targeted programmes, while regressive fuel subsidies shrank.

Next, we turn to China. China experienced periods of upgrading industrialization between 1978–1991 and 2002–2011 and in between (1992–2001), China experienced advanced industrialization. ST was rapid and average incomes rose substantially from 1978–1991. The 1978–1985 period was one of an ambiguous Kuznetsian tension (KT) with steady inequality. The period from 1986–2001 was one of weak/adverse KT with rising inequality. And the period 2002–2011 was one of a strong KT with rising inequality. The third period (2002–2011), however, is more associated with policies to address inequality. In the first period, many workers moved to manufacturing, though not to urban centres but to rural industrial sites, township and village enterprises (TVEs), which were set up by township and village-level governments. ST policies in this period included the abolition of the commune system and the establishment of the Household Responsibility System. The new arrangement allowed rural households to have land use rights and to claim residuals after paying tax. Alongside this, non-state-owned enterprises and TVEs flourished and expanded remarkably from the late 1980s, absorbing surplus rural labour. In terms of inequality, the government implemented nine years of free and compulsory schooling, in addition to relaxing the Hukou system to allow urban migration. In the 1990s, the policies of restructuring/privatizing state-owned enterprises (SOEs) began, resulting in lay-offs of workers and an expansion of private enterprises, as private ownership was further legalized in the late 1990s. From 1999 onwards, higher education was expanded. ST policy entered a new period in 2002 with China's entry into the World Trade Organization (WTO). Trade and investment liberalization ensued, and local governments competed for foreign and domestic investments by offering low tax rates and weaker labour rights. Concern over widening inequality led to more redistributive policies in the late 2000s covering education, labour law (including minimum wage strengthening), health insurances and pensions, and a poverty eradication programme.

Finally, we consider Thailand. Thailand experienced some industrialization between 1981 and 1987, then upgrading industrialization during the boom period of 1988–1996, then weaker industrialization from 2000–2017. The pre-boom period 1981–1987 was shaped by rising inequality. In contrast, during 1988–1996, inequality was stable/declining and ST strong. The post-2000 period was one of falling inequality and weak ST.

In terms of ST policies, up to 1988 the Thai government supported private-sector development, favouring a small group of businesses through tax exemptions, tariff protection, and subsidized credit. Import substitution further strengthened financial and industrial elites and was pursued alongside export-orientated industrialization. There was substantial infrastructure investment in and around Bangkok. Key agencies of the developmental state provided the institutional framework.

External conditions deteriorated due to the oil shocks of the late 1970s/early 1980s, leading to debt-burden-induced austerity adjustment and the opening of the Thai economy through deregulation. The late 1980s to the mid-1990s saw large FDI inflows and an FDI-led export boom following the currency devaluation and the introduction of FDI-attracting incentives. To support export industries, export processing zones with relaxed labour laws were established, tax incentives applied, and infrastructure rolled out. A series of financial sector reforms was enacted, including the opening of the Bangkok International Banking Facility, which stimulated the capital market and supported Thai firms in borrowing overseas. Thai firms borrowed heavily, and often short-term, unhedged, and unregulated, and large capital inflows ensued. This led to stock market and real estate bubbles and a currency appreciation. The Asian Financial Crisis hit hard in Thailand. A severe IMF austerity package commenced in 1997. This, in part, led to the emergence of populist-nationalist politics and protectionist measures for domestic capital, and populism following elections and the introduction of an industrial policy based on tax incentives linked to output targets and local content requirements, as well as on cheap credit in a small set of strategic sectors (automobiles, computers, textiles, food, and tourism).

In terms of inequality policies, there were rice price interventions. These can be characterized as taxation, at declining rates until 1986 and rising subsidies through input (not output) subsidies until the early 2000s and then an overt period of overt output subsidies (the 'rice-pledging' scheme) during almost all of the period 2001–2014. After the military coup in 2014, the output price subsidies were removed but the input subsidies continued. In short, the story is a steady movement from taxing to subsidizing the rice sector.

The government helped smallholders to develop alternatives in cassava, chicken, fruit, and vegetables. Thailand also introduced the Tambon rural development programme. The welfare components of this programme focused on agriculture and rural areas, aiming to ensure cheap staple foodstuffs. Redistributive policies were introduced alongside economic nationalism in the 2000s, enacting a rural up-lift programme based on debt relief, spending programmes, and most significantly a universal health insurance scheme. The basis of funding in general taxation made it highly redistributive given out-of-pocket costs for health care for much of the population prior to its introduction.

3.2 South Asia

In South Asia our case studies were India and Bangladesh. India experienced advanced industrialization from 1960 to 1980, though limited in magnitude, and then primary industrialization from 1980–2010. The first period was one of an ambiguous KT with steady inequality. The second period was one of a strong KT with rising inequality. Policies aiming to promote ST between 1960 and 1980 relied on industrialization through massive investment in the public sector, import controls, and import substitution. However, these policies largely failed to spur ST. Between 1980 and 2010, ST was pursued via trade reforms and industrial delicensing. While these policies led to an increase in the manufacturing employment share, they did not cause a sustained increase in the manufacturing value-added share, thus contributing to primary industrialization. This period was characterized by tertiarization, with strong growth in construction and information technology. Inequality increased between 1980 and 2010, which could be an indirect consequence of the movement of labour from agriculture to services.

India implemented several policies to address inequality in the first period of ST. These included a licensing regime for the industrial sector, and small-scale industry reservation, anti-poverty programmes, expansion of rural infrastructure, social banking, and provision of food at subsidised prices. Indirectly, these policies might have had an adverse impact on growth-enhancing ST, as public expenditure was mostly focused on consumption, rather than investment. In the second period, there was no explicit focus on redistributive policies except for the National Rural Employment Guarantee Act in the second part of the 2000s, which guaranteed employment to poor rural workers.

In contrast, Bangladesh experienced advanced industrialization from 1991–2000 and then two periods of upgrading industrialization from 2001–2010 and 2011–2018, with the second period leading to stronger growth in the share of manufacturing employment than the first period. The first period was one of a weak/adverse KT with rising inequality. The second and third period were both periods of a strong KT with rising inequality alongside strong, growth enhancing ST.

Policies used to promote ST included rapid trade liberalization since 1991, along with policies to attract FDI. This led to an increase in ready-made garments (RMG) exports, which contributed to a very high share of manufacturing exports in total exports (above 90 per cent) and an increase in manufacturing employment and value added. The growth of the RMG sector was the primary reason behind upgrading industrialization since 2001. Given that the RMG sector is characterized by low-skilled labour, low wages, poor working conditions, and a relaxed execution of labour laws, the ST policies may have contributed to higher inequality since 1991 and since 2001.

Bangladesh has not implemented policies to directly reduce inequality in any significant manner. Social protection is minimal, with Bangladesh spending less than 2 per cent of its GDP on social protection. Inequality may have been indirectly impacted by significant human capital accumulation, as there has been a large increase in gross enrolment in primary education among both males and females. However, the NGO provision of schooling also made important contributions to the accumulation of human capital as the government policies on the provision of primary education remained rather inadequate.

3.3 Sub-Saharan Africa

In sub-Saharan Africa, we considered Ghana and South Africa. Ghana experienced stalled industrialization in general, or stalled primary industrialization specifically, for much of the period under study. All three periods were of weak/adverse KT with rising inequality. Policies in the first period of ST were socialist in nature, with strict control of the private sector. It was also a period of political instability with frequent changes of government and military coups. During the second period, from 1983 onwards, economic reforms were implemented, including trade liberalization, privatization of SOEs, policies to attract FDI, tax reforms, and a shift from import-substitution industrialization (ISI) to an export-led industrialization strategy. The third period saw a watershed moment in Ghana's industrialization agenda as a result of the discovery and production of oil in commercial quantities.

In the early 2010s, the government pursued the Ghana Shared Growth and Development Agenda (GSGDA I), which coincided with the beginning of the oil production. In addition to ensuring continued macroeconomic stability and enhancing the competitiveness of the private sector, GSGDA I aimed at changing the structure of the economy to favour the services and industrial sectors. The specific strategies under GSGDA I included the development of infrastructure, as well as petrochemical-based industries to support oil and gas production. GSGDA I was succeeded by GSGDA II in 2014. GSGDA II aimed to sustain the shared growth while the economy continued on the path of transformation and was to be implemented up to 2017. The administration that took over in 2017 has emphasized agricultural mechanization, productivity enhancement, and industrial transformation.

In the 1980s and 1990s, the Ghanaian government received considerable external financial assistance, leading to increased expenditure on education, health, and social protection programmes. While there was a sharp fall in poverty, inequality rose during this period and continued to increase during the 2000s. One potential reason is that although the agricultural sector's share in employment declined, the released labour was absorbed by the low-productivity informal sector. With the onset of the oil production in 2010, the policy direction of GSGDA I and GSGDA II was informed by the desire to make the growth process more inclusive. However, due to the capital-intensive nature of the oil and mining sector, growth did not translate into increased job creation, which may have contributed to increased inequality.

South Africa experienced a period of upgrading industrialization between 1960 and 1980, followed by two periods of secular deindustrialization: 1981–1993 and 1994 onwards. In the first period, the Kuznets tension was weak/benign, as inequality was steady alongside strong ST. The two later periods of secular deindustrialization are both associated with rising inequality. ST was weak between 1981 and 1993 and strong afterwards. For almost five decades (1925–1973), South Africa experimented with import-substitution policies to pursue ST. Around the same time, it also developed a 'mineral energy complex' that linked manufacturing to available resources via various state supports, including cheap energy. During this period, until the 1980s, inequality was stable, though high, under apartheid. One of the key reasons could be the increased unionization of workers, particularly Black unions. Import-substitution policies continued until 1993, but unlike in the previous period, failed to deliver strong growth. Due to weakened external competitiveness and efficiency, South Africa entered an era of poor growth and deindustrialization that is correlated with increasing inequality. In the post-apartheid era (from 1994 onwards), South Africa implemented the Industrial Policy Action Plan (IPAP), aiming to reindustrialize without success. Deindustrialization and tertiarization persisted and inequality continued to rise towards the end of the 2000s.

Among the first important initiatives to address soaring inequalities in the post-apartheid era was the Broad-Based Black Economic Empowerment (B-BBEE) programme from 2003. As a key component, it attempted to dismantle the White control of the South African economy. However, its outcomes remain unclear. In addition, there were other active labour market policies in the form of a job-retraining scheme, some variants of a public employment scheme, and a firm-based wage subsidy intervention. While these schemes have seen some success, they have had limited impact on the pervasive unemployment levels. One further, more prominent pro-poor policy has been the widening and deepening of social security and social transfers. However, all these measures have not been successful in addressing the rising inequality of the post-apartheid era.

3.4 Latin America

Brazil and Chile were our case studies in Latin America. Brazil has experienced several different periods of ST. Brazil had upgrading industrialization between 1950 and 1964. Two periods following this (1964–1994 and 1994–2011) were ones of what can be labelled non-uniform secular deindustrialization (meaning that there were some signs of other varieties of industrialization within the period). The period of 1964–1972, was one of a strong KT, as inequality rose and there was strong growth-enhancing ST. The period of 1973–1993 was one of weak/benign KT, as inequality was steady. And the period of 1994 onwards was a period of weak ST and declining inequality, thus the KT was ambiguous.

Brazil implemented an import-substitution policy to promote domestic industrialization up to the 1980s. The manufacturing industry flourished and triggered internal migration from poorer regions in the north and north-east to the south-east, where most manufacturers were concentrated. During this period, productivity growth was quite high. The Brazilian government also invested quite heavily in infrastructure projects in the 1960s and 1970s, which may have helped the process of ST in creating higher growth. However, during the same period inequality rose. One potential reason for this was Brazil's limited attention to developing human capital and its predominant focus on building physical capital.

Brazil's history of economic development is marked by a decline in inequality in the 1990s and 2000s. This, to a large extent, is attributed to a combination of policies, especially the acceleration of schooling, stronger social policies, and rising minimum wages. In 2004, Brazil introduced the *Bolsa Familia*, a large, conditional cash transfer programme. Furthermore, the minimum wage rose dramatically. In other words, a mix of improved social policies and progressive labour market policies supported inclusive growth.

Chile experienced periods of stalled industrialization and secular deindustrialization. The period of 1960–1973 was one of a weak/benign KT. The periods of 1973–1989 and 1990–1999 were periods or weak/adverse KT with rising inequality. The period 2000–present was one of an ambiguous KT. Since the second half of the twentieth century, Chile's economic growth has been mainly led by the labour-intensive yet low-productivity services sector at the expense of manufacturing. The latter contributed more than 30 per cent of economic growth in the early 1960s but only 15 per cent in the early 2010s. During the same period, absolute poverty has fallen sharply, yet inequality has remained high. Chile's ST is also affected by the persistent dependence on the mining sector, a sector that plays only a minor role in the dynamics of labour re-allocation in the context of ST. From 1960 up to the 2000s, Chile's economy did not encounter a strong KT. Strong growth-enhancing ST only occurred between 1960 and 1973, a period during which inequality remained stable. During 1973–1999, Chile experienced a weak adverse KT, with little growth-enhancing ST but rising inequality.

In the 1970s, post-coup, the Chilean government introduced various neoliberal economic reforms, including exchange rate evaluation, privatization of public enterprises, opening up to international trade, and curtailment of labour unions. However, this did not lead to growth-enhancing ST. Rather, the share of the manufacturing sector remained stable, or even declined after the introduction of these policies. The privatization of public assets in the 1970s, 1980s, and some in the 1990s led to a concentration of wealth. Following these free-market-orientated reforms, Chile introduced so-called 'market-orientated social policies' in the 1980s, which led to the privatization of social services. The new laws allowed for-profit providers to operate in the education, health, housing, and pension-fund management sectors.

Up to the 2000s, policies to promote inclusive growth focused on reducing absolute poverty, not inequality. Chile relied on aggregate economic growth complemented by subsidies targeted at the poor. In the early 2000s, some new programmes in the health sector were put in place, which provided financial resources to patients for the treatment of a list of illnesses. In 2008, a partial reform of the pension system was carried out, which created minimum pensions and supplementary subsidies for people with small pensions. These reforms, however, were limited.

4. Structural transformation and income inequality: a comparison of country episodes

Our cross-country analysis covers the history of economic development of nine countries from the 1950/60s to the 2010s. We distinguish different episodes of economic development for each country. We distinguish a range of different country episodes, each of which can classified by the variety of ST: upgrading industrialization, primary industrialization, secular deindustrialization, advanced industrialization, and stalled industrialization (Figure 13.1). We also distinguish a range of different country episodes that can be classified into our types of KT: weak/adverse, strong, ambiguous, and weak/benign (see Figure 13.2).

In terms of the varieties of ST, we can make three conclusions. First, six of the nine countries studied have experienced at least one episode of upgrading industrialization, a period of an increase in both the share of manufacturing value added and employment. Three East Asian countries—Indonesia, China, Thailand—experienced episodes of upgrading industrialization. Bangladesh also experienced two episodes of upgrading industrialization. We also find that five of the nine countries have experienced, at some point, an episode of stalled industrialization or deindustrialization. Second, we find that few countries experienced

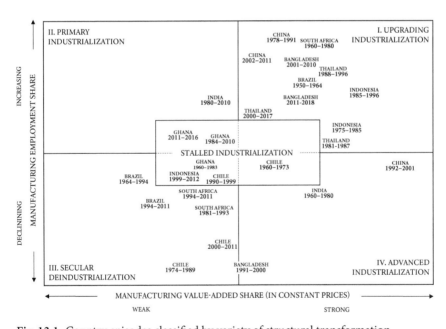

Fig. 13.1 Country episodes classified by variety of structural transformation

Source: authors' illustration based on country case studies in this volume. Classification based on authors' chapters.

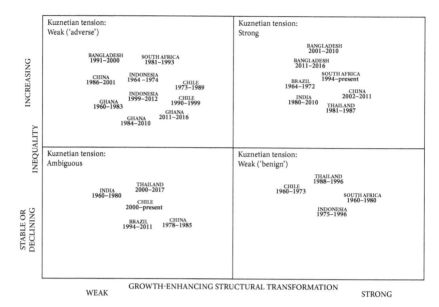

Fig. 13.2 Country episodes classified by Kuznetsian tension

Notes: (i) Classification based on authors' chapters; (ii) strong growth-enhancing structural transformation is defined as more than 2 per cent GDP growth (using data from World Development Indicators (World Bank 2019) and authors used other criteria such as changes in value-added and employment shares in manufacturing along with GDP growth; (iii) Brazil 1973–1994 does not appear in our bottom-right quadrant of this summary figure due to data concerns on inequality data for the 1970s noted in the Brazil chapter (notably, poor coverage of household surveys, missing or imputed years, high inflation, and discrepancy among nominal values of labour income).
Source: authors' illustration based on country case studies in this volume.

primary industrialization—a period of rising employment share of the manufacturing sector, and declining value-added share—or an episode of advanced industrialization. Third, some countries have spent some considerable length of time in one quadrant. For example, Chile has experienced four decades of secular deindustrialization or stalled industrialization since the mid-1970s. South Africa was in the deindustrialization quadrant for more than thirty years since the early 1980s. In contrast, Indonesia, and Bangladesh both spent approximately twenty continuous years in the upgrading industrialization quadrant, Indonesia from 1975–1996 and Bangladesh from 2001–2018.

If we turn to the KT (Figure 13.2), we can also make three conclusions. First, the political regimes are not—in our case studies—deterministic. Democracies are not necessarily better at managing the tension between ST and income inequality. Second, if we focus on the bottom-right quadrant—the desirable place to be—of strong ST and steady inequality, we can see an East Asian story and a Latin American story. Third, we can see that there are clearly some limitations to our approach related to group inequality—specifically racial inequalities—that need exploring further in the case of South Africa. In the weak/benign KT quadrant, there is the

East Asian story (Indonesia 1975–1996; Thailand 1988–1996). This story is one of a strong policy focus on rural and agricultural development through public investments, technology, and a focus on food prices and availability, which acted to constrain, to some extent, the urban–rural income divergence and thus upward pressure on inequality during ST. Further, there is the strong policy focus on primary, and later secondary, education expansion, which acted to constrain, to some extent, the higher skilled–lower-skilled worker income divergence (in short, redistributing future incomes) and upward pressure on inequality during ST. One could also add the clear focus on access to health evident in each period, too. In short, the government enacted policies which weakened any potential income divergences across urban–rural incomes and higher-skilled–lower-skilled workers. One can also note the large number of jobs created in manufacturing in Thailand and Indonesia in these periods, providing many people with higher incomes and an equalizing effect, given movements would likely have been from relatively less equal economic sectors (agriculture or traditional services).

In the same weak/benign KT quadrant, there is also a Latin American story of Chile, 1960–1973. In the case of Chile, the benign outcome in the KT quadrant may be attributed to the strong labour union movement in the 1960s and early 1970s (culminating in the election of the left-of-centre Popular Unity government of Salvador Allende in 1970), as well as the launch of agrarian reforms from the mid-1960s until 1973. Furthermore, there was increasing degree of universalism in the provision of social services through the access of the middle and working classes to public education, public health, housing, and social security schemes in this period.

Finally, in that same quadrant is South Africa (1960–1980), which shows some of the limits of our approach. In that period, South Africa experienced strong ST with stable (albeit very high) inequality. Our focus on the Gini misses racial and presumably other group inequalities.

5. Conclusion

What would Lal Jayawardena make of our findings? Or, for that matter, Simon Kuznets or W. Arthur Lewis? All of them, in their own ways, were dedicated to identifying strategies for developing countries to build societies that are more just. Each would thus be surprised about the multiple variations of ST beyond the 'traditional' pathway. Each would likely pick up on the fact that rising inequality during economic development is not inevitable and seek to bury that falsehood once and for all. Finally, each would remind us that they themselves had written about how broad-based, or inclusive, economic development requires public policies to address any upswing in inequality and to spread the benefits of economic development to those people and areas left behind. In sum, to echo Lal's approach, public policies remain essential not only to building a society, but also to building one that is foundationally more just.

References

Kanbur, R. (2019). 'Structural Transformation and Income Distribution: Kuznets and Beyond'. In C. Monga and J.Y. Lin (eds), *The Oxford Handbook of Structural Transformation*. Oxford: Oxford University Press, 96–108.

Kim, K., and A. Sumner (2019). 'The Five Varieties of Industrialization: A New Typology of Diverse Empirical Experience in the Developing World'. ESRC GPID Research Network Working Paper 18. London: ESRC Global Poverty and Inequality Dynamics Research Network (GPID).

Singh, A. (2005). 'Lal Jayawardena: Crafting Development Policy', *Development and Change* 36(6): 1219–1223.

World Bank (2019). 'World Development Indicators' (data base). Washington, DC: World Bank.

Index